The Fatherhood of God in Matthew

Biblical Hermeneutics Rediscovered

The Series as the name suggests will focus on Biblical Hermeneutics, i.e., literary works concerned with methods of interpreting the Old and New Testaments of Bible via different stream of topics like Literature & Poetry, Indigenous Philosophizing, Ethical response towards Ecology, Health & Healing, Science & Technology, Feminist Theology, Sociological approach towards Human Rights, Law & Politics, Arts, History of Ideas, Ancient Civilizations, Cultural Contiguity, Religious Cosmologies & Mysticism, Appraisal of various Theologians, World Peace & Harmony, Global Capitalism, Network Marketing, Cybertheology, Population & Demographics, Epigraphic Studies, Contextualized Education, and many others. We welcome a Mss. on any topic/s mentioned, whether they are original works, scholarly monographs, collections of conference papers, revised dissertations, or translations of historical documents. Through the Series we, the Publishers, are striving to put forward published works that may help Institutions, Academic Bodies, Researchers, Scholars and the World at large in furthering their respective knowledge and understanding on the concerned subject. We welcome your comments on our efforts and further suggestions on how we can enshrine new ray of analysing & explaining the written Texts through our upcoming books.

Biblical Hermeneutics Rediscovered - 22

The Fatherhood of God in Matthew

Towards a Theology of God in the Synoptic Gospels in Indian Context

I. Limatemsu Ao

CWI

Christian World Imprints

First Published in 2019 by

Christian World Imprints
Christian Publishing & Books from India
C-3, Shop No. 14, Ground Floor
Wazirpur Industrial Area, **Delhi-110052**
cwidelhi2017@gmail.com
www.ChristianWorldImprints.com
Phone: +91 11 41526079

ISBN: 978-93-5148-372-4 (HB)
ISBN: 978-93-5148-373-1 (PB)

Printed in India.

DEDICATION

Dedicated to my beloved parents
Mr. Imtichawa (1940 - February 2019) and Mrs. Temjensola (1944 -)
whose unceasing prayers and tears led me to full time God's ministry

The book, in its original form, is the thesis submitted to the Senate of Serampore College, towards the Doctor of Theology degree, accepted in the Senate in December 2016. It is published with written permission. The original title of the thesis is unchanged. The candidate is solely responsible for the title, contents and opinions expressed in it.

Contents

Acknowledgements

This book is the outcome of my D.Th dissertation on which I worked while studying at United Theological College, Bangalore (2011-2015) and was accepted by the Senate of Serampore College on 7th December 2016.

I am happy that it comes out as a book and hope that this book has a particular contribution to make to the scholarly world in the area of New Testament Theology – focusing on the nature and the work of God in the Synoptic Gospels, which is too infrequent in New Testament studies. The study has also made effort to re-conceptualize the theology of God in the Indian religion and theology. I expect that this book will make a contribution to a fresh understanding of God of the Synoptic Gospels in the Indian situation.

Indeed, I am glad to acknowledge those who have greatly helped me in the completion of this work. I express my sincere thanks to the authority of the United Theological College, the Principal and the Dean of Doctoral Studies, for giving me admission and family accommodation throughout my research period.

My deep gratitude goes to Rev. Dr J. G. Muthuraj, my supervisor, for his patient guidance and scholarly supervision in preparing and completing the dissertation. My gratitude also goes to the Faculty, Staff, Librarian and students of United Theological College with whom I had great time of interaction during my stay in the UTC campus.

I acknowledge my thanks to Rev. Dr. H. Vanlalauva, the then Dean, Department of Research/SATHRI and his office, for arranging Consolidated and Bursary scholarship supports from Global Ministries' South Asia Scholarship Fund and EMW (Germany) for three academic years of my research work. I also would like to thank Fr. Dr. P. G. George, the incumbent Dean of Research / SATHRI, and the SATHRI staff for their supportive role to accomplish my research. I am also very grateful to Rev. Dr. Santanu K. Patro, the Registrar of the Senate of Serampore, for the kind permission to publish the thesis.

I am greatly indebted to Dr. Paul Wiebe and his wife Mrs. Donna Beth (Mennonite Ministries, US) who has been source of help for our family. I also acknowledge our prayer partner Ms. Amenla Imsong (Bethel Prayer Home

Ministry, Dimapur) for the much needed support during our residential period of studies at UTC, Bangalore.

I acknowledge my friends for processing books and articles related to my research work. A special word of gratitude to Thomas Breitzkreuz and his family (Dietenheim, Germany) for his sustained effort in helping me with valuable materials related to my research work.

My sincere gratitude goes to my wife Mrs. Moakala, who has been the backbone while I was doing my research and to my two sons Bendangsungit Yaden and Jason Yaden who has been the motivation and happiness.

I acknowledge my close family members, relatives, friends, Church members, prayer partners and well wishers for their prayer and financial support during my studies. Above all I thank Almighty God and our loving heavenly Father.

May 24, 2019
I. Limatemsu Ao
Trinity Theological College, Dimapur

List of Abbreviations

I. Miscellaneous abbreviations and symbols

B.C.E.	Before Common Era
c.	circa
C.E.	Common Era
cf.	compare
ch	chapter
ed.	editor
eds.	editors
e.g.	for example
et al	and others
i.e.	that is
lit.	literally
LXX	The Septuagint
[*sic*]	thus
trans	translated by
v	verse
vv	verses
vol	volume
vols	volumes
//	parallels

II. Publications

AB:	Anchor Bible
ABD:	*Anchor Bible Dictionary*
ANRW:	*Aufstieg und Niedergang der romischen Welt*
ATR:	*Anglican Theological Review*

APOT:	*The Apocrypha and Pseudepigrapha of the Old Testament*
BAGD:	*A Greek-English Lexicon of the New Testament*, edited by W. Bauer, W.F. Arndt, F.W. Gingrich, T.W. Danker
BECNT:	Baker Exegetical Commentary of the New Testament
Bib:	*Biblica*
BR:	*Biblical Research*
BT:	*The Bible Translator*
BTESSC:	Board of Theological Education, Senate of Serampore College
BTTBPSA:	The Board for Theological Text Books Programme of South Asia
BZ:	*Biblesche Zeitschrift*
CBQ:	*Catholic Bible Quarterly*
CSS:	Christava Sahitya Samithy
DJG:	*Dictionary of Jesus and the Gospels*
DBI:	*Dictionary of Biblical Imagery*
DNTB:	*Dictionary of New Testament Background*
ECNT:	Exegetical Commentary of the New Testament
EDNT:	Exegetical Dictionary of the New Testament
ExpT:	*The Expository Times*
HTR:	*Harvard Theological Review*
IBS:	*Irish Biblical Studies*
ICC:	International Critical Commentary
IJT:	*Indian Journal of Theology*
Int:	*Interpretation*
IVP:	InterVarsity Press
JAAR:	*Journal of the American Academy of Religion*
JAOS:	*Journal of the American Oriental Studies*
JBL:	*Journal of Biblical Literature*
JSNT:	*Journal of the Study of the New Testament*
JSOT:	*Journal of the Study of the Old Testament*
JTS:	*Journal of Theological Studies*
LCL:	Loeb Classical Library
LXX:	The Septuagint
NCBC:	New Cambridge Bible commentary
NICNT:	New International Commentary of the New Testament
NICOT:	New International Commentary of the Old Testament
NIDNTT:	New International Dictionary of New Testament Theology

NIDOTT: New International Dictionary of Old Testament Theology
NIGTC: New International Greek Text Commentary
NovT: Novum Tetsamenteum
NRSV: The New Revised Standard Version
NTS: *New Testament Studies*
OCD: The Oxford Classical Dictionary
OTP: The Old Testament Pseudepigrapha
PTCA: Programme for Theology and Cultures in Asia
RevQ: *Revue de Qumran*
RSV: The Revised Standard Version
SATHRI: South Asia Theological Research Institute
SBL: Society of Biblical Literature
SE: *Studia Evangelica*
SJ: Studia Judaica
SHBC: Smyth and Helwys Bible Commentary
SPCK: Society for Promoting Christian Knowledge
ISPCK: Indian Society for Promoting Christian Knowledge
TDNT: Theological Dictionary of the New Testament
TS: *Theological Studies*
TToday: Theology Today
TPI: Theological Publications of India
TynBul: *Tyndale Bulletin*
WBC: Word Biblical Commentary
ZECNT: Zondervan Exegetical Commentary on the New Testament

Chapter 1

Introduction
Methodological Considerations

1.1. The Problem

The fatherhood of God represents one of the major strands of Matthean theology. This is evident not only from the fact that the designation 'Father' for God occurs the most in Matthew among the Synoptic Gospels, but that the idea of the fatherhood of God is very much emphasized in several unique narratives in Matthew. However, this is also the area that has received the least attention so far.[1] Hence, the purpose and aim of this research is to examine the theological significance of the fatherhood of God in Matthew, as he reveals it in the structure and composition of the various parts of his text. Such a research would enable us to see Matthew's unique contributions to the theocentric nature of New Testament theology and its relevance for doing theology and mission in India.[2]

Since the term 'Father' is seen mainly in the speech attributed to Jesus in the Synoptic Gospels, many scholars have studied the theme of the fatherhood of God from historical Jesus' perspective. The most influential work has been that of J. Jeremias. Looking from the perspective of Jesus, J. Jeremias argued that *Abba*, Father is an address to God and is typical of Jesus' prayers and so unique

---

[1] It is curious that to date there seems to be no detailed study of "God" in Matthew. We have to date only two small articles that deals specifically with theology of God in Matthew, in particular reference to the use of the term Father for God: R.L. Mowery, "*God, Lord and Father: The Theology of the Gospel of Matthew*," in *BR* 33 (1988), 24-36; and Julian Sheffield, "The Father in the Gospel of Matthew," in *A Feminist Companion to Matthew*, edited by Amy-Jill Levine (Cleveland: The Pilgrims Press, 2001), 52-69.

[2] As the centrality of the fatherhood of God in Matthean theology seems to be the right place to relate to and for doing theology from Indian perspective.

to Jesus.[3] Several scholars follow Jeremias' thesis. R.G. Hamerton-Kelly, in line with Jeremias, studied the use of Father for God in the teaching of Jesus and so the theology of Jesus and argued that Father usage is unique to Jesus.[4] For him *Abba* expressed a relationship with God characterized purely by intimacy and that this experience is the starting point of Christology, and the key to his eschatology.[5] In 1989, Edgar Krentz reaffirmed the position of Jeremias that Jesus' address to God as *Abba* Father is unique to Jesus, and that it expresses closeness to God because it is an intimate familial term.[6] In 1992, Mary Rose D' Angelo, while examining the use of *Abba* and Father in the Gospels in general, however, argued that "the Gospels do not and cannot support the claim that Jesus always addressed God as 'Father.'"[7] However, she argued that "if indeed the title 'Father' was important to Jesus, it may have been in the context of spiritual resistance to imperial pretensions."[8]

M. M. Thompson (2000),[9] in her study of God as Father in the New Testament brought out a careful and balanced assessment of the claim of J. Jeremias about Jesus' use of *Abba* as prayer-address for "God." She argued that Jesus did use the expression but that the use of the expression *Abba* reflects more of continuity with Judaism.[10] She insists that the New Testament designation of 'God' as 'Father' reflects both a christological and an ecclesiological emphasis: God as 'Father of the Son' and 'Father of a people.'[11]

From the above review it is observed that most of the scholars who dealt on the Fatherhood of God in the Gospels and the New Testament, look at the level of Jesus and his theology. They concentrate on the sayings of Jesus as regard to his *Abba* expression and experience and thus look at the fatherhood of God idea from christological perspective. But as we will see, the usage of the term 'Father' and the idea of God's fatherhood in many cases, do not go back to Jesus lips, but rather to

---

[3] J. Jeremias, *The Prayer of Jesus* (London: SCM Press, 1967), 53-54, 57; J. Jeremias, *New Testament Theology* I (London: SCM Press, 1971), 36, 61-67.

[4] Robert Hamerton-Kelly, *God the Father: Theology and Patriarchy in the Teaching of Jesus* (Philadelphia: Fortress Press, 1979), 83.

[5] Hamerton-Kelly, *God the Father*, 101.

[6] E. Grentz, "God in the New Testament," in *Our Naming of God*, edited by Carl E. Braaten (Minneapolis: Fortress, 1989), 88-89; J.D.G. Dunn (*Jesus and the Spirit: A Study of the Religious and Charismatic Experience of Jesus and the First Christians as Reflected in the New Testament* [Philadelphia: Westminster Press, 1975], 26) draws much the same conclusion saying that Jesus *Abba* experience was unique to him.

[7] M. R. D'Angelo, "Abba and 'Father:' Imperial Theology and the Jesus Traditions," in *JBL* 111/4 (1992), 617.

[8] D'Angelo, "Abba and 'Father:' Imperial Theology and the Jesus Traditions," 628.

[9] M.M. Thompson, *The Promise of the Father: Jesus and God in the New Testament* (Louisville: Westminster John Knox, 2000).

[10] Thompson, *The Promise of the Father*, 21-34.

[11] Thompson, *The Promise of the Father*, 156.

do with the theology of the Evangelists and their communities. This is where this research would like to focus.

Moreover, since there is no detailed study on the theme of 'God' in Matthew so far, there are very important theological issues yet to be addressed in Matthew, particularly in relation to the theme of God's fatherhood: Why God as Father attracted so much to Matthew? What is the context that contributed to the increasing importance of 'Father' as a designation for God in Matthean community? Does Matthew provide an anti-type to the Greco-Roman father? What does 'Father' mean in Matthean usage in the Gospel? Whether Matthean emphasis on God's fatherhood is particular or universal? Is the designation 'Father' for God in Matthew and the Synoptic Gospels the same deity described in the Old Testament? Does the term 'Father' in Matthew reflect Jewish notion of God as Father or Greco-Roman tradition or Hellenistic thought? Is there any distinct emphasis about God as Father in Matthew? In what way Matthew differs from the rest of the Synoptic Gospels? How can this theology-laden Matthew's Gospel be utilized for doing theology from an Indian perspective?

Before explaining the basis and importance of this research we need to be aware of the contemporary challenges in relation to the use of the term 'father,' particularly from the feminist theologians.

1.1.1. The Feminist Challenge to the Fatherhood of God and Patriarchy

The language of God particularly the categorical projection and view of God as Father[12] in the biblical tradition receives strong criticism from the feminist theologians. For example, asserting that the biblical texts and faith are inevitably and intolerably patriarchal, Mary Daly made a radical dictum, "If God is male, then the male is God."[13] Rosemary Radford Ruether too made a revolutionary statement against the patriarchy and hierarchy found in the Bible. She avoids all designations for God that presuppose some sort of hierarchical rule or authority. Instead, she defines God, whom she calls 'God/ess' as 'the Primal matrix' the "great womb within all things, gods and humans, sky and earth, human and nonhuman beings are generated."[14] Daphne Hampson in similar vein, argues that male conceptualization of God of the Bible is "an ideology which is biased against half of humanity."[15] Further, Hampson intensifies her argument by attacking the very affirmation of the centrality of Jesus Christ and the unique revelation

---

[12] For a categorical statement on patriarchy in Jesus' tradition, see R. Hamerton-Kelly, "God the Father in the Bible," in *God as Father?* Edited by Johannes-Baptist Metz and Edward Schillebeeckx (New York: T & T Clark, 1981), 101.

[13] M. Daly, *Beyond God the Father: Toward a Philosophy of Women's Liberation* (Boston: Beacon, 1973), 19.

[14] R.R. Ruether, *Sexism and God-talk: Toward a Feminist Theology* (Boston: Beacon, 1983), 48-49.

[15] D. Hampson, *Theology and Feminism* (Oxford: Basil Blackwell, 1990), 53.

through him.[16] For her the very patriarchalism lies in the very designation of God as the Father of Jesus of Nazareth.

Accordingly, several feminist scholars see the apparent patriarchy, particularly pointing to the language of Jesus in the Synoptic Gospels (e.g., Mk 14:36; Mt 6:9; Lk 11:2). By contrast, Elisabeth Schussler Fiorenza, a noted feminist theologian, finds the corrective to patriarchy and hierarchy within Jesus' own use of God as Father. She finds in Jesus' statement in Matthew 23:9, "a critical subversion of all structure of domination."[17] For her, by envisioning God as the only Father all disciples are equal as brothers and sisters.[18]

Hence, it is seen that the issue on fatherhood and patriarchy centers mainly on Jesus' *Abba* experience, that is, at the level of Jesus and his theology. However, as stated earlier, our task is mainly at the level of the author and his interpretation and theology. So, rather than speculating on Jesus' personal experience of God as Father, which is the root of the debate on patriarchy, we will concentrate instead on Matthew's context, where the usage of the term 'Father' and so the idea of God's fatherhood seems to be connected most probably with the socio-political realities of the time.

1.2. Basis and Importance of the Research

The basis behind this proposal is that Matthew appeared to have a special interest in portraying God as Father. For example, the term 'Father' occurs in Matthew more than the other Synoptic writers combined: 44 times against 4 times in Mark and 17 times in Luke.[19] Moreover, there are several pericope mostly unique to Matthew that focus on the fatherhood of God. It is only in the portrayal of Matthew that the heavenly Father "makes his sun rise on the evil and on the good, and sends rain on the righteous and on the unrighteous" (5:45-48). It is also in Matthew that God is projected as: All-seeing (6:4, 6[x2], 18[x2]) and All-knowing (6:8, 32) heavenly Father. It is Matthew alone who talks about peacemaking in connection with children of God (5:9).

The chart below shows the occurrences of the term 'Father' in Matthew vis-à-vis his Synoptic counterparts. The words or phrases in bold in the last column of the below illustration shows the redactional activities of Matthew, thus points to his theological emphasis.[20]

---

[16] Hampson, *Theology and Feminism*, 8.

[17] E.S. Fiorenza, *In Memory of Her: A Feminist Theological Reconstruction of Christian Origins* (New York: Crossroad, 1983), 151.

[18] Fiorenza, *In Memory of Her*, 151.

[19] Out of the total 63 occurrences of the word 'Father' in Matthew; see J.R. Kohlenberger III, E.W. Goodrick & J.A. Swanson, *The Exhaustive Concordance to the Greek New Testament* (Grand Rapids: Zondervan Publishing House, 1995), 771-772.

[20] Text in this illustration is NRSV.

Matthew	Mark	Luke	Source/Redaction[21]
5:16, 45; 6:1 your Father in heaven	x	x	**M**
5:48 your heavenly Father is perfect	x	6:36 your Father is merciful	Q
6:4, 6[x2], 18[x2] your Father … in secret	x	x	**M**
6:8 your Father knows what you need	x	x	**M**
6:9 Our Father in heaven	x	11:2 Father	Q
6:14 your heavenly Father	11:25 your Father in heaven	x	Mk
6:15 your Father	x	x	**M**
6:26 your heavenly Father feeds	x	12:24 God feeds	Q
6:32 your heavenly Father knows	x	12:30 your Father knows	Q
7:11 your Father in heaven	x	11:13 the heavenly Father	Q
7:21 my Father in heaven	x	6:46	**additions to Q**
10:20 Spirit of your Father	x	12:12 the Holy Spirit	Q
10:29 apart from your Father	x	12:6 in God's sight	Q
10:32, 33 my Father in heaven	x	12:8, 9 angels of God	Q
11:25-27 [x5] Father	x	10:21-22 Father [x5]	Q
12:50 the will of my Father in heaven	3:35 the will of God	8:21the word of God	Mk
13:43 like the sun in the kingdom of their Father	x	x	**M**
15:13 my heavenly Father	x	x	**M**

[21] 'M' = Matthean; Q=Quelle; Mk=Mark

16:17 but my Father in heaven	x	x	**M**
16:27 the glory of his Father	8:38 the glory of his Father	9:26 the glory of the Father	Mk
18:10 my Father in heaven	x	x	**M**
18:14 your Father in heaven	x	15:7 in heaven	Q
18:19 my Father in heaven	x	x	**M**
18:35 my heavenly Father	x	x	**M**
20:23 prepared by my Father	10:40 it has been prepared	x	**expansion of Mk**
23:9 one Father – the one in heaven	x	x	**M**
24:36 but only the Father	13:32 but only the Father	x	Mk
25:34 come, ... blessed by my Father	x	x	**M**
26:29 my Father's kingdom	14:25 the kingdom of God	22:18 the kingdom of God	Mk
26:39 My Father	14:36 Abba, Father	22:42 Father	Mk
26:42 My Father	14:39	x	**expansion of Mk**
26:53 appeal to my Father	x	x	**M**
28:19 in the name of the Father	x	x	**M**

The above chart demonstrates that Matthew has deliberate interest on the theme of the fatherhood of God. Out of these 44 occurrences of 'Father,' as seen in the illustration above, only in four instances Matthew has parallels with Mark (6:14//Mk 11:25; 16:27//Mk 8: 38; 24:36//Mk 13:32; 26:39//Mk 14:36); nine instances with Luke (5:48//Lk 6:36; 6:9//Lk 11:2; 6:32//Lk 12:30; 7:11//Lk 11:13; 11:25-27[5x]//Lk 10:21-22 [5x]; while in three instances with both Mark and Luke (16:27/ /Mk 8:38//Lk 9:26; and 26:39// Mk 14:36//Lk 22:42).

20 times the term 'Father' for 'God' is occurring in the special Matthean (M) material (5:16,45; 6:1,4,6[2],8,15,18[2]; 13:43; 15:13; 16:17; 18:10,19,35; 23:9; 25:34; 26:53; 28:19); while on several occasions 'Father' are Matthean

redactions. On six occasions Matthew replaced 'God' with 'Father' to his sources Mark (12:50//Mk 3:35; 26:29//Mk 14:25) and Q (6:26//Lk 12:24; 10:29//Lk 12:6; 10:32//Lk 12:8; 10:33//Lk 12:9) thus exhibiting a particular fondness for 'Father' over other ways of referring to God. In one occasion Matthew replaced 'Holy Spirit' with 'Father' to his source Q (10:20//Lk 12:12); while in four occasions Matthew added 'Father' to his source Mark (20:23//Mk 10:40; 26:42// Mk 14:39) and Q (7:21//Lk 6:46; 18:14//Lk 15:7) Consequently, it is clear that Matthew emphasizes the fatherhood of God, retaining occurrences found in his sources Mark and Q, and adding several others from his own special sources (M), as well as by way of addition or expansion (redaction) to his sources. This clearly shows Matthew's interest on the fatherhood of God.

It is also interesting to see that in Matthew God as Father is identified as 'heavenly' or 'in heaven' 20 times (5:16,45,48; 6: 1,9,14, 26, 32; 7:11,21; 10:32,33;12:50; 15:13; 16:17; 18:10,14,19,35; 23:9). Out of these occurrences only two have parallels (6:14 //Mk 11: 25; 7:11//Lk 11:13).

Matthew's distinct theological emphasis on the fatherhood of God is all the more evident as in several narratives, mostly in parables unique to him, Matthew has portrayed God in several imageries of God in close relation to the fatherly nature of God. They are: God as the landowner (20:1-16); the king (18:23-35); the shepherd (18:10-14); parent (7:9-11). In all these the focus on the fatherliness or fatherhood of God is very clear. There are also in Matthew 'divine passives,'[22] for example, ἁγιασθήτω (6:9//Lk 11:2), γενηθήτω (6:10) and δεῖ constructions occurring in connection with the theme of the fatherhood of God. These δεῖ constructions occur some 8 times in Matthew (16:21; 17:10; 18:33; 23:23; 24:6; 25:27; 26:35, 54).[23] This construction, usually occurring in the third person singular neuter δεῖ ('it is necessary' or 'it must'), expresses the character of necessity or compulsion in an event.[24] In a unique parable in Matthew (18:23-35) we see the usage of this construction in relation to God's character: "Should you not have had (οὐκ ἔδει) mercy on your fellow slave, as I had mercy on you?" (18:33), thus pointing to God's fatherly nature.

While the idea of the fatherhood of God is the most prominent in Matthew among the Synoptic Gospels, yet as highlighted in the illustration above, the usage of 'Father' for God and the idea of God's fatherhood is also present in Mark and Luke (Q). That simply means, 'Father' is used by all the Synoptic authors as an appropriate address for God and it reflects the usage of the early Christian communities and for whom the Gospels were written.

As explained above Mark has 4 instances of 'Father' usage for God (Mk 8:38; 11:25; 13:32; 14:36), among which Mark 14:36 is the only instance of

---

[22] The divine passive was a typical Jewish way of speaking about God.

[23] Kohlenberger, *The Exhaustive Concordance*, 188.

[24] W. Popkes, "δεῖ," in *EDNT* I, edited by H. Balz and G. Schneider (Grand Rapids; Michigan: Wm B. Eerdmans, 1990), 279-81.

Aramaic prayer supposed to be uttered by Jesus, "*Abba*, Father ...." Most of the 'Father' usage seems to occur in Mark in the context of prayer (e.g., Mk 11:22-25; 14:36). Is then for Mark the 'Father' usage to do with spiritual experience of the community?[25] Likewise, the 'Father' usage for God too occurs 17 times in Luke;[26] and like other Synoptic Gospels we see in Luke the occurrences of 'Father' for God in prayer contexts (Lk 11:2-4;10:21-22; 22:42). Particularly noteworthy is the similarity yet striking differences between Matthean and Lukan version of the Lord's Prayer. In the Lukan version Jesus is addressing God simply as 'Father' (Lk 11:2), while Matthean version has 'Our Father in heaven' (Mt 6:9). The same pattern of employing 'Father' (without any qualifying expression 'in heaven' or 'heavenly') is seen in other instances in Luke as well (Lk 6:36//Mt 5:48; Lk 12:30//Mt 6:32). This seems to do with their respective theology of God.

It is interesting to observe that all the three Synoptic authors recorded Jesus' prayer addressing God as his own Father in Gethsemane: 'My Father' (Mt 26:39); '*Abba*, Father' (Mk 14:36); 'Father' (Lk 22:42). So, also in a discourse on discipleship found in all the Synoptic Gospels (Mk 8:34-9:1; Mt 16:24-28; Lk 9:23-27), we see the occurrences of exclusive Father-Son idea in the lips of Jesus: "For the Son of Man is to come with his angels in the glory of his Father" (Mt 16:27); the parallels in Mark says "when he (Son of Man) comes in the glory of his Father" (Mk 8:38) ; while Luke has "when he (Son of Man) comes in the glory of the Father" (Lk 9:26). Such instances show the unanimity of the Synoptic Gospels in portraying filial relationship between God and Jesus, and thereby pointing to the centrality of God in the Synoptic Gospels and so in the theology of the Evangelists.

Thus, having all these data in mind and seeing Matthean perspectives on the fatherhood of God, Matthew's Gospel deserves a detailed research, in order that his unique contribution to the subject might be revealed in a systematic way. Moreover, by placing the very idea of the fatherhood of God within the context of the Synoptic Gospels, the very similarities and distinctiveness within the Synoptic Gospels will be projected and thereby drawing attention to the theology of the Synoptic Gospels in addition to Matthean theology.

1.3. Definitions of Terms

1.3.1. Fatherhood of God

According to the *Random House Unabridged Dictionary*,[27] 'fatherhood' basically means 'the state of being a father.' It also means 'the qualities or Spirit of a father.' A father is one that establishes or is head of a household; an originator or

---

[25] D' Angelo, "Theology in Mark and Q: Abba and 'Father' in Context," in *HTR* 85/2 (1992): 160.

[26] Lk 2:49; 6:36; 9:26; 10:21-22; 11:2, 13; 12:30, 32; 22:29, 42; 23:34, 46; 24:49.

[27] Second Edition (New York: Random House, 1993), 702.

generator. He feeds his household, physically and spiritually. He loves and cares for his household because it is his. The Greek term πατήρ is used in both literal and figurative sense.[28] In literal sense 'father' is connected with paternity, that is, as originator (or begetter); while in the figurative sense, 'father' is connected with fatherhood, one responsible for the welfare of the child. When the word 'father' is connected with the idea of paternity, it means no more than the person fathered the child. On the other hand, when the word 'father' is connected with the idea of fatherhood, it describes a relationship of closeness and intimacy and love. It describes a relationship in which the father cares for the child in body, mind and spirit, in which the father nourishes the child with food, guides the child, advices, surrounds and strengthens the child with continual love.[29] It is in this latter sense that the fatherhood idea is used for God in both Old and New Testament.

1.3.2. Patriarchy/Patriarchal

The term 'patriarchy' or 'patriarchal' both formed with the combination of two Greek words *pater* (father) and *arche* ('first' or 'beginning'). The term patriarchy thus refers to the structure of male superiority in the household functioning. Patriarchy thus implies hierarchy and male superiority.[30]

1.3.3 Theology of God

The word 'theology' is used here in the narrow sense of the term. It thus focuses on who God is and what God has done.[31]

1.4. Limitation and Scope

The major concern of this research is to examine the theological significance of the fatherhood of God as portrayed in Matthew. As such this study proposes to make a detailed analysis of the following passages that talk about God's fatherhood both explicitly and implicitly in Matthew and examine how Matthew redacted, keeping his theological perspectives: 2:13-15; 5:9, 43-48; 6:1-6, 9-13;

---

[28] W.C. Trenchard, *A Concise Dictionary of New Testament Greek* (Cambridge: Cambridge University Press, 2003), 122.

[29] W. Barclay, *The Mind of Jesus* (London: SCM Press, 1960), 120.

[30] According to Rosemary Radford Ruether (*Sexism and God-talk*, 61) patriarchy is not merely mean subordination of females to males, but the whole structure of father-ruled society. For Gerda Lerner (*The Creation of Patriarchy* [New York: Cambridge University Press, 1986], 239) sexism and patriarchy are inseparable. According to her sexism is the manifestation and institutionalization of male dominance over women and children in the family and the extension of male dominance over women in society in general. However, for J.W. Miller (*Biblical Faith and Fathering: Why We Call God "Father"* [New York: Paulist Press, 1989], 24-25) in the ancient West Asian society, including the Jewish society, the term 'patriarchal' was basically meant the tracing of lineage through the male line.

[31] As J.D.G. Dunn in his recent work (*New Testament Theology: An Introduction* [Nashville: Abingdon Press, 2009], 41) rightly talks about theology as first and foremost *theo-logy*, that is, God, being the foundation in every New Testament writings, as the main theme for any theology.

6:24-34; 7:7-11; 18:10-14; 18:23-35; 20:1-16; 25:31-46; 26:36-42, 47-56. The passages concerning God's fatherhood common to all the Synoptic Gospels will also be considered so as to examine their common theological perspectives. It would be necessary to have background studies from the Greco-Roman writings and philosophical discourses, the Old Testament, Palestinian and Hellenistic Judaism and Jesus' traditions as regard to the theme of God's fatherhood. After this investigation, its relevance and applicability to current studies about God, especially for doing theology in Indian context shall be discussed.

1.5. Previous Studies

Before we present our strategy for analyzing the fatherhood of God theme in Matthean theology, a brief survey of recent discussions - on how the theme of God fared in New Testament and Matthean studies - is necessary. It will prepare us to think about the importance of the fatherhood of God idea in Matthew and New Testament thinking than is previously recognized.

It is a fact that the New Testament studies including the many works of the New Testament theology is dominated by the study of the person and work of Christ (Christology). And it is only in the recent few decades that scholars began to address the theme of God (theology) in New Testament studies. A clear recognition of God as the principal force of the New Testament is found in the work of N.T. Wright,[32] J.D.G. Dunn[33] and L.W. Hurtado.[34] Prior to these scholars, most New Testament theologies are found in Bultmannian mould, that is, christocentric focus.[35] Consequently, in all these major New Testament theologies till the 1980s the theme of 'God' is subsumed under Christology. Even in recent times most New Testament theology works, though theocentric in focus

[32] It was N.T. Wright who observed that the question of God is fundamental to all the issues of New Testament; see his work *The New Testament and the People of God* (London: SPCK, 1992), 1992), 471.

[33] Dunn, *New Testament Theology: An Introduction*, 41.

[34] L.W. Hurtado, *God in New Testament Theology* (Nashville: Abingdon Press, 2010), 26.

[35] R. Bultmann (*Theology of the New Testament* [complete in one volume; trans. Kendrick Grobel; New York: Charles Scribner's Sons, 1955], 3) talks about the kerygma, that is, Christology, as the beginning of New Testament theology and thus sidelined the importance of theology (God). Several noted New Testament theology works follow in the same Bultmann trend. Alan Richardson, *An Introduction to the Theology of the New Testament* (London: SCM Press, 1958); H. Conzelmann, *An Outline of the Theology of the New Testament* (New York: Harpers & Row, 1969); W.G. Kummel, *The Theology of the New Testament According to Its Major Witnesses: Jesus-Paul-John* (London: SCM Press, 1974); L. Goppelt, *Theology of the New Testament I: The Ministry of Jesus In Its Theological Significance* (trans John E. Alsup and ed. Jurgen Roloff; Grand Rapids: William B. Eerdmans, 1981); G.E. Ladd, *A Theology of the New Testament* (London: Lutterworth Press, 1974); D. Guthrie, *New Testament Theology* (London: Inter-Varsity Press, 1981).

yet the importance of the theme of the fatherhood of God has not often been specifically pointed out.[36]

The scene is starker when we survey the Matthean studies as regard to the theme of God. It is surprising that to date there is no extended study of God in the Gospel of Matthew, particularly when we compare Matthew to his Synoptic counterparts Mark and Luke, as both have received certain amount of attention as regard to the theme of God.[37] This neglect of Matthew is all the more curious by the absence of a treatment of it in the recent work on New Testament Theology *Forgotten God: Perspective in Biblical Theology*.[38] With the exception of two small articles contributed on the subject of God in Matthew by Robert L. Mowery (1988)[39] and Julian Sheffield (2001)[40] respectively, there is no work on Matthew focusing on God (theology). It is seen that most of the works on Matthew and Matthean theology are dominated by christological focus. In the early 1980s two

[36] E.g., I. H. Marshall, *New Testament Theology: Many Witness, One Gospel* (Illinois: Intervarsity Press, 2004); F.J. Matera, *New Testament Theology: Exploring Diversity and Unity* (Louisville: Westminster John Knox Press, 2007); U. Schnelle, *Theology of the New Testament* (trans. M.E. Boring; Grand Rapids: Baker Academic, 2009); Thomas R. Schreiner, *New Testament Theology: Magnifying God in Christ* (Grand Rapids; Michigan: Baker Academic, 2008).

[37] Some of the works on the theme of God in Mark Gospel see J.R. Donahue, "A neglected factor in the Theology of Mark," in *JBL* 101 (1982), 563-94; P. Danube, "The Narrative Function of Mark's Characterization of God," in *NovT* 43 (2001), 12-30; J.D. Kingsbury, "God within the Narrative World of Mark," in A. Andrew Das and F. J. Matera (eds.), *The Forgotten God: Perspectives in Biblical Theology* (Louisville: Westminster John Knox Press, 2002), 75-89. For the Gospel of Luke see R.L. Brawly, *Centering on God: Method and Message in Luke-Acts* (Louisville: Westminster John Knox Press, 1990); Diane G. Chen, *God as Father in Luke-Acts* (SBL 92; Bern/Frankfurt: Peter Lang, 2006); R. C. Kawlni, *Lord God Most High My Savior: Theocentricity in Lukan Theology: An exploration into the Portrayals of God in Luke-Acts* (Delhi: ISPCK, 2009).

[38] The volume has essays on Mark, Luke-Acts, John, Romans and Galatians, the Corinthians, Colossians and Ephesians, The Pastoral Epistles, Hebrews, James and the Petrine Epistles and the book of Revelations, plus four more essays on 'God' in Old Testament writings.

[39] His article ("God, Lord and Father: The Theology of the Gospel of Matthew," in *BR* 33 [1988], 24-36) is an analysis of the uses of God, Father and Lord in Matthew. However he did not draw theological conclusions from the data he collected.

[40] Julian Sheffield, "The Father in the Gospel of Matthew," in *A Feminist Companion to Matthew*, edited by Amy-Jill Levine (Cleveland: The Pilgrims Press, 2001). She made a data analysis of the occurrences and usage of the term 'Father' (Sheffield, "The Father in the Gospel of Matthew," 53-55). While using feminist interpretative tools she talks about how the human father is displaced in favor of God-as-Father. Thus she observed that the word 'Father' has a special meaning for Matthew as it is exclusively applied to the heavenly Father. For her the picture of a caring Father in heaven is of maternal in nature (Sheffield, "The Father in the Gospel of Matthew," 69). Thus her study on God as Father is done mainly to underline Matthew's inclusive and egalitarian perspective.

leading Matthean scholars namely G. Stanton[41] and Donald Senior[42] come out with comprehensive survey of leading Matthean scholarship from the end of the Second World War (1940s) to the 1980s. Their survey show that the major focus in almost all the leading works on Matthew during these decades were on the Setting of Matthew, Sources and Structure, Salvation History, Fulfillment, The Law, Christology, Discipleship and Church (Ecclesiology).[43] In line with their observations it is noticed that even in the current Matthean scholarship, most of the works in Matthean theology is dominated by Christology and the theme of God finds no place. One of the most noted works on Matthean theological themes is by R.T. France *Matthew - Evangelist and Teacher* (1989), which is a systematic and comprehensive treatment on Matthew, covering several themes of Matthew. But he subsumed the theme of God under Christology.[44] This preoccupation with Jesus or giving primacy to Christology is evident in the works of several Matthean scholars in the recent past. J. D. Kingsbury's 1988 monograph *Matthew as Story* project Jesus as the major character and Christology as the key theme in Matthew.[45] So also in his earlier work *Matthew: Structure, Christology, Kingdom* (1975), Kingsbury considered the 'Son of God' as the key christological title in Matthew.[46] Another noted Matthean scholar U. Luz too views Christology as the overarching theme in Matthew. In his 1995 monograph *The Theology of the Gospel of Matthew*, following literary narrative approach, he presents Matthew as "a *story* of Jesus."[47] He views Matthew with christological lens as he clearly noted right at the introduction that "the entire Gospel is bracketed by the fundamental Christological motif of 'God with us' (Immanuel) in 1:23 and 28:20."[48] Thus we see that the theme of God finds no proper emphasis in his work. The same neglect of God is evident in the work of Donald Senior (1997) who asserts that "virtually every aspect of the gospel (of Matthew) relates to its Christology."[49] So, also is the work of R. Schnackenburg (2002) who subsumed the theme of God under Christology.[50] It seems then that virtually almost all the scholars sidelined

---

[41] G. Stanton, "The Origin and Purpose of Matthew's Gospel: Matthean Scholarship from 1945-1980," in *ANRW* II.25.3 (1985), 1889-1951.

[42] D. Senior, *What Are They Saying About Matthew?* (New York: Paulist Press, 1983; *Revised and Expanded Edition*, 1996).

[43] Senior, *What Are They Saying About Matthew? Revised and Expanded Edition*, 7-104.

[44] R.T France, *Matthew - Evangelist and Teacher* (Exeter: The Paternoster Press, 1989), 279-317.

[45] J.D. Kingsbury, *Matthew As Story* (Philadelphia: Fortress Press, 1988), 10-11.

[46] J.D. Kingsbury, *Matthew: Structure, Christology, Kingdom* (Philadelphia: Fortress Press, 1975), 41, 80-82.

[47] U. Luz, *The Theology of Matthew* (Cambridge: Cambridge University Press, 1995), xi.

[48] Luz, *The Theology of Matthew*, 4.

[49] D. Senior, *The Gospel of Matthew* (Nashville: Abingdon Press, 1997), 53.

[50] R. Schnackenburg, *The Gospel of Matthew* (Grand Rapids; Michigan: Wm B. Eerdmans, 2002), 143-145.

the theme of God and focused on Jesus' significance, though God is the main agent and the prime force behind every narrative in the Gospel. The same neglect is apparent in M. Hannan's work on Matthew (2006). She contends that the central theological concern of Matthew is *he basileia* or the sovereignty of God.[51] According to her Matthew structures his work as a biography of Jesus and that the sovereignty of God is the core subject matter of Jesus' teaching.[52] As such her focus is more on the nature of the kingdom and that the question of God emerges only in relation to the Kingdom proclamation of Jesus.

It is clear from these reviews that very little explorations seem to have been undertaken on the theme of God particularly in Matthew. As explained above, most Matthean scholars focus on Jesus but not on God. As such there are important theological issues yet to address: What is the place of God in the Matthean thinking and emphasis? Why God is not given his due place in spite of the fact that God holds the overarching and fundamental place in all the presentations of Jesus (Christology)? How about the fatherhood of God?

1.6. Method of Approach

The particular methodological approach to exploring Matthew's distinct theological perspective concerning the theme of the fatherhood of God will comprise a combination of traditional historical-critical method and comparative-historical analysis.

Historical-critical tools will be used in the exegesis of the selected passages that deal with the theme of God's fatherhood, with particular utilization of Source and Redaction criticism. Obviously traditions about Jesus namely Mark and Q, together with other traditions about the early church account for the main sources of information for Matthew. What we perceive in Matthew is the result of Matthew's selection, arrangement and redaction of these materials. In other words, we will look at Matthew's Gospel as complete documents and see the Evangelist Matthew as individual theologian in his own right. So, redaction criticism will be used to identify what are the unique Matthean emphases on the fatherhood of God and thus his theological intentions behind these usages.[53] As stated above comparative-historical analysis, which is also called the history of religions perspective,[54] will be necessary as in the process of exegesis, we will compare Matthew's idea with his broader cultural, religious and political milieus, that is, Greco-Roman and Jewish understanding of the same idea of God's

[51] M. Hannan, *The Nature and Demands of the Sovereign Rule of God in the Gospel of Matthew* (New York: T & T Clark, 2006), 5.

[52] Hannan, *The Nature and Demands of the Sovereign Rule of God*, 230.

[53] Redaction critics believe that the changes to the source or tradition provide a clue to the Evangelist's theological intentions and the life-situation of his community.

[54] Scholars employing this approach looked at the sources of Christianity in terms of the surrounding religions.

fatherhood. This approach is exhibited by several noted scholars and theologians particularly in the early twentieth century onwards. Martin Hengel sees in the Jewish idea of a universal sovereign God as depicted in the Gospels, e.g., Matthew 5:44-45, some elements of the Greek, universalist conception of God.[55] The striking similarities of Christianity to the Oriental religions were observed by many noted scholars of religions.[56] According to J.G. Muthuraj, the New Testament as a religion has its roots in the oriental religions and piety.[57] He thus strongly advocates a New Testament hermeneutic from the perspective of history of religions in order to explore the common bond and mutual influence existed between New Testament and the oriental religions. Using this approach attempt will be made to put Matthew and the Synoptic Gospels within the surrounding Greco-Roman cultural, religious and political milieus, keeping their idea of God as Father in mind. We believe that these conceptual worlds too shaped Matthew's idea of God's fatherhood, in addition to Jesus' traditions and other sources of information that the author had on hand.

1.7. Plan of the Research

Keeping these above perspectives in mind this study will have three broad sections. The first section will cover the background study keeping in mind the theme of God's fatherhood in Matthew. The second section will form the core part of the research, the exegetical section, examining the passages that deal with God's fatherhood in Matthew. The examination will cover both teaching and narrative sections of Matthew. In all these the focus will be on the convictions of the Evangelist about God. That is, the theology of Matthew, particularly the fatherhood of God. The final section will be the on the significance of the fatherhood of God, so centrally placed in Matthew, as a source for doing theology, mission and witness in religiously pluralistic context of India.

The first section covers three chapters with chapter one introducing the thesis and dealing with the methodological considerations. The second chapter

[55] Martin Hengel, *Judaism and Hellenism; Studies in their Encounter in Palestine during the Early Hellenistic Period* (London: SCM Press, 1974), 264.

[56] E.g., R. Otto (*Indian Religion of Grace and Christianity Compared and Contrasted* [New York: The Macmillan Company, 1930], 64) sees close affinity of Indian devotional religious traditions with New Testament Christianity. Noted church historian and New Testament scholar S. Neill (*Jesus Through Many Eyes: Introduction to the Theology of the New Testament* [Philadelphia: Fortress Press, 1976], 12) sees remarkable resemblances of the origin of Christianity to that of the origin of Buddhism, as both founders wrote nothing yet are extraordinary in terms of maintaining their historicity and faith traditions.

[57] J.G. Muthuraj, "Reading New Testament with a Pluralist Mindset," in *Light on Our Dusty Path*, edited by Israel Selvanayagam (Bangalore: BTESSC / SATHRI, 2008), 30-57; J.G. Muthuraj, "New Testament and Methodology: An Overview," in *Interweaving Methodology and Praxis – Exploring Disciplinary Options in Today's World*, edited by I. John Mohan Razu (Bangalore: BTESSC/SATHRI, 2007), 112-118.

will be entirely devoted to the broader environments of Matthew – the Greco-Roman and Hellenistic-Jewish social, religious and political milieus - in order to grasp the significance of Matthew's theology of God. That means we will cover Platonic-Stoic philosophical treatises and extra-canonical literatures of early Judaism - the Apocrypha, the Old Testament Pseudepigrapha, the Dead Sea Scrolls, Josephus, Philo and Rabbinic literatures - with the hope that they will shed light on Matthew and the Synoptic writers' idea of the fatherhood of God. We will also look at the Roman history to examine how the fatherhood idea prevailed in social political sphere. While in the third chapter we will focus on Matthew's immediate source Mark, Luke (Q) and Paul, focusing on the words of Jesus on God as Father and so the fatherhood idea in Jesus' traditions. Our focus will be to examine whether the idea is in continuity with the Old Testament Jewish traditions or unique to Jesus.

The second section contains the core part of the research; with chapter four dealing with the exegetical analysis, examining the passages that deal with God's fatherhood in Matthew. The examination will cover both teaching and narrative sections of Matthew. The fifth chapter will be dealing with the meaning and functions of the fatherhood of God in Matthew. In this chapter we will also touch upon the broader New Testament God-discourse and examine the status of the theme of the fatherhood of God, which is the core theological motif of Matthew, in the overall New Testament thinking and theology.

The third section will cover the implication part of the research, with the sixth chapter devoting to how the theme of the fatherhood of God can be utilized for doing theology in a multi-faith context of India. As such we will delve into the major religious traditions of India and examine how God's fatherhood idea is portrayed in Vedic traditions, Upanishads, the Bhagavad Gita, Quran and the popular and later religious traditions of both Hinduism and Islam. So, also we will cover traditional tribal religious traditions of the Ao Nagas, and examine how the idea of God's fatherhood is portrayed in the belief in the supreme God *Tsungrem* and its functional names. Getting insights from some of the prominent theologians and secular thinkers of India we will argue how the fatherhood of God idea so central in Matthew and the Synoptic Gospels can be carried forward in Indian thinking, theology and mission. In the final chapter, we will give the overall summary of the study and also highlight the main findings and functions of God's fatherhood in Matthew.

Chapter 2

The Fatherhood of God in Greco-Roman and Jewish Literatures

2. 1. The Fatherhood of God in Greco-Roman Literatures

In order to understand the idea of God's fatherhood in Matthew we need to understand first the broader context of Matthew, the surrounding Greco-Roman cultural, religious and political milieus. We believe that these conceptual worlds explicitly and implicitly shaped Matthew's view of God and the idea of God's fatherhood. Before looking into the religious and philosophical idea of the fatherhood we will first look into the social context of the use of father with the assumption that the philosophical-theological symbolization draws on family figure and relationships, as family being the basis of any society.

2.1.1. Sources

A wealth of information about Greco-Roman fathers and the idea of fatherhood can be obtained from a wide range of Greek and Roman literary sources including historical accounts, biographies, moral essays, plays, poetry and philosophical treatises. As such for our purpose, apart from the classical philosophers like Plato and Aristotle (fourth century B.C.E.), we will consider Greek writers like Plutarch (46 -119 C.E.),[58] Epictetus (55 -135 C.E.);[59] while the Roman writers

---

[58] Plutarch, *Moralia*, trans Frank C. Babbitt, 15 vols (Cambridge; Mass: Harvard University Press 1927-1969).

[59] Epictetus, *The Discourses as Reported by Arrian, The Manual and Fragments*, trans W.A. Oldfather, 2 vols (Cambridge; Mass: Harvard University Press, 1925-1928).

like Seneca (4 B.C.E.- 65 C.E.),[60] Suetonius (b. 69 C.E.),[61] and Ovid (43 B.C.E. – 17 C.E.)[62] are the main sources. Most of these writers were active from the end of the first century B.C.E. to the latter part of the first century C.E. thus provided contemporaneous perspectives on the characteristics of the father and fatherhood idea.

2.1.2. The Father in Secular Context

In ancient Greco-Roman society, a very strong father-figure flourished. The father was the head of the household (*paterfamilias*). His role was monarchical, and the main duty of the children was to honor and obey him. Being the head and protector of the household, the father had an overwhelming power (*patria potestas*). This power was life-long, that is, it lasted until the father's death.[63] A person could do nothing without the father's consent. Even adults under his paternal roof had no legal right to property. A person could not sign a contract, free a slave or draw up his or her will. In other words, a person could not become free under the law, until his or her father died.[64] There were of course some lifelines for the children in the midst of such strong paternal power. A son could get a *peculium*, for instance, in the form of a house, money or slaves which he could administer as his own.[65] The wife was in a position of subordination to her husband. This was according to Greco-Roman tradition.

2.1.3. Characteristics of the Greco-Roman Fathers

2.1.3.1. Paternal Authority and Piety

The respect and reverence for the father was very much prevalent in Greco-Roman society. Children were expected to give reverence in words and in deeds to their fathers absolutely.[66] For Seneca, obedience is the highest respect that a child can bestow on his or her parents and that one must submit to parental authority, whether just or unjust. Since the father is the very source of the child's existence,

---

[60] Seneca, *Moral Essays*, trans John W. Basore, 3 vols (Cambridge; Mass: Harvard University Press, 1928-1935).

[61] Suetonius, *The Twelve Caesars*, trans Robert Graves (Great Britain: Penguin Books, 1957), 7.

[62] S.G. Owen, 'Ovid [Publius Ovidius Naso],' in *OCD*, edited by M. Cary, A.D. Nock, W.D. Ross, et al. (Oxford: Clarendon Press, 1968), 630-632; Geraldine Herbert-Brown, *Ovid and The Fasti: A Historical Study* (Oxford: Clarendon Press, 1994).

[63] B. Rawson, "The Roman Family," in *The Family in Ancient Rome: New Perspectives*, edited by B. Rawson (London: Routledge, 1992), 7-8.

[64] Paul Veyne (ed.), *A History of Private Life I: From Pagan Rome to Byzantium* (Cambridge: Harvard University Press, 1987), 28.

[65] Paul Veyne (ed.), *A History of Private Life I*, 27-28.

[66] See Laws 4.717D, in *Plato* I, 299, trans R. G. Bury (Cambridge; Mass: Harvard University Press, 1926).

the child is expected to reciprocate with respect, obedience and filial piety to the father (*De Beneficiis* 3.29.2-8).[67]

2.1.3.2. Father as Loving, Affectionate and Humane

The fathers in the Greco-Roman society were generally loving and humane. Such image of a father is seen in the writings of the Greco-Roman secular writers and philosophers. Diogenes Laertius talks about father as having affectionate and loving in nature (*Zeno* 7.120).[68] Epictetus once said, "How, then, can we still be social beings, if affection for our own children is not a natural sentiment? … once a child is born, it is no longer in our power not to love it or to care for it" (*Discourses* 1.23.3-5).[69] The natural sentiment is grounded on the fact that the father is the source of his child's life (*Nicomachean Ethics* 8.12).[70] Seneca too says that a father loves his children simply because they are his own (*Epistle* 66.26-28).[71] Children should be reared and nurtured (*De Beneficiis* 3.11.1),[72] which logically rules out the unethical exposure of infants.

2.1.3.3. Father as Provider of Material Needs

A father's love is channeled through the care and nurture of his children. Parents are expected to provide for their children's needs of food and shelter, heap benefits on them, and put their needs before their own, as Seneca put forth, "like the best of parents, who only smile at the spiteful words of their children, the gods do not cease to heap their benefits upon those who are doubtful about the source of benefits, but distribute their blessings among the nations and peoples with unbroken uniformity" (*De Beneficiis* 7.31.4).[73] Here Seneca compares God with the goodness of the earthly father.

2.1.3.4. Father as Provider of Moral and Intellectual Needs

Among the parents it is the father who contributes in upbringing and teaching the children by education, disciplining and planning for his children's future. In the discourse on household management, Aristotle says, "It is the mother

[67] Seneca, *Moral Essays* III, 181-183.

[68] *Diogenes Laertius* II, trans R. D. Hicks (Cambridge; Mass: Harvard University Press, 1925), 225.

[69] *Epictetus* I, 149-151.

[70] *Aristotle* XIX, 499; It is commonly held by the ancients that parental affection is ordained by nature. As such Aristotle equates the instinctive love in human beings for their young with that found in animals and bird; See *Nicomachean Ethics* 8.1.3, in *Aristotle* XIX, trans H. Rackham (Cambridge; Mass: Harvard University Press, 1926), 451-453.

[71] Seneca, *Ad Lucilium Epistulae Morales* II, trans Richared M. Gummere (Cambridge; Mass: Harvard University Press, 1920), 19.

[72] Seneca, *Moral Essays* III, 147.

[73] Seneca, *Moral Essays* III, 523.

who nurtures, and the father who educates" (*Oeconomica*1.3.4).[74] So also in his discourse on Law regarding the disciplining of children Plato writes on father, "To his children it behoves a man to bequeath modesty, not money, in abundance ... the most effective way of training the young ... is not by admonition, but by plainly practicing throughout one's own life the admonitions which one gives to others" (*Laws* 5.729 B-C).[75] In the account of Plutarch, we see a good example of a father who invests on his child's education, so much so "by instruction, by threats, by entreaties pointing out examples of men who through ... their steadfastness, have gained for themselves approval and good repute."[76]

2.1.3.5. Disciplining and Merciful Father

We also see the nature of a wise father who holds affection and discipline in a complementary tension. Seneca suggests that a good parent reproves sometimes gently and at other times with threats and lashes. In his own words:

> What, then, is his duty? It is that of the good parent who is wont to reprove his children sometimes gently, sometimes with threats, who at times admonishes them even by stripes. Does any father in his senses disinherit a son for his first offence? Only when great and repeated wrong-doings has overcome his patience ... but first he makes many an effort to reclaim a character that is still unformed ... when the case is hopeless, he tries extreme measures. No one resorts to the exaction of punishment until he has exhausted all the means of correction (*De Clementia* 1.14.1).[77]

As seen in this discourse, for Seneca, maintaining a balance between freedom and control is the key to sound education. The goal is to prevent a father from breaking his children's spirits by being too harsh, or fostering laziness and disregard for others by being too permissive (*De Ira* 2.21.1-7).[78] Thus we find in the Greco-Roman writings a father having the characteristics of both paternal authority and affection. The father figure symbolized power and authority as well as providence and beneficence. As such both sides of fatherhood, patriarchal authority and compassionate and caring nature coexisted in a positive tension.

---

[74] *Oeconomica and Magna Moralia*, in Aristotle XVIII, trans G. Cyril Armstrong (Cambridge; Mass: Harvard University Press, 1935), 333.

[75] *Plato* I, 329-331.

[76] *De Liberis Educandis* 12 C, in Plutarch's *Moralia* I, trans F.C. Babbitt (Cambridge; Mass: Harvard University Press, 1927), 57-59.

[77] Seneca, *Moral Essays* I, 399.

[78] Seneca, *Moral Essays* I, 209-211.

2.1.4. The Father Imagery in Greco-Roman Imperial Context

The Romans showed an affinity by using family concepts metaphorically, that is, they used family concepts to describe relationships outside the family spheres. Since the family is considered the basic unit of Greco-Roman society, it is a short step to move from the *paterfamilias* as the head of the household to emperor as the head of the state.[79] Both occupy the most authoritative position in their respective realm of influence. Just as the role of a father as *paterfamilias* the emperor was called the 'Father of the Fatherland' (*Pater Patriae*). It would seem that such title expressed that complete confidence which respectful children (subjects) should have in their father (emperor).[80] The paternal authority of monarchs and rulers were thus accepted as right. The respect for and obedience to royal authority was based on the commandment to respect the parents, particularly the father.[81]

The father metaphor is found mentioned in several ancient authors particularly used in the political realm. And we see in several texts prominent elements about the fatherly role of the Roman emperor. In Seneca we find extensive comparison of an emperor to a father:

> This is the duty of a father, and it is also the duty of a prince, whom not in empty flattery we have been led to call "the Father of his Country." For other designations have been granted merely by way of honor ... but to "the Father of his Country" we have given the name in order that he may know that he has been entrusted with a father's power, which is most forbearing in its care for the interests of his children and subordinates his own to theirs (*De Clementia* 1.14.2-3).[82]

Seneca here speaks of the paternal authority of the emperor, stressing the importance of extending mercy, even in the midst of wielding one's power. According to him, the obligation that comes with possessing *patria potestas* is the wise use of that power. Calling emperor *Pater Patriae* is an expression of trust on the part of the citizens, who put their corporate interests in the hands of a man who can bring as much harm to them as he can benefits. Because the emperor is like a father who has the power over the life and death of his political children, he "ought to use this great gift of the gods in a noble spirit" (*De Clementia* 1.21.2).[83] Precisely because the emperor's *patria potestas* is a divine mandate, it must be carried out with care and integrity. And this integrity is measured by the way in which the emperor uses his power. As such Seneca portrays Caesar speaking:

---

[79] See the argument of W.K. Lacey that Roman state as a family and the gods of the state as the gods of a family; Lacey, "Patria Potestas," in *The Family in Ancient Rome: New Perspectives*, 125-130.

[80] As Aristotle likens the ruler-subject relationship in a monarchy to that of a father and his children; see *Pol.* 1.5.2.

[81] See e.g., Plato, *Laws* 4.71; Seneca, *De Beneficiis* 3.29. 2-8.

[82] Seneca, *Moral Essays* I, 399.

[83] Seneca, *Moral Essays* I, 417.

> Have I of all mortals found favor with heaven and been chosen to serve on earth as vicar of the gods? I am the arbiter of life and death for the nations; it rests in my power what each man's lot and state shall be ... With all things thus at my disposal, I have been moved neither by anger nor youthful impulse to unjust punishment, nor by the foolhardiness and obstinacy of men which have often wrung patience from even the serenest souls, nor yet by that vain glory which employs terror for the display of might – a dread but all too common use of great and lordly power (*De Clementia* 1.2-3).[84]

For Seneca, mercy is thus a crucial quality to cultivate for an emperor who lives up to his title as *Pater Patriae*. This is all the more evident as in another instance he says:

> Yet of all men none is better graced by mercy than a king or a prince. For great power confers grace and glory only when it is potent for benefit; it is surely a baneful might that is strong only for harm. He alone has firm and well-grounded greatness who all men know to be much their friend as he is their superior; whose concern they daily find to be vigilant for the safety of each and all (*De Clementia* 1.3.3.).[85]

Mercy is thus for Seneca the virtue most befitting of the *Pater Patriae*. It allows the emperor to exercise his *patria potestas* in a benign manner for the benefit of all.

From the above views we see the rulers as good fathers, with generous nature towards their subjects. As a father of the whole nation his impartial nature is seen in that he generously provides for all regardless of their social status. However, as seen in the description of Seneca, granting mercy does not diminish but in fact enhances the greatness of the emperor's authority. Just as a father's love is reciprocated by his children's respect, the emperor's mercy will earn the loyalty and affection of his subjects. The image of a ruler or a leader as father is thus associated with his generosity and attentiveness to the interest of the people. With this we will briefly trace the development of the use of the father metaphor for leaders in Rome's political history.

2.1.4.1. The Roman Emperor as *Pater Patriae*

It is said that Cicero was the first Roman to receive the title *Parens Patriae* (Parent of his country) officially.[86] The title was "the greatest honours conferred and

---

[84] Seneca, *Moral Essays* I, 357-359.

[85] Seneca, *Moral Essays* I, 365-367.

[86] Cicero 23.6, in *Plutarch's Lives* VII (Cambridge; Mass: Harvard University Press, 1919), 139.

called him the father of his Country"[87] given by the Senate after he successfully suppressed the Catiline conspiracy.[88]

2.1.4.1.1. Julius Caesar

Caesar was also conferred the title 'Father of the Fatherland' officially. Like Cicero he was honoured as father because he saved his country. More so Caesar was greatly honoured as a father who showed mercy. Despite the ruthless means by which Julius Caesar rose to power, at the end of the civil war he implemented an unprecedented policy of clemency by granting amnesty to political opponents and sparing the lives of defeated enemies.[89] Eventually when Caesar died, his followers extolled him greatly so much so that they set up a twenty-foot-high column in the Forum with the inscription, 'To the Father of His Country.'[90] The Roman Senate even made the decision to call the day of Caesar's murder as 'The Day of Parricide.'[91] Even in the coins the very title *Parens Patrai* was stamped with the implication that the Father of the country was not merely a savior, but a merciful savior.[92] His murder thus resulted in his divinization, spontaneously enacted by the people and later sanctioned by the Senate, which officially accepted Caesar among the gods of the state and erected an altar for him in the city. Thus the very idea of imperial and paternal imagery 'father' was strongly associated with Caesar.[93]

2.1.4.1.2. Augustus

According to Suetonius the Roman Senate decided to confer the title *Pater Patriae* on Augustus on behalf of the entire Senate and the people. Thus in the account of Suetonius, Valerius Messala, speaking for the whole body said: "Caesar Augustus, I am instructed to wish you and your family good fortune and divine blessings; which amounts to wishing that our entire City will be fortunate and our country prosperous. The Senate agree with the people of Rome in saluting you as Father of your Country."[94] On giving such great honour, Suetonius narrates, Augustus was moved to tears saying: "Fathers of the Senate, I have at last achieved my highest ambition. What more can I ask of the immortal gods than that they may permit

[87] Cicero 23.6, in *Plutarch's Lives* VII, 139.

[88] Cicero 22.7-8, in *Plutarch's Lives* VII, 137.

[89] Julius Caesar 75, in *Suetonius: The Twelve Caesars*, 40-41.

[90] Julius Caesar 85, in *Suetonius: The Twelve Caesars*, 48.

[91] Julius Caesar 88, in *Suetonius: The Twelve Caesars*, 48.

[92] Stefan Weinstock, "The Father," *Divus Julius* (Oxford: Clarendon Press, 1971), 239.

[93] On the idea of Roman political leaders as father-figure and Imperial Cult, see also H. Koester, *Introduction to the New Testament I: History, Culture, and Religion of the Hellenistic Age* (New York: Philadelphia, 1982), 366-371.

[94] Augustus 58, in *Suetonius: The Twelve Caesars*, 83.

me to enjoy your approval until my dying day?"[95] Why was Augustus so deeply moved? To accept the title meant to accept a tremendous responsibility. Thus his response revealed the seriousness with which he regarded this honour. As an emperor he was having benign authority of a father.

Following the footsteps of his predecessor Julius Caesar, Augustus too showed clemency towards defeated enemies and fellow citizens. He spared all those who seek pardon both citizens and foreigners, and rehabilitate those who complete their military services.[96]

At one time he showed mercy to his own daughter and her lover who committed adultery, which according to the law deserved capital punishment but Augustus showed mercy and "banished them for their greater safety, and gave them their credentials" (*De Clementia* 1.10.3-4).[97] As such in the account of Seneca, Augustus "well deserved the name of father" (*De Clementia* 1.10.3). As a fatherly figure in the whole empire Augustus showed tremendous mercy not only to his kid and kin but also to others including his enemies. As such Augustus also extended clemency to his enemy Cinna, the grandson of Pompey. Twice Augustus spared Cinna's life, the first time as a defeated foe and the second time for sedition. While Augustus was deliberating whether to give Cinna his just desert or to spare this man of noble birth, his wife Livia advised him not to execute Cinna, because since the latter had already been arrested, he could do no further harm. Besides, pardoning Cinna could even enhance Augustus' reputation as a merciful father. So by extending friendship instead of vengeance, Augustus earned Cinna's loyalty and gained much more than if he were to sentence him to death (*De Clementia* 1.9.2-12).[98]

Another illustration of Augustus' mercy in the account of Seneca is that Augustus spared the life of Tarius' son, who was accused of attempted patricide, a crime that deserved capital punishment, but Augustus recommended exile. When Tarius' son committed that crime, Augustus went to Tarius' house, sat next to him at the hearth as a member of the consilium, and did not usurp the latter's prerogative as *paterfamilias*. He did not bypass Tarius, the head of the household, though he had the power and capacity to do so, thus showing the deeds worthy of the title 'Father of his country' (*De Clementia* 1.15.3-1.16.1).[99]

2.1.4.1.2.1. Augustus Paternal Gestures

Not only has the merciful nature that describes Augustus as Father but that his reforms and developments of the city underscore his father image. He instituted

---

[95] Augustus 58, in *Suetonius: The Twelve Caesars*, 83.

[96] *Res Gestae Divi Augusti* 3, in *Roman Civilization: Sourcebook II: The Empire*, edited by N. Lewis and M. Reinhold (New York: Harper & Row, 1966), 10.

[97] Seneca, *Moral Essays* I, 389.

[98] Seneca, *Moral Essays* I, 381-387.

[99] Seneca, *Moral Essays* I, 401-403.

a series of urban projects to beautify Rome and improve the infrastructure of the city.[100] He used his own funds to restore eighty-two temples, built numerous new shrines and temples, and personally conducted rituals and made sacrifices in the capacity of *pontifex maximus*.[101] Augustus thus used the position *pontifex maximus* to enhance his father image.[102] He introduced Apollo as the State god. At the very place where the imperial palace stood he elevated the temple of Apollo. The essence of his religious policy was a close union of the throne and the altar. He connected his imperial house directly with the temple of Apollo and holding many state functions in the temple precincts.[103] Thus the worship of the deity and the emperor become very close. In fact many writers compare Augustus' fatherhood to that of Jupiter. Comparing Augustus' fatherhood to that of Jupiter, Ovid writes: "You bear on earth the name which Jupiter bears in high heaven, you the father of men, he of gods" (*Fasti* 2.37-40).[104] His birthday was celebrated throughout the empire.[105] Games were organized in his honour and sacrifices were offered to the gods.[106] Consequently with the introduction of state religious activities on the person of the emperor, and the development of the imperial cult in the background, the *Pontifex maximus* came to be elevated above his priestly position to a level closer to the gods.

Just as a father generously provides for his children, Augustus instituted large scale distributions of money and grain to his subjects on several occasions to the benefit of thousands and thousands of common people each time. Some of these occasions were celebrations of triumphs at war, during which the spoils were shared with the soldiers and the people. On several occasions he came to the rescue of the treasury and pays his own money in disbursement of bonuses to the soldiers. He covered the shortfall in tax revenues with his own funds. He donated to both the public and the military treasuries, and bought land in Italy and in the provinces to resettle retired soldiers.[107] Augustus thus exercised his role as father on a grant scale. He lived and demonstrated by his deeds of what it means to be *Pater Patriae* in a more comprehensive way. He was the savior and founder of Roman peace (*Pax Romana*).[108] He put an end to years of bloodshed and brought Rome back to a time of peace and prosperity. Every level of Roman

---

[100] Suetonius, Augustus 28, in *The Twelve Caesars*, 83.

[101] *Res Gestae Divi Augusti* 19-20, in *Roman Civilization; Sourcebook II: The Empire*, 15.

[102] *Res Gestae Divi Augusti* 7-10, in *Roman Civilization; Sourcebook II: The Empire*, 12.

[103] "Restoration of the State Religion," in *Roman Civilization; Sourcebook II: The Empire*, 55.

[104] Cited in G. Herbert-Brown, *Ovid and The Fasti: a Historical Study*, 47.

[105] "Emperor Worship," in *Roman Civilization; Sourcebook II: The Empire*, 61-66.

[106] "The Secular Games," in *Roman Civilization; Sourcebook II: The Empire*, 56-61.

[107] *Res Gestae Divi Augusti* 15-18, in *Roman Civilization; Sourcebook II: The Empire*, 14-15.

[108] See M.P. Charlesworth, *The Roman Empire* (London: Oxford University Press, 1961), 27.

society recognized his paternal authority.[109] To accept the title meant to accept a tremendous responsibility. Accordingly it is said that Tiberius, who was the successor of Augustus, indeed refused the title, according to Suetonius, "for fear that his shame would be intensified when he turned out to be unworthy of such honours."[110] In Augustus we see the characteristics of a good father and patron. He was honoured with the title *Pater Patriae*, which did not come automatically to any emperor but was earned by benefactions, political contributions and military victories. Augustus used his power for the good of his people. Thus, the very title 'father' was an imperial title and that the imperial fatherhood was very much at force during the reign of Augustus.[111]

The image of father is therefore a powerful one with which to view the emperor, having paternal love and tremendous authority hence demanded allegiance, piety and worship.

2.1.5. Fatherhood of God in Greco-Roman Religious and Philosophical Literatures

2.1.5.1. Sources

The sources for learning about Greek and Roman religions and philosophies dealing with the fatherhood of God are mainly found in the works of Homer, Hesiod, Aeschylus, Euripides and Sophocles and the philosophical treatises of Plato, Aristotle as well as the Roman Stoic philosopher Epictetus.

2.1.5.2. Father as an Epithet for the Deity

Invocation of deity under the name of father is one of the basic phenomena of religious history.[112] And according to Greek religious traditions Zeus is considered as the foremost and the supreme deity.[113] The vocative Zeus Father can be traced to Indo-European *Dyaus Pitar* who was the god of light and the air, master of thunder and lightning, dwelling in the heavens.[114] The address of Zeus as Father

---

[109] Thus at one time when he was passing by the sea-port town of Puteoli, even the crew and passengers of a ship from Alexandria paid tribute to him, worshiped him and crying, "Through thee we live, Through thee we sail the seas, Through thee we enjoy our freedom and our fortunes." See M.P. Charlesworth, *The Roman Empire* (London: Oxford University Press, 1961), 27-28.

[110] Suetonius, Tiberius 67, in *The Twelve Caesars*, 143.

[111] According to Mary Rose D'Angelo "the assumption of the titles *parens patriae* and *pater patriae* was a major step in the emergence and solidification of the new world order Augustus constructed as the basis of his rule." See M. Rose D'Angelo, "Abba and 'Father:' Imperial Theology and the Jesus Traditions," 623.

[112] Schrenk, "Πάτερ," in *TDNT V*, edited by G. Friedrich (Grand Rapids: Wm B. Eerdmans, 1967), 951.

[113] M.P. Nilsson, *A History of Greek Religion* (Oxford: Clarendon Press, 1949), 145.

[114] M.P. Nilsson, "Zeus," in *OCD*, 966; Alain Hus, *Greek and Roman Religion*, trans S. J. Tester (New York; Hawthorn Books, 1962), 23; E.O. James, *The Cult of the Mother-Goddess, An Archaeological and Documentary Study* (London: Thames and Hudson, 1959), 111; M. Eliade, *The*

is found in numerous instances in the *Iliad* and *Odyssey* of Homer[115] as: 'Father Zeus,'[116] 'the Father of gods and human beings,'[117] 'the Father'[118] and 'the Father of the gods.'[119] The address of Zeus as Father is also found outside of Homer, for example, the *Hymn of Cleanthes to Zeus.*[120] From all these appellations used in addressing Zeus we see the idea of divine fatherhood, particularly in Homer's portrayal of Zeus. Homer portrays Zeus as the head of the Olympian family of gods.[121]

2.1.5.3. Zeus as the Father of Gods and Humankind

In the Homeric poem *Iliad* Zeus is called 'Father of gods and of men' (e.g., *Iliad* 1.544 cf. *Odyssey* 1.45). He is the head of the Olympian patriarchal family.[122] And according to Murray, Zeus have fathered many gods and mortals. Apollo and Athena are the son and daughter among several children of Zeus and his wife Hera.[123] While Moore categorized the Olympian family in hierarchical order with Zeus as the chief with Athena and Apollo in the same rank, Hera and Poseidon hold the second rank, while Hephaestus, Ares and Aphrodite belong to the third rank.[124] Thus Zeus' fatherhood can be understood both in the sense of fathering children as well as in the sense of headship (*paterfamilias*).

However, the name of father expresses above all god's absolute authority. That means, Zeus' fatherhood is seen primarily in his power and authority. In the writings of Homer, Zeus' paternal authority, a typical patriarchal feature, is evident in that upon his arrival on Olympus, "the whole company of gods rose from their chairs in deference to their Father. There was not one that dared to keep his seat as he approached; they all stood up to greet him" (*Iliad* 1.533-535).[125] The

---

Encyclopedia of Religions vol 6 (New York: Macmillan Publishing Company, 1987), 103; See also W. Kaufman, *Religions in Four Dimensions: Existential, Aesthetic, Historical, Comparative* (New York: Reader's Digest Press, 1976), 210.

[115] The phrases and expressions are all from Homer, *The Iliad*, trans E.V. Rieu (Great Britain: Penguin Books, 1950) and *The Odyssey*, trans E.V. Rieu (Great Britain: Penguin Books, 1946).

[116] E.g. *Iliad* 1.587; 3.365; 4.288; *Odyssey* 4.341; 5.7; 7.311. So also the address, 'O Father' (*Iliad* 22.178) and 'Father' (*Iliad* 3.350).

[117] E.g., *Iliad* 1.544; 4.68; 5.426; 8.49; *Odyssey* 18.137.

[118] E.g., *Iliad* 1.535; 8.69;17.648; 22. 209.

[119] E.g., *Iliad* 15.12,47.

[120] *Stobaeus Eclogae* 1.1.12; see, F.C. Grant, *Hellenistic Religions: The Age of Syncretism* (New York: The Liberal Arts Press, 1953), 152-154.

[121] C.H. Moore, *The Religious Thought of the Greeks: From Homer to the Triumph of Christianity* (Cambridge: Harvard University Press, 1916), 15.

[122] G. Murray, *Five Stages of Greek Religion* (Oxford: Clarendon Press, 1925), 25; Moore, *Religious Thought*, 14-15.

[123] Murray, *Greek Religion*, 25.

[124] Moore, *Religious Thought*, 18.

[125] Homer: *The Iliad*, trans E.V. Rieu, 37.

sons and daughters begotten by him have to obey his fatherly authority without qualification (*Iliad* 15.197). Since Zeus is the Sky Father, his power is symbolized by the formidable thunderbolt, which he holds in his right hand. When he hurls his thunderbolt, it is frightening and irresistible (e.g., *Iliad* 14.414-418). Here we find the despotic aspect of the fatherhood of Zeus.

Similar expression of sovereignty and powerful nature of Zeus is also found in the works of Hesiod. Zeus is the king of the gods, and his sovereignty is complete and final: thus sings the Muses at the beginning of the *Works and Days*:

> Muses of Pieria who give glory through song, come hither, tell of Zeus your father and chant his praise. Through him mortal men are famed, sung or unsung alike, as great Zeus wills. For easily he makes strong, and easily he brings the strong man low; easily he humbles the proud and raises the obscure, and easily he straightens the crooked and blasts the proud – Zeus who thunders aloft and has his dwelling most high (*Works and Days*, 1-8).[126]

In spite of Zeus being seemingly characterized as aloof in his power and sovereignty, yet Zeus is very much earth-bound, as Nilsson put forth that Hesiod's Zeus is "the champion of justice. His eyes see everything and notice everything; he fixes a penalty for the haughty who commit wickedness and shameful deeds ... he sends out watchers who move invisibly about the earth and observe the doings of mankind."[127]

Similarly the very high conception of Zeus is also found in the works of Aeschylus, who enhances his righteousness and overwhelming power. As the opening line of the play, 'The Supplicant Maidens' begins:

> Zeus, the Suppliant's God, be gracious to us,
> pitifully behold us, for fugitives are we;[128]

He goes on praising the sovereignty of Zeus thus:

> King of kings, among the Blest
> In thy bliss, among the blessedest,
> Mighty, mightiest by far,
> Happy Zeus, that prayer receive,
> And the even our wish achieve.[129]

Thus, Zeus is also having a good fatherly nature. Even in the Homeric *Iliad* and the *Odyssey* there are prayers addressed to Father Zeus for deliverance, for

---

[126] Cited by A. Hus, *Greek and Roman Religion*, 43.

[127] M.P. Nilsson, *Greek Piety*, trans H. J. Rose (Oxford: Clarendon Press, 1948), 35.

[128] The Suppliant Maidens 1, The Plays of Aeschylus, trans G.M. Cookson, in *Encyclopedia Britannica* 5 (Chicago: University of Chicago, 1952), 1.

[129] The Suppliant Maidens 513-515, in *Encyclopedia Britannica* 5, 7.

protection against, and victory over one's enemies.[130] Zeus acts as the guardian of oaths and of hospitality,[131] the protector of all justice, of the stranger and the suppliant.[132] He sets the balance of the golden scales of Fate to show his impartiality.[133] Thus the name of Father for Zeus expresses his merciful, love, goodness and care. In him we see the Father *par excellence*. We find similar development in the philosophical treatise to which we now turn.

2.1.6. Fatherhood of God in Philosophical Treatises

2.1.6.1. The Cosmological Fatherhood of Plato

The idea of the fatherhood of God is given a philosophical interpretation in Plato. In his cosmological elaboration of the Father idea, Plato emphasizes the creator relationship of God, the 'universal Father,' to the entire cosmos (*Timaeus* 28c, 41a). He speaks of God as 'fatherly' in his generative powers and contrasted passive, 'maternal' matter with the active and creative male principle. In his *Timaeus* we find explaining 'fatherhood' thus:

> And that which has come into existence must necessarily, as we say, have come into existence by reason of some Cause. Now to discover the Maker and Father of the Universe were a task indeed; and having discovered Him, to declare Him unto all men were a thing impossible.[134]

The first important principle in the doctrine of creation in the *Timaeus*, is the creator-god, commonly known as the Demiurge, even though Plato's terminology is more rich and varied. The Creator is definitely called Demiurge, but more frequently God. He is also called Father and Creator.[135] In the *Timaeus* Plato says that which is to receive the resemblances of eternal things must be devoid of any particular Form (51a). Therefore, matter is the Mother and Receptacle of Form. In itself it cannot be any sensible thing, like the elements: fire, air, water, or earth. Matter, so far, is that pre-cosmic condition in which there is not yet received any semblance of Form, and which therefore is invisible and completely unshaped.[136]

It is seen that the idea of fatherhood is connected with the mother metaphor in Plato. While God is the Father and begetter (28c) of the cosmos and the metaphor father is here understood as the primary moving power that contributes what in an essential way is formative of the new entity that is to be born, the

[130] e.g., *Iliad* 3.350-352; 15.372-376; 17.645-647.

[131] e.g., *Iliad* 3.276-280; 4.235-239.

[132] e.g., *Iliad* 15.12; 17.648; 22.166-176.

[133] e.g., *Iliad* 8.69; 22.209.

[134] *Timaeus 28c, Plato* IX, 51.

[135] He is called God in 30a, b, d, 31b, 32b, 34a, 55c, 69b, 73b, Demiurge in 41a, 42e, 68e, 69c, Demiurge and Father in 41a, Creator and Father in 28c.

[136] *Timaeus* 51a, *Plato* IX, 119.

mother is the receiver (receptacle) of the fatherly influence.[137] Hence in the understanding of Plato God's fatherhood has strong feminine aspect and it covers the whole cosmos.

2.1.6.2. Fatherhood of God in Stoicism

2.1.6.2.1. Fatherhood and Creation

When we come to the Stoic literatures and philosophy we see that the very idea of the fatherhood of God is understood in relation to the whole of humanity and creation. Cleanthes (331-232 B.C.E.), a leading figure of Stoic theology,[138] in his hymns to Zeus clearly sees his convictions about God's universal fatherhood:

> Most glorious of immortals, Zeus
> ...
> From thee was our begetting; ours alone
> Of all that live and move upon the earth
> The lot to bear God's likeness.
> Thee will I ever chant, thy power praise![139]

Similarly according to Epictetus, one of the well-known Stoic philosophers of the Hellenistic period, God's authority as father pervades the universe. For him God is the creator, father and sustainer of all who are his children related to him. On the issue of kinship of God and mankind Epictetus cites an example in Socrates who replied, on being asked whether he is an Athenian or a Corinthian, that he is a citizen of the universe (*kosmois*).[140] Epictetus continues his discourse on the issue of kinship of God and mankind thus:

> [T]hat from Him have descended the seeds of being, not merely to my father or to my grandfather, but to all things that are begotten and that grow upon earth, and chiefly to rational beings, seeing that by nature it is theirs alone to have communion in the society of God, being intertwined with him through the reason - Why should not such a man call himself a citizen of the universe? Why should he not call himself a son of God? And why shall he fear anything that happens among men? ... in fear of nothing whatsoever, but to have God as our maker, and father, and guardians, shall this not suffice to deliver us from grief and fears?[141]

---

[137] *Timaeus* 50d-51a, *Plato* IX, 117-119.

[138] See, Kurt von Fritz, "Cleanthes," in *OCD*, 199.

[139] *Stobaeus Eclogae* I.1.12, cited in F.C. Grant, *Hellenistic Religions: The Age of Syncretism*, 152.

[140] *Discourses* 1.9.2, *Epictetus* I, 63.

[141] *Discourses* 1.9.3-7, *Epictetus* I, 65.

Similarly in another earlier discourse he clearly talks about human beings as God's (Zeus) children by virtue of their ability to think and reason, having filled with intelligence by their divine Father:

> We are all primarily begotten of God, and that God is the father of men as well as of gods ... if you know that you are a son of Zeus, will you not be elated? ... inasmuch as these two elements were comingled in our begetting ... reason and intelligence, which we have in common with the gods.[142]

From the above discourses we can see two main ideas as regard to the fatherhood of God.

2.1.6.2.1.1. God as Primary Cause of Beings

It is understood that all are children of God, particularly human beings who are endowed with reason. The expression 'son of God' refers here to each and everyone, humankind, the rational beings. As God's children everyone has a share in the same divine origin (divine sonship). So we find here a clear instance of universal fatherhood of God. That is, God's fatherhood is understood in universal sense, and so God as universal Father.

2.1.6.2.1.2. God as Provider

God is the benevolent and loving custodian of all humankind, who provides for their needs and guards their destinies. According to Epictetus, God is not only maker and Father but guardians and that such a high sense of relationship to God gives freedom from worry and fear (*Discourses* 1.9.7). Concerning God's providential care he says:

> Consider what it would be for us to have to take thought not for merely ourselves, but also for our sheep and our ass, how they are to be clothed and shod, how they are to find food and drink. But just as soldiers appear before their general, all ready for service, shod, clothed and armed ....[143]

Here we see that by nature and general providence animals are well-equipped and so the owners of them need not to worry for their clothing. God in his fatherly goodness cares and provides already in nature, as he continues, "Take the mere fact that milk is produced from grass, and cheese from milk, and that wool grows from skin – who is it that has created or devised these things?"[144] Thus we find clearly in the Stoic teaching God as the provider and nourisher. God's fatherhood is seen in the gifts of nature. As a father God cares for all. We will see

[142] *Discourses* 1.3.1-3, *Epictetus* I, 25.

[143] *Discourses* 1.16.3-5, *Epictetus* I, 109.

[144] *Discourses* 1.16.8, *Epictetus* I, 111.

such strikingly similar idea of the universality of God in his providence and so God as the Father of all in the Synoptic Gospels, particularly in Matthew.

2.1.7. Summary

We have seen that the father-figure was very strong in the Greco-Roman society, both within the family and in the public (political) sphere. While the fathers in the Greco-Roman society were having absolute power over the family yet we also see them as being affectionate, compassionate and humane. The father-figure became an important part of the image of the political leader, especially with Caesar and Augustus. The imperial rule flourished in the pattern of *paterfamilias* with the Roman emperor as *Pater Patriae* (emperor as father of the country or empire). Such a context of imperial ideology or theology may have permeated the whole of the region including Matthean communities. Hence, it will help us to inquire how far such a characterization of the Greco-Roman father has informed Matthew's idea of God's fatherhood. So, also the idea of God's providence and the universal fatherhood of God found in the Greco-Roman philosophies can be of help to explain the idea of God's fatherhood in Matthew.

While the idea of the Greco-Roman father and imperial fatherhood may be of strong help to see Matthew and his idea of God's fatherhood but we also need to look into the more narrower and immediate context of Matthew, that is, the Old Testament and early Judaism and their idea of God's fatherhood, so as to understand the complete idea of God's fatherhood in Matthew and the Synoptic Gospel. Therefore, before dealing with Matthew and the Synoptic Gospels' idea on God's fatherhood, we must consider another important element that constitutes Matthew's conceptual world, namely, the fatherhood of God in Judaism.

2.2. The Fatherhood of God in Old Testament and Palestinian-Hellenistic Judaism

2.2.1. Fatherhood of God in the Old Testament

Since the Old Testament is Scripture for Jesus, Matthew, and his readers, it provides the basic materials for their reflection of God as Father. The Old Testament, over and above all other Jewish literature of the time, occupies an authoritative position as the trustworthy witness to God and his promises to Israel. In this section our task is to sketch the picture of God as Father that we believe Matthean Jesus found when they read the Old Testament. But before we turn to the idea of the fatherhood of God in the Old Testament, that is, the theological context of the use of Father in the Old Testament, we will first look into the social context of the use of father and so the characteristics about a father in Israelite society which shed light on the reference in the Old Testament to God as Father.

2.2.1.1. Fatherhood in Social Context

2.2.1.1.1. The Father as Head of the Household

In ancient Israel the father played a very significant role in the structuring of the family, which formed the basis of the larger tribal organization of the Israelite society. The smallest familial unit is typically referred to as the father's house (*bet ab*).[145] The family system was therefore patriarchal and the relationship on the father's side was a hereditary one (e.g., Num 27:8-11). The significance of the father is seen in the patrilineal structure of biblical genealogies in which it is the male ancestor who gives his name to a tribe or family.[146]

2.2.2.1.2. Paternal Authority

The father had supreme authority over his children (e.g., Gen 22:1-14; Jud 11:39). Children were regarded as the property of the father and could be seized for debt (2 Kings 4:1). The father could sell his daughter into marriage (Ex 21:7-11). Father must be respected at any cost (Ex 21:15, 17; Prov 20:20). However the element of authority is always exercised within the context of paternal love. Thus, this paternal authority is a combination of firmness (Prov 13:24; 3:11-12) and compassion (Ps 103:13).

2.2.1.1.3. Obedience and Respect of the Father

As head of the family and an authority it is the duty for the children to give respect and honour under all circumstances (Ex 20:12; 21:15, 17; Prov 23:22). Children are bidden to look upon them as God's representatives on earth, as their greatest benefactors (Lev 19:3; Prov 1:8).[147]

2.2.1.1.4. Protector and Provider

Being the one most responsible for the welfare of the family members, the role of the father within the family structure was primarily that of protector and provider. The role of father as protector is implied in frequent references to the plight of those fatherless and orphans (e.g., Lam 5:3; Ps 68:5).

---

[145] In the book of Genesis alone the term 'father's house,' 'father's household,' 'father's family' occur some 18 times (12:1; 20:13; 24:7, 23, 38, 40; 28:21; 31:14, 19, 30; 34:19; 38:11[x2]; 41:51; 46:31[x2]; 47:12; 50:8, 22; See J. R. Kohlenberger III, J. A. Swanson, *The Hebrew-English Concordance to the Old Testament* (Grand Rapids: Zondervan, 1998), 1-2.

[146] e.g., Genesis chapter 5; however, according to Carol Meyers such naming refers to the descend reckoning along male lines but not necessarily to male dominance in the household functioning. See C. Meyers, "The Family in Early Israel," in *Families in Ancient Israel*, edited by Leo G. Perdue, J. Blenkinsopp, J.J. Collins, C. Meyers (Louisville: Westminster John Knox Press, 1997), 34.

[147] On the aspect of the privilege and honour of a Jewish father, see Caspar Levias, "Father," in *The Jewish Encyclopedia* V, edited by Isidore Singer (New York: Funk & Wagnalls, 1925), 351-352; see also Adolf Guttmacher, "Family and family life," in *The Jewish Encyclopedia* V, 336-338.

2.2.1.1.5. Compassionate and Caring Father

The fathers in the Old Testament were loving and compassionate. Such image of a father is inferred from the narratives and biographies of the patriarchs and kings of Israel. For example, the anguish of Jacob at the loss of Joseph (Gen 37:34-36), his passionate love for Benjamin (Gen 42:36-38), and David's lament over his son (2 Sam 18:33 and 19:4) vividly portray the loving and compassionate nature of a father. The nature of a father as caring is also implied in Deuteronomy 1:31; while the Psalmist compares God with a compassionate father as he says, "As a father has compassion for his children, so the Lord has compassion for those who fear him" (Ps 103:13).

2.2.1.1.6. Father as Educator

The father is responsible for seeing that family life is in accordance with the covenant and that the children receive religious instruction. The father in the family educate the children about their history (Ex 12:26-27; 13:14), nurture them in the Law (Deut 6:7; 32:7; Isa 38:19). The father is a strict disciplinarian. This aspect of fatherhood is emphasized in the Wisdom Literature, which speaks of the duty of a father to educate and discipline his children (Prov 3:12; 4:1-4 cf. Deut 8:5). Thus, the social meaning for 'father' in Old Testament Israel has to do with authority, care, discipline, and protection.

With these characteristics of a human father as found in the Old Testament we will turn to the theological idea of the fatherhood of God. We believe that these ideas and expressions of God were drawn from the family relationships.

2.2.1.2. Fatherhood in Theological Context

2.2.1.2.1. Introduction

The theological-metaphorical language of God as Father can be located mainly in contexts that speak of his deliverance, provision, discipline and restoration of Israel. Two main events in Israel's history – the exodus and the exile - provide the background for Old Testament writers to reflect on God as the Father of Israel.

2.2.1.2.2. Occurrences of the term 'Father' for God

As such one does not necessarily need to have the word 'father' present to argue that the idea of God's fatherhood lies behind a particular passage. For example, passages that speak of God's 'begetting' of Israel or beloved son of God (Ps 2:7) can be taken as implicitly suggestive of God's fatherhood. Still then the passages in which the actual term 'Father' does occur often tend to serve as the most helpful avenues into the depiction of God as Father in the Old Testament. The word 'Father' is used for God only 16 times in the whole of the Old Testament,[148] while

[148] 11 times as Father of Israel (Deut 32:6; Isa 63:16[x2]; 64:8; Jer 3:4,19; 31:9; Mal 1:6; 2:10; Ps 68:5; 89:26) and 5 times as Father of Israel's kings (2 Sam 7:14; I Chr 17:13; 22:10; 28:6; Ps 2:7).

in 4 instances God as Father is inferred by way of comparing with an earthly father.[149]

2.2.1.2.3. God as Father of Israel

2.2.1.2.3.1. Paternal Authority and Love

In the Old Testament the idea of God's fatherhood basically has to do with God's relationship with the people of Israel. Although, it does not specifically name God as "Father," Hosea contains one of the most cited passages portraying God's paternal love: "When Israel was a child, I loved him, and out of Egypt I called my son" (Hos 11:1). For Hosea God chose Israel to be his son.[150] Of course already in the event of the Exodus itself we see God having revealed himself as a compassionate and a saving God: "The LORD, the LORD, a God merciful and gracious, slow to anger, and abounding in steadfast love and faithfulness" (Ex 34:6). And Hosea seems to have developed this thought of God.[151] This very verse is all the more important for us because it is one of the passages in the Old Testament that talks about the fatherhood of God which Matthew quoted among several of the passages (called 'fulfillment quotations') from the Old Testament prophet.[152] While the compassionate fatherly nature of God is implicit in this very expression in Hosea and Matthew's use of this very quotation seems also to do with his theology of God, that is, his emphasis on God's purposes and activity.

This usage is rooted in the covenantal functions of creating a bond of kinship between two parties. God directs Moses to tell Pharaoh that "Israel is my firstborn son" (Ex 4:22). The same idea is found in Jeremiah's highly charged description of the return of the exiles, both to their land and to their God:

> With weeping they shall come, and with consolations I will lead them back, I will let them walk by brooks of water, in a straight path in which they shall not stumble; for I have become a father to Israel, and Ephraim is my firstborn (Jer 31:9).

Similarly we also find in the book of Exodus in the description of God's instruction to Moses the notion of the very sonship of Israel, "Israel is my firstborn son" (Ex 4:22). The understanding of God as Father in these passages has to do with adoption and redemption, as Hofius remarks, "To be a child of God is not

---

[149] Ps103:13; Prov 3:12; Deut 1:31; 8:5.

[150] In this case the father image denotes God's covenant relationship with Israel.

[151] H.H. Rowley, *The Faith of Israel* (London: SCM Press, 1973), 62-63.

[152] Ten times in Matthew has the formula 'this was to fulfill ....' or 'then was fulfilled ....' after which comes a quotation from the Old Testament prophet: Mt 1:22-23; 2:15, 17-18, 23; 4:14-16; 8:17; 12:17-21; 13:35; 21:4-5; 27:9-10; See R.H. Gundry, *The Use of Old Testament in St. Matthew's Gospel* (Leiden: Brill, 1967).

a natural state or quality, rather it grounded in the miracle of divine election and redemption."[153]

Even where, in connection with God's fatherhood, the language of creating and begetting is used, in several instances the reference is to the historical saving action of God towards a particular people Israel, thus pointing to God's fatherhood in the sense of adoption or redemption.[154] This idea is clearly seen in Deuteronomy 32:6: "Do you thus repay the LORD, O foolish and senseless people? Is not he your Father, who created you, who made you and established you?"

In Isaiah 64:8, the term' Father' and 'potter' (so creator) occur together as the prophet compares God with a potter (maker) who shapes the clay in his hands, "Yet, O LORD, you are our Father; we are the clay, and you are our potter; we are all the work of your hand." Here we see the idea of God's fatherhood in the sense of both his sovereignty and care. Sovereignty in the sense that just like the absolute power of the potter over the clay being molded as he likes, so also the power and authority of the Father (God) over his children (Israel), who has neither the right to challenge the actions of the parent or the maker.[155] But because God is Israel's Father, he cares about his children as a potter cares about the work of his hands. Accordingly God is Israel's Father in the sense that he gives them life in the sense of redemption: "For you are our father, though Abraham does not know us and Israel does not acknowledge us; you, O LORD, are our father; our Redeemer from of old is your name (Isa 63:16)."

In Malachi too, God's fatherhood and his creatorship are set in parallel: "Have we not all one father? Has not one God created us? Why then are we faithless to one another, profaning the covenant of our ancestors?" (Mal 2:10). In all these references we see that what is created or begotten is none other than Israel itself - pointing to the particularity of God's fatherhood - thus returning to the covenant context for the use of the term father for God.[156]

Similarly in the context of Israel's unfaithfulness the prophet Jeremiah talks about merciful and forgiving love of God in his fatherliness: "I thought

---

[153] O. Hofius, "Father," in *NIDNTT* I, edited by Colin Brown (Exeter: Paternoster Press, 1975), 617.

[154] For more elaborate discussion on soteriological understanding of creation in the Old Testament, see G. von Rad, *Old Testament Theology* I (London: SCM Press, 1975), 136-139.

[155] Such God's absolute authority is implied in the rhetorical questions in Deutero-Isaiah, "Does the clay say to the one who fashions it, 'What are you making'? ... Thus says the LORD, the Holy One of Israel, and its Maker: Will you question me about my children, or command me concerning the work of my hands?" (Isa 45:9c-11).

[156] According to Paul Ricoeur, "the designation of God as father proceeds from the other designations of Yahweh in the Covenant" and thus fatherhood has to do with adoption but nothing to do with begetting, See, P. Ricoeur, "Fatherhood: From Phantasm to Symbol," in *The Conflict of Interpretations: Essays in Hermeneutics*, edited by Don Ihde (Evanston: Northwestern University Press, 1974), 487.

how I would set you among my children, and give you a pleasant land, the most beautiful heritage of all the nations. And I thought you would call me, My Father, and would not turn from following me." As such God's fatherhood is again understood in the sense of care and protection. God is Israel's Father in the sense that he is their redeemer.

The motifs of creation, begetting and redemption are woven together by various Old Testament writers to illustrate God's paternal power over his children and his concern for them. God chose Israel by divine initiative to be his firstborn son.[157] As Israel's loving and faithful Father, he redeemed his people from captivity and established them as a nation. In this sense God is the Father of Israel; he is the one to whom Israel owes its origin. Lodged in the context of God's historical deliverance in the Exodus, the motifs of creation, begetting and redemption signify the foundational characteristics of the father-son relationship and Israel, namely, his election, love, authority and salvation.[158] This is a significant strand in Old Testament theology that seems to have informed Jesus' and the New Testament's concepts of sonship.[159]

2.2.1.2.3.2. God's Fatherly Care: Sustenance, Protection and Guidance

If the idea of God's fatherhood in the Old Testament is mostly understood in the sense of God's relationship with the people of Israel, then the Exodus and the wilderness experience provide the context for the Old Testament writers to describe the ways in which God cared for Israel, his 'firstborn son' (Ex 4:22). Like any responsible father, God fed his children, gave them an inheritance, and taught them to keep his commandments. Looking back at what God did for Israel, Moses says to the Israelites:

> [I]n the wilderness, where you saw how the LORD your God carried you, just as one carries a child, all the way that you traveled until you reached this place. But in spite of this, you have no trust in the LORD your God (Deut 1:31-32).

So also in Deuteronomy 32:10-13, we see Moses reminding the people of the attentiveness with which their Father took care of them in the wilderness:

---

[157] Rex Mason, *Old Testament Pictures of God* (Georgia: Smyth & Helwys Publishing Inc., 1993), 56.

[158] The same is true with Israel's king, as in some instances 'father' is used for God in relation to Israel's kings; and it is striking that the term 'father' always appear in the context of God's covenant relationship with Israel's king (see 2 Sam 7:14; I Chr 17:13; 22:10; 28:6; Ps 2:7). As such the themes that pertain to God as the Father of Israel – adoption, firstborn, redemption, paternal love and authority – are also true to God as Father of Israel's king.

[159] C.J.H. Wright, *NIDOTT* I, edited by Willem A. VanGemeren (Carlisle: Paternoster Press, 1997), 222; C.J.H. Wright, *Knowing Jesus through the Old Testament* (London: Marshall Pickering, 1992), 118-135.

He sustained him in a desert land, in a howling wilderness waste; he shielded him, cared for him, guarded him as the apple of his eye. As an eagle stirs up its nest, and hovers over its young; as it spreads its wings, takes them up, and bears them aloft on its pinions, the LORD alone guided him; no foreign god was with him. He set him atop the heights of the land, and fed him with produce of the field; he nursed him with honey from the crags, with oil from flinty rock ....

This passage vividly portrays God as the Father who protected, trained, guided, and fed his children until they arrived at the Promised land. The picture of a parent eagle further adds to the father metaphor. The eagle imagery points to God's protection and instruction of Israel by portraying as young, immature, and dependent. This strongly projects God's fatherhood, who alone led the Israelites though the desert. In addition to the miraculous supply of water, manna, and quail in the wilderness (Ex 16:1-17:7; Num 20:2-13; Deut 8:15-16), God brought his children to the "land flowing with milk and honey" (Ex 33:3; Lev 20:24; Deut 31:20; cf. 32:13-14). Indeed. Israel lacked nothing under their father's care.

2.2.1.2.3.3. The Feminine Nature of God in the Old Testament

While we have seen above that the fatherhood of God in the Old Testament is understood metaphorically or figuratively in the sense of adoption and redemption, there are several references in the Old Testament which talk otherwise. For example, the Song of Moses of Deuteronomy chapter 32, which is said to be one of the oldest of the poetic texts in the Hebrew Bible, is one clear instance where the term fatherhood of God occurs along with the imagery of mother to describe God.

Like in the primitive and natural religions, where we find the idea of a relationship with deity based on begetting or birth, in several instances such idea is preserved in the religion of Israel.[160] In Numbers 11:12 the idea of God as mother is evident. Moses complains about the unbearable burden which the people are to him:

> Did I conceive all this people? Did I give birth to them, that you should say to me, 'Carry them in your bosom, as a nurse carries a sucking child,' to the land that you promised on oath to their ancestors?

The idea of motherhood is expressed here very clearly. Divine motherhood seems to have been very much part of the ancient Israelite and Judean piety.[161] Similarly in Deuteronomy 32:18, the author of the Song of Moses talks about God giving birth:

You were unmindful of the Rock that bore you; you forgot the God who gave you birth.

---

[160] Quell, "The Father Concept in the Old Testament," in *TDNT* V, 967-968.

[161] P. A. H. De Boer, *Fatherhood and Motherhood in Israelite and Judean Piety* (Leiden: E.J. Brill, 1974), 35.

Here we find both male and female imagery for Yahweh. Similarly, in Genesis 49:24-26, we find feminine nature of God, "blessings of the breasts and the womb" when talking about God. So also several other texts in the Old Testament reflect the idea of begetting, when talking about God. In Psalms 27:10, the Psalmist declares:

> If my father and mother forsake me, the Lord will take me up.

Here the Psalmist is comparing between Yahweh and a father or mother. Yahweh stands in contrast to either a mother or a father. The prophet Ezekiel talks about the marriage of Yahweh (23:4), that Yahweh begets sons and daughters through two women Oholah and Oholibah. Similar marriage imagery of God is also found in Psalms 19:5, "In the heavens he has set a tent for the sun, which comes out like a bride groom from his wedding canopy."

Pointing to such presence of feminine traits of God in the later prophets and other wisdom literatures many scholars see the influence of neighboring deities and their religions. For example, W.F. Albright talks about strong Phoenician-Canaanite influence at the beginning of Israel's history.[162] P.A.H. De Boer too observed a very close connection between the cult of Yahweh and the Astarte cult. According to him, God and Goddess stood side by side in Israel and Judea in the 9th century B.C.E.[163] M.S. Smith too observed that such presence of female and maternal traits of God seems to project Israel's Canaanite heritage, as Israelite and Canaanite cultures shared a great deal in common including religion.[164] B. Vawter sees syncretistic element in Gen 49:24-26, particularly with Canaanite deity Asherah.[165] S.M. Olyam too sees some role of Asherah in the cult of Yahweh. He remarks: "The prohibitions and polemics against Asherah and her cult symbol attest to their popularity in the cult of Yahweh in Iron Age Israel."[166] O. Keel and C. Uehlinger too observed that the Israelite-Judean God and Goddess symbol system had the same relationship with the Canaanite system. For them the religious symbol systems of the ancient Israel were marked by images of fertility

---

[162] W.F. Albright, "The Role of the Canaanite in the History of Civilization," in *The Bible and the Ancient Near East*, edited by G. Ernst Wright (New York: Double Day Company, 1961), 351.

[163] De Boer, *Fatherhood and Motherhood in Israelite and Judean Piety*, 44.

[164] M.S. Smith, *The Early History of God: Yahweh and other deities in Ancient Israel* (New York: Harper & Row Publishers, 1990), 7; He identified the major deities in the territory of Israel during the period of the Judges as Yahweh, El, Baal and Asherah, See *The Early History of God*, 6.

[165] B. Vawter, "The Canaanite Background of Genesis 49," in *CBQ* 17 (1955): 16.

[166] S. M. Olyan, *Asherah and the Cult of Yahweh in Israel* (SBL Series 34; Atlanta: Scholars Press, 1988), 74; M.S. Smith sees more than the Canaanite deity El's elements, the traits of the goddess Asherah in Yahweh's description in Genesis 49, which talks about the maternal and nurturing character of God (See *The Early History of God*, 98).

and sexuality and talks about openness to "the buried feminine aspects of the Judeo-Christian image of God."[167]

T. Jacobsen sees Sumerian influence in some of the Old Testament poetic texts. For example, Psalm 27:10, where the combination of father and mother roles for a single deity Yahweh is evident. In his prayer to Gatumdug, the city-goddess of Lagash, Gudea says:

> I have no mother – you are my mother,
> I have no father – you are my father,
> You implanted in the womb the germ of me,
> Gave birth to me from out of the vulva (too),
> Sweet, O Gatumdug is your holy name![168]

In another Akkadean didactic and wisdom text we see similar expression in the lament of individual sufferers; (Sufferer 1):

> My father and mother left me without anyone to be my guardian ....[169]

And the lament ends with another individual (sufferer 27) saying:

> May the god who has abandoned me give help, May the goddess who has [forsaken me] show mercy, The shepherd, the sun of the people, pastures (his flock) as a god should.[170]

So also an ancient Hittite prayer likewise attributes both parental roles to Istanu, the sun-god:

Thou, Ishtanu, art father and mother of the oppressed, the lonely [and the] bereaved person.[171]

These poems combine parental imagery of mother and father. Thus by implication, when compared to Gudea's and Hittite prayer as seen above, Psalms 27:10 suggests that Yahweh assumes the role of father and mother, thereby affirming divine care. Moreover the imagery of the marriage of God found in prophetic literatures of Ezekiel, Hosea and Psalms also reminisce the ancient

---

167 O. Keel and C. Uehlinger (eds), *Gods, Goddess, and Images of God In Ancient Israel* (Edinburgh: T&T Clark, 1998), 409.

168 T. Jacobsen, *The Harps That Once ...: Sumerian Poetry in Translation* (New Haven: Yale University Press, 1987), 361.

169 "Sumerian Wisdom Text," trans by S.N. Kramer, in *The Ancient Near East: Supplementary Texts and Pictures Relating to the Old Testament,* edited by J.B. Pritchard (Princeton: Princeton University Press, 1969), 602-603.

170 "Sumerian Wisdom Text," trans by S.N. Kramer, in *The Ancient Near East: Supplementary Texts,* 604.

171 H. Guterbock, "The Composition of Hittite Prayers to the Sun," in *JAOS* 78 (1958), 240.

West Asian Hittite cult of sacred marriage (*hieros gamos*).[172] These striking parallel examples illustrate the larger West Asian background to the combination of parental roles for Yahweh.

Thus, the fatherhood and motherhood of God are inseparably related in the Old Testament, that the motherly nature of God is seen in the imagery of a father God. And as the above parallels show, these parental descriptions of God seem to have assimilated gradually in interaction with its surrounding religions. It is important that we keep this idea in mind as we look ahead to the New Testament concept of the fatherhood of God particularly as portrayed in Matthew. With this we will now turn to the literatures of Palestinian and Hellenistic Judaism, and examine how the fatherhood of God is portrayed.

2.2.2. Fatherhood of God in Palestinian and Hellenistic Judaism

The literary works during this period (c. 300 B.C.E. - 100 C.E.) encompasses a collection of writings that are largely heterogeneous in provenance, date, genre, and subject matter. They include wisdom literature, hymns, prayers, historical writings, apocalyptic literature, novellas, apocryphal writings, legends and so forth. Many of these literatures are included in either the Old Testament Apocrypha[173] or the Old Testament Pseudepigrapha.[174] The rest will be found in the Dead Sea Scrolls,[175] Josephus, Philo and Rabbinic literatures. For our study these literatures

---

[172] I. Engnell, *Studies in Divine Kingship in the Ancient Near East* (Oxford: Blackwell, 1967), 60; See also similar idea of sacred marriage and the goddess of the Greek pantheons, E.O. James, *The Cult of the Mother-Goddess*, 141-145.

[173] The term 'Old Testament Apocrypha' refers to the Jewish documents that originated between the 3rd century B.C.E. and the 1st century C.E. and that were incorporated into the LXX (Greek translation of the Old Testament) but not the Hebrew Bible. These Apocryphal works includes: Judith, the Wisdom of Solomon, Tobias or Tobit, the book of Jesus ben Sirach or Ecclesiasticus, the book of Baruch with the Letter of Jeremiah, 3 Ezra, 1 and 2 Maccabees, the Additions to the Greek book of Esther, and the Additions to the Greek book of Daniel (consisting of the stories of Susanna and Daniel and of Bel and the fiery furnace), and finally the late Prayer of Manasseh. For more details on the historical and theological treatment of each of these Apocryphal books, see O. Kaiser, *The Old Testament Apocrypha: An Introduction* (Peabody: Hendrickson Publishers, 2004).

[174] 'Pseudepigrapha' (from the Greek for 'pseudonymous writings') is a term applied to other non canonical Jewish literature, though all of it is written under a false name. For a detail categorization of each of these Pseudepigraphal literatures under different genres: Apocalyptic Literatures, Testaments, Expansions of the Old Testament, Wisdom and Philosophical Literature, Prayers, Psalms and Odes and The Supplement; see J. H. Charlesworth, *The Old Testament Pseudepigrapha and the New Testament* (Cambridge: Cambridge University Press, 1985), 41-44.

[175] The term 'Dead Sea Scrolls' refer to the more than 900 manuscripts and thousands of manuscript fragments which were found in eleven caves at Qumran and elsewhere in the Judean desert (discovered 1946 onwards). These scrolls in Hebrew, Aramaic, and Greek, were thought to have written between 250 B.C.E and 68 C.E. These manuscripts contain biblical books, commentaries and interpretations on some of the biblical books, Rules of the Community which produced the writings, hymns, and similar religious writings. For overview of its literatures and surveys, see James C. VanderKam, *The Dead Sea Scrolls Today* (Grand Rapids: Wm B. Eerdmans,

are indispensable as they help us understand the worldview, symbols, metaphors, and concepts in the New Testament writings. Our focus in these diverse literatures will be on how these Jewish and Hellenistic writers understood God's fatherhood, which may perhaps shed light on Matthew and the Synoptic writers' idea of the fatherhood of God.

2.2.2.1. God as Israel's Father

First of all what we observe is that there is continuity with the Old Testament as is evident in several ancient Jewish works. Several writings stress on God as Israel's Father. Affirming God's fatherhood in close relation to God's parental discipline, we find a Qumran text saying, "For you called [I]srael 'my son, my first-born,' and have corrected us as one corrects his son" (4Q504 1-2 III, 5-7).[176] Similarly, another prayer text from Qumran states that while God disciplines because of Israel's disobedience, he has not deserted his children:

> ...F]or you have not forsaken your servant [...] my father and my Lord .... (4Q460 5 I, 4-6).[177]

Similar address to God as Father in the context of troubles is found in 3 Maccabees, when the Jews are standing "at the gates of death" (3 Macc 5:51), Eleazar the priest pleads for deliverance in a long prayer, in the course of which he twice addresses God as Father: "Look upon the descendants of Abraham, O Father" (3 Macc 6:3); and again "And Jonah, wasting away in the belly of a huge, sea-born monster, you, Father, watched over and restored unharmed to all his family" (Macc 6:8). So here God is invoked as Israel's Father, that he will have mercy on them and save them from their enemies. Similarly in Tobit, in his thanksgiving to God, expresses the very idea of God as Israel's Father thus:

> Acknowledge him before the nations, O children of Israel; for he has scattered you among them. He has shown you among them. He has shown you his greatness even there. Exalt him in the presence of every living being, because he is our Lord and he is our God; he is our Father and he is God forever (13:3-4).[178]

In the Book of *Jubilees* 'Father' appears in covenant language:[179]

1994); G.W.E. Nickelsberg, *Jewish Literature between the Bible and the Mishnah* (Second edition; Minneapolis: Fortress Press, 2005), 119-189.

[176] Trans F.G. Martinez and Eibert J.C. Tigchelaar, *The Dead Sea Scroll* vol 2 (Leiden: Brill, 2000), 1015.

[177] Trans F.G. Martinez and Eibert J.C. Tigchelaar, *The Dead Sea Scroll* 2, 937-938.

[178] All English translations of Old Testament apocryphal works are taken from *The Holy Bible containing Old and New Testaments with the Apocryphal/Deuterocanonical Books* (NRSV; Nashville: Thomas Nelson, 1989).

[179] For theology of the author and God and Israel relationship in the Book of *Jubilees*, See James C. Vander Kam, *The Book of Jubilees* (Sheffield: Sheffield Academic Press, 2001), 120-125.

> And their souls will cleave to Me and to all My Commandments ... and I will be their Father and they shall be My Children. And they all shall be called children of the living God, and every angel and every spirit shall know, yea, they shall know that these are My Children, and that I am their Father in uprightness and righteousness, and that I love them (*Jubilees*1:24-25).[180]

The affirmation of God as Israel's Father is also implicit in the acknowledgement of Israel as God's 'firstborn son' in another reference in the Book of *Jubilees*[181] and also in Sirach: "Have mercy, O Lord, on the people called by your name, on Israel, whom you have named your firstborn" (Sir 36:17).

There are also places in the literature of this period where individuals are shown to address God as 'Father' and pray for forgiveness and protection in the same way as Israel does as a nation. For example, a Qumran prayer text says:

> For my father did not know me, and my mother abandoned me to you. Because you are father to all the [son]s of your truth. You rejoice in them, like her who loves her child, and like a wet-nurse you take care of all your creatures on (your) lap (1QH 17. 35-36).[182]

This prayer recalls Psalms 27:10, affirming that God's affection for his children often surpasses that of one's earthly parents. There is another interesting hymn from Qumran, where both the fatherhood of God and maternal traits of God are expressed together, as the psalmist proclaims in complaining that his parents abandoned him:

> For my father knew me not and my mother abandoned me to Thee. For Thou art a father to all [the sons] of Thy truth, and as a woman who tenderly loves her babe, so dost Thou rejoice in them; and as a foster-father bearing a child in his lap so carest Thou for all Thy creatures (IQH 9.35).[183]

Here the psalmist appears to compare the unkindness of his human father to the care and love of God. The most important element of this description of God's fatherhood is the prominence given to parental, indeed maternal, affection manifest in the hymn. Another text from Qumran (4Q372 I) which was published

[180] Trans R.H. Charles in *APOT* II, edited by R.H. Charles (Oxford: Clarendon Press, 1969), 12-13.

[181] "I will sanctify the people for myself ... They will become my people and I will become their God. I have chosen the descendants of Jacob among all of those whom I have seen. I have recorded them as my first-born son and have sanctified them for myself throughout the ages of eternity." See, *Jubilees* 2:19-20, trans R.H Charles, *APOT* II, 14-14.

[182] Trans F.G. Martinez and Eibert J.C. Tigchelaar, *The Dead Sea Scroll* 1, 185.

[183] Trans G. Vermes, *The Dead Sea Scrolls in English* (4th Edition; London: Penguin Books, 1995), 219.

by Eileen Schuller in 1990 called the Psalm of Joseph includes a prayer. In it Joseph prays to God as Father and asks for protection in the context of trouble at the hands of the unbelieving Gentiles:

> My father and my God, do not abandon me into the hands of nations; do justice for me, lest the afflicted and the poor perish. You have no need for any nation or people for any help; [your fin]ger is greater and stronger than anything in the world.[184]

There are also references to God as Father in other Pseudepigraphal works. In the *Testament of Job* 33:3-9, a psalm of affirmation, the term 'Father' for God occurs in the first and last units of the psalm:

> My throne is in the upper world, and its splendor and majesty come from the right hand of the Father ... But my kingdom is forever and ever, and its splendor and majesty are in the chariot of the Father.[185]

So also in another text of same *Testament of Job* 40:2-3, which is a lament psalm, we see a certain Sitis praying:

> I sang praises to the Father. And after the prayer I said to them, "look up with your eyes to the east and see my children crowned with the splendor of the heavenly one."[186]

The occurrence of the term 'Father' is important here, as all these references are mostly to be found in prayers. There is also in the Pseudepigraphal *Joseph and Aseneth*,[187] a long prayer in which Aseneth confesses her sin of idolatry and asks God to be her father, replacing the father and mother who rejected her because of her conversion to Judaism:

> And I am now an orphan and desolate, and I have no other hope save in you, Lord, and no other refuge except your mercy, Lord, because you are the father of the orphans, and a protector of the persecuted and a helper of the afflicted. Have mercy upon me, Lord, and guard

[184] See E. Schuller, "4Q 372 I; A Text about Joseph," in *Rev Q*14/55 (1990), 343-370; See also Schuller, "The Psalm of 4Q 372 I Within the Context of Second Temple Prayer," in *CBQ* 54 (1992), 68.

[185] Trans R.P. Spittler, "Testament of Job," in *OTP* I, edited by J.H. Charlesworth (New York: Doubleday, 1983), 855-857.

[186] Trans R.P. Spittler, "Testament of Job," in *OTP* I, 859-860; because of the presence of mystical expressions in these psalms, Spittler assume its origin in the Merkabah mysticism in Hellenistic Judaism of the New Testament times; see R.P. Spittler, "Testament of Job," in *OTP* I, 858 n. 'm;' while Nickelsberg support an origin among Therapeutae group of Egyptian Judaism; see Nickelsberg, *Jewish Literature between the Bible and the Mishnah*, 321.

[187] For a detail discussion of its provenance and survey, see Nickelsberg, *Jewish Literature between the Bible and the Mishnah*, 332-338.

> me, a virgin [who is] abandoned and an orphan, because you, Lord, are a sweet and good and gentle father (*Joseph and Aseneth* 12.13-14).[188]

Here God is depicted as a loving Father of humankind, assuring the welfare of those who adhere to him and hating those who worship idols; but always he is prepared to receive in mercy those who repent earnestly.

These above texts indicate that the personal addresses of God as "my Father" was prevalent in the literature of Palestinian Judaism prior to Jesus, Matthew and the Gospel writings, which means that the fatherhood of God was a prominent idea in the early Jewish writings, in continuity with the Old Testament idea of God's fatherhood. However, we also see a distinct trend in process, that is, from the understanding of the nationality as the criterion of sonship to God to something that is individual and personal and thus moves towards universality of God's fatherhood.

2.2.2.2. God as Father of Righteous Individuals

In the later Judaism we witness a note of development, where the references to God as Father are not tied explicitly to Israel as a whole or Israel's king, but the appeal to God as Father is made on a personal and individual basis. Stress came to be laid upon the loving and authoritative Fatherhood of God in relation to individuals who obey him, and not merely to the nation. In the context of a prayer for help against sinning, Sirach address God: "O Lord, Father and Master of my life, do not abandon me ...." (Sir 23:1); and again "O Lord, Father and God of my life, do not give me haughty eyes" (23:4). Elsewhere Sirach expresses the same affirming God's fatherhood, "Lord, you are my Father; do not forsake me in the days of trouble, when there is no help against the proud" (51:10).[189]

Such idea of individual claim of God as Father is found in Wisdom of Solomon, in its second chapter group of wicked Jews are shown to plot evil against a righteous person, whom they consider as boastful because "he professes to have knowledge of God, and calls himself a child of the Lord ... and boasts that God is his father" (2:13-16). Though the Father address is not occurring we see the same idea in 3:1: "But the souls of the righteous are in the hands of God" (cf. 11:26). Here God appears as Father of the righteous persecuted by the unjust.

It came to be seen that there is a shift from the national and particularity of Old Testament to something that is individual and universal in these Jewish writings; and that the righteousness of the individual not nationality as the

---

188 Trans C. Burchard, in *OTP* II, edited by J.H. Charlesworth (New York: Doubleday, 1985), 222.

189 However in the light other text in Sirach (e.g., 4:10 - "Be a father to orphans, and be like a husband to their mother; you will then be like a son of the Most High, and he will love you more than does your mother") some understood it in corporate sense of God as the Father of Israel or the Father of all righteous Israelites, see Henry J. Wicks, *The Doctrine of God in the Jewish Apocryphal and Apocalyptic Literature* (New York: Ktav Publishing House, 1971), 344.

criterion of sonship to God. Thus we see the emergence of a very strong emphasis on universality of God in the later period of Judaism.

This means that in Judaism prior to Jesus, Matthew and the Gospel writers, it is observed that God is addressed as 'Father,' not merely in the collective sense but also in the personal and individual sense (e.g., 4Q372; 3 Macc 6:3, 8; Sir 23:1, 4; Wis 14:3).[190]

2.2.2.3. The Feminine Nature of God

Mother imagery in relation to God is also mentioned in some of the writings in this period. In talking about human wretchedness Sirach 40:1 says, "Hard work was created for everyone, and a heavy yoke is laid on the children of Adam, from the day they come forth from their mother's womb until the day they return to the mother of all living." There is a hint of the mother-goddess idea here when Sirach talks about earth-mother idea. So also in 4 Maccabees chapter 15, a passage of praising 'the Mother of the Seven,' we find similar inference of mother goddess and fertility.

2.2.2.4. God's Fatherhood and Providence

Earlier in the Greco-Roman religions and philosophical context we have seen the idea of universal fatherhood of God and it is not surprising that such idea is found in the Hellenistic-Jewish writings (which were written for and in the Hellenistic world). In the Wisdom of Solomon 14:3 we see in the prayer of a navigator, a typical Stoic idea of God as Provident Father: "But it is your providence, O Father, that steers its course, because you have given it a path in the sea, and a safe way through the waves, showing that you can save from every danger, so that even a person who lacks skill may put to sea." The occurrence of the word 'providence' along with 'Father' is striking. The implication here is that God as the benevolent and loving custodian of all humankind provide their needs and guard their destinies.[191] This is a significant development as far as the fatherhood of God is concerned, which will also be found in the New Testament particularly in the theology of Matthew and Q.

2.2.2.4.1. God as Father of All

In the *Sibylline Oracles*, which is a Hellenistic Apocalyptic in genre, the emphasis on the idea of God as universal Father is evident by the several expressions of God as 'the Great Father' (3.96), 'Father of all men' (3.50, 604), 'God, the great Father of all' (5.406), 'the Immortal Father of gods and all men' (3.278), 'the Father,

---

[190] Some New Testament scholars, however, argue that the individual address of God as 'Father' is unique to Jesus; see Jeremias, *The Prayer of Jesus*, 57; A.W. Argyle, *God in the New Testament* (London: Hodder & Stoughton, 1965), 58.

[191] H.W. Montefiore, "God as Father in the Synoptic Gospels," in *NTS* 3/1 (Nov 1956), 32.

Sustainer of souls' (5.500).[192] Of course the acknowledgment of the particularity of Israel's sonship is not entirely absent (3.702; 5.202, 328), but the presentation of God as the Father in general underscored God's supremacy over all people and gods, which was propelled by Jewish monotheistic polemic.[193] Accordingly, one very important feature of this work is the shift of the attribute of Zeus, as the Father of gods and mortals, to God as the Father of all humanity, as the very purpose and function of the *Sibylline Oracles* was primarily to establish common ground between the Jewish and gentile worlds.[194]

The same universalizing tendency is seen in another Jewish-Hellenistic literature, *the Letter of Aristeas.* One of the main theological emphases of this work is that Jewish monotheism is not in contradiction to the Greek idea of universalism. It is implied in the request of Aristias to Ptolemy to release Jewish captives. He appeals thus:

> Let it never be unreasonable to be refuted by events themselves, O King … But out of your unsullied and magnanimous soul release those who are subject to misery; the (same) God who appointed them their Law prospers your kingdom, as I have been at pains to show. These people worship God the overseer and creator of all, whom all men worship including ourselves, O King, except that we have a different name. Their name for him is Zeus or Jove. The primitive men, consistently with this, demonstrated that the one by whom all live and are created is the master and Lord of all ….[195]

The most remarkable in this passage is the identification of the God of the Jews with Zeus, a very clear instance of assimilation and syncretism.[196] And even though God is not called 'Father' in the *Letter of Aristeas*, the fatherhood of God is implicit here. It is through God that all things are endowed with life and come into being (*Letter of Aristeas* 16). God's fatherhood is here understood as the source and origin of all beings which is quite in line with Greek-Stoic philosophy.

---

[192] All the phrases are from The Sibylline Oracles, trans H.C.O. Lanchester, in *APOT* II, 368-406.

[193] H. Koester, *Introduction to the New Testament II: History, Culture, and Religion of the Hellenistic Age* (New York: Philadelphia, 1982), 258.

[194] J.J. Collins, *The Sibylline Oracles of Egyptian Judaism* (SBL Dissertation Series 13; Missoula: Montana University Press, 1972), 117-118.

[195] *The Letter of Aristeas* 15-16, trans R.J.H. Shutt, in *OTP* II, 13.

[196] According to F.C. Grant, the main characteristics feature of Hellenistic religion was syncretism - the tendency to identify the deity of various peoples and to combine their cults, See F.C. Grant, *Hellenistic Religions: The Age of Syncretism*, viii; Alain Hus puts the term 'syncretism' and 'aspiration towards monotheism' in the same line; see Alain Hus, *Greek and Roman Religion*, 81; Martin Hengel too would expressed this syncretistic trend as 'monotheizing tendency.' See M. Hengel. *Judaism and Hellenism: Studies in their Encounter in Palestine during the Early Hellenistic Period* (Philadelphia: Fortress, 1974), 262.

Aristeas further expresses about God "that there is only one God and that his power is manifested throughout the universe, hence every place is filled with his sovereignty and none of the things which are wrought in secret by men upon earth escapes His knowledge" (132).[197]

As such again the nature of God is such that his power is manifested throughout the universe and every place is filled with his sovereignty. He is an all-seeing God, and so nothing can be hidden from Him. This idea of an all-seeing God is also found in the New Testament only in Matthew. The Letter goes on expressing that "God bestows his benefits on the human race, providing for them health and food and all other things in due season."[198] In this typical Hellenistic-Stoic expression, God's fatherly nature is clearly expressed as the source of all the endowments and blessings of life. God is also described as the one who sways the lives of mankind (17) and grants answers to their prayers (192). This letter presents one of the most positive views of the Greeks, their culture and of the possibility for peaceful and productive coexistence between Jews and Greeks.[199] We will find similar idea in Philo, another prominent Jewish-Hellenistic writer of the period, to which we now turn.

2.2.3. Fatherhood of God in Philo[200]

2.2.3.1. Cosmic Father

Though there are a few places where Philo recognizes God's relationship with Israel apart from the rest of the humanity,[201] yet his main idea of God's fatherhood is closely related with creation and reflects a Platonic-Stoic understanding of God as universal Father. It is clearly evident in his frequent references to God as

---

[197] *The Letter of Aristeas* 132, trans H.T. Andrews, in *APOT* II, 107.

[198] *The Letter of Aristeas* 190, trans H.T. Andrews, in *APOT* II, 112.

[199] Nickelsberg, *Jewish Literature between the Bible and the Mishnah*, 196.

[200] Philo (c. 15 B.C.E. – 50 C.E.) was born in a Hellenized Jewish family in Alexandria (Egypt). He was the most learned and most productive author of Hellenistic Judaism. He marks the endpoint of Hellenistic philosophy as well as of the development of Hellenistic Judaism. While the main form of his writing was exposition of the biblical text, yet its content was thoroughly informed by Greek philosophical speculation. He thus drew eclectically from Platonic and Stoic traditions. He is significant not only for our understanding of first-century Judaism, but also for the interpretation of the New Testament. Philo's writings thus helps us understand early Christianity as a religious phenomenon that has synthesized biblical religion and Hellenistic religion and culture; For an excellent overview, see G.W.E. Nickelsberg, *Jewish Literature between the Bible and the Mishnah*, 212-221; Peder Borgen, "Philo of Alexandria," *ABD* V, 333-342.

[201] E.g., in his work *De Legatione ad Gaium* 3, Philo says, "...the deity takes thought for men, and particularly for the suppliant's race which the Father and King of the Universe and the Source of all things has taken for his portion. Now this race is called in the Hebrew tongue Israel" (See *Philo* X, 3-5.). All translations are from F.H. Colson and G.H. Whitaker, *Philo with an English Translation* 12 vols (LCL; Cambridge: Harvard University Press, 1929-62).

"Father and Maker."[202] In his work *De Opificio Mundi* we find Philo explaining God's fatherhood in line with Plato's understanding of the fatherhood of God in *Timaeus*.[203] Echoing Homeric epithet of Zeus as universal Father and Plato's metaphysical fatherhood, Philo develops the thought of the generation of the cosmos and the soul. He makes considerable use of the term 'Begetter,' 'Father Begetter,' and 'Father and Begetter' in relation to creation, whether with reference to the heavens, humankind, the soul or mind.[204] He even describes the Universe specifically as the son in *De Specialibus Legibus* 1.96. Thus for Philo, everything is understood as God's son. So for him God's fatherhood is understood in universal, metaphysical sense. Because God created all that is, God is therefore the Father of all "created things, in so far as they are created, are brothers, since they all have one Father, the Maker of the universe."[205] God's fatherhood is thus understood in general, universal sense.[206]

For Philo God, the Father of all, is also the Husband of Wisdom, as he clearly describes in *De Cherubim* that:

> He is the father of all things, for he begat them, and the husband of Wisdom, dropping the seed of happiness for the race of mortals into good and virgin soil ... as the husband not of a virgin, for a virgin is liable to change and death, but of virginity, the idea which is unchangeable and eternal.[207]

The main idea here is the ethical one that virtues are begotten in her. As such when Philo talks about God's fatherhood, the understanding is more in ideal sense. From this foundational claim, Philo develops the idea of God's fatherhood in several ways.

2.2.3.2. God as Father-Creator

God is Father-Creator because he is the source of all life and the cause of all things. This emphasis on the creative activities of the Father is also strengthened by his usage of other expressions such as "Father and Creator" (e.g., *De Vita Mosis* 2.256), "Father and Begetter" (e.g., *Quod Deus Immutabilis Sit* 47), and "Creator and Maker of all" (e.g., *De Specialibus Legibus* 1.30). God is the Father who begets

---

202 The titles occur frequently – together, apart and in reverse order, see e.g., *De Opificio Mundi* 10, 20-21, 72-75.

203 "Just such a power is that by which the universe was made, one that has as its source nothing less than true goodness. For should one conceive a wish to search for the cause, for the sake of which this whole was created, it seems to me that ... the Father and Maker of all is good." See *De Opificio Mundi* 20-21, in *Philo* I, 17-19, trans F.H. Colson and G.H. Whitaker.

204 e.g., *De Specialibus Legibus* 1.30; 2.30-31; 3.189; *De Opificio Mundi* 84.

205 *De Decalogo* 64, in *Philo* VII, 39, trans F.H. Colson and G.H. Whitaker.

206 which means everyone has a share in the same divine origin.

207 See *De Cherubim* 50, in *Philo* II, 39, trans F.H. Colson and G.H. Whitaker.

the material as well as the immaterial, mortal beings, happiness,[208] and time.[209] However, above all other created things, human beings can claim special kinship with God because their soul and mind are conformed to God their begetter.[210]

2.2.3.3. God as Authoritative Father

Secondly, God's parental sovereignty is implied in his creatorship. As sole and supreme Ruler, God has authority over his entire creation.[211] Parental authority reflects God's rule over the world.[212] So also rebuke and admonition, which are indicative of the closeness between God and human beings, as caring fathers discipline their children for their good.[213] In response to the Father's benevolence and authority, God's children ought to revere their Father-Creator-Ruler with honour, praise, fidelity, and to allow their souls to draw near to him.[214]

2.2.3.4. God as Protector and Provider

God protects his children and provides for their sustenance. He is aware of the needs of his creatures and is the giver of all good things. In a discourse on God's providence in nature Philo talks about God who protects and provides for all as a father; that he cares for all as his own children.[215] This discourse on God's fatherly protection and providence in nature anticipates the words of Jesus in Q (Mt 6:25-33//Lk 12:22-31). Again on a discourse on thanksgiving and temperance, Philo talks about people who give thanks in their heart saying, "We have gladly received and are storing the boons of nature, yet we do not ascribe our preservation to any corruptible thing, but to God the Parent and Father and Savior of the world and the right to nourish and sustain us by means of these or without these."[216] In the description of Philo, God's fatherly nature is also seen in his compassion

208 *De Cherubim* 49-50, in *Philo* II, 39, trans F.H. Colson and G.H. Whitaker.

209 As Philo in his discourse in the *Quod Deus Immutabilis Sit* 31-31 says, "But God is the maker of time also, for he is the father of time's father, that is of the universe ... For this universe, since we perceive it by our senses, is the younger son of God. To the elder son, I mean the intelligible universe, he assigned the place of firstborn, and purposed that it should remain in His own keeping." See *Philo* III, 25-27, trans F.H. Colson and G.H. Whitaker.

210 Thus for Philo, "The mind alone in all that makes us what we are is indestructible. For it is mind alone which the Father who begat it judged worthy of freedom ... For the other living creatures in whose souls the mind, the element set apart for liberty, has no place, have been committed under yoke and bridle to the service of men, as slaves to a master." See *Quod Deus Immutabilis Sit* 47 in *Philo* III, 33, trans F.H. Colson and G.H. Whitaker.

211 *De Decalogo*155; *De Specialibus Legibus* I.14.

212 *De Specialibus Legibus* 2.225.

213 *De Congressu quaerendae Eryditionis gratia* 177; *De Fuga et Inventione* 83-84.

214 *De Specialibus Legibus* 2.256.

215 *De Specialibus Legibus* 1.318 in *Philo* VII, 285, trans F.H. Colson and G.H. Whitaker.

216 *De Specialibus Legibus* 2.198 cf. 1.318; *De Cherubim* 44; *De Fuga et Inventione* 62.

towards widows and orphans, and his merciful nature who forgives the sins of the penitent.[217]

2.2.4. Fatherhood of God in Josephus[218]

2.2.4.1. Fatherhood and Begetting

The works of Josephus reveal clearly the influence of the Greek concept of the universal Father. While in some occasions he stresses on God as "the Father and Lord of the Hebrew nation" (*Antiquities* 5.93 cf. 7.380),[219] yet his main emphasis is on the universal fatherhood of God. At the very preface of his *Antiquities*, while giving account of the divine operatives in the events surrounding Moses' life, he talks about God as "the Father and Lord of all things" (*Antiquities* 1.20). God is also described as "Father of all" by Judah as he pleads with Joseph for forgiveness for himself and the other sons of their father Jacob (*Antiquities* 2.152). In the context of Moses' discourse for young men on the need of obedience and respect to the parents, Josephus talks about God as "the Father of the whole race of mankind" (*Antiquities* 4.262). So also in the narrative regarding King David and his son Solomon and their preparation for building the temple, God is described as "the Father and Parent of the universe, and the Author of human and divine things" (*Antiquities* 7.380).

In all these expressions the characterization of God's fatherhood has to do with origin and source, quite in line with Greek-Hellenistic concept of God's fatherhood. That means, we see here a departure from the Old Testament particularistic understanding of God's fatherhood, to something that is universal, that God is the Father of all literally, that all things owe their existence to him. When Josephus says that God is "the Father and Parent of the universe, and the Author of human and divine things" (7.380), he is echoing the Greek-Homeric characterization of Zeus as "Father of gods and human beings" (e.g. *Iliad* 1.544). Accordingly, God's fatherhood means God is the source or creator of all living things. For Josephus, God is also the all-seeing and authoritative Father who has the power to bless the faithful and punish the wicked (*Antiquities* 1.20). Here in the projection of Josephus, the primary characteristic of God as universal Father pertains to his supreme authority.

---

[217] *De Vita Mosis* 2.24; 2.238; *De Providentia* 2.6; *De Specialibus Legibus* 4.180.

[218] Flavius Josephus was a Jewish historian (37-105 C.E.), who participated actively in the Jewish War (66-70 C.E.) and wrote about it using the conventional method of writing of the time (historiography). His three major works includes; *The Jewish War* (c.79 C.E.); *Jewish Antiquities* (c. 93/94 C.E.); and *Against Apion*, an apologetic and polemical work, favoring the virtues of the Jewish people and their religion and way of life completed around 96-100 C.E.; for details of his life, career and works see, J.R. Bartlett, *Jews in the Hellenistic World: Josephus, Aristeas, The Sibylline Oracles, Eupolemus* (Cambridge: Cambridge University Press, 1985), 72-191.

[219] All English translations of Josephus works are from W. Whiston, *Josephus: The Complete Works* (Nashville: Thomas Nelson Publishers, 1998).

2.2.4.2. Fatherhood and Providence

Josephus gives strong emphasis to the providence of God, which is a theme that he underlined when describing his own escape from death after the siege of Jotapata by the Romans under Vespasian (*The Jewish War* 3. 337-339). In his own narrative about his life in dilemma whether to commit suicide instead of being killed in the hands of the enemies we see his discourse on God's providence. He argues:

> What are we afraid of ... that it is a manly act for one to kill himself. No, certainly, but a most unmanly one; as I should esteem that pilot to be an arrant coward who, out of fear of a storm, should sink his ship of his own accord. Now, self-murder is a crime most remote from the common nature of all animals, and an instance of impiety against God our creator ... And do not you think that God is very angry when a man does injury to what he hath bestowed on him? for from him it is that we have received our being; and we ought to leave it to his disposal to take that being away from us ... and while God, who is their father, punishes those that offend against either of them in their posterity .... (*The Jewish War* 3.366-375).

The occurrence of the word 'father' when Josephus is talking about God's providence is important here. As Josephus contemplates about taking his life by himself, he realizes that God is in control of everything and God has a purpose even for his own life. As such he affirms that God is the benevolent and loving custodian of all humankind who is in guard of their destinies. His life was saved by the providence of God (*The Jewish War* 3.391).

The same emphasis is also found in his account of the virtues of the Israelite leaders and heroes, that Abraham submitted to God's will and took Isaac away to be sacrificed because he thought "that it was not right to disobey God in anything, but that he was obliged to serve him in very circumstances of life, since all creatures that live enjoy their life by his providence, and the kindness he bestows on them" (*Antiquities* 1.225).

This theme of providence is also stressed in the stories of Jacob (*Antiquities* 2.8), Joseph (*Antiquities* 2.60) and the rebellion of Korah (*Antiquities* 4.47). In *Antiquities* 10 Josephus uses the prophecies of Daniel and demonstrates "how the Epicureans are in an error, who cast providence out of human life, and do not believe that God takes care of the affairs of the world, nor that the universe is governed and continued in being by that blessed and immortal nature, but say that the world is carried along of its own accord, without a ruler and a curator" (*Antiquities* 10.277-278).

In the expressions 'God takes care of the affairs of the world,' and 'the universe is governed and continued in being by that blessed and immortal nature,' we see the central theological emphasis of Josephus. And this emphasis on providence makes Josephus in line with the Stoic philosophers who talk about

God's fatherhood as seen in the gifts of nature.[220] Josephus uses events in history to demonstrate God's providential care for the moral order of things.

2.2.5. Fatherhood of God in Rabbinic Judaism[221]

Rabbinic Judaism shows several references and expression relating to the use of 'Father' for God. Due to the difficulties in dating of its vast literatures, scholars however tend to exclude it from the possible influence on Jesus and the Gospel writers.[222] However, Rabbinic Judaism is very important particularly from the point of view of Matthew's Gospel, to help us understand the context of the use of 'Father' for God and so the idea of God's fatherhood.

2.2.5.1. An Ever-Present Prayer-Answering Father

In a number of rabbinic texts God is addressed with the title 'our Father in heaven.' Most of these expressions are found in the context of prayer in the aftermath of the fall of Jerusalem temple.[223] A text found in *Mishnah* describes the laments of R. Eliezer ben Hyrcanus over the pathetic situation of life after the fall of the Jerusalem Temple. His account of the woes goes thus:

> Since the day that the Temple was destroyed the Sages began to be like school-teachers, and the school-teachers like synagogue-servants, and the synagogue-servants like the people of the land; and the people of the land waxed feeble, and there was none to seek [compassion for them]. On whom can we stay ourselves? – on our Father in heaven (*Sotah* 9.15).[224]

---

[220] Cf. Epictetus, who talks about divine providence in nature (e.g., *Discourses* 1.16.3-5).

[221] It is said that while rabbinic period begun with the demise of Hillel and Shammai (c. 10 C.E.). However the real emergence of rabbinism as the guiding force in Judaism began with the fall of Jerusalem in 70 C.E., with the rabbis (or *tanna*, hence the age of Tannaim) as the center of learning. The father of this new stage in rabbinism was Rabbi Johannan ben Zakkai who established a flourishing centre of Jewish learning at Jabneh (Jamnia). For more details on the literature of rabbinic Judaism, See M. McNamara, *Intertestamental Literature* (Delware: Michael Glazier, Inc., 1983), 241-275.

[222] E.g., Diane G. Chen, *God as Father in Luke-Acts*; while M.M. Thompson mentioned its literatures in the footnote; See her work, *The Promise of the Father: Jesus and God in the New Testament*, 52 n. 34.

[223] And according to Jeremias the term 'Father' for God occurs more frequently, especially after Johanan ben Zakkai (50-80 C.E.) who began to favor the address 'our heavenly Father.' The phrase is attributed to him twice: *Mekilta Exodus* 20.25//*Sifra Leviticus* 20.16 and *Tosephta Baba Qamma* 7.7; See Jeremias, *The Prayer of Jesus*, 16. n. 8.

[224] Danby, *The Mishnah*, 306. Another rabbi called R. Cadoq (c.70 C.E.) said in a prayer lamenting over the helpless situation: "My Father who art in heaven, Thou hast destroyed thy city and burnt thy temple and remainst untroubled and calm." See G. Schrenk, "God as Father in Judaism," in *TDNT* V, 980 n. 215.

In another text in Yoma, which largely describes rituals of atonement which could no longer be enacted after the fall of the Temple, the redactors cite a blessing of R. Akiba:

> Blessed are ye, O Israel. Before whom are ye made clean and who makes you clean? Your Father in heaven as it is written, *And I will sprinkle clean water upon you and you shall be clean* (*Yoma* 8.9).[225]

This blessing seems to function in the same way as a number of comments that offer consolation for the destruction of Jerusalem.

2.2.5.2. God as Father and King

In several rabbinic prayers, God as Father is frequently connected with the idea of God as King. A prayer, offered by R. Akiba in a time of drought, has been preserved and reads:

> Our Father, our King, we have sinned before Thee. Our Father, our King, we have no king beside Thee. Out Father, our King, have compassion upon us.[226]

So also a prayer in the Hebrew liturgy opens with the words:

> With great love hast Thou loved us, O Lord our God, with great and exceeding pity hast Thou pitied us. Our Father, our King, for our father's sake, who trusted in Thee, and whom Thou didst teach the statues of life, be also gracious unto us and teach us.[227]

The address of God as 'Father' is thus seen as conventional expression of the time of rabbinic Judaism.[228]

2.2.5.3. God as Universal Father

We can also infer the idea of God's universal fatherhood in the rabbinic writings. For example, it is implied in a saying of R. Akiba:

Beloved is man for he was created in the image [of God]; still greater was the love in that it was made known to him that he was created in the image of God, as it is written, *For in the image of God made he man.* Beloved are Israel for they were called children of God; still greater was the love in that it was made known to them that they were called children of God, as it is written, *Ye are the children of the Lord your God.*[229]

---

[225] Danby, *The Mishnah*, 172.

[226] *Taan.* 25b, see A. Cohen, *Everyman's Talmud* (London: J.M. Dent & Sons Ltd., 1961), 21.

[227] A. Cohen, *Everyman's Talmud*, 21

[228] This is also the view of G. Schrenk, see Schrenk, "God as Father in Judaism," in *TDNT* V, 978-981.

[229] *Aboth* 3.15 in Danby, *The Mishnah*, 452.

The inference from this saying is that God is the universal Father and so his love and goodness is to all. This logically implies that human beings, who are children of the same Father, should respond through the general love of all. This ethical implication is very clear from the commentary on the same text by R. Judah, while giving theological explanations on the expression 'Ye are the children of the Lord your God,' he said:

> At the time that you conduct yourselves as dutiful children, you are called God's children; but when you do not so conduct yourselves, you are not called God's children.[230]

2.2.6. Summary

From our examination of the various literatures of Judaism, from the Old Testament to the Palestinian-Hellenistic literatures, we have observed that the fatherhood of God idea is found in almost all the literatures. Our observations thus reveal how central and pervasive is the idea of God's fatherhood in all these writings. As we have attempted to derive the meaning of God's fatherhood, from a close reading of the many primary texts, we can make a few observations in connection to what the fatherhood of God means. *First,* God's fatherhood is collective or corporate; this is the idea we see in the Old Testament. That means, in the Old Testament the use of God as Father has to do exclusively with God as Father of Israel. *Secondly,* God's fatherhood is understood in the sense of God's providence in nature. This idea is seen mainly in the Hellenistic literatures. It is in this very idea of God-nature as inseparable and so cosmic idea that the feminine aspect of God comes in. *Thirdly,* God's fatherhood is also individual. While, in continuity with Old Testament, the corporate sense is also seen in the later Judaism, but a new trajectory on the idea of God's fatherhood in individual sense - and so a trend towards universality of God as Father of all humanity - is found in the Hellenistic writings. *Fourth,* God's fatherhood is also seen in close connection with the idea of God as king; this is particularly seen in rabbinic Judaism.

With such a composite picture of God's fatherhood idea we will now turn to Mark, Luke and Paul and examine their own usage and understanding of God's fatherhood.

---

230 Cohen, *Everyman's Talmud,* 20.

Chapter 3

The Fatherhood of God in Mark, Luke and Paul

Introduction

We have seen in the preceding chapter that the idea of the fatherhood of God is found in almost all the literatures of the Greco-Roman world and Judaism, in which environment Jesus, Matthew and New Testament writers' idea of the fatherhood of God sprang. We will now turn to Matthew's Synoptic counterparts Mark and Luke and so also Paul with whose traditions Matthew shares including the idea of God's fatherhood,[231] and pay attention to the narrative of each of them and the presentations of the fatherhood of God embodied within them.

---

[231] The Gospel of John was written later than the Synoptic Gospels. This is the view of the majority of the New Testament scholars. See C.K. Barrett, *The Gospel According to St. John* (London: SPCK, 1967), 14-18; R.H. Fuller, *A Critical Introduction to the New Testament* (Letchworth: The Garden City Press, 1971), 176-178; Kummel, *The Theology of the New Testament* , 203-205; H. Koester, *Introduction to the New Testament 2: History and Literature of early Christianity* (Philadelphia: Fortress Press, 1982), 178; M.M. Thompson, 'The Gospel of John,' in *DJG*, 370-371. Nevertheless, the emphasis on the theme of God's fatherhood is very strong in John. The term 'Father' for God occur the most in John (120 times). John sets its christological tone right from the very beginning of his gospel. At the prologue itself John highlights the unique relationship of God as Father to Jesus as Son (Jn 1:14, 18). That means for John God is specifically the Father of the only Son, Jesus. Moreover, Johannine Jesus frequently refers to himself as Son and to God as "my Father," "the Father," or "the Father who sent me." This emphasis on the Father-Son correlation is seen in several instances (e.g., 5:23; 8:19; 14:10; 10:30; 14:9). As such the emphasis on the theme of God's fatherhood is very strong in John. For an exhaustive treatment on the theme of God's fatherhood in John, see M.M. Thompson, *The God of the Gospel of John* (Grand Rapids; Michigan: Wm B Eerdmans, 2001).

3.1. The Fatherhood of God in Mark

3.1.1. Occurrences of the term 'Father'/ 'Son'

The theme of God's fatherhood is found in the Gospel of Mark, which is one of the primary sources that Matthew and Luke used. However before dealing with the significance of the idea of the fatherhood of God we need to look at the data, that is, on the occurrences of the term 'Father' for God. Of course mere occurrences of term 'Father' for God are not the only indicator to see the idea of God's fatherhood, yet it is in such passages that the fatherhood of God idea is explicitly seen. In Mark there are only four occurrences of the term 'Father' for God (8:38; 11:25; 13:32; 14:36),[232] and all these occurrences have parallels in one[233] or both[234] of the Synoptic Gospels.

There are several passages in Mark where the very notion of God's fatherhood is implied in the expression 'Son of God' for Jesus. Mark portrays Jesus as the 'Son of God' in his role as 'Messiah, Son of God' (1:1; 14:61-62; 15:32, 39). At the same time, in Mark's projection, Jesus as God's Son has a special relationship with God that sets him apart: 'my Son, the Beloved' (1:11; 9:7); 'Abba, Father' (14:36); the Father and the Son (13:32 and 14:36); 'the beloved son' of the vineyard owner in the parable of the tenants (12:6). Other passages where sonship is implicit are found in the rhetorical questions posed by the religious leaders, crowds, demons and others in the activities of Jesus (e.g., 1:27; 2:7; 4:41; 5:7).

3.1.2. The Significance of the Fatherhood of God in Mark

3.1.2.1. "Abba, Father" (14:32-42)

One of the most significant expressions found in the lips of Jesus recorded in Mark is *Abba*, which plays a vital role in understanding the fatherhood of God in the Synoptic Gospels and in the whole of the New Testament. This expression is found in the Markan passion narrative. Jesus, while moving towards his final destination, along with his disciples "went to a place called Gethsemane" (Mk 14:32; Mt 26:36), and there he prays for God's will to be done. He prays:

[232] Out of these four occurrences twice Markan Jesus refers to God as "Father" in the context of eschatological teachings (8:38; 13:32). The other two passages that have the term 'Father' occurring in the lips of Jesus are Mark 11:25 and 14:36 respectively. The occurrence of the term *Abbà* in 14:36 is the epitome in explaining the significance of the idea of God's fatherhood in Mark, which occurs as a word of address in prayer and as the only occurrence of the word in the Gospels. It is the only time the Gospel writers attribute the words "Abba, Father" to Jesus. This very expression *Abba* has generated a lot of debate on Jesus' idea of the fatherhood of God, particularly post Jeremias' 1967 work, *The Prayer of Jesus*.

[233] Mk 11:25//Mt 6:14; Mk 13:32//Mt 24:36.

[234] Mk 8:38//Mt 16:27//Lk 9:26; Mk 14:36//Mt 26:39//Lk 22:42.

> Abba, Father, for you all things are possible; remove this cup from me; yet, not what I want, but what you want (Mk 14:36).[235]

This prayer, which is the core expression of the Gethsemane episode, is found in all Synoptic Gospels (Mk 14:32-42; Mt 26: 36-46; Lk 22:40-46) but it is Mark alone that retains this very Aramaic term *Abba*, which Greek translates as πατήρ. And some scholars observed that this expression though occurs only in Mark, is likely to preserve Jesus' genuine mode of address to God when requesting help.[236] Such an address seems to imply a sense of sonship on the part of Jesus with God. In this direction, one of the most influential contributions has been that of J. Jeremias. Basing on this very expression *Abba*, found in the lips of Jesus in Mark (14:36), he talks about Jesus' special consciousness of sonship:

> The complete novelty and uniqueness of *Abba* as an address to God in the prayers of Jesus shows that it expresses the heart of Jesus' relation to God. He spoke to God as a child to its father: confidently and securely, and yet at the same time reverently and obediently.[237]

That means for Jeremias *Abba* was Jesus' preferred and exclusive mode of address to God and hence his unique experience of God. Several scholars in line with Jeremias support this as clear instance of Jesus' unique and distinct experience of God. J.D.G. Dunn sees Jesus' *Abba* experience as distinctive experience.[238] For Edgar Krentz, this very *Abba* expresses Jesus' close and intimate relationship with God as his Father.[239] Feminist theologian Elizabeth A. Johnson too speaks of Jesus' *Abba* experience as a special and original experience of God, an intimate and close relationship.[240]

However there are questions to this linking of Jesus' *Abba* expression and his unique experience of God. As we have seen in the previous chapter that *Abba* is not without analogy as an address to God, that the address of God as Father was prevalent in Judaism of Jesus day, as is evident in several Jewish and Hellenistic literatures. In Judaism prior to Jesus, it is seen that God is commonly addressed

---

[235] All English translations of the New Testament texts are from *The Holy Bible* (NRSV; Grand Rapids; Michigan: Zondervan Bible Publishers, 1990).

[236] Notably G. Vermes, see Vermes, *The Religion of Jesus the Jew* (London: SCM Press, 1993), 161; similarly J.H. Charlesworth says that Jesus pray to God was *Abba* in disheartening times. See his work, "Jewish Prayers in the Time of Jesus," in *The Lord's Prayer: Perspectives for Reclaiming Christian Prayer*, edited by D.L. Migliore (Grand Rapids: Wm B. Eerdmans, 1993), 37.

[237] Jeremias, *New Testament Theology* I, 67.

[238] J.D.G. Dunn, *Jesus and the Spirit: A Study of the Religious and Charismatic Experience of Jesus and the First Christians as Reflected in the New Testament* (London: SCM Press, 1975), 26.

[239] E. Krentz, "God in the New Testament," in *Our Naming of God*, edited by C.E. Braaten (Minneapolis: Fortress, 1989), 88.

[240] Elizabeth A. Johnson, *Consider Jesus: Waves of Renewal in Christology* (New York: Crossroad, 1994), 57.

as 'Father,' in personal and individual sense. Particularly in the prayer of Eleazar in 3 Maccabees 6:3 and 6:8 we do find 'Father' is used in the absolute form. So also in Qumran[241] and rabbinic literatures[242] invocation of God as "our Father" is found. Thus, Jesus' use of Father put him squarely within the practices of first-century Judaism, and so this very expression '*Abba*' need to be read within that first century Jewish milieu, as Geza Vermes asserts:

> One of the distinguishing features of ancient Hasidic piety is its habit of alluding to God precisely as 'Father.' The ancient Hasidim spent an hour (in recollection before praying) in order their hearts towards their Father in heaven ... that for the charismatic, as for Jesus, God is *Abba*.[243]

That means, for Vermes, there is nothing unique in Jesus' use of *Abba*. What he meant by *Abba* is what it meant in Judaism. That if Jesus had filial relationship with God so also the Jewish Hasid.[244] Thus in the view of Vermes, Jesus' use of *Abba* for God and so his conception of God seems to be quite in line with the contemporary Jewish custom of addressing God as "our Father." The same stance is found in the work of J.H. Charlesworth who observes that there is not a world of difference between 'our Father' in the lips of Jesus and 'Father' in the address of the rabbis to God, as both languages evoke a loving and intimate God.[245]

---

241 As E. Schuller has shown in a Qumran text a clear cut pre-Christian Palestinian prayer in seen in which God is addressed as father. It reads, "My father and my God, do not abandon me into the hands of nations; do justice for me, lest the afflicted and the poor perish. You have no need for any nation or people for any help; [your fin]ger is greater and stronger than anything in the world (4Q372 I).". See Schuller, "The Psalm of 4Q372 I Within the Context of Second Temple Prayer," in *CBQ* 54 (1992), 79.

242 In a version of the second benediction before the Shema in the morning synagogal service, namely the Ahabah Rabbah in pre-70 Palestinian Jewish liturgical settings, it reads: "Our Father (*abinu*), merciful Father, thou who art ever compassionate, have pity on us and inspire us to understand and discern, to perceive, learn and teach, to observe, do, and fulfill gladly all the teachings of thy Torah." See *Daily Prayer Book* (trans P. Birnbaum, New York: 1977), 73-76.

243 G. Vermes, *Jesus the Jew* (London: SCM Press, 1994), 210-211.

244 Vermes particularly noted the striking similarities between the prayer of Jesus and Hanan, a Jewish holy man, in whose prayer the term *Abba* for God occurs, though indirectly as recorded in the Babylonian Talmud (*b. Taan.* 23 b.). The account goes, "When the world was in need of rain, the rabbis used to send school-children to him, who seized the train of his cloak and said to him, *Abba, Abba*, give us rain! He said to God: Lord of the universe, render a service to those who cannot distinguish between the *Abba* who gives rain and the *Abba* who does not." See Vermes, *Jesus the Jew*, 211.

245 J.H. Charlesworth, *Jesus Within Judaism: New Light from Exciting Archaeological Discoveries* (London: SPCK, 1990), 134.

However, comparing particularly to the colourful, beautifully-arranged liturgical forms of addresses to God in Jewish prayer,[246] Jesus' address of God in absolute simplicity is striking.[247] In this direction a very straightforward observation is found in E. Schillebeeckx thus:

> Jesus' uniqueness in his relationship to God undoubtedly lies in its unaffected simplicity; and the marks of that in late Judaism, though not absent, were rally rare. But we cannot build on it an awareness on Jesus' part of some 'transcendent' sonship and still less a Trinitarian doctrine, as has often happened in the exegetical and theological writings deriving therefrom. For that, more is needed. If we can find it, then in Jesus' unaffected intercourse with God as *Abba* we may justifiably perceive the natural consequences of it; not, however, the other way round.[248]

In the same vein, N.T. Wright too argues:

> It is doubtful whether one can actually *start* with the expression '*Abba*,' found as it is in only one gospel text, and build upon it a whole theory as to the uniqueness of Jesus' experience of, and teaching about, Israel's God. However, it should not be supposed that Jeremias has been disproved completely: there *is* a striking phenomenon to be observed in the prayers of Jesus, and, once we relieve it of the strain of being the load-bearing wall in a much larger construction, it can relax and make a valuable contribution to a different one.[249]

As both Schillebeeckx and N.T. Wright observed, just one instance in the whole of the Synoptic Gospels of the occurrence of *Abba* in the lips of Jesus may not be sufficient to arrive at a conclusion that his experience was the very starting point or source of his understanding of God as Father. Yet, when we examine the overall theological presentations of Mark it is seen that Jesus' experience of sonship to God and the kingdom activities of Jesus as projected in Mark are

---

[246] For instance, in the prayer of Eighteen Benedictions (*Shemoneh Ezreh*), God is address as, "Blessed are thou, Lord our God and God of our fathers, God of Abraham, God of Isaac and God of Jacob, the God who is great, mighty and awesome, God sublime who lavishes tender goodness. Master of all ... King who dost succor, save, and shield, blessed are thou, Lord, shield of Abraham." See *The Traditional Prayer Book for Sabbath and Festivals*, edited and translated by David De Sola Pool (New York: Behrman House Publishers, 1960), 8.

[247] For Michael H. Crosby (*Thy Will be Done: Praying the Our Father as Subversive Activity* [Maryknoll: Orbis Books, 1977], 21) Jesus address of God as 'Father' is a highly subversive prayer because he was undermining the institutional expressions of their religion.

[248] E. Schillebeeckx, *Jesus: An Experiment in Christology* (trans H. Hoskins; New York: Crossroads, 1981), 260.

[249] N.T. Wright, *Jesus and the Victory of God: Christian Origins and the Question of God* 2 (Minneapolis: Fortress, 1996), 649.

inseparably connected. In fact the sonhood of Jesus seems to be the overarching theological-christological perspective of Mark. As such when we view this very expression along with other sayings and deeds of Jesus in Mark, we see that there are indications of Jesus' consciousness of his sonship to God, as Schillebeeckx correctly puts:

> It is not from Jesus' *Abba* experience in itself that conclusions may be drawn, but only from that experience as the soul, source and ground of Jesus' message, praxis and ministry as a whole, which alone serve to illuminate the exceptional and peculiar character of the *Abba* experience.[250]

The point is that Jesus' experience of God's fatherhood directed his life and determined his ministry.

In order to put in perspective let us be reminded with the definite context of this very *Abba* occurrence. It occurs at the Gethsemane prayer (14:32-42), at the height of the Markan passion narrative (14:1-15:47). And it is in this very passion narrative we observe the continuity of Mark's theological-christological focus, particularly in relation to the activities of Jesus prior to the passion. It is thus evident that Jesus undergoes suffering as God's Son. Mark returns to this theme at the end of chapter 15 where the centurion confesses that Jesus is the Son of God (15:39). Jesus, acknowledging that all things are possible with God, asks his Father to let the hour pass (v35) and to 'remove this cup' (v36). The hour and the cup refer to Jesus' suffering, which includes the denial, betrayal, shame, rejection and subsequent death.[251] In the apocalyptic discourse, Markan Jesus tells the disciples to watch and pray because no one knows, including the Son, the day or the hour when the events described in that discourse will take place (13:32-37). The passion is the hour of final suffering for Jesus. It foreshadows the events mentioned in his apocalyptic discourse.[252]

Thus, the cup points to Jesus' death. When James and John ask him for the seats at his right and his left (10:35-37), Jesus responds, "Are you able to drink the cup that I drink, or be baptized with the baptism that I am baptized with (10:38)?" The imagery points to the suffering.[253] In this moment of anxiety, Jesus

[250] Schillebeeckx, *Jesus: An Experiment in Christology*, 266.

[251] P.S. Minear, *The God of the Gospels: A Theological Work Book* (Atlanta: John Knox Press, 1988), 110.

[252] For details of this strong correspondence between the Gethsemane pericope (14:32-37) and the preceding chapter, that is, the Olivet discourse (Mark chapter 13), particularly the apocalyptic sayings in verses 32-37, see P.S. Minear, *Commands of Christ: Authority and Implications* (Nashville: Abingdon Press, 1972), 157-164.

[253] In line with the Old Testament understanding of the cup as an image for God's judgment and salvation, E. Best (*Mark: The Gospel as Story* [Edinburgh: T&T Clark, 1983], 70) notes "men drink the cup of salvation which is reach to them in the eucharist. Because Jesus has borne God's wrath they will enjoy God's salvation." However, R.E. Brown (*The Death of the Messiah: From*

would avoid the suffering, provided it accorded with God's will ("yet not what I want, but what you want"). Thus, the fact that the cup of suffering is pictured as being given to Jesus by his Father (who is thus able also to remove it) strikingly expresses the conviction which underlies Mark's narrative of the passion that God controls the whole process culminating in Jesus' death. Thus God wills Jesus' death. This very expression discloses the actuality of fatherhood/sonship.[254] This very notion of sonship of Jesus is implicit in the activities or the 'deeds' of Markan Jesus to which we now turn.

A close observation of Mark shows that the activities of Jesus as a healer and exorcist are inseparably linked to an awareness of sonship and of the Spirit of God active through him.[255] We will now turn to some of these powerful deeds of Jesus (cf. Mk 1:7) in Mark and examine his theological-christological emphasis.

3.1.3. The Dawning of God's Fatherly Rule in Jesus' Deeds

For Mark, Jesus' ministry centers on the coming of the kingdom of God. He affirms that Jesus is the Son of God (1:1), who inaugurated God's kingdom through his ministry (1:14, 15). The exorcisms of the demoniac (e.g., 1:21-27; 9:14-29), the healing of the sick (e.g., 2:1-12), the nature miracles (e.g. Mk 4:37-41; 6:45-51), all these activities bear evidence to the coming of the kingdom of God (cf. 1:15). Thus, there is a direct connection between the miracles Jesus performed and his proclamation of the coming of God's kingdom in Mark. Not only that the miracles of Jesus are integrally related to the coming of the kingdom, but that they also support and promote the identity of Jesus as the Son of God. That means, in Mark, Jesus' kingdom activities (theology) and his identity (Christology) are inseparably related.[256] In other words, who he is and what he does are inseparable. What he does reveal who he is, and who he is entails what he does.[257] We will

---

Gethsemane to the Grave: A Commentary on the Passion Narratives in the Four Gospels [London: Chapman, 1994], 168-70 wishes to separate the ideas of suffering and of judgment, and sees the former as the primary focus here.

[254] Minear, *God of the Gospels*, 110.

[255] As J.D.G. Dunn (*Jesus and the Spirit*, 67) remarks, referring to the many extraordinary healings and exorcisms done by Jesus, "the heart of Jesus' religious experience was his experience of God as Father ... that through this sense of sonship to God, of God as his Father, Jesus drew the convictions which in very large part governed his life and determined his mission." For further details on the strong connection of the power and authority of Jesus (his miracles) with his *Abba* experience, see Dunn, *Jesus and the Spirit*, 68-92; J.D.G. Dunn, *Unity and Diversity in the New Testament: An Inquiry into the Character of Earliest Christianity* (London: SCM Press, 1977), 184-189; so also on Jesus as son of God=miracle worker, see G. Vermes, *Jesus The Jew*, 202-210.

[256] As U. Schnelle (*Theology of the New Testament* [trans M. Eugene Boring; Grand Rapids: Baker Academic, 2007], 403) observes: "In Mark, kingdom theology and Christology are not antitheses or alternatives, but Christology has a theocentric foundation."

[257] R. Bauckham, *Jesus and the God of Israel* (Grand Rapids; Michigan: Wm B. Eerdmans, 2008), 262.

look at some of the deeds of Jesus, the 'deeds of power' (Mk 6:2, 5), where Jesus' identity is the centre of focus and so God's fatherhood is implicit.

3.1.3.1. Who Then Is He? (4:35-41)

In one of Jesus' well-known activities, that is, stilling the sea storm, recorded in all the Synoptic Gospels we see in Jesus' deeds, the fatherly rule of God, his power and compassion:

> On that day, when evening had come, he said to them, "Let us go across to the other side." And leaving the crowd behind, they took him with them in the boat, just as he was. Other boats were with him. A great windstorm arose, and the waves beat into the boat, so that the boat was already being swamped. But he was in the stern, asleep on the cushion; and they woke him up and said to him, "Teacher, do you not care that we are perishing?" He woke up and rebuked the wind, and said to the sea, "Peace! Be still!" Then the wind ceased, and there was a dead calm. He said to them, "Why are you afraid? Have you still no faith?" And they were filled with great awe and said to one another, "Who then is this, that even the wind and the sea obey him?"

Unlike the parallel pericope in Matthew, which Matthew coloured with the focus on discipleship,[258] Mark reports this incident simply as a miracle story with his typical narrative interest.[259] When we compare this pericope with its Matthean parallel pericope and observe the changes made by Matthew to suit his perspective on discipleship, it is obvious that Mark's projection of the scenes 'they took him with them' (v36), coupled with the word of address to Jesus as 'teacher' (v38) seems to be original. Unlike Matthew who seems to modify the pericope with ecclesiological interest Mark is seen focusing on its theological-christological aspect of the narrative.[260] The vivid details of the episode including the projection of Jesus being asleep in the midst of storm also heighten his theological interest. Matthew lacks these details, but Mark vividly narrated how Jesus was sleeping (v38). Although, this storm clearly appeared to be a life-threatening situation, Jesus continued to sleep peacefully because of his complete trust in God's protective power. In the Old Testament such sleep is evidence of a trust in God's protection (cf. Job 11:18, 19; Ps 3: 5-6; 4:8). In the Ancient West Asian literatures sleeping

---

[258] G. Bornkamm, "The Stilling of the Storm in Mathew," in G. Bornkamm, G. Barth, H. J. Held, *Tradition and Interpretation in Matthew* (London: SCM Press, 1963), 55.

[259] J.P. Meier (*A Marginal Jew II: Rethinking the Historical Jesus* [New York Doubleday, 1994], 928) categorized it as a sea-rescue miracle rather than a sea-rescue epiphany, though the epiphany element is not altogether absent.

[260] For Christology as a major aspect of Mark's overall purpose, see N. Perrin, "The Christology of Mark: A Study in Methodology," in W.R. Telford (ed.), *The Interpretation of Mark* (Edinburgh: T&T Clark, 1995), 125-140.

is a symbol of divine rule.[261] Thus, there is a clear theological-christological aspect here ("Who then is this," v41): Jesus is at perfect peace anywhere, even in the midst of storm, apparently untroubled by normal anxieties, unlike the disciples, who got panicked. Thus Jesus' rest in the midst of the storm is a sign of his divine sovereignty.[262]

In Mark Jesus brought the storm to silence first and then rebukes his panicky disciples. That means the miracle occurs first and the words of rebuke second. In Matthew this scene occurs in reverse order. The explanation is that, unlike Matthew, who seems to emphasize more on the faith of the disciples in a difficult situation, Mark's focus is on the actual act of stilling the storm by displaying the power of God. Thus, for Mark Jesus woke up and rebuked the storm and the sea saying: "Peace! Be still!" (v39).[263]

And in the following verses it is seen that, unlike in Matthew who tone it down, as he cannot picture discipleship without faith (Mt 8:26), we see in Mark the natural harsh rebuke of the disciples (Mk 4:40). And at the end of the pericope (v41) the disciples marveled. Thus, the main emphasis of Mark is the utterance of the disciples in astonishment: "Who then is this, that even the wind and the sea obey him?" (v41). The answer is obvious: He is the very Son of God, who with the fatherly authority and compassion protects his disciples in times of stress and danger.

Thus, the theological-christological aspect is the main emphasis in this pericope. In this miracle of stilling of the storm on the Sea of Galilee we see demonstrated the power and the compassion of God exercised in love for disciples. In the midst of a terrifying upheaval the presence of the Son of God and his mighty works in stilling the situation, and thus it is in this person the disciples ought to relate and depend in the crisis of life, even so for Mark who intends to encourage his community in hardships with the same assurance.[264] We find

---

[261] B. Batto, "The Sleeping God: An Ancient Near East Motif of Divine Sovereignty," *Bib* 68 (1987), 153-77.

[262] This divine power over the sea is found in the Old Testament, in the Psalms, where God is described as the one who makes the storm of the sea and the waves calm down and redeem those in trouble (Ps 107:23-32 cf. 104:7).

[263] A miracle similar to this is found in the Mishnah, in the deeds of certain holy man named Onias, the Circle-drawer (though Jesus did not pray for rain but his miracle of controlling the storm is similar to Onias' performance - who in making the rain happen by his prayer to God – affect the weather). His action is depicted in this way: "He drew a circle and stood within it and said before God, 'O Lord of the world, thy children have turned their faces to me, for that I am like a son of the house before thee. I swear by thy great name that I will not stir hence until thou have pity on thy children.' Rain began falling drop by drop…" (*m. Taanith* 3:8 in H. Danby, *The Mishnah* [Oxford: Oxford University Press, 1933], 198). And in the same paragraph (*m. Taanith* 3:8 in Danby, *The Mishnah,* 198), Simon ben Shetah commented that Onias' filial relationship with God is in the manner of a son with his father.

[264] R.P. Martin, *Mark: Evangelist and Theologian* (Exeter: The Paternoster Press, 1979), 133.

similar display of God's authority and love in another pericope, a rescue-epiphany of Jesus, to which we now turn.

3.1.3.2. Walking on the Water (6:45-51)

In another of Jesus' activities recorded in Mark and Matthew the same loving and compassionate nature of God is displayed:

> Immediately he made his disciples get into the boat and go on ahead to the other side, to Bethsaida, while he dismissed the crowd. After saying farewell to them, he went up on the mountain to pray. When evening came, the boat was out on the sea, and he was alone on the land. When he saw that they were straining at the oars against an adverse wind, he came towards them early in the morning, walking on the sea. He intended to pass them by. But when they saw him walking on the sea, they thought it was a ghost and cried out; for they all saw him and were terrified. But immediately he spoke to them and said, "Take heart, it is I; do not be afraid." Then he got into the boat with them and the wind ceased.

The focus of this pericope is on the sea-rescue epiphanic character of Jesus,[265] unlike its parallel pericope in Matthew where the faith element of the disciple seems to be the central emphasis (Mt 14:22-33) with an additional episode of having Peter walking on the water (Mt 14:28-31).

After the miracle of the feeding (6:30-44), Jesus compels his disciples to get into the boat and go before him to the other side while he dismisses the crowd (v45). Meanwhile he ascends to the mountain to pray privately (v46). The disciples were drifting in the sea with their boat being beaten by the adverse wind (v48). So they are in the midst of hardships. Then Jesus comes to their rescue walking on the sea (v48). Mark emphasizes Jesus' purpose in performing this miracle by stating that "he intended to pass them by" (v48d). Trampling the waves and walking on the water top is something that God alone does in the Old Testament (Job 9:8; Ps 77:19; Isa 43:16). Thus, the use of the expression 'to pass by someone' in Old Testament narratives of theophany illuminates the point Mark is making in v48d: Jesus wanted to reveal himself to his disciples in all his divine majesty and power by demonstrating his dominion over the unruly forces of wind, sea, and waves. He acts toward them as God acts in the Old Testament.[266] The disciples did not recognize Jesus, rather thinking it to be a ghost and cried out in fear (v50a). Thus they were terrified, but Jesus came to their rescue saying: "Take heart, it is I: do not be afraid" (v50b). The expression "It is I" (ἐγώ εἰμι) literally is "I [I] am." In the Old Testament, the expression "I am" is generally a self-proclamation of God

[265] G. Theissen (*The Miracle Stories of the Early Christian Tradition* [Edinburgh: T&T Clark, 1983], 101) labeled it as an epiphany which bring rescue.

[266] Meier, *A Marginal Jew* II, 907.

(cf. Ex 3:14-15). It echoes the theophany of the Old Testament, as Jesus utters the revealing word ἐγώ εἰμι (v50c) as he come towards the disciples by walking on the water.[267] Thus, ἐγώ εἰμι has to do with the presence of God in Jesus.

Mark's focus seems to be equally on the action of Jesus - trampling on the water in manifestation of God's power - and on his words, "Take heart, it is I; do not be afraid." In this reassuring words of Jesus Mark wanted to convey his theological-christological intent: He is the Son of God, who demonstrated the power and the compassion of God in love for the disciples, bringing hope and deliverance to them. We will find similar compassionate and merciful nature of God's fatherly rule in Jesus' activities of healings and exorcisms, to which we now turn.

3.1.3.3. Man with an Unclean Spirit (1:21-27)

In this healing activity of Jesus which Mark share with Luke (4:33-35), we see similar traits of compassion and merciful nature of God:

> They went to Capernaum; and when the sabbath came, he entered the synagogue and taught. They were astounded at his teaching, for he taught them as one having authority, and not as the scribes. Just then there was in their synagogue a man with an unclean spirit, and he cried out, "What have you to do with us, Jesus of Nazareth? Have you come to destroy us? I know who you are, the Holy One of God." But Jesus rebuked him, saying, "Be silent, and come out of him!" And the unclean spirit, convulsing him and crying with a loud voice, came out of him. They were all amazed, and they kept on asking one another, "What is this? A new teaching – with authority! He commands even the unclean spirits, and they obey him."

The framework of this pericope is a sabbath visit to the synagogue, where Jesus' teaching leaves the congregation amazed by his authority, so that his reputation spread far and wide. But woven in with this straightforward motif is the story of a dramatic exorcism, which offers a more visible display of authority and which leads to a remarkable exclamation by the congregation (v27), which seems to be the central focus of Mark: the theological-christological aspect.

It is interesting to see here a strikingly similar pattern with the pericope of the stilling of the storm (4:35-41). Similar to the life-threatening storms countered by Jesus, a counter force is seen in the form of a man with an unclean spirit (v23). The comparison of this pericope with the pericope of the stilling of the storm is so compelling as in both situation Jesus is seen rebuking the spirit (v25) and the storm (4:39); and just as the storm was stilled, so also "the unclean spirit, convulsing him and crying with aloud voice, came out of him" (v26).

---

[267] Meier, *A Marginal Jew* II, 907.

For Mark the rebuking words of Jesus – "Be silent, and come out of him!"(v25) - is important. Here in this very act of driving out of the unclean spirit, for Mark, the 'time of salvation' has come near (1:15). God's rule is already present. God himself is active in Jesus, as R. Otto, in dealing with Jesus and the kingdom of God, put forth that "it was not he but rather God himself who achieved the first great divine victory over Satan."[268] Thus, for Mark, in the very deeds of Jesus, God's fatherhood is implied. In the very action of Jesus we see the loving and compassionate rule of God and the dethronement of the reign of Satan (cf. 3:23-27).

The subsequent amazement on the part of the disciples (4:41) and the crowds (1:27) culminate the episode in both the pericope; which seems to be the deliberate design of Mark keeping his theological-christological interest:

> Mk 1:27: They were all amazed, and they kept on asking one another, "What is this? A New teaching – with authority! He commands even the unclean spirits and they obey him."
>
> Mk 4:41: And they were filled with great awe and said to one another, "Who then is this, that even the wind and the sea obey him?"

The answer is obvious: he is not an ordinary person but a person having the power and authority of God. This is quite in line with what Mark affirms at the very beginning of his Gospel, that Jesus is the Son of God (1:1); and that it is he who inaugurated God's kingdom through his ministry (1:14,15). In other words, christology has a theocentric foundation: God's kingdom constitute the framework and content of Jesus' own preaching.[269] In the projection of Mark the mighty deeds of Jesus support and promote who Jesus is. He is the beloved Son of God, who participates in his Father's own divine identity, and it is he who brings about God's fatherly rule.[270] Thus the theological significance is seen in the fact that implicit in the deeds of Jesus demonstrates the fatherhood of God. A similar pattern is seen in another healing narrative, to which we now turn.

3.1.3.4. Jesus, Son of the Most High God (5:1-20)

While this episode is also found in Matthew (8:28-34) and Luke (8:26-39), but Mark has the most detail elaborations of the whole episode (20 verses) as compared to Matthew (7 verses) and Luke (13 verses). In this healing narrative Mark's theological emphasis is seen in that he has not only the most vivid description of the act of Jesus' exorcism but some recurring expressions, found in other miracle story of Markan Jesus is also seen. For example, the words of rebuke - "Come out

---

[268] R. Otto, "The Kingdom of God Expels the Kingdom of Satan," in *The Kingdom of God*, edited by B. Chilton (London: SPCK, 1984), 31.

[269] U. Schnelle, *Theology of the New Testament*, 403.

[270] R. Bauckham, *Jesus and the God of Israel*, 262.

of the man, you unclean spirit!" (v8) - is found only in Mark, which seems to be a recurring expressions of Mark (cf. 4:39; 1:25 above); so also the amazement at the culmination of the episode (v20b), another recurring pattern of Mark (cf. 4:41; 1:27 above), is again found only in Mark.

Mark has lengthy details of the nature of the spirit-possessed man on the way to meeting Jesus (vv2-5), and Mark alone has the possessed man bowed down before Jesus (v6) thus hinting at the divine identity of Jesus (v6). Subsequently in verse 7 we see the possessed man uttering Jesus as the 'Son of the Most High God.' However, in the view of G. Vermes, when Jesus is addressed as the Son of God by the possessed man here, it is not a unique recognition but in the manner of the Jewish *Hasidims* who were recognized to possess charismatic powers and therefore called as sons of God.[271] Accordingly for Vermes, Jesus is one of the Jewish holy man (*Hasid*) who performed miracles.[272]

However, when we see this episode within the overall narrative in Mark, the author's perspective is clearly seen. For Mark, the idea of Jesus' sonship to God is linked with key moments in the life of Jesus – at the baptism (1:11), at his transfiguration (9:7), and at his crucifixion and death (15:39). From beginning to end he is Son of God,[273] and now as is seen in this very episode, the sonship of Jesus is affirmed in his ministry or kingdom activities. Thus Mark's theological program is very clear. For Mark, the whole of the episode, including the vivid details of the possessed and the confession of the demoniac, in which is implied Jesus' divine identity (v7), is secondary to the authoritative words of Markan Jesus: "Come out of the man, you unclean spirit!"(v8). The demonic rule is subdued and in the very authoritative words of Markan Jesus, the rule of God came into

---

[271] G. Vermes, *Jesus The Jew* (London: SCM Press, 1994), 206-210.

[272] According to Vermes (*Jesus the Jew*, 208-209), referring to Babylonian Talmud text, *Pesahim* 112b, there were several holy men who performed miracles and there is a strikingly similar account to this Markan miracle account in Babylonian Talmud, which talks about Hanina ben Dosa, a Jewish miracle worker, and his encounter with the queen of demons, who was leading a vast army of evil spirits. Once when Hanina was walking at night alone, he met the "queen of the demons." She claimed that had he (Hanina) not enjoyed heaven's protection, she would have harmed him. Hanina then banned her from passing through inhabited places. We see here that even Hanina was recognized by the queen of demons as having heavenly (God's) approval. See also in M. Hengel, *The Son of God* (Philadelphia: Fortress Press, 1976), 41-43.

[273] For details on 'Son of God' as Mark's overarching theological emphasis, see J.D. Kingsbury, *The Christology of Mark's Gospel* (Philadelphia: Fortress, 1983), 155; J.D. Kingsbury, *Jesus Christ in Matthew, Mark, and Luke: The New Testament Witness for Preaching* (Philadelphia: Fortress, 1981) 33-38. Of course it was W. Wrede (*The Messianic Secret* [London: J. Clarke, 1971]), who was the first to see a Christological motif as giving shape to Mark's Gospel, as Mark projects that until a Gentile centurion confession of Jesus' divine sonship in 15:39, Jesus divine sonship is veiled from humans, all the confessions of Jesus as the Son of God is uttered from supernatural beings: from heaven (at baptism and transfiguration) or demons during Jesus healing ministry (e.g., 5:7). For a detail discussions on the theology of Mark, see R.P. Martin, *Mark: Evangelist and Theologian* (Exeter: Paternoster House, 1979), 84-106.

force.[274] For Mark the very presence of Jesus conveys a message – the message of God's rule – in speech and action.[275] In other words, the fatherly rule of God, his care and mercy (v19) became a reality in Jesus' presence.

In verse 9, the dialogue continues with Jesus' reciprocal demand for the demon's name (v9), to which came the reply: "My name is Legion; for we are many." Legion was a division of the Roman army, comprising some 4200 to 6000 soldiers.[276] However, here the significance of the 'name' Legion need not focus on the actual number of troops in a Roman legion, as verse 13 says that the unclean spirits entered to 2000 swine. The function of the name in this narrative is rather to provide a graphic indication of the multiple possessions involved in this case. What Mark wanted to emphasize is that Jesus is not confronted by one demon, but by an army of them.[277] Some scholars see in this very choice of Mark's of "the region of the Gerasene" as a site of symbolic confrontation with the "legions" takes on new and specifically political meaning. For C. Meyers this exorcism of the demons at Gerasa are symbolic of the political repudiation against the Roman military occupation of Palestine.[278] In the same light U. Schnelle too see in this usage, in conjunction with the Son of God christology elsewhere in Mark, a polemic against the claim of the Roman emperor.[279]

In verses 14-17 Mark has given a long account of the crowd reaction, after which has again the possessed man appear begging Jesus to be with him (v18), and to which Markan Jesus replied: "Go home to your friends, and tell them how much the Lord has done for you, and what mercy he has shown you"(v19). In this narrative context 'the Lord,' used in Jesus' words as a third-person designation of the one who is the source of mercy, must refer to God rather than Jesus himself (cf. Lk 8:39). While it is in Luke that we see Jesus acknowledging God as the source of healing (6:39b), yet-it is Mark alone who put into the lips of Jesus, expressing the fatherly compassionate nature of God:

[274] This is also the view held by those who adhere to Jesus as an eschatological prophet and his theology as realized eschatology; e.g., Schillebeeckx, *Christology*, 185; For details on these different views, see also W.R. Telford, *Mark* (Sheffield: Sheffield Academic Press, 1995), 127-134.

[275] Schillebeeckx, *Christology*, 192.

[276] U. Schnelle, *Theology*, 407.

[277] R.T. France, *The Gospel of Mark* (NIGTC; Grand Rapids; Michigan: Wm B Eerdmans, 2002), 229.

[278] As it is in this very place that Romans retaliated during Vespasian's reconquest of northern Palestine during the late years of the Jewish Revolt; See C. Myers, *Binding the Strong Man: A Political Reading of the Story of Jesus* (Maryknoll; New York: Orbis Books, 1988), 191.

[279] U. Schnelle, *Theology*, 407; Looking at the level of Jesus R.A. Horsley ("Jesus and Empire," in *In The Shadow of Empire: Reclaiming the Bible as a History of Faithful Resistance*, edited by R.A. Horsley [Louisville: Westminster John Knox Press, 2008], 86) finds the exorcisms as part of anti-imperial tactics of Jesus.

> Mk 5:19: Go home to your friends, and tell them how much the Lord has done for you, *and what mercy he has shown you.* (italic added)

> Lk 8:39: Return to your home, and declare how much God has done for you.

So also the amazement at the culmination of the episode is again found only in Mark:

> Mk 5:20: And he went away and began to proclaim in the Decapolis how much Jesus had done for him; *and everyone was amazed.* (italic added)

> Lk 8:39b: So he went away, proclaiming throughout the city how much Jesus had done for him.

For Mark, Jesus' works of healing are acts of God's compassion. For him, these activities show the reality of God's love and power that Jesus brings into human life. Thus, once again the theological significance is seen in the fact that God's fatherly authority and compassion is implicit in the very words and deeds of Jesus. We find the same pattern with similar perspectives in another healing narrative, the healing of a paralytic man.

3.1.3.5. Sins Forgiven (2:3-12)

This episode is again found in Matthew (9:2-8) and Luke (5:17-26), but Mark has the most detail elaborations of the whole episode (10 verses) compared to Matthew (7 verses) and Luke (9 verses). In this healing narrative once again Mark's theological-christological emphasis is seen more prominently than his Synoptic counterpart Matthew and Luke. As such it is seen that prior to the acts of forgiveness (healing), the persistent faith of the helpers is projected (v4). On seeing their faith in actions Jesus pronounced, "Son, your sins are forgiven" (v5). Of course, this scene is found in all the three Gospels (Mk 2:5//Mt 9:5//Lk 5:20). This statement of Jesus is found in divine passive, that is, as Herman Hendricks puts, "a veiled hint at an action on the part of God."[280] This construction (ἀφίενταί - present indicative passive) indicates divine action: God forgives. The persistent faith activity of the bearers appears more than trust in the miracle-worker, as faith in God, who forgives sins, that is, faith in the merciful Father, whom Jesus proclaims. And as the pericope proceeds, some redactional activities are seen. Thus in the very expressions of the scribes in Mark, following that pronouncement of Jesus (which is also seen in Luke), we see his theological convictions:

> Mk 2:7: Why does this man speak thus? It is blasphemy! Who can forgive sins but God *alone*? (RSV) [italic added]

[280] H. Hendricks, *The Miracle Stories of the Synoptic Gospe*ls (San Francisco: Harper and Row, 1987), 115.

Lk 5:21: Who is this that speaks blasphemies? Who can forgive sins but God only? (RSV)

As observed carefully, particularly in the very use of εἷς ὁ θεός (Mk 2:7), rather than μόνος ὁ θεός as in Luke (Lk 5:21), Mark has let the scribes accorded primacy to God and to his authority, and which echoes the Jewish creedal statement that 'God is one' (Deut 6:4). The conviction is that only God can forgive sins.[281] For the scribes a man who claims to do what only God can do threatens that unique status, and that is a blasphemy.[282] To claim to do what only God could do, and to constitute himself as God's spokesman in declaring sins forgiven, was to infringe upon the divine prerogative.[283] However, for Mark, what matters is that in the very reactions of the scribes, implicit in their rhetorical questions, is his theological-christological convictions that this Jesus is indeed the Son of God, and he has the authority to forgive sins: "so that you may know that the Son of Man has authority on earth to forgive sins" (v10). Thus, for Mark, Jesus belongs to the divine identity,[284] and so he is able to extend to people the help of God.[285]

Furthermore, Markan Jesus goes on saying to the paralytic, "I say to you, stand up, take your mat and go to your home" (v11). Then the paralytic was instantly healed and started walking and the people were amazed (v12), in the same pattern as in the stilling of the storm (4:39) and in the subduing of the demons (5:8). For Mark, forgiveness is a sign of the coming of God's kingdom. It therefore offered ample reason to glorify God (v12). For Mark, God's rule or God's fatherhood is manifested in the very speech and action of Jesus. God's rule is but the reign of love and forgiveness. In other words, the fatherly rule of God, his love, forgiveness and acceptance (v15) became a reality in Jesus' presence. It is not surprising that elsewhere in the teaching of Markan Jesus the notion of pardon is one of the central ingredients of the Father image of Jesus. (Mk 11:25). Thus once again the conviction of Mark, his idea of a loving, compassionate and forgiving Father is clearly seen in this healing narrative. With this we will turn to another pericope, the cleansing of a leper (1:40-42), where the compassion of God seems to be the focus again for Mark.

3.1.3.6. Cleansing of a Leper (1:40-42)

While this very brief episode lacks the usual Markan structure of explicit theological-christological expressions in the mouth of the supplicant or crowd, yet certain traits are seen hinting at his christological focus: the suppliant, a leper,

[281] The convictions is that they (the scribes) 'considered sin a sin against God and therefore more serious than paralysis or other sickness' (See Minear, *God of the Gospels*, 77).

[282] For the Jews blasphemy was a capital offence (Lev 24:10-16).

[283] France, *The Gospel of Mark*, 126.

[284] Bauckham, *Jesus and the God of Israel*, 265.

[285] Schillebeeckx, *Christology*, 200.

approaches Jesus 'kneeling,' requesting a healing (v40); Jesus complies, healing the supplicant with a touch and a word (v41); and the fact and immediacy of the cure are then affirmed (v42). The Gospel parallels of the same verse reveals that the expression 'moved with pity' is seen only in Mark, and which seems to be quite in line with his theological-christological focus, which is also seen elsewhere in Mark (6:34):

> Mk 1:41: *Moved with pity*, Jesus stretched out his hand and touched him, and said to him, "I do choose. Be made clean!"(Italic added)
>
> Mt 8:3: He stretched out his hand and touched him, saying, "I do choose. Be made clean!" Immediately his leprosy was cleansed.
>
> Lk 5:13: Then Jesus stretched out his hand, touched him, and said, "I do choose. Be made clean." Immediately the leprosy left him.

A leper came to Jesus praying for his cleansing (v40). It is generally agreed that *lepra* in the Bible is used for a wider range of diseases including 'leprosy.'[286] Probably the leper was suffering from a kind of skin disease that was thought to be contagious, and his suffering seems to be related with social and religious reason, rather than physical.[287] This is inferred from the fact that the leper does not ask to be healed but to be made clean.[288] Jesus' fame (v28) has reached this man, who was probably living in isolation, and as we see in verse 40, the leper has unquestioning trust in Jesus' authority. Since for Mark, Jesus is the one in whom God is present and active, the leper is projected as coming towards him "kneeling" (v40a), which is much beyond ordinary respect. Markan Jesus then 'moved with pity'[289] (σπλαγχνισθεὶς) and touched the leper with his hand stretched out (ἐκτείνας τὴν χεῖρα αὐτοῦ ἥψατο). The participle σπλαγχνισθεὶς (cf. 6:34; 8:2; 9:22) which means 'have pity' or 'feel sympathy,' from the verb σπλαγχνίζομαι denotes a feeling that is felt physically - an emotion. Literally σπλαγχνίζομαι means "to be moved in one's bowels."[290] Thus it means that Jesus was emotionally affected by the encounter. The intensity of the suffering both socially and physically, caused by the disease, moved Jesus to such compassion. And that inward feeling led to action and the very action was but care and concern towards the needy and the helpless like the leper. Here once again we find the

[286] France, *The Gospel of Mark*, 116.

[287] Such people were segregated from the mainstream society; not only isolated from family and friends but were also excluded from public worship.

[288] D.A. Hare, *Mark* (Louisville: Westminster John Knox Press, 1996), 34.

[289] In some manuscripts it is 'anger' which is not widely attested (See France, *The Gospel of Mark*, 115).

[290] The Jews regarded the bowels as the center of the tender affections, especially kindness and pity; See D.J. Williams, "Mercy," in *DJG*, edited by J.B Green, S. McKnight, I.H. Marshall (Leicester: IVP, 1992), 542-543.

very idea of God's fatherhood in this healing pericope, as James Moffat explains, "These works of healing represent the pity and power exercised upon men; they are cures which are meant to deepen faith in the merciful and strong character of the Father, whose kingdom Jesus has come to establish. Furthermore, the miracles ... witness to the truth that the reign of God concerns the physical as well as the spiritual well-being of men, and that the goodwill of the Father embraces all sides of human nature (cf. Matt. xi.4f.), with the power of reaching and healing it at every point."[291]

As such the healing miracles of Jesus are the revelation of God's power and compassion; they are the sign that God cares. In the action of Markan Jesus we see the power and the compassion of God combine to deal with the human situation. Thus God's fatherhood is strongly implied in this pericope. The same trait of a compassionate and caring God is strongly emphasized in another pericope, the feeding of the 5000, to which we now turn.

3.1.3.7. Compassionate God (6:34-44)

The given pericope is again found in all the Synoptic Gospels but there are some slight yet striking differences in the account. A parallel of the three Synoptic Gospels of the same verse reveal the distinct emphasis of Mark:

> Mk 6:34: As he went ashore, he saw a great crowd; and he had compassion for them, *because they were like sheep without a shepherd; and he began to teach them many things.* (italic added)
>
> Mt 14:14: When he went ashore, he saw a great crowd; and he had compassion for them and cured their sick.
>
> Lk 9:11: When the crowds found out about it, they followed him; and he welcomed them, and spoke to them about the kingdom of God, and healed those who needed to be cured.

It is interesting to see that Mark has the expression 'sheep without shepherd' in a narrative of Jesus' 'deeds of power,' the feeding of the multitude, which is not found in the same pericope in Matthew as seen in the parallel, though found elsewhere in a didactic context (Mt 9:36). Mark tells us that, as a result of his compassion, Jesus began to teach them many things (v34c). Ched Myers sees in this very pericope 'a political polemic' of Markan Jesus, particularly pointing to the presence of the expression 'sheep without shepherd' here. He saw this background in Ezekiel 34 where the prophet is seen criticizing the leadership of Israel using the shepherd-sheep analogy.[292] Thus for him, "linking Jesus – as one who attends to the hunger of the crowds in the wilderness – with these prophetic

[291] J. Moffat, *The Theology of the Gospels* (London: Duckworth & Co, 1912), 92.

[292] Myers, *Binding the Strong Man*, 207-209.

traditions is meant as a criticism of the political economy of Palestine and the ruling class who profits from it."[293]

The exact expression here in Mark may be found in the Old Testament languages of Ezekiel (34:5), Numbers (27:17) and I Kings (22:17); but the echoes of the Psalmist seems to be stronger in Mark as regard to his sheep-shepherd expression. Mark seems to have Psalm 23 in his mind as he retells this miracle account of Jesus.[294] Not only that he alone has the expression 'sheep-shepherd' in this episode of Jesus' miraculous feeding in the wilderness, but that he alone records the apparently small detail that Jesus commanded them to sit down on the green grass (Mk 6:39), as shown in the parallels of the same verse below:

> Mk 6:39: Then he ordered them to get all the people to sit down in groups on the *green* grass. (italic added)
>
> Mt 14:19a: Then he ordered the crowds to sit down on the grass.
>
> Lk 9:14b: And he said to his disciples, "Make them sit down in groups of about fifty each."

The presence of the nurturing and guiding element in Psalm 23 and here in this narrative is striking. In Psalm 23 God is affirmed as Shepherd as the Psalmist says, "The Lord is my shepherd, I shall not want" (v1). And in the following verses it is seen that God leads the flock to where there is green pasture, concerned to feed them, not himself (v2). He leads and guides his flock on those right paths that lead to shelter and security (v3). So also in Mark the idea of sustenance and guidance is equally strong in this pericope (vv34-44). It is all the more striking as we observe that the very actions of Jesus in verse 41 in the manner of blessings at a table fellowship - 'taking' the loaves, 'blessed,' 'broke' and 'gave'[295] - is in agreement again with Psalm 23 that God as a shepherd would prepare a table for his people in the very sight of their enemies (v5). Thus the theological interest of Mark in this pericope is very clear. As Mark retells this feeding activity of Jesus, the idea of God's fatherhood is clearly seen. For him implicit in the very deeds of Jesus is the idea of God's fatherhood, a caring, selfless and compassionate God.

3.1.4. Summary

In Mark the fatherhood of God is mostly understood in the sonship activities of Jesus. In the several miracles of Jesus recorded in Mark, in the 'deeds of power'

---

[293] Myers, *Binding the Strong Man*, 209.

[294] Rex Mason, *Old Testament Pictures of God* (Oxford: Regent's Park College, 1993), 155.

[295] Which is said to be common actions and expressions of the Jewish head of the family at a meal, taking bread, pronouncing the blessing, breaking it, and distributing it; See J. Jeremias, *The Eucharistic Words of Jesus* (trans N. Perrin; London: SCM Press, 1966), 48-49); yet in these expressions many find Eucharistic echoes; See R.T. France, *The Gospel of Mark*, 262; W.R. Telford, *Mark*, 128; R.M. Fowler, *Loaves and Loaves* (California: Scholars Press, 1981), 85-86.

(Mk 6:2, 5), Jesus' identity is the centre of focus. That means, in Mark Jesus' activities are signs of God's fatherly rule or God's compassion in action. Among the very few instances of the usage of 'Father' for God it is in Mark alone that we also see the very theologically significant term *Abba* in the lips of Jesus. While in one instance in Mark (11:25) the fatherhood of God is seen in relation to disciples ('your Father'), but in the rest the idea of God's fatherhood is understood in relation to the sonship of Jesus and his proclamation of the kingdom of God. As such quite in line with the *Abba* expression in the lips of Jesus, the whole activity of Markan Jesus has linked to the person and work of Jesus. All in all, for Mark, the powerful activities of Jesus demonstrated God's compassion, love and mercy. In this case Mark's understanding of the fatherhood of God has universal significance. With this we will now turn to Luke and examine how the same aspect of God's fatherhood is highlighted.

3.2. The Fatherhood of God in Luke

We have seen that in Mark the idea of God's fatherhood is understood mainly in relation to the sonship of Jesus to God, that is, fatherhood implicit in the kingdom activities of Jesus. We will now turn to Luke and examine the material he shares in common with Matthew (so Q[296]); and also the materials unique to Luke (L) and highlight how the very idea of God's fatherhood is expounded.

3.2.1. Occurrences of 'Father' for God

In Luke 'Father' for God occur 17 times,[297] out of which 2 occurrences are from Mark,[298] 9 are from Q,[299] and 6 instances are found in Lukan special material (L).[300] The nine instances that Luke shares with Matthew (so Q) are seen in the following pericope: the teaching on imitating the Father (6:36); the saying regarding the mutual knowledge of Father and Son (10:21-22); the way of praying to God (11:2); the query about a father's provision for his children (11:13); the promise that the heavenly Father will provide for his children as he does for the grass and the birds (12:28-30). Moreover within Luke special material (L), he contributes several sayings linking the Father and the kingdom (12:32; 22:29-30) and the Father and the Spirit (11:13 [Q]; 24:49). There are also multiple instances of prayer - of thanksgiving to God as 'Father' (10:21 [Q]); in intercession for himself

[296] This source (from *Quelle*) was a collection of sayings of Jesus that Matthew and Luke drew upon, in addition to Mark, when they wrote their gospels (though both also had access to other sources).

[297] Out of the total 56 occurrences of the term 'father' in Luke; see Kohlenberger III, *The Exhaustive Concordance to the Greek New Testament*, 772-773.

[298] 9:26//Mt 16:27//Mk 8:38; 22:42//Mt 26:39//Mk 14:36.

[299] 6:36//Mt 5:48; 10:21-22[x5]//Mt 11:25-27[x5]; 11:2//Mt 9:6; 11:13//Mt 7:11; 12:30// Mt 6:32.

[300] 2:49; 12:32; 22:29; 23:34, 46; 24:49.

(22:42[Mk]); and for others (23:34, 46). There is of course also the parable of the prodigal son (Lk 15:11-32), though we cannot count the 'father' occurrences there, yet the description of the fatherly nature of God is very clear. The parable is told in response to the complaint of the Pharisees that Jesus welcomed and ate with sinners, thus the story implies compassion, forgiveness and acceptance of God.

3.2.2. Jesus and God Correlation: The Significance of the Fatherhood of God

In dealing with Luke's presentation of the fatherhood of God it is logical to begin with Luke 10:21-22, where the idea of God's fatherhood is seen prominently and particularly in the occurrences of the Father/Son correlation.

3.2.2.1. Father and Son: An Intimate Knowledge (10:21-22)

This pericope, found in both Luke and Matthew (so Q), has strong emphasis on the Father-Son correlation. As a culmination of the discipleship and mission sermons of Jesus (9:51-10:24), Lukan Jesus addresses the Father in a prayerful expression of rejoicing in the Holy Spirit:

> I thank you, Father, Lord of heaven and earth, because you have hidden these things from the wise and the intelligent and have revealed them to infants; yes, Father, for such was your gracious will. All things have been handed over to me by my Father; and no one knows who the Son is except the Father, or who the Father is except the Son and anyone to whom the Son chooses to reveal him.[301]

It is interesting to note that five of the nine occurrences of 'Father' for God in Luke are found in this very pericope. It is also in this very pericope that Jesus is seen indicating himself as 'the Son' three times in verse 22. While this pericope is also found in Matthew (Mt 11: 25-27), but Lukan colouring is also seen at the very beginning of the pericope that Jesus "rejoices in the Holy Spirit" (cf. Lk 1:14, 44). Scholars see this pericope as redactional compilation of two sayings,[302] with verse 21 as Palestinian-Jewish,[303] since Jesus is seen rejoicing in the Holy Spirit in wisdom language that God's revelation comes to the simple, not to the wise; while verse 22 as typical Hellenistic revelation saying.[304] But the unity of

---

[301] Due to the presence of the idea of strong mutual Father-Son correlation in this pericope, a trait so common to John's Gospel, some scholars called it as 'Johannine thunderbolt.' See H.W. Montefiore, "God as Father in the Synoptic Gospels," in *NTS* 3/1 (1956), 37; Jeremias, *New Testament Theology*, 56.

[302] R. Bultmann, *History of Synoptic Tradition* (New York: Harper and Row, 1976), 159-160; I. H. Marshall, *The Gospel of Luke* (NIGTC; Grand Rapids; Michigan: Wm B. Eerdmans, 1978), 431.

[303] G. Vermes, *The Religion of Jesus the Jew*, 162.

[304] Bultmann, *History of Synoptic Tradition*, 160.

this pericope is very strong with the clear connections of expressions "Father," "hidden," "these things" in verse 21 with the corresponding expression "Father," "all things," "reveal" in verse 22.

In verse 21, we see a prayer of the blessing and thanksgiving: "I thank you, Father, Lord of heaven and earth, because you have hidden these things from the wise and the intelligent and have revealed them to infants." The content of this thanksgiving prayer contains wisdom motif which insists that true wisdom belong to God alone.[305] It is therefore a typical Palestinian-Jewish in form.[306] And here in this very context of Luke (Q), the 'hidden' is the revelation of divine powers seen in the healing and exorcism by the disciples (10:9). So what was happening remained obscure in its significance to one group of people, but to the disciples it constituted a revelation of God's saving action. The former group is described as 'wise and the intelligent,' while the latter group is described as 'infants' (νηπίοις). That is, "the childlike, innocent ones, unspoiled by learning with whom God is pleased."[307] There is an implicit condemnation of the religious leaders of the community who despite their wisdom have failed to gain a true perception of God and his will. Jesus takes up the thought that God addresses himself to the poor and simple who are prepared to listen to him because they have no wisdom of their own (cf. Sir 3:19; Wis 10:21). Jesus gives thanks not "because 'these things' are reserved for a select group of people but because they are revealed to those humanly speaking could not have expected it."[308] Thus, for Jesus, the childlike and poor are not the meticulous performers of law and rituals but the needy and downtrodden who accept the Gospel.[309]

And it is seen that the term 'Father' and 'Lord (of heaven and earth)' occur together when Q Jesus is talking about the 'gracious will' of God. Such pairing, however, is not new to Jesus alone. There are such expressions in Jewish-Hellenistic tradition of prayers. A strikingly similar to this expression is found in the prayer of Eleazar in 3 Maccabees chapter 6, where the same pairing of Father and Ruler occur (vv2-3, 5-8). As such according to D' Angelo, this very expression "exhibits God's will and providence as the governor of history."[310] However, in the second sentence of the prayer (Lk 10:21c) the address 'Father,' which occurs alone without any additional expression, seems to be in line with intimate address of God as 'Father' in Luke 22:42, which parallels Mark 14:36. Thus the address of God as Father here may reflect an original use by Jesus, that is, 'Abba, Father' (Mk14:36; 'Father,' Lk 22:42), which expresses an intimate filial relationship with God, and

---

[305] F.W. Burnett, "Wisdom," in *DJG*, 875.

[306] See Jeremias, *New Testament Theology*, 190; Schillebeeckx, *Jesus: An Experiment in Christology*, 265.

[307] G. Bertram, "νηπίοις," *TDNT IV*, 912.

[308] H. Conzelmann, "συνίημι," *TDNT VIII*, 893 n. 46.

[309] Marshall, *Luke*, 434.

[310] D'Angelo, "Theology in Mark and Q: *Abba* and 'Father' in Context," 167.

which is clearly expressed in the next verse (v22). Jesus thanks God, who is his own 'Father.' He rejoices that the mystery of the kingdom has been revealed to the infants; and this was God's good and gracious will.

The next verse talks about the mutual knowledge of Father and Son: "All things have been handed over to me by my Father; and no one knows who the Son is except the Father, or who the Father is except the Son and anyone to whom the Son chooses to reveal him." This phrase says that Jesus, as God's Son, is the only recipient and mediator of God's wisdom. Scholars see striking parallels to this saying in Hellenistic mysticism. For example, Bultmann sees this having its possible background in Akhnaton's hymn to the Sun, "No other knows thee save thy son Akhnaton. Thou hast initiated him into thy plans and thy power."[311] Bentley Layton, in his treatment of Gnosticism and its context, describes a common 'Hellenistic' myth in which the soul awakens to the knowledge of its true origin and destiny in God.[312]

However, the typical Jewish root of this expression is seen in the strong Semitic characteristic language and style of this verse. G. Dalman noted that the two clauses in this verse referring to the mutual knowledge of the Father and the Son "really constitute a detailed Oriental mode of expressing the reciprocity of intimate understanding."[313] T.W. Manson too finds strong Semitic language and style in this saying.[314] The idea of mutual knowledge is found in Exodus 33:12-13 and E. Schweizer finds here Jewish covenantal roots of "election by the Father and acknowledgement by the Son."[315] But the closest to this idea is found in Tobit 5:2, though in a secular context of mutual trust and insight.[316] So also in Jewish wisdom piety, knowledge of God and the claim on God as Father were already connected (Wis 2:12-20). In Philo also we see the language of sonship, but the term is 'first-born' and there is no thought of a Father-Son personal relationship.[317] While wisdom language is clear yet the Father-Son relationship language in verse 21 and 22 is quite in line with another tradition found in Q, that is, in Luke 11:2 and Matthew 9:6, where the fatherhood of God and so the Sonship of Jesus to God is strongly implied. Nolland thus rightly commented that Luke and his

---

[311] Bultmann, *History of Synoptic Tradition*, 160. n. 1.

[312] Bentley Layton, *The Gnostic Scriptures: A New Translation with Annotations and Introduction* (New York: Double day, 1987), 360.

[313] G. Dalman, *The Words of Jesus* (Edinburgh: T&T Clark, 1909), 283.

[314] T.W. Manson, *The Teaching of Jesus* (Cambridge: Cambridge University Press, 1955), 109-12.

[315] E. Schweizer, "υἱὸς," in *TDNT* VIII, 373.

[316] In the context of a father giving instruction to his son, Tobias, the son responded to his father Tobit regarding some amount of money left in trust with certain Gabael (Tob 5:2): "But how can I obtain the money from him, since he does not know me and I do not know him?"

[317] *De Somniis* 215 in Philo V, 412-413, trans F.H. Colsen and G.H. Whitaker; *De Confusione Linguarum* 146 in Philo IV, 88-89, trans F.H. Colsen and G.H. Whitaker.

source "have understood the address from the beginning as an expression of Jesus' distinctively intimate relationship with God."[318]

Finally, Lukan Jesus blesses those who see and hear what prophets and kings did not (vv23-24). The main emphasis here is on the realization of God's kingdom. The disciples had witnessed a unique event. They lived in the time of fulfillment. What prophets and kings of past generations had longed for had come to fulfillment (v24). The new age had begun. This was revealed to the disciples by the Son (v21). Thus the private address to the disciples underlines more clearly that the beatitude – "Blessed are the eyes that see what you see!" (v23) - is applicable mainly to the disciples because they are the ones who have been able to see the events surrounding Jesus for what they really were. Thus Luke has in mind the mighty works which the disciples reported in 10:17. The language of seeing is literal here, it means "see with insight and response" (cf. Lk 8:10).[319] The personification of eyes is paralleled in 2:30, and as such the language used here "stresses the element of real, personal experience (cf. Job 19:27; 42:5)."[320]

It is clear that stress is placed on the filial relationship between God and Jesus. So Jesus (the Son) knows God as Father. And Jesus (the Son) can decide to share his knowledge of God. Such sharing brings others into this family of Father and Son. As Father, God chooses to share 'all things' with the Son, and through him, with the disciples, the family.[321] Such an understanding of God's fatherhood is also stressed by Luke in a unique pericope in the Lukan infancy narratives to which we now turn.

3.2.2.2. Being in the Father's House (2:48-49)

Both Luke and Matthew introduce us to Jesus by means of their version of birth narratives, and in Luke's narratives we see his distinctive emphasis on the theme of God's fatherhood. In the pericope on 'the annunciation to Mary concerning Jesus' birth' (1:26-38), which is unique to Luke, the angel Gabriel is seen telling Mary that Jesus would be the Son of God (1:32, 35). And in this pericope, again found only in Luke, Jesus is seen speaking of God as his Father. In countering Mary's words of distress ("Look your father and I have been searching for you in great anxiety," v48), Lukan Jesus replies:

---

[318] J. Nolland, *Luke 9:21-18:34* (WBC vol 35b; Dallas: Word Books Publishers, 1993), 572.

[319] Nolland, *Luke*, 576.

[320] Marshall, *Luke*, 438.

[321] In such an understanding of God's fatherhood in exclusive sense, J. Moffat (*The Theology of the Gospels*, 99) commented that Jesus did not teach "God as the Father of men, but that God as His Father; it was in virtue of this unique consciousness of sonship that he called men to come to Him and learn the secret of sonship, and He mediated the knowledge of it by His life and death and resurrection, no less than by His words." So also Jeremias (*New Testament Theology*, 180) commented that the fatherhood of God is not an automatic possession of all humankind but a privilege enjoyed by the disciples of Jesus.

> Why were you searching for me? Did you not know that I must be in my Father's house?

For Luke, "the tensions between the claims of physical and spiritual allegiance are evident when Mary speaks of Jesus' father (Joseph) and Jesus replies in terms of his actual Father (God)."[322] Thus both physical and spiritual aspect of fatherhood is seen here. From the physical aspect of fatherhood, it is seen that Jesus' childhood was just like that of any other children of dedicated parents (v48); growing in maturity (v52), and being obedient to his earthly parents (v51). But Luke's primary purpose is seen in the very words in the lips of Jesus about the fatherhood of God.

Most of the arguments in regard to this verse centers around the very expression ἐν τοῖς τοῦ πατρός μου. In most translations the phrase is rendered either as "in my Father's house" or "about my Father's affairs."[323] The first translation seems to fit the logic of the narrative. That is, the immediate situation in the story seems to suit this rendering. Jesus is found inside the temple area, the house of God. For Jesus, to refer to the temple as "my Father's house" may suggest an obvious claim to sonship and belonging. However, when we examine this phrase within the context of Old Testament as well as New Testament usages, it has no convincing supports. While denoting a person's family of origin or clan the Old Testament expression is ὁ οἶκος τοῦ μου ("my father's house," e.g., Gen 28:21; Jud 11:7); and within Luke too, ἐν τοῖς τοῦ πατρός μου is an unusual expression to use for the temple. The common term for temple in Luke-Acts is ἱερόν (e.g., 2:27; 4:9; 18:10; 20:1). Thus, the expression ἐν τοῖς τοῦ πατρός μου can best be translated as 'in the things of my Father's (works),' as De Jonge suggests εἶναί as "to be occupied in."[324] So here the 'things of (my Father)' can be interpreted as the activities as deeds of God which Jesus helped to carry out, for example, the proclamation of the kingdom of God (4:43).

The occurrence of a typical Lukan motif δεῖ also points toward this direction. This idea of divine necessity is most frequent in Luke among the Synoptic Gospels, occurring some 18 times.[325] According to Grundmann, the expression δεῖ is at home in Greek and Hellenistic usage and Luke is familiar with this term from his Hellenistic background.[326] It is striking to see that it occurs in relation to the fatherhood of God here. It expresses a sense of divine necessity or compulsion. As such in the depiction of Luke Jesus sees his whole life and activity and passion

---

[322] B. Witherington III, 'Birth of Jesus,' in *DJG*, 74.

[323] For thorough discussions on various options for translating this verse, see Patrick J. Temple, "'House' or 'Business' in Lk. 2:49?" in *CBQ* 1 (1939), 342-52; Henk J. De Jonge, "Sonship, Wisdom, Infancy; Luke 2:41-51a," in *NTS* 24/3 (April 1978), 317-354.

[324] De Jonge, "Sonship, Wisdom, Infancy; Luke 2:41-51a," 335.

[325] See J.R. Kohlenberger III, *The Exhaustive Concordance to the Greek New Testament*, 188-189.

[326] Grundmann, "δεῖ," in *TDNT* II, 21.

under this will of God (δεῖ) - in his childhood, under this divine compulsion Jesus is in the temple, in the locus of God's presence (2:49); leads him to suffering and death (9:22;17:25; 24:7, 26); determines his activity (4:43;13:33;19:5); it has its basis in the will of God concerning him which is laid down in Scripture (22:37; 24:44). The result of the saying is thus to show that Jesus is indeed the Son of God.

It is interesting to note in this very expression ἐν τοῖς τοῦ πατρός μου, Jesus does not say that he had to be in the affairs of 'God' but of 'my Father.' Clearly here Lukan Jesus is speaking of God as his Father. This seems to be the deliberate work of Luke. The relationship with the earthly parents is placed beneath the relationship of the Father and the Son.[327] Seeing from the lens of gender, Elisabeth S. Fiorenza argues that the use of the term 'Father' for God here in verse 49 "relativizes all claims of earthly fatherhood and rejects all power of a patriarchally institutionalized society."[328] That means for her this very expression of Lukan Jesus does not affirm patriarchal fatherhood but stands in criticism of it and against it. Interestingly, Lukan genealogy of Jesus is also traced to Adam (3:37), which demonstrates that it is not the earthly father (Joseph) who is the father of Jesus but God who is the Father of Jesus. Thus for Luke, even genealogy is guided by his emphasis on God's fatherhood. As such here in his version of the infancy narratives Luke has brought the fatherhood of God into the forefront: Jesus is depicted as one who is uniquely related to God as Son to Father.[329] That means, for Luke, Jesus is the Son who stands in an exclusive relationship to the Father.

However, in Luke it is also seen that the one whom Jesus addresses exclusively as Father is also the one whose realm of reign is universal. This is clearly implied in several narratives in Luke to which we now turn.

3.2.3. Fatherhood of God and Kingdom of God

The theme of the kingdom of God is seen in close relation with the idea of God's fatherhood in the teaching of Jesus in Luke. We will now examine some of the passages where the idea of God's fatherhood and kingdom are inseparably linked in Luke.

3.2.3.1. "Father … Your kingdom come." (11:2-4)

This prayer of Jesus is recorded both in Luke and Matthew (hence Q), and according to Jeremias, Luke preserves an earlier form of the prayer, which seems

---

[327] De Jonge ("Sonship, Wisdom, Infancy: Luke 2:41-51a," 335, 352) while seeing strong christological character here, but says that the tradition which influenced Luke 2:49 was not that of the Son of God but that of "'the Son,' or 'the Son and the Father'" in line with Luke 10:22.

[328] E.S. Fiorenza, "Luke 2:41-52," in *Int* 36 (1982), 402-403.

[329] On the expression 'Son of the Father' as metaphorical or analogical and as rooted in Jesus' own unique experience, See Dunn, *New Testament Theology: An Introduction*, 60.

to be correct as expansions are more likely than omission. Whatever it may be we see in this very expression strong theocentric emphasis.

The address of God as 'Father' is highly theological. *Pater* is Greek for the Aramaic *Abba* and according to J. Jeremias, the regular use of *Abba*, especially in its absolute form 'Father' is typical of Jesus' prayers and so unique to Jesus in terms of his intimate experience with God.[330] However, the use of 'Father' for God as well as addressing God as Father in prayers has a long history in both Old Testament Judaism and later Judaism. God is represented metaphorically as Father of the chosen people in both the Old Testament (e.g., Jer 3:9; Isa 64:8) and Apocryphal literature (e.g., *Jubilees* 1:24-25). Prayers in ancient Judaism are rich in invocations to God the Father. Long before Jesus' time strikingly similar invocations of God as Father are found. For example, in 3 Maccabees, we see God is being addressed as both 'Father' and 'King' in the prayer of Eleazar:

> King of great power, Almighty God Most High, governing all creation with mercy, look upon the descendants of Abraham, O Father, upon the children of the sainted Jacob, a people of your consecrated portion who are perishing as foreigners in a foreign land (3 Macc 6:2-4).[331]

Similarly in Sirach 'Lord' and 'Father' combine occurs even in invocation: "O Lord, Father and Master of my life" (23:1, 4; 51:10). The phrase also occurs in Tobit (13:4), 3 Maccabees (5:7) and Wisdom of Solomon (11:10). Similarly, 'Father' appears in the Wisdom of Solomon (14:3), where an explorer preparing to set out to sea in a ship addresses God as "O Father" in prayer.

In the rabbinic Judaism the combination of 'Father' and King' in invocation is common. The Jews during the synagogue morning service pray to God with the fixed formula: "Our Father, our King!"[332] The same expression is found in the New Year prayer *Abinu malkenu*. It is said that it was R. Akiba who pronounces the beginning of this prayer at a service of fasting: "Our Father, our King! [Thou art our Father, and] we have no king but Thee. Our Father, our King for thine own sake have compassion upon us!"[333] Another ancient Jewish prayer whose earliest form probably goes back to the time of Jesus is the *Qaddish* prayer. It may have some influence on Jesus as he formulates the prayer (Lk 11:2-4) for his

[330] Jeremias, *The Prayers of Jesus*, 11-67.

[331] All English translations of Old Testament apocryphal works are taken from *The Holy Bible containing Old and New Testaments with the Apocryphal/Deuterocanonical Books* (NRSV; Nashville: Thomas Nelson, 1989).

[332] See *The Authorized Daily Prayer Book of the United Hebrew Congregations of the British Empire*, with a new translation by S. Singer (Ninth edition; London: Eyre and Spottiswoode, Ltd., 1912), 55.

[333] G.F. Moore, *Judaism in the First Centuries of the Christina Era The Age of the Tannaim*, vol II (Cambridge: Harvard University Press, 1932), 209, citing *b. Ta'anit* 25b.

disciples. There are striking similarities between Jesus' teaching on prayer and the *Qaddish*. The prayer began thus:

> Magnified and sanctified be his great name in the world which he hath created according to his will. May he establish his kingdom during your life and during your days, and during the life of all the house of Israel, even speedily and at near time, and say ye, Amen.[334]

On looking at the broader surrounding milieu we see that the designation 'Father' was not a solely Jewish or Q title for God. There are other striking parallels of prayers addressing God as Father in the Ancient West Asian religions as well as in the Greco-Roman writings. In a hymn to the moon god, addressed by his Sumerian name Nanna, God is addressed as Father: "O Lord, hero of the gods, who in heaven and earth is exalted in his uniqueness, Father Nanna, Lord Anshar, hero of the gods."[335] The Greeks refer to the chief deity as 'Father.' It is evident in Homer, who pictures human calling on Zeus in prayer as Father.[336] From the earliest written period Greek religions recognized Zeus or Jupiter as "Father of gods and men."[337]

Thus the invocation of God as 'Father' seems to be a common invocations and practice of the time,[338] yet the expression of Jesus addressing God as Father with the eschatological overtone is striking:

> Father, hallowed be your name. Your kingdom come (Luke 11:2)[339]

The petition is forward looking. Jesus instructs his disciples to call upon the one who is Father to bring his kingdom. Here we see that while welcoming the nearness of God's own rule the emphasis of Jesus is of a loving Father, who is asked to let his 'kingdom come.' This linking of eschatological expression with the invocation of God as 'Father' is striking here as Udo Schnelle observes:

> Jesus's eschatology is the proper framework within which to locate his Father-language for God, so that his theocentric message is structured

---

334 *The Authorized Daily Prayer Book of the United Hebrew Congregations*, 86.

335 James B. Pritchard (ed.), *The Ancient Near Eastern Texts relating to the Old Testament* (3rd edition; Princeton: Princeton University Press, 1955), 385.

336 E.g., *Iliad* 3.320-23.

337 E.g., *Iliad* I. 544.

338 Thus for Moore (*Judaism* II, 211) the invocation of 'Father' or 'Father in heaven' has nothing to do with the conception of God but refers to an inward and ethical attitude on the part of the pious Israelite towards God. In his owns words, "That God is so often called our Father who is in heaven, or invoked in prayer, O our Father! does not indicate that the age had a new conception of God, or put a new emphasis on one element of the conception. What these phrases express is not an idea of God, but a characteristic attitude of piety in which Jesus and his immediate disciples were brought up, and the Gospel of Matthew is a most instructive illustration of it."

339 Its parallel in Matthew 6: 9b-10 has, "Our Father in heaven, hallowed be your name. Your kingdom come. Your will be done, on earth as it is in heaven."

> eschatologically. The eschatological perspective shapes Jesus's picture of God, so that in Jesus's teaching one can speak of a coinciding of "upward look" (*Aufblick*) and "forward look" (*Ausblick*), of theology and eschatology, of a mutual interpenetration of the upward look to the Father and the forward look to the coming of the kingdom. Jesus proclaims the one God as the Father who is acting eschatologically, whose lordship is already experienced in the present.[340]

As Schnelle correctly observes the proclamation of the imminent kingdom coincides with the revelation of God's loving care and compassion. Thus God's fatherhood gets directly connected to the announcement of the kingdom of God. In addressing God as Father while talking about God's kingdom to come at the same breath, it is seen that, Jesus in Q combines the theme of fatherhood of God and kingdom of God. That means in the theology of Q the kingdom of God is no more than God's fatherly rule of grace at the present. And it is in the surrender of the self to God's will (theocentric) that his sovereignty is realized on earth,[341] which is quite in line with Q conception of God's fatherhood in relation to creation and providence elsewhere (e.g., Lk 12:22-32//Mt 6:24-33).

The first petition saw the occurrence of divine passives in the expressions, "hallowed be your name (ἁγιασθήτω). Your kingdom come (ἐλθέτω)." The divine passive was a typical Jewish way of speaking about God. And it is interesting to observe that this expression is seen in relation to the fatherhood of God here. This theocentric petition means that the sacredness of God's name be magnified in every area of life. To hallow God's name means to acknowledge God for who He is. "To acknowledge God to be God connotes by definition something about God's person as well as one's relationship to him and his will. Honor, glory, awe, obedience belong inherently to God as God."[342] The second theme is to pray that God's kingdom may come. That is, asking for God to act by setting up his rule, echoing the Jewish *Qaddish* prayer as seen above. The emphasis is on the sovereignty of God, thus going back to the opening word 'Father.'

The next petition again talks about God's fatherly concern for his creation, as the very petition is for the provision of daily bread which is based on faith in the Father's providential care (v3): "Give us each day our daily bread" (ἐπιούσιον δίδου ἡμῖν τὸ καθ' ἡμέραν). In Matthew too the same petition is found (6:11): "Give us this day our daily bread" (ἐπιούσιον δὸς ἡμῖν σήμερον). Here the emphasis in Luke's form of the prayer (Q) is that of continual daily basis, as the very present tense δίδου ("keep on giving us") shows and as he has "each day" unlike Matthew,

340 U. Schnelle, *Theology*, 84-85.

341 G. Vermes, *Jesus and the World of Judaism*, 39.

342 R.A. Guelich, *The Sermon on the Mount: A Foundation for Understanding* (Waco: Word Books, 1982), 289.

who has "today."[343] It thus emphasizes the day-by-day, dependence of the prayers on God's provision.[344] That means for Jesus in Q God in his loving fatherly care gives continual nourishment and sustenance. However, whether it has to do with physical or spiritual is still a matter of debate. R.E. Brown, taking the word ἐπιούσιος as derived from ἐπι plus εἶναι, explains the expression as 'the bread for the coming day, for the future,' thus understands the petition as non-literal eschatological sense.[345] Fitzmyer, taking the expression as noun ἐπιούσιος (which means 'substance' or 'being' or 'essence'), understands the expression in the sense of '(bread for) subsistence,' that is, 'necessary for existence,'[346] while Catchpole,[347] Nolland,[348] Balch[349] and Muthuraj[350] stand for material aspect of the petition, referring to the ordinary bread. Whatever be the precise emphasis, the petition is a powerful expression of trust and dependence on God. And it is basically material things in view and which implies that God, in his fatherly kindness, is concerned for the provisions of these needs.[351] For Luke (Q) God is the provider of daily needs. That means, for Luke, God is very much near and present so as to attend to such needs. The same care and concern of a fatherly God is clearly explained in another pericope of Luke (Q) to which we now turn.

3.2.4. *Imitatio Dei*: Universality of God's Fatherhood

3.2.4.1. Being Merciful (6:32-36)

In one of the most concise sayings, Jesus in Luke speaks of mercy not only as the primary quality of God, but also as the primary quality of a life lived in accord

[343] For a detail discussions on various meanings in relation to the word ἐπιούσιος, see Colin Hemer, "ἐπιούσιος," in *JSNT* 22 (1984), 81-94.

[344] Dunn, "Prayer," in *DJG*, 622; Cullmann, *Prayer in the New Testament* (London: SCM, 1995), 51-54.

[345] R.E. Brown, "The Pater Noster as an Eschatological Prayer," in R.E. Brown, *New Testament Essays* (Milwaukee: Bruce Publishing Company, 1965), 243.

[346] J.A. Fitzmyer, *The Gospel according to Luke X-XXIV* (AB 28a; New York: Doubleday, 1985), 900.

[347] D.R. Catchpole (*The Quest for Q* [Edinburgh: T & T Clark, 1993], 223-224) argues strongly that the petition refers to ordinary, everyday food, not to eschatological nourishment.

[348] Nolland, *Luke 9:21-18:34*, 617.

[349] D.L. Balch ("Luke," in *Eerdmans Commentary of the Bible*, edited by J.D.G Dunn and J. W. Rogerson [Grand Rapids: Eerdmans, 2003], 1128) favors this as economic component referring to the ordinary bread for the hungry.

[350] J.G. Muthuraj ("Economic Scenarios of the NT Christianity: A Socio-Economic Reading of Luke-Acts," in *IJT* 38/1 [1996], 56) pointing to the emphasis of Luke on material aspect of this petition, argues that Luke portrays God as 'the giver of food' to humanity.

[351] Dunn, "Prayer," in *DJG*, 622.

with God.[352] In remarkably few words, theology and ethics are combined, when Lukan Jesus says:

> But love your enemies, do good, and lend, expecting nothing in return. Your reward will be great, and you will be children of the Most High; for he is kind to the ungrateful and the wicked. Be merciful, just as your Father is merciful (Lk 6:35-36).

Found in slightly different form in Matthew 5:45-48, this passage affirms an ethic known as imitation of God (*imitatio dei*).[353] The ethical imperative is to live in accord with God's character. As the context in Luke indicates, this means imitating the God, who "is kind to the ungrateful and the wicked" (Lk 6:35). Whereas in Matthew God is kind to both righteous and unrighteous (Mt 5:45), but for Luke God's goodness is to those who will show no return (ἀχαρίστους καὶ πονηρούς). The key word in this pericope is 'merciful' (οἰκτίρμων, v36). The basis for behaviours found here is also attested in Old Testament. In the Old Testament the Psalms of thanksgiving for God's goodness too talks about a merciful and gracious God (Ps 103:8, cf.111:4). The notion of 'compassion' also occurs in the same passage, as the Psalmist compares the compassion of God to the compassion of a human father (103:13). Accordingly, I. Howard Marshall is of the view that while this very concept is close in meaning to 'mercy' (ἔλεος, Lk 1:50; 10:37), but stresses more on the idea of sympathy and pity shown to the unfortunate and needy.[354] Even in some versions[355] we see this Greek word οἰκτίρμων rendered as "compassionate." And this usage accord well with Luke's emphasis elsewhere. For example, in another parable of Jesus recorded only in Luke, the emphasis on the compassion and humanitarian aspect is projected in the parable of the Good Samaritan (Lk 10:29-37). The extension of love and compassion is grounded in God's goodness and mercy.

In what way then is God merciful? The answer is clear in verse 35: "But love your enemies, do good, and lend, expecting nothing in return" (ἀγαθοποιεῖτε καὶ δανίζετε μηδὲν ἀπελπίζοντες). Here Q Jesus' teaching is that of loving enemies and do good without expecting any return (ἀπελπίζοντες). The next expression then talks about the goodness of God – God is kind to both ungrateful and the wicked. On being such a God as the Father Lukan Jesus give the ethical imperative to

---

352 M.J. Borg, *Jesus: Uncovering the Life, Teachings, and Relevance of a Religious Revolutionary* (New York: Harper Collins Publishers, 2006), 175.

353 For details on the concept of imitation of God in Mediterranean milieu, See C.H. Talbert, *Reading the Sermon on the Mount: Character Formation and Decision Making in Matthew 5-7* (Grand Rapids; Michigan: Baker Academic, 2004), 96-98; W.D. Davies and Dale Allison, *The Gospels According to St. Matthew*, vol I (Edinburgh: T&T Clark, 1988), 560-64.

354 I. H. Marshall, *The Gospel of Luke: A Commentary on the Greek Text* (Grand Rapids; Michigan: William B. Eerdmans, 1978), 265.

355 E.g., *The Jerusalem Bible, The New English Bible.*

live in accord with God's character: "Be merciful, just as your Father is merciful" (6:36). The Matthean parallel has 'perfect' (τέλειός) instead of 'merciful' (Mt 5:48). Many see Luke term as the original expression.[356]

God is merciful in the sense that he does good in spite of the fact that the ungrateful and the wicked people will not appreciate his benefits; they will remain enemies even though he keeps doing good to them. God's mercy is thus defined by treatment of the ungrateful and the wicked.[357] There is no motive of rewards whatsoever and thus no expectation of reciprocity here as one does good (mercy), as Lukan Jesus again says:

> If you love those who love you, what credit is that to you? For even sinners love those who love them. If you do good to those who do good to you, what credit is that to you? For even sinners do the same. If you lend to those from whom you hope to receive, what credit is that to you? Even sinners lend to sinners, to receive as much again (Lk 6:32-34//Mt 5:46-47).

The call to "be merciful as your heavenly Father is merciful" implies that the children of God, too, can become merciful by imitating God in dealing with their own enemies. Thus, the implication here in verse 36 is that those imitating such a character of God are God's children. Of course, we find similar idea in both Jewish and Greco-Roman literatures. Philo says: "Kinship is not measured only by blood, but by similarity of conduct and pursuit of the same objects" (*De Virtutibus* 195).[358] So also in Sirach, while dealing with the duties toward the poor and the oppressed, Sirach 4:10 expresses: "Be a father to orphans, and be like a husband to their mother; you will then be like a son of the Most High." Similar expressions are also found in rabbinic literatures. In *Targum Pseudo-Jonathan*, Leviticus 22:28 says: "My people, children of Israel, as our Father is merciful in heaven so shall you be merciful on earth."[359]

The centrality of mercy or compassion in the ethical teaching of Lukan Jesus is again strongly underlined in the parable of the good Samaritan, a parable found only in Luke (10:30-37). In this parable, the inaction of a priest and a Levite when confronted by the needs of a wounded man is set in contrast to the responsiveness

---

[356] Marshall, *Luke*, 265; for Mary Rose D' Angelo ("Theology in Mark and Q: Abba and 'Father' in Context," 166), this expression, where 'father' occurs first time in Q, belongs to the sapiential speech that forms the basis of Luke's Sermon on the Plain (Lk 6:20-49), and considers this Lukan version as the original.

[357] P.S. Minear, *God of the Gospels*, 39.

[358] *Philo* VIII, 283-285, trans F.H. Colson and G.H. Whitaker.

[359] Cited in C.A. Evans, *Ancient Texts for New Testament Studies: A Guide to the Background Literature* (Peabody: Hendrickson Publishers, 2005), 188.

of a Samaritan, a despised one in the eyes of the Jews.[360] While all three are shown to have seen the man lying on the road-side (vv31-33), the priest and the Levite do nothing to help. Both of them bypass him (v32). By contrast, the Samaritan saw him and "was moved with pity" (v33). He takes specific action to show kindness to the injured man. Luke describes the compassionate action of the Samaritan in vivid details; he tends to the wounds of the victim, takes care of him overnight, and arranges for his care with the innkeeper (vv34-35). At the end of the parable, Lukan Jesus asks, "Which of these three, do you think, was a neighbor to the man who fell into the hands of the robbers?" (v36).The answer: "The one who showed him mercy." Jesus said to him, "Go and do likewise" (v37). Thus in this parable of Lukan Jesus the Samaritan has acted in a manner that God's children ought to do, that is, showing mercy (v37), in line with the words of Lukan Jesus: "Be merciful as your Father is merciful" (6:36). And elsewhere in Luke Jesus himself is presented as one who loves his enemies (23:34 cf. 6:27-28). That means, for Luke, Jesus embodied the mercy of God; he was God's compassion in action. Jesus is portrayed as one who discloses the Father's compassion (cf. 6:32-36).

Here we find strong emphasis on the universality of God's fatherhood. God is depicted as a merciful Father, whose fatherly love and care is for all. The question arises whether the sonship and obedience go together, as some believe, most notably W. Barclay, who commented, "God is the father of the good and of the righteous in a way in which he cannot be the father of the disobedient and the rebellious."[361] Quite contrary to such an exclusivistic understanding of God's fatherhood, we find here in Lukan Jesus an inclusive Father who shows compassion to all. In support of this inclusive understanding is also the fact that the very audience of this very exhortation, which is part of the Lukan Jesus' sermon on the plain, is not only the disciples of Jesus but also "a great multitude of people from all Judea, Jerusalem, and from the coast of Tyre and Sidon" (6:17). It is to these people that Jesus directs the exhortation: "Be merciful, just as your Father is merciful" (6:36). Similar nature of God as a loving and compassionate Father is strongly emphasized in a parable found only in Luke, to which we now turn.

3.2.4.2. A Loving Father and His Wayward Son/s (15:3-32)

God as a loving Father is remarkably displayed in a series of parables of Jesus in Luke 15. The first pericope is on the lost sheep, which is also found in Matthew (Lk 15:3-7//Mt 18:12-14), so probably from Q; while the other two parables are found only in Luke: the lost coin (15:8-10), and the lost son/s (15:11-32). In these parables God's action is compared to the actions of a shepherd, a housewife

---

[360] The Samaritans were considered by the Jews as unclean like the Gentiles because they intermarried with foreigners. For a details on this background, See G. Balla; *The Four Centuries Between the Testaments* (Vallejo; CA: Bibal Press, 1993), 50-51. Elsewhere in Luke a Samaritan is again projected in positive light (17:11-19).

[361] W. Barclay, *The Mind of Jesus*, 122.

and a father. The context of these parables is clear right at the very beginning of the chapter. In the face of grumbling by Pharisees and scribes, Lukan Jesus intended these parables to defend his table fellowship with social outcasts and sinners (15:1-2).[362] Particularly noteworthy is the last pericope, the story of a father and his two sons, where the fatherhood of God found its classic expression. The story unfolds in three scenes.

In the first scene Lukan Jesus vividly describes the younger son's plight, who lavishly spent his share of wealth taken from his father. The details of the story underline the depth of his descent: after he spent his money on loose living, famine struck the foreign land and he fell into poverty and yet no one gave him anything. His hunger became so desperate that he earns his living by feeding pigs of a foreigner (vv1-16).

In the second scene, the son returns from exile to the delight of the waiting father (vv17-24). The father does not bear a grudge against his returning son by recalling how he wasted his wealth. But filled with compassion, he runs to greet his son and embraces him with a kiss. The expression 'compassion' (of the father) here clearly reflects divine compassion.[363] And the father does not allow the son to finish his confession of sin (vv18-24). He celebrates his son's return by clothing him with the best robe and with shoes and a ring, and by preparing a fattened calf for a celebratory feast. The projection of Luke is thus of a God as a seeking Father, who did not wait for the son to come back, but who went out to seek and to search for him. Here we also see God as a loving and forgiving Father, who rejoices for and with each penitent sinner.

In the final scene, the elder son reacts but the father lovingly persuades him (vv25-32). Having felt a sense of unfairness, the elder son sidelined himself but the father goes to him and listens to his complaint. The father's compassion extends to his dutiful son as well: he goes outside to invite him to join the celebration. The story thus ends with the father's simple justification: "But we had to celebrate and rejoice, because this brother of yours was dead and has come to life; he was lost and has been found" (v32). For Lukan Jesus this parable illustrates the nature of God. God is a loving Father whose love and forgiveness is unconditional.[364] That means God is a compassionate Father who extends his love and compassion to all. In this story God's action is compared to the action of a loving and forgiving

[362] However, R.H. Stein (*An Introduction to the Parables of Jesus* [Philadelphia: Westminster Press, 1981], 117-118) while discussing whether this parable is an allegory or not see it as a story parable (but not an allegory) with a basic point of comparison. Luise Schottroff (*The Parables of Jesus* [Minneapolis: Fortress Press, 2006], 142-143) too rejected the allegorical reading of this parable but he see it "as a social-historical source for a hierarchy-critical awareness in regard to the relationship between father and son in a patriarchal household."

[363] As elsewhere in Luke this same expression 'compassion' occurs expressing the divine compassion revealed in Jesus (Lk 17:13); See A.J. Hultgren, *The Parables of Jesus: A Commentary* (Grand Rapids; Michigan: Wm B. Eerdmans: 2002), 78.

[364] Hultgren, *The Parables of Jesus: A Commentary*, 87.

father. The fatherhood of God is thus strongly implied in this very parable of Jesus reported by Luke.[365] Such an emphasis on a compassionate and forgiving Father is found in another pericope as Luke retells the passion of Jesus, to which we now turn.

3.2.5. The Death of Jesus and the Fatherhood of God

3.2.5.1. Forgiving Father (23:32-43)

The merciful and forgiving Father is also strongly emphasized by Luke in the passion narrative. While giving account of the crucifixion and death of Jesus, Lukan Jesus is portrayed as praying for pardon for his executioners, saying:

> Father, forgive them; for they do not know what they are doing (23:34)

This pericope which relates how Jesus is crucified along with the two criminals is found in all the three Gospels in almost the same number of verses of description: Mark 10 verses (15:22-32); Matthew 11 verses (27:33-44); and in Luke 10 verses (23:33-43). Yet Lukan distinct emphasis is evident in that the very prayer in the lips of Jesus, asking God for forgiveness at this moment of suffering, is found only in Luke. However, since within Luke itself this very utterance of Jesus (v34a) is missing in several ancient manuscripts, its Lukan origin is often challenged.[366] But Marshall[367] and Nolland[368] argued for its Lukan hand, as this very prayer of Jesus accord well with Lukan motif of ignorance (Acts 3:17; 13:27; 17:30), mercy and forgiveness (Lk 6:27-28, 36; 24:47).

Even at the dying moment at the cross Jesus prayed for the forgiveness of the people who crucify him, "Father, forgive them." Luke understands the suffering of Jesus as integral to Jesus' identity as Son of God or sonship to God. After entering Jerusalem, as Jesus struggles in prayer on the Mount of Olives, he addresses God as "Father" (22:42); as a true Son, he does so obediently in order to represent the will of the Father in the course of his own life (22:42-44). The Father will honor the Son's request because their wills have become one, as P.S. Minear puts, "the grace of the one has become the grace of the other."[369] For Luke this prayer clearly expresses the power of the cross in God's forgiveness of his enemies, proving that the power of God is greater than that of his enemies.[370] It is precisely while he is at the cross that he explicitly turns to the world in compassion and forgives

---

[365] Stein (*An Introduction to the Parables of Jesus*, 124) too has rightly pointed out that this parable of the gracious father fits well into the key emphasis in Luke-Acts on salvation to all.

[366] For details on its textual problems and its authenticity, see B.M. Metzger, *A Textual Commentary on the New Testament: A Companion Volume to the United Bible Societies' Greek New Testament* (London: United Bible Societies, 1971), 180; Fitzmyer, *Luke X-XXIV*, 1503.

[367] Marshall, Luke, 867-868.

[368] Nolland, *Luke*, 1141-1144.

[369] Minear, *God of the Gospels*, 112.

[370] Minear, *God of the Gospels*, 112.

them their sins. Thus, Jesus is portrayed as the one who discloses the Father's compassion (cf. 6:32-36). In other words, for Luke, Jesus embodied the mercy of God; he is God's compassion in action. God's fatherhood is hence revealed on the cross. The same idea is seen in another pericope of the passion narrative, 'the death of Jesus.' It is to this we now turn.

3.2.5.2. The Death of the Father's Son (23:44-47)

This pericope is found in all the Synoptic Gospels but Luke alone has the utterance of Jesus expressing his trust in God's faithfulness and provides dramatic signs at the threshold of Jesus' death. Luke describes:

> It was now about noon, and darkness came over the whole land until three in the afternoon, while the sun's light failed; and the curtain of the temple was torn in two. Then Jesus, crying with a loud voice, said, "Father, into your hands I commend my spirit." Having said this, he breathed his last. When the centurion saw what had taken place, he praised God and said, "Certainly this man was innocent."

The Lukan passion narrative contains material not found in Mark and this pericope is no exception. As such his portrayal of Jesus' death differs significantly from the scene in Mark. In Mark Jesus is seen uttering in despair and abandonment, "My God, my God, why have you forsaken me?" (Mk 15:34 cf. Ps 22:1), but Luke does not project Jesus in such a manner of dying as the abandoned Son of God. In other words, Luke has deliberately omitted the cry of dereliction in the lips of Jesus from the cross, but added the very words of Jesus addressing God as Father, thereby strengthening the emphasis of Father-Son relationship (v46), which is so prominent throughout Luke,[371] consequently pointing to the central emphasis on the fatherhood of God.

As mentioned above, Luke has deliberately omitted Jesus' cry of dereliction from the cross (cf. Lk 23:46; Mk 15:34; Mt 27:46), as this very cry is expressive of a sense of distancing from God felt by Jesus, so the notion of a forsaken God.[372] For Luke, there is no room for giving such a notion of a forsaken God but rather he put the centre of focus on the trust and faithfulness of a loving Father. As found in verse 46, Luke reports that at his death Jesus prayed to God addressing as Father which echoes the words of Psalm 31:5. But whereas the Psalm reads, "Into your hand I commit my Spirit," Lukan Jesus says, "Father, into your hands I commend my spirit." The Psalmist prays for deliverance from enemies,

[371] 2:49; 9:26; 10:21-22; 11:2,13; 12:30, 32; 22:29, 42; 23:34; 24:49.

[372] However, as France (*The Gospel of Mark*, 652) rightly observes, even Markan Jesus prays here addressing God not as 'Father' but 'God,' which is one of bewilderment and separation; while M.A. Tolbert (*Sowing The Gospel : Mark's World in Literary-Historical Perspectives* [Philadelphia: Fortress Press, 1996], 283) found this prayer ironic, as an element of trust is still present even in this very utterance of Jesus, that "Jesus is forsaken by God, and at the same time God is available to be called upon."

expressing his confidence in God; and it is striking to see that in the preceding verses (Ps 31:1-4), the Psalmist speaks of God as rock, refuge and fortress. The same language of trust and faithful relationship is also found in Luke as Jesus utters at the moment of his death, "Father, into your hands I commend my spirit" (23:46b). This language of trust marks the eternal unity of Father and Son, as P.S. Minear puts, "God as Father is source and home of Jesus' 'spirit.'"[373]

Jesus' death is climatic evidence of his sonship and so of God's fatherhood, inducing the centurion to praise God, "Certainly this man was innocent" (v47). While Mark has apparently stronger statement in Jesus' confession as the Son of God (Mk 15:39), yet Luke's expression ὄντως ὁ ἄνθρωπος οὗτος δίκαιος ἦν (lit. 'righteous') contains equally strong christological emphasis, that is, in line with 'the righteous sufferer' in the Old Testament, as Luke also depicted Jesus as the 'Righteous one' elsewhere in his writings (Acts 3:14; 7:52; 22:14).[374] Therefore, for Luke, the ultimate sense of the centurion's statement is that it is Jesus, not his persecutors, who stands in the right covenant relationship to God; he is the truly righteous person portrayed in the Psalms of the righteous sufferer.[375] However, the main focus of Luke is seen in Jesus' final utterance of his faithful relationship to God, "Father." And this very expression also implies that God cares, as earlier in the passion narrative, it is Luke who alone depicts Jesus as giving reassuring words to one of the criminals crucified along with him (23:43). That means, Jesus, who is the Son to the Father, continues to save others even at the moment of death. Thus for Luke the fatherhood of God is fully revealed at the cross, in the death of Jesus.

3.2.6. Summary

In Luke the trend found in Mark of the sonhood of Jesus to God is seen more explicitly in the occurrences of 'Father' for God in absolute ('Father') and exclusive ('my Father') sense mostly in the teachings of Jesus. That means for Luke, father/son expressions is used almost exclusively to speak about the relationship between God and Jesus (e.g., 10:21-22). Right from the beginning of the infancy narratives Luke gives strong emphasis on the fatherhood of God. This is evident not only in his projection of God as the originator of Jesus' line ('son of Adam, son of God,' 3:38), but also in the projection of Jesus himself as being aligned with God's purpose (δεῖ), even if this affairs appears to compromise his relationship with his earthly parents (2:49). We also see in Luke strong theocentric focus as Lukan Jesus talks about the fatherhood of God ('your Father') and the kingdom of God in the same breath. In Luke God is also depicted as a merciful Father, whose

---

373 Minear, *God of the Gospels*, 113.

374 For a discussion of this point, see Robert J. Karris, "Luke 23:47 and the Lucan View of Jesus' Death," in *JBL* 105/1 (March 1986), 65-74; See also Fitzmyer, *Luke X-XXIV*, 1520.

375 Frank J. Matera, *Passion Narratives and Gospel Theologies: Interpreting the Synoptics Through Their Passion Stories* (New York: Paulist Press, 1986), 187.

fatherly love and care is for all. So a strong emphasis on a compassionate Father is clearly seen. In this case God's fatherhood has universal implication. This is heightened by a unique parable found only in Luke (15:1-32), where once again the nature of God as a loving and compassionate Father is the focal point of the parable. The passion narrative too has exceptional emphasis on the fatherhood of God. In a unique expression found only in Luke Jesus utters words of forgiveness for his killers from the cross, and thereby portrays Jesus as the one who discloses God's love and mercy (6:27-36). For Luke, the cross is the embodiment of Jesus' own teaching on God's love and mercy. The fatherhood of God is fully revealed on the cross for Luke. Thus the theme of the Fatherhood of God is an important theological emphasis of Luke.

3.3. Fatherhood of God in Paul

The earliest written documents in the New Testament are Paul's letters. These letters then give us the earliest ideas on the theology and faith of the early Christians including Matthew.

3.3.1. Occurrences of the term 'Father' for God

There are 40 references to God as Father in Paul's letters.[376] Every one of the Pauline letters begins with some form of greeting or opening blessing that refers to God as either "our Father" (Rom 1:7; I Cor 1:3; 2 Cor 1:2; Gal 1:3-4; Eph 1:2; Phil 1:2; Col 1:2; 2 Thess 1:1), or "the Father" (Gal 1:1; I Thess 1:1; I Tim 1:2; 2 Tim 1:2; Titus 1:4), or more expansively "the Father of our Lord Jesus Christ" (2 Cor 1:3; Eph 1:3; Col 1:3). The references to God as Father in Paul's letters tend to be found either in the opening remarks or in benedictions, or in quotations of confessional formulas such as the christological hymn in Philippians 2.

3.3.2. The Significance of the Fatherhood of God in Paul

3.3.2.1. "Abba! Father!"- Fatherhood of God in Experience

One of the significant expressions of the fatherhood of God idea in Paul is "Abba! Father!" This very expression occurs in the context of Paul's teaching on 'life in the Spirit' (Rom 8:1-17). He emphatically states, "For all who are led by the Spirit of God are children of God" (v14). He then goes on speaking explicitly of a sense of sonship to God as Father borne in upon believers as they pray the "Abba" prayer (v16). For him the gift of the eschatological Spirit of God to believers in Christ is the first part of the redemption of the whole person. It is the Spirit who enables a person to make a true confession that Jesus is the risen Lord (I Cor 12:3) and it is also the Spirit who enables a person to pray to God as "Abba." In Paul's view fatherhood of God is thus a subjective experience of the believers.[377] That means

[376] Thompson, *The Promise of the Father: Jesus and God in the New Testament*, 118.

[377] J.D.G. Dunn, *The Theology of Paul the Apostle* (Grand Rapids: Wm B Eerdmans, 2006), 49.

to say that the presence of God in the person of the Spirit replicates the spiritual life of Jesus in his followers' lives, conforming them to Jesus' image. This includes enabling the believer to have the same intimate relationship with God as Jesus did. Indeed, for Paul, the presence of this Spirit conforms a person to the image of Jesus such that he or she becomes a child of God (Rom 8:16; Gal 4:6). Paul goes even further, suggesting that the presence of this Spirit not only prompts prayer like Jesus' prayer but enables one, as a child of God, to become fellow heirs with Jesus of the eschatological blessings (Rom 8:17; Gal 4:7).[378] Thus we find a strong christological anchorage in Paul's idea of God's fatherhood here. We will find similar idea in several instances in Paul.

3.3.2.2. The God and Father of Our Lord Jesus Christ

This christologically focused fatherhood of God idea dominates his discourse on God's fatherhood. For example, in Romans 6:4 in a striking phrase Jesus is said to have been raised from the death by the glory of the Father. In I Corinthians 15:24 Paul explains that after the second coming and after the Son has subdued the earth, he will turn the kingdom over to God the Father. So also when Paul uses, in addition to "God the Father" and "God our Father," the phrase "the God and Father of our Lord Jesus Christ" as he frequently does (e.g., Rom 15:6; 2 Cor 1:3; 11:31), he is emphasizing that God has revealed himself as Father in Jesus Christ and can hence be recognized as such only in him. The fatherhood of God idea is thus a christological-eschatological miracle for Paul.

3.3.2.3. One God and Father of All

However, in Paul we also see the idea of God's fatherhood in relationship to creation. God is the 'Father' of the world. This is implicit in several instances in his authentic letters. In his first letter to the Corinthian Church, in the context of his discourse on food matters, he talks about the whole world as God's creation, "there is one God, the Father, from whom are all things and for whom we exist, and one Lord, Jesus Christ, through whom are all things and through whom we exist" (I Cor 8:6). While Paul here describes Christian monotheism, echoing the "one God' and "one Lord" of the regularly cited *Shema* (Deut 6:4),[379] yet he is also in agreement with Hellenistic religious philosopher Maximus of Tyre, who talks about one God, who is the king of all and father.[380]

---

[378] Ben Witherington III and Laura M. Ice, *The Shadow of the Almighty: Father, Son, and Spirit in Biblical Perspective* (Grand Rapids; Michigan: Wm B Eerdmans, 2002), 29.

[379] Craig S. Keener, *1-2 Corinthians* (NCBC; Cambridge: Cambridge University Press, 2005), 73.

[380] According to Maximus of Tyre (*Diss.* 17, 5) there is universal consent to the proposition that there is one God, the king of all and father, and that there are many gods, sons of God, co-existing with God. See R.M. Grant, *The Early Christian Doctrine of God* (Charlottesville: University Press of Virginia, 1966), 5.

Another passage in Romans (1:18-21) suggests that like other Hellenistic thinkers Paul had considered the question of God's self-disclosure in natural phenomena. Paul categorically states that 'the known of God' (τὸ γνωστὸν τοῦ θεοῦ) is evident, for God made it evident (Rom 1:19). Here Paul talks about human capability of knowing God through the creation of God (God's revelation in nature).[381] The inference is that without special revelation people know God through his creation.[382] The idea of the universality of God's fatherhood is implicit here.

The same idea is very strong in Ephesians.[383] Here in several instances we see the idea of God's fatherhood in cosmic, universal sense.[384] A clear instance is Ephesians 4:6 where Paul talks about God's fatherhood in relation to all (πάντων). For him, there is "one God and Father of all who is above all and through all and in all." The expression εἷς θεὸς καὶ πατὴρ πάντων is quite similar to the cosmic Father idea of Philo.[385] In this expression Paul is referring to the divine presence in all creation. That means, like in Hellenistic literature of Philo, here the reference is to God who is the cosmic Father.

In line with this, in Ephesians 2:11-18 God is again depicted as 'the Father' to whom both Jew and non-Jew have access through Jesus (2:18). Thus the cosmic creator is the Father whom all people can now approach. This is supported by the idea of God as Father of "every family in heaven and on earth" again in Ephesians 3:14. Here the idea of God's fatherhood is without a christological anchor. The understanding here is that God in his capacity as creator of the world is called the Father of "every family in heaven and on earth." The occurrence of this expression πᾶσα πατριὰ ἐν οὐρανοῖς καὶ ἐπὶ γῆς clearly helps us understand that God's fatherhood idea here has to do with God as maker and creator.

3.3.3. Summary

We have seen that in Pauline writings, the fatherhood of God is seen in two ways. First, the fatherhood of God idea has strong christological anchorage. This is the very notion of God's fatherhood that Paul talks about in Romans (8:16-17) and Galatians (4:6). For him, God has, through the Spirit, made Jews and non-Jews alike pray to God "Abba! Father!" (Rom 8:15), thereby made them "heirs, heirs of

---

[381] Grant, *The Early Christian Doctrine of God*, 6-7.

[382] A. Nygren, *Commentary on Romans*, translated by Carl L. Rasmussen (Muhlenberg Press: Philadelphia, 1949), 107.

[383] Several scholars, however, considered Ephesians as a Deutero-Pauline writing and argue that this letter emerged within a Pauline school of thought. For detail discussions, see P.T O' Brien, *The Letter to the Ephesians* (Grand Rapids; Michigan: Wm B Eerdmans, 1999), 38; Andrew T. Lincoln, *Ephesians* (Waco; Texas: Word Books, 1990), lv-lxxiii; Andrew T. Lincoln and A.J.M. Wedderburn, *The Theology of the Later Pauline Letters* (Cambridge: Cambridge University Press, 1993), 83.

[384] For detail on the cosmic dimension in the language about God in Ephesians, see Edgar M. Krentz, 'God in the New Testament,' in *Our naming of God*, 82-83.

[385] See *De Specialibus Legibus* 1.96.

God and joint heirs with Christ" (Rom 8:17a). It is complimented by his inclusive expression "God and Father of our Lord Jesus Christ" seen in several instances (e.g., 2 Cor 1:3 cf. Rom 1:8; I Cor 1:3). Secondly, the idea of God's fatherhood is also understood in Paul in the sense of universality of God's fatherhood. That is, God as the Father of all creation (e.g., I Cor 8:6; Phil 2:6-11; Rom 1:19-21; Eph 2:11-18). The emphasis on the theme of God's fatherhood thus finds a prominent place in Paul.

3.3.4. Concluding Remarks

This chapter provides us with the theological explanations of the fatherhood of God in Mark, Luke and Paul. And we have seen that while the roots of their God-language, particularly the identification of God as Father may be found in the Old Testament and Jewish traditions, yet the idea of God's fatherhood portrayed in Mark, Luke and Paul seem to be equally rooted in the filial relationship between Jesus and God as Son and Father. All of them have shown their focus on the relationship between Jesus and God as Son and Father, that is, fatherhood of God understood in the projection of Jesus' relationship to God as Son of the Father, but one aspect that Mark emphasizes on God's fatherhood is seen in the activities of Jesus as Son of God, in which the fatherhood of God is strongly implied. While in Luke the theme of the fatherhood of God is seen prominently in the discourse of Lukan Jesus, projecting a loving Father whose care and concern is for all. In Paul one of the interesting facets of the idea of God's fatherhood is that he stands with his fellow believers in Christ in referring to God as "our Father." As such we see the presence of a strong christologically focused fatherhood of God idea in Paul. Yet, the idea of the universality of God's fatherhood is also seen in Paul. And as we are arguing that the idea of the fatherhood of God is the most prominent in Matthew, this present chapter will be of immense help for the coming chapter, that is, on the fatherhood of God in Matthew, particularly to examine the very distinct emphasis of Matthew on the fatherhood of God while placing it within the context of the Synoptic Gospels. So with this we will now turn to the Gospel of Mathew and examine in what unique way Matthew, the Evangelist and theologian, emphasizes the theme of the fatherhood of God.

Chapter 4

The Fatherhood of God in Matthew

Introduction

We have observed in the previous chapter the idea of the fatherhood of God in Mark, Luke and Paul with whom Matthew shares Jesus' traditions with regards to the idea of God's fatherhood. We will now turn to Matthew and examine how the very idea of God's fatherhood is given a central emphasis. The focus of our investigation will be the narratives and discourses of Matthew where the idea of Gods' fatherhood is both explicit and implicit. Before dealing with the theological explanations of the theme of God's fatherhood in Matthew the occurrences of the terms and ideas related with the fatherhood of God will be considered.

4.1. Occurrences of 'Father' and Related Terms in Matthew

4.1.1. Father

The term 'Father' occurs in Matthew more than the other Synoptic writers combined, 44 times.[386] In several instances Matthew used his sources or redacted in most cases with the use of the term 'Father' in line with his theological perspective. It shows that Matthew has keen interest on the theme of the fatherhood of God. Of course mere occurrences of the term 'Father' may not be the real indicators; however, it is in these places that the theme of God's fatherhood is the most explicit. Out of the forty-four occurrences of 'Father' for God in Matthew, thirty one occurrences are found only in Matthew. That means only thirteen

[386] Kohlenberger, *The Exhaustive Concordance to the Greek New Testament*, 771-772. They are 5:16, 45,48; 6:1,4, 6 [x2], 8, 9, 14, 15, 18, 26, 32; 7:11, 21; 10:20, 29, 32, 33; 11:25-27 [x4], 27; 12:50; 13:43; 15:13; 16:17, 27; 18:10, 14,19, 35; 20:23; 23:9; 24:36; 25:34; 26:29, 39, 42, 53; 28:19.

occurrences are from his sources Mark and Q: four from Mark[387] and nine from Q (so Luke).[388] Out of these thirty one instances in Matthew, twenty times the term 'Father' for 'God' is occurring in the special Matthean (M) material;[389] while in several occasions 'Father' are Matthean redactions. On six occasions Matthew replaced 'God' with 'Father' to his source Mark[390] and Q,[391] thus exhibiting a particular fondness for 'Father' over other ways of referring to God. In one occasion Matthew replaced 'Holy Spirit' with 'Father' to his source Q;[392] while in four occasions Matthew added 'Father' to his source Mark[393] and Q.[394] It is thus seen that Matthew clearly emphasize on the theme of the fatherhood of God, retaining occurrences found in his sources Mark and Q, and adding several others from his own special sources (M), as well as by way of addition or expansion (redaction) to his sources.

His projection of God as 'Father in heaven' or 'heavenly Father' is also worth noting. This expression is found twenty times in Matthew, with the construction ὁ πατὴρ ὁ ἐν [τοῖς] οὐρανοῖς (Father in heaven) occurring thirteen times[395] and ὁ πατὴρ ὁ οὐράνιος (heavenly Father) seven times.[396] The fatherhood of God is reaffirmed with the expression of 'Son of God' for Jesus and that Jesus addressing God as 'my Father.'

4.1.2. Son of God

The idea of the sonhood of Jesus found expressed in Matthew also indicates his strong emphasis on the fatherhood of God. This is clearly seen in the several occurrences of 'my Father' on the lips of Jesus. It is striking to see that out of the total of seventeen occurrences of the address of God as 'my Father' on the lips of Matthean Jesus, sixteen occurrences are found only in Matthew[397] and only in one instance he shares with Luke.[398]

---

[387] 6:14//Mk 11:25; 16:27//Mk 8:38; 24:36//Mk 13:32; 26:39//Mk 14:36.

[388] 5:48//Lk 6:36; 6:9//Lk 11:2; 6:32//Lk 12:30; 7:11//Lk 11:13; 11:25-27[5x]//Lk 10:21-22 [5x].

[389] 5:16, 45; 6:1, 4, 6[2], 8, 15, 18[2]; 13:43; 15:13; 16:17; 18:10, 19, 35; 23:9; 25:34; 26:53; 28:19.

[390] 12:50//Mk 3:35; 26:29//Mk 14:25.

[391] 6:26//Lk 12:24; 10:29//Lk 12:6; 10:32//Lk 12:8; 10:33//Lk 12:9.

[392] 10:20//Lk 12:12.

[393] 20:23//Mk 10:40; 26:42//Mk 14:39.

[394] 7:21//Lk 6:46; 18:14//Lk 15:7.

[395] 5:16, 45; 6:1, 9; 7:11, 21c; 10:32, 33; 12:50; 16:17; 18:10c, 14, 19.

[396] 5:48; 6:14, 26, 32; 15:13; 18:35; 23:9.

[397] 8 in Matthew's special material (13:43; 15:13; 16:17; 18:10; 18:19; 18:35; 25:34; 26:53) and 8 in redactional alteration (7:21; 10:32; 10:33; 12:50; 20:23; 26:29; 26:39; 26:42).

[398] Mt 11:27//Lk 10:22.

Apart from the explicit occurrences of 'Father' for God in Matthew as seen in the above statistical analysis, the very idea of God's fatherhood is implicit throughout the discourse and narratives of Matthew. The very notion of God's fatherhood is implied in the several occurrences of the expression 'Son of God' in Matthew. In fact Kingsbury argues that the title 'Son of God' is the key Christological title in Matthew.[399] Matthew not only retains almost all of Mark's statements regarding the sonship of Jesus[400] but has additional emphasis of the idea of the Son of God in several pericope thus heightening his emphasis on God's fatherhood.

In the pericope of Jesus' walking on the water (14:22-33//Mk 6:45-52), it is Matthew alone who has added the confession of the disciples, "Truly you are the Son of God" (14:33). Again it is Matthew alone who added the expression "the Son of the living God" (16:16) to his source Mark, where Peter confesses simply saying "Your are the Christ" (Mk 8:29). So also in 26:63, it is Matthew alone who has the more articulated expression "I adjure you by the living God, tell us if you are the Christ, the Son of God," against his source Mark's expression "Are you the Christ, the Son of the Blessed" (Mk 14:61). At the passion narratives, again it is Matthew alone having the expression on the lips of the bystanders (27:40) and religious leaders confessing of Jesus as the Son of God (27:43 cf. Mk 15:32). The sonship is also seen emphasized in the unique occurrence of the Matthean expression "in the name of the Father and of the Son and of the Holy Spirit" (28:19). At the infancy narrative the idea of sonship is implicit in the unique Matthean quotation of Old Testament Scriptures in 1:23 ('God is with us') and in 2:15 ('Out of Egypt I have called my son').

4.1.3. Sons of God/Children of God

Matthean emphasis on the theme of God's fatherhood is also seen in the several unique occurrences of the expressions like 'sons of God' (5:9, 45) and 'these little ones' (18:10, 14).

Moreover his distinct theological emphasis on the fatherhood of God is all the more evident as in several narratives, mostly in parables unique to him, Matthew has portrayed God in several imageries in close relation to the fatherhood of God. They are: God as the landowner-householder (20:1-16); the king (18:23-35); the shepherd (18:10-14). In all these the focus on the fatherhood of God is very strong.

4.2. The Fatherhood of God in Matthew: Exegesis

Creative use and well defined structure of the Gospel narratives and discourses is obvious for a reader. Matthew does not simply follow Mark which is his main

---

[399] Kingsbury, Matthew, *Structure, Christology, Kingdom*, 41, 80-82; Kingsbury, *Mathew as Story*, 10-11.

[400] e.g., 3:17; 8:29; 17:5; 26:63; 27:54.

source.[401] These narratives and discourses have a central emphasis on the theme of the fatherhood of God. This is clearly evident right from the infancy narratives to the passion narratives of Matthew.

4.2.1. The Fatherhood of God in Matthean Infancy Narratives

4.2.1.1. "Out of Egypt I have called my Son" (2:13-15)

Matthew introduces us to Jesus by means of his version of birth narratives. Stressing the involvement of God in the events surrounding Jesus' birth in this unique Matthean pericope (2:13-15), Matthew narrates:

> Now after they had left, an angel of the Lord appeared to Joseph in a dream and said, "Get up, take the child and his mother, and flee to Egypt, and remain there until I tell you; for Herod is about to search for the child, to destroy him." Then Joseph got up, took the child and his mother by night, and went to Egypt, and remained there until the death of Herod. This was to fulfill what had been spoken by the Lord through the prophet, "Out of Egypt I have called my son."

4.2.1.1.1. Matthean Redaction

While both Matthew and Luke introduce us to Jesus by means of their version of birth narratives, but Matthew has some unique pericopes where the idea of the fatherhood of God is obvious. In an earlier pericope on 'the birth of Jesus the Messiah' (1:18-25), Matthew has explicit references to God's intervention in Jesus' conception (1:18) and naming (1:21). In chapter 1 verse 23 Matthew introduces the first of his fulfillment quotations,[402] which dramatically verifies the role of God in the birth and naming of the child. Matthew projects "an angel of the Lord" telling Joseph that his wife Mary will bear a son in fulfillment of the "'Emmanuel,' which means 'God is with us'" (1:23) prophecy. It is important for Matthew's theological purposes that the child, born of the virgin, is known as

[401] W.D. Davies and D.C. Allison, *A Critical and Exegetical Commentary on the Gospel of Matthew* I (ICC; Edinburgh: T&T Clark, 1988), 61; Of course, it was Bacon who first identified that Matthew has patterned his Gospel into five discourses of Jesus in the manner of the five books of Moses, and thus compared Jesus as the new Moses. These five-fold discourses are: the Sermon on the Mount (5:1-7:29), the mission discourse (10:1-42), discourse on parables (13:1-52), the discourse on the Church (18:1-35) and the eschatological discourse (24:1- 25:46). See B. W. Bacon, *Studies in Matthew* (New York: Hort, 1930).

[402] The formula quotations (cf.1:23; 2:6, 15, 17-18, 23; 4:15-16; 8:17; 12:18-21; 13:35; 27:9-10) are a series of citations from the Hebrew Scriptures, which are mostly peculiar to Matthew's Gospel. The term 'formula quotations' derives from the very expression or formula that Matthew attaches to them, "This was to fulfill what had been spoken by the Lord through the prophet" (2:15). For an exhaustive theological analysis on these formula quotations specifically in Infancy Narratives, see G. M. Soares Prabhu, *The Formula Quotations in the Infancy Narrative of Matthew* (Rome: Biblical Institute Press, 1976); R.E. Brown, *The Birth of the Messiah: A Commentary on the Infancy Narratives in the Gospels of Matthew and Luke* (New York: Doubleday, 1993), 96-104.

both Jesus and Emmanuel. Both names are theologically significant for Matthew. His use of both names emphasizes his conviction that God has appointed Jesus as the one who will manifest God's saving presence among the people. And in this pericope 'the escape to Egypt' (2:13-15), again found only in Matthew's Gospel, Matthew explains concerning divine interventions in the life surrounding Jesus, that is, God extending this special care and protection to the family of Jesus. Moreover, unlike other fulfillment quotations, Matthew deliberately put this quotation before the departure of Jesus from Egypt, to which it refers. Generally, fulfillment formulas are inserted after the narration of the events to which they refer. But Matthew did not place the formula before the event here because he intended to stress God's care for Jesus while he was in Egypt, thus heightening his (Matthew's) emphasis on the fatherhood of God.

4.2.1.1.2. Theological Explanation

4.2.1.1.2.1. Divine Plan

This pericope is the core part of Matthean infancy narrative, the primary purpose of which is to establish the sonship of Jesus to God. Right at the beginning verse Matthew traces Jesus' lineage to David (1:1), that is, the Messianic lineage. He also identifies Jesus as the one conceived by the Holy Spirit (1:20), as savior (1:21), as Emmanuel, 'God with us' (1:23). Having explained Jesus' identity in chapter one, in chapter two he goes on explaining that Jesus was born in Bethlehem in accordance with the ancient prophecy,[403] of which the present pericope is a sequel. Because of Herod's jealousy, however, the infant Messiah must flee to Egypt (2:13-14). So at the level of the infancy story, the withdrawal to Egypt preserves Jesus from Herod's plot, but Matthew has a deeper purpose in mind, that is, the divine programme.[404] In the birth of Jesus, the Son of God, he sees biblical history repeating itself.[405] The reader is thus immediately reminded of a similar order given by a certain Pharaoh of Egypt, who, threatened by the growing numbers and strength of the Hebrews and a possible challenge to his power, ordered Egyptian midwives to kill any new-born males. Hence, Matthew deliberately intends his readers to notice the parallel and to connect God's providential care of the child

---

[403] "And you, Bethlehem, in the land of Judah, are by no means least among the rulers of Judah; for from you shall come a ruler who is to shepherd my people Israel" (2:6).

[404] On the idea of God-centered or divinely aided interpretation of the New Testament Scriptures see also R. Glenn Wooden, "Guided By God: Divine Aid in Interpretation in the Dead Sea Scrolls and the New Testament," in *Christian Beginnings and the Dead Sea Scrolls*, edited by J.J. Collins and C.A. Evans (Grand Rapids; Michigan: Baker Academic, 2006), 101-120.

[405] Some scholars see it as typology, see D.C. Allison, *The New Moses: A Matthean Typology* (Minneapolis: Fortress Press, 1993); C. A. Evans, *Matthew* (NCBC; Cambridge: Cambridge University Press, 2012), 47; Nolland, Matthew, 123.

Jesus with that of God's earlier providential care of Moses.[406] By relating God's warnings to Joseph in a dream to take the child and his mother to Egypt, because Herod has designs on his life, Matthew intimates God's overarching care of the child of promise.[407]

The occurrence of the term 'Lord' (κύριος) in the expression 'an angel of the Lord' is important here. This expression simply means 'a messenger of God.' So it has to do with the action of God. The term 'Lord' is employed here by Matthew, in relation to God's activity and providence thus related to God's fatherhood. The expression 'Lord' is used for God in Matthew 45 times,[408] out of which 27 occurrences are unique to Matthew.[409] Furthermore, it is striking to see that out of these 27 unique occurrences of the term 'Lord' for God in Matthew, 6 occurrences fall in the Matthean infancy narratives (1:20, 22, 24; 2:13, 15, 19). This shows strong Matthean emphasis on the activity of God. The action of the angel is in 'historical present' tense[410] φαίνεται ('appears'). It heightens the emphasis on the vividness or rather activeness of the divine providence for Matthew, as God intervenes on behalf of the family of Jesus.

4.2.1.1.2.2. The Sonhood of Jesus

The obedience of Joseph is for Matthew in fulfillment of a well-known biblical pattern, which alludes to the new significance of the event described in Hosea 11:1 "Out of Egypt I called my son." The introductory formula is identical to the one that occurs in 1:22 and denotes the accomplishment of God's purpose in his word through the prophetic channel. Matthew cites only the last clause of Hosea 11:1 and it seems here he follows the Hebrew more closely than it does the LXX.[411] A parallel look at the two texts clearly reveals that the LXX

---

[406] Brown (*The Birth of the Messiah*, 113-115) has thus emphasized the parallels in this Matthean birth story with the story of Moses in Exodus. As Pharaoh sought to do away with Moses, so Herod tried to do away with Jesus (Mt 2:13//Ex 1:22). Herod massacred all the boys under age two in Bethlehem in the same manner that Pharaoh killed every male born to the Hebrews (Mt 2:116//Ex 1:22). Both Herod and the king of Egypt died (Mt 2:19//Ex 2:23). Jesus' father Joseph and Moses are commanded to return either to Israel or to Egypt because it is now safe (Mt 2:19// Ex 4:19; Mt 2:21//Ex 4:20).

[407] M. Hannan, *The Nature and Demands of the Sovereign Rule of God in the Gospel of Matthew* (New York: T & T Clark, 2006), 30.

[408] 1:20, 22, 24; 2:13,15, 19; 4:7,10; 5:33; 9:38; 11:25; 13:27; 18:23-35[x5]; 20:8; 21:9, 30, 40, 42; 22:37, 44; 23:39; 24:45-50 [x4]; 25:11 [x2], 14-30 [x10]; 31-46 [x2]; 27:10; 28:2.

[409] 1:20, 22, 24; 2:13, 15, 19; 5:33; 13:27; 18:23-35 [x5]; 20:8; 21:30; 25:11[x2], 14-3 0[x6], 31-46 [x2]; 27:10; 28:2.

[410] This is the first occurrence of the historical present constructions in Matthew. For details on data and its functions, see D.L. Turner, *Matthew* (BECNT; Grand Rapids: Baker Academic, 2008), 89, n. 1.

[411] See R.H. Gundry, *The Use of the Old Testament in St. Matthew's Gospel* (Leiden: Brill, 1967), 93-94.

has the compound aorist verb μετεκάλεσα whereas Matthew has ἐκάλεσα. More significantly, the LXX has God summon "his children" (τὰ τέκνα αὐτοῦ), not "my son" (τὸν υἱόν μου) from Egypt.[412]

It seems this very concept of sonship/fatherhood is the reason Matthew was attracted to Hosea. While, as both R.E. Brown and D.C. Allison[413] have shown, a strong typological interplay between the notion of Jesus as Son of God and that of Israel as God's Son is seen here, but the sonship of Jesus or the fatherhood of God is the main focus for Matthew. The initial words of Hosea 11:1, though not cited by Matthew, are also crucial for the fatherhood theme. In fact throughout this chapter, Hosea talks about God's love in spite of Israel's ingratitude (Hos 11:1-12). Particularly, in the first four verses Hosea compares God's care for the nation since its infancy in Egypt with that of a father proudly and tenderly guiding his child to its first steps holding firmly in its arms as support for walking:

> When Israel was a child, I loved him, and out of Egypt I called my son ...
>
> Yet it was I who taught Ephraim to walk, I took them up in my arms ...
>
> I led them with cords of human kindness, with bands of love (Hos 11:1-4).

The verse as a whole affirms that God loved Israel and called him from Egypt when he was a child (Hos 11:1a). Thus Hosea 11:1, in its historical context, is a reference to the Exodus, of God's past redemptive act of bringing the nation of Israel out of Egypt. According to J. Nolland there is no emphasis on 'my son' here at this point as distinct from any other designation for Israel for Matthew.[414] But it seems that the very emphasis of Matthew is on divine sonship here. Matthew sees in Hosea a strong theological motif, that is, divine sonship, which attracted him. This language of sonship will recur at Jesus' baptism (3:17) and subsequent temptation in the wilderness (4:1-11).

In Hosea, the idea of God's fatherhood has to do with God's relationship with the people of Israel. For Hosea God chose Israel to be his son. In this case the Father image denotes God's covenant relationship with Israel. So God's fatherhood is understood in a metaphorical sense but not literal sense. Of course, already in the event of the Exodus itself we see God having revealed himself as a compassionate and a saving God : "The LORD, the LORD, a God merciful

---

[412] The text is from *The Septuagint Version of the Old Testament with an English Translation and with Various Readings and Critical Notes* (New York: Harper and Brothers).

[413] For D.C. Allison ("The Son of God as Israel: A Note on Matthean Christology," *IBS* 9 [1987], 76) this very expression in Hosea clearly refers to Israel and in Matthew points to the close parallels between Jesus' story and Israel's. Moreover Allison (*The New Moses: A Matthean Typology*) sees Israel's history of exodus, wanderings in the desert and revelation on the mountain as clearly mirrored in Jesus' story in Matthew.

[414] J. Nolland, "No Son-of-God Christology in Mathew 1.18-25," in *JSNT* 62 (1996), 3-12.

and gracious, slow to anger, and abounding in steadfast love and faithfulness" (Ex 34:6). We also find in the book of Exodus in the description of God's instruction to Moses the notion of the very sonship of Israel, "Israel is my firstborn son" (Ex 4:22). The understanding of God as Father in these passages has to do with adoption and redemption. And Hosea seems to have developed this thought of God.[415] Elsewhere, Hosea also stresses on God's love and loyalty to his people (Hos 1: 6-7; 2:1, 23; 11:1, 8). Hosea's allusion to this theological motif of divine sonship attracted Matthew and brought the former's theological motif of covenant relationship and used it in a familial context, that is, the sonship of Jesus to God ("my son"). Thus in this unique Matthean fulfillment quotation of Hosea 11:1 the fatherhood of God is strongly implied in the very expression "my son." This is in line with his emphasis on the divine sonship of Jesus, as found expressed in key moments in Jesus' life: at baptism and at the transfiguration Matthew has the divine voice addressing Jesus as "My beloved Son," (3:17; 17:5) and at the death of Jesus Matthew has put in the lips of the bystanders and the centurion uttering Jesus as the Son of God (27:40, 54). This is strongly complimented by the several unique occurrences of 'my Father' for God in the lips of Matthean Jesus, occurring 17 times, out of which 16 times are unique in Matthew.

Clearly Matthew is here stressing of the sonship of Jesus to God, that is, God as his Father. As such here in his version of the infancy narratives Matthew has brought the fatherhood of God into the forefront: Jesus is depicted as one who is uniquely related to God as Son to Father. That means, for Matthew, Jesus is the Son who stands in an exclusive relationship to the Father.

However, in Matthew it is also seen that the one whom Jesus addresses exclusively as Father is also the one who is addressed inclusively as 'our Father.' This is particularly seen in his version of the Sermon on the Mount to which we now turn.

4.2.2. The Fatherhood of God in Matthean Sermon on the Mount

The Sermon on the Mount is the first and the lengthiest of the five discourses, which Matthew had composed and compiled carefully. That means, this discourse is not preached by Jesus on a single occasion but it is Matthew's carefully constructed discourses keeping his theological perspective. It is clearly evident in that the speeches of Matthean Jesus (5-7) is followed by a series of miracles (8-9) and scholars see here clear Matthean intention projecting Jesus as both the Messiah of words and deeds.[416] Interestingly, in this discourse itself the term 'Father' for God occur the most, a staggering 17 times. It shows Matthean strong emphasis on the fatherhood of God. While mere occurrences of the term 'Father'

[415] H.H. Rowley, *The Faith of Israel* (London: SCM Press, 1973), 62-63.

[416] G. Bornkamm, "The Stilling of the Storm in Matthew," in G. Bornkamm, G. Barth and H.J. Held, *Tradition and Interpretation in Matthew* (London: SCM Press, 1963), 53.

may not be the real indicators, as mentioned earlier, yet it is in these places that the theme of God's fatherhood is the most explicit.

4.2.2.1. Father of All (5:43-48)

The pericope is the last of the six contrasts (5:21-48) which Matthew has put as antithesis of ethics "You have heard that it was said … but I say to you" that repeats every pericope – on anger (5:21-26); adultery (5:27-30); divorce (5:31-32); oaths (5:33-37); retaliation (5:38-42) and culminates on love of enemies (5:43-48). This very pericope is climatic in its emphasis on loving one's enemies and in its concluding call to the perfection of the Father (v48). Thus Matthean Jesus says:

> You have heard that it was said, 'You shall love your neighbor and hate your enemy.' But I say to you, Love your enemies and pray for those who persecute you, so that you may be children of your Father in heaven; for he makes his sun rise on the evil and on the good, and sends rain on the righteous and on the unrighteous. For if you love those who love you, what reward do you have? Do not even the tax collectors do the same? And if you greet only your brothers and sisters, what more are you doing than others? Do not even the Gentiles do the same? Be perfect, therefore, as your heavenly Father is perfect.

4.2.2.1.1. Matthean Redaction

As mentioned above, this pericope (5:43-48) is the last of the six antithesis that form the core part of the Sermon on the Mount (Mt 5-7), and which is a compilation of the sayings of Jesus by Matthew, rather than something spoken by Jesus on a single occasion. In other words, the teaching is that of Jesus, but the arrangement is that of Matthew. This very pericope has parallel in Luke but in quite different order and wording (cf. Lk 6:27-28, 32-36). While verses 43 and 44 have parallels in Luke (Lk. 6:27-28) with almost verbatim agreement on the command to 'love your enemies,' but verse 45 has no parallel. This shows that this particular verse is a deliberate Matthean redaction, with a definite purpose. Then Matthew 5:46-47 has its parallel in Luke 6:32-33, although there are some slight changes. The concluding verse 48 is paralleled in Luke 6:36, where, however, Luke has 'be merciful as your Father is merciful.' Thus the very theocentric expression 'perfect' (τέλειός) is uniquely Matthean.

As mentioned above, it is seen that while verse 44 has parallel in Luke 6:27-28 with almost verbatim agreement on the command to 'love your enemies,' but the next verse which talks about the fatherhood of God is unique to Matthew:

> Mt 5:44-45: But I say to you, Love your enemies and pray for those who persecute you, *so that you may be children of your Father in heaven;*

for he makes his sun rise on the evil and on the good, and sends rain on the righteous and on the unrighteous. (italic added)

Lk 6:27: But I say to you that listen, Love your enemies, do good to those who hate you, bless those who curse you, pray for those who abuse you.

A close look at the parallel above shows that the expression on loving enemies is also found in Luke (Q)[417] so it may be traced to Jesus, but the additional expression on the fatherhood of God idea in relation to nature is peculiar to Matthew, as nowhere in other Synoptic Gospels and in the whole of the New Testament has this parallel. The theocentric expression υἱοὶ τοῦ πατρὸς ὑμῶν τοῦ ἐν οὐρανοῖς ('sons of your Father in heaven') is distinctively Matthean. As we have seen in the earlier section, Matthew's use of 'Father (in heaven)' is carefully shaped to emphasize the fatherhood of God, and thus Matthew puts the term 'Father' rather than 'God' or 'Lord' in several instances on Jesus' lips. Moreover, Matthew has insistently located that Father in heaven. That means God as heavenly Father is a deliberate Matthean redaction. Here identifying God as the 'Father in heaven' also highlights, for Matthew, God's authority and sovereignty. This is confirmed by the observation elsewhere in Matthew that heaven is God's throne (5:34; 23:22). However, our main interest is the next expression, "for he makes his sun rise on the evil and on good, and sends rain on the righteous and on the unrighteous" (5:45bc). This expression is seen only here in Matthew and nowhere else in the whole of the New Testament.

4.2.2.1.2. Theological Explanation

4.2.2.1.2.1. God's Fatherhood Expressed in Creation and Nature

In this unique expression (5:45bc), Matthean Jesus teaches that the Father in heaven "makes his sun rise on the evil and on the good." This expression occurs in the context of teaching on love of one's enemies and thus in the verse immediately prior to this expression Matthean Jesus says that if one loves one's enemies, one is a child of God (v44-45a). This is proven in the simple fact of nature for Matthean Jesus: God "makes his sun rise on the evil and on the good, and sends rain on the righteous and on the unrighteous." This logical illustration, found only here, is where our interest lies. Moreover, Matthew's uses of 'Father in heaven' and 'sun' in the same breath strike our attention. Interestingly, the term 'sun' occurs five times in Matthew (5:45; 13:6; 43; 17:2; 24:29). For Matthew the 'sun' and 'rain' signifies the all-embracing love of God towards his creation, and that both the good and the bad also receive God's blessings. God lavishes the sun and rain

[417] Of course, this expression is nothing new to Jesus. There are similar statements in Judaism, among the Greeks, particularly the Stoics and Indian religions (See, Luz, *Matthew 1-7*, 340, n. 18). For an exhaustive analysis on the rabbinic Jewish discourse on loving of one's enemies, see C. G. Montefiore, *Rabbinic Literature and Gospel Teachings* (London: Macmillan and Co, 1930), 59-111.

on both good and bad, just and unjust. Similar to this Matthean expressions are also prevalent in the Greek philosophy, particularly in the Platonic and Stoic tradition, describing God's beneficence expressed in creation that is experience by both good and bad. Thus Seneca says:

> If you are imitating the gods … then bestow benefits also upon the ungrateful; for the sun rises also upon the wicked and the sea lies open also to Pirates (*De Beneficiis* 4.26.1).[418]

For the Greeks, particularly the Stoics, the logic is that "everyone has a share in the same divine origin so that universal love of human beings is in agreement with nature."[419] Such a universal Father whose love and goodness is to all (that is, universally just as sun and rain) is presupposed in Matthew. In this regard the occurrence of the expression 'sons of your Father in heaven' (υἱοὶ τοῦ πατρὸς ὑμῶν τοῦ ἐν οὐρανοῖς) is striking. The word 'sons' here implies that the relationship between the Father and his children defines the children as taking on the character of the Father. The expression 'sons of God' is also found in the Stoic writings. Epictetus in his discourse clearly talks about human beings as God's children thus:

> We are all primarily begotten of God, and that God is the father of men as well as of gods ... if you know that you are a son of Zeus, will you not be elated? … inasmuch as these two elements were comingled in our begetting … reason and intelligence, which we have in common with the gods.[420]

The inference from this expression is that all are children of God, particularly human beings who are endowed with reason. Thus the expression 'son of Zeus (God)' refers here to each and every human being, the rational beings. As God's children everyone belong to the same divine origin. So the occurrence of the very expression 'sons of heavenly Father' here in Matthew seems to be used in similar sense. So here we see a clear emphasis of Matthew on the universal fatherhood of God. The second act (v45c) indicates that rain is God's activity: "and sends rain on the righteous and on the unrighteous." In Greek religion, rain comes from Zeus, the weather-god. Zeus is thus the giver and god of fruitfulness.[421] For Aeschylus, the Greek tragedian, Helios is the nourisher of life.[422]

The relation of God with sun is equally strong in the literatures of Hellenistic-Judaism and Hans D. Betz is of the opinion that this very idea of Matthew can be traced in ancient hymns to the sun called 'solar mythology 'or

[418] Seneca, *Moral Essays* III, 257.

[419] Luz, *Matthew 1-7*, 431.

[420] *Discourses* 1.3.1-3, *Epictetus* I, 25.

[421] M.P. Nilsson, *A History of Greek Religion*, 121.

[422] M.P. Nilsson, *A History of Greek Religion*, 122.

'solar theology.'[423] In a text in *Odes of Solomon* there are hymns that describe God's activities in relation to creation: "And the Lord (is) like the sun upon the face of the land."[424] Similarly, in another Hellenistic literature called *Hellenistic Synagogal Prayers*, there are hymns in praise of God in linking with sun:

> While light and sun, for days and (for) fruits, came birth ... then earth grew green, engraved with all sorts of flowers, and with embroidery of different trees, and (the) all-blazing luminaries are nourishers of these.[425]

As we have noticed in these hymns, God's nature in likened to the activities of the sun (creation), similarly, the very unique expression in Matthew too describes God's activity. It seems Matthew's idea of God particularly the concept of an impartial God as expressed here in verse 45 seems to have some influence from its surrounding Greek-Hellenistic religions.

Furthermore, on examining this very idea of Matthew in his more immediate milieu, the Old Testament, it is also seen that there are several references of close association of sun with God (Yahweh) in the Old Testament[426] among which Psalm 84:11 is one. Here God's nature is expressed in solar language: "For the Lord God is a sun and shield; he bestows favor and honor." According to Mark M. Smith, solar cult or theology has originated as a gradual assimilation of Canaanite and Ancient West Asian tradition, pointing to the cult of foreign deity. He found striking similarities between Old Testament solar imagery of Yahweh (e.g., Ps 50:1-3; Ezek 43:1-5) and the Babylonian deity Ningirsu (the warrior god whose divine nature is expressed with storm and solar language) and Marduk (to whom Enuma Elish I:101-102,157, and II: 128-29 applies solar and storm qualities).[427] According to Smith, solar language for Yahweh "originated as part of the Canaanite, and more generally Near Eastern, heritage of divine language as an expression of general theophanic luminosity."[428] He goes on saying that "the sun became one component of the symbolic repertoire of the chief God in Israel just as it did in Assur, Babylon, and Ugarit."[429] This logically says that even if Matthew is relying on the Old Testament, which is Matthew's more direct source for his God-language,[430] the syncretistic element is not ruled out, as Smith has observed, the Old Testament too has influences from the surrounding religions.

---

[423] H.D. Betz, *The Sermon on the Mount* (Hermenia; Minneapolis: Fortress Press, 1995), 316.

[424] *Odes of Solomon* 11.13, Trans J. H. Charlesworth, in J. H. Charlesworth, *OTP*, 745.

[425] *Hellenistic Synagogal Prayers* 3. 6-13, trans D.R. Darnell, in J. H. Charlesworth, *OTP*, 679.

[426] E.g. Deut 33:2; Isa 60:1-3; Ps 84:11; 89:15; 104:2.

[427] Smith, *The Early History of God*, 117.

[428] Smith, *The Early History of God*, 120.

[429] Smith, *The Early History of God*, 120.

[430] Jeremias, *The Prayers of Jesus*, 12.

It is therefore seen that the very Matthean idea of God's fatherhood, particularly in relation to creation and nature, has certain measures of foreign influences, particularly that of Greek-Hellenistic idea of a cosmic Father. Thus the inference from this expression is that God is universal Father and so his love and goodness is to all and that human beings, being children of the same Father, should respond through the general love of all. That is how Matthean Jesus talks about imitating the heavenly Father, who is perfect in his love and beneficence so God's children must reciprocate in loving all without any discrimination.

4.2.2.1.2.2. Imitators of God as God's Children

When Matthean Jesus culminated this very particular pericope with the expression "Be perfect, therefore, as your heavenly Father is perfect" (v48), Matthew is thinking concretely of the love of enemies in particular. When Matthew is speaking of the perfection of God, he probably refers to God's fatherly goodness on the basis of verse 45. This concluding verse is paralleled in Luke 6:36, where, however, Luke has 'be merciful as your Father is merciful.' While Luke's version has several rabbinic parallels,[431] Matthew's phrase has no parallels in the whole of rabbinic literatures, and thus C.G. Montefiore observed that the expression is original to Matthew.[432] It seems then that this very theocentric expression τέλειός has to do with Matthean theology. Yet looking Matthew within the broader Greco-Roman literatures help us to see that this principle arose perhaps not without Hellenistic influence, as Matthew is very much part of that of Hellenistic-Jewish milieu. Statements about the perfection of God are found particularly among the Greeks. First century C.E. philosophers used similar concept of (imitation of) God. Epictetus says:

> We must learn what the gods are like; for whatever their character is discovered to be, the man who is going to please and obey them must endeavor as best he can to resemble them. If the deity is faithful, he also must be faithful; if free, he also must be free; if beneficent, he also must be beneficent; if high-minded, he also must be high-minded, and so forth; therefore in everything he says and does, he must act as an imitator of god.[433]

The logic behind such ethical imperative for the stoics is their belief in the presence of an all-knowing god.[434] Matthean Jesus teaching here has striking

---

[431] E.g., in *Targum Pseudo-Jonathan Leviticus* 22:28 says: "My people, children of Israel, as our Father is merciful in heaven so shall you be merciful on earth."

[432] C.G. Montefiore, *Rabbinic Literature and Gospel Teachings*, 110.

[433] *Discourses* II.14.12-13, *Epictetus* I, 309.

[434] As the same ethical imperative (Epictetus, *Discourses* II, 309) goes on saying that "there is a God, and that he provides for the universe, and that it is impossible for a man to conceal from Him, not merely his actions, but even his purposes and his thoughts."

similar to such stoic-Hellenistic idea. For Matthew, God is perfect, the one who gives gifts to righteous and unrighteous alike (v45). And therefore to such a compassionate and impartial God Matthew calls him '(your) heavenly Father.'

The term τέλειός occurs only in Matthew (twice in 5:48 and once in 19:21). The occurrence twice in verse 48a can be understood as an attribute of human persons (cf. 19:21) and in verse 48b as an attribute of God.[435] The adjective τέλειός is derived from τέλεω, (verb, meaning 'to finish,' 'to complete') and τέλός (noun, meaning 'end,' 'goal').[436] The basic meaning, therefore, is 'having attained the end' or 'purpose,' 'complete,' 'perfect.'[437] As noted above the only parallel to this verse is found in 19:21, where Matthean Jesus talks about attaining perfection by selling one's possessions and distribute to the poor. The term τέλειός occurs again only in Matthew's version of the story of the rich young man found in his source Mark (Mk 10:17-22//Mt 19:16-22//Lk 18:18-23). When Jesus, according to Mark, says to the young man, "You lack one thing" (Mk 10:21), Matthew changes this to, "If you wish to be perfect." Here we see the rich young man seeking guidance on conduct that will lead to eternal life (Kingdom of God), but when he is advised to sell his possessions and give to the poor, he turns away. He was unwilling to sell his goods and help the poor. In that case he finds difficult to pursue righteousness or perfection. Hence there is quantitative element in the Matthean conception of righteousness which is already sounded in 5:20 (better righteousness) and once more in 5:47 with the word περισσὸν. This makes it probable that the quantitative element must not be neglected as we ponder on God's perfection.

God's perfection, for Matthew, is seen in his indiscriminate goodness. He bestows the benefits of his creation continuously on the bad and the good and on the righteous and the unrighteous. He is perfect in the sense that he does good in spite of the fact that the evil and the ungrateful ones (enemies) will not appreciate his benefits; they will remain enemies even though he keeps doing good to them.[438] According to C.H. Talbert, 'perfect' in this Matthean context means 'inclusive in one's love.'[439] The implication from this ethical imperative of Matthean Jesus ("Be perfect as your heavenly Father is perfect") is that the children of God, too, can become perfect by imitating God[440] in dealing with their own enemies. In other words, it is a call to live in agreement with God's character, that is, goodness. The call here is consequently a call to do good without expecting any result. That is,

---

435 Luz, *Matthew 1-7*, 346.

436 Trenchard, *A Concise Dictionary of New Testament Greek*, 156.

437 Betz, *The Sermon on the Mount*, 322.

438 Betz, *The Sermon on the Mount*, 324.

439 Talbert, *Reading the Sermon on the Mount*, 96.

440 For details on the concept of imitation of God in Mediterranean milieu, See Davies and Allison, *A Critical and Exegetical Commentary on the Gospel of Matthew* I, 560-64; Talbert, *Reading the Sermon on the Mount*, 96-98.

without looking for rewards or results, the children of God will by their conduct serve as 'salt of the earth' and 'light of the world,' and they will do so whether or not they are appreciated (5:13-16).[441] God's love is unconditional. It is spontaneous and constant. It is unlimited in very way. It is like the sun which is for everybody (v45). Such is the idea of God's fatherhood portrayed by Matthew. This idea is unique to Matthew. Some noted New Testament scholars, most notably, Moffatt and Jeremias have overlooked this very idea of God's cosmic fatherhood found in Matthew. The former categorically rejected the idea of God's fatherhood in relation to creation, saying that "there is no reference in the New Testament to the idea that God is to be loved as our Maker and Creator."[442] God's fatherhood, for Moffatt, has nothing to do with creation. The comments of Jeremias implies the same as he says, "being a child of God is not a gift of creation."[443]

Matthew indeed portrays a God who is impartial as the sun and the rain. God's fatherly love cannot be limited to the people of God; he demonstrates his love in sending sunlight and rain to all. That is what Matthew meant by being perfect which is nothing but being 'whole' or 'totality' or 'undivided' in love. As such God for Matthew is the cosmic benevolent Father, whose providence is universal in its scope (universal benevolence of the heavenly Father). Thus, we see here a strong emphasis of Matthew on the fatherhood of God as seen in the gifts of nature whose goodness is for all. One of the qualifications to be sons of God is peacemaking (or loving of enemies) which is explicit in a unique beatitude in Matthew (5:9) to which we now turn.

4.2.2.2. Children of God: The Peacemakers (5:9)

Following the kingdom preaching and activities (4:17-25) Matthean Jesus went up the mountain and began to speak to his disciples saying:

> Blessed are the poor in spirit, for theirs is the kingdom of heaven.
> Blessed are those who mourn, for they will be comforted.
> Blessed are the meek, for they will inherit the earth.
> Blessed are those who hunger and thirst for righteousness, for they will be filled.
> Blessed are the merciful, for they will receive mercy.
> Blessed are the pure in heart, for they will see God.
> Blessed are the peacemakers, for they will be called children of God.

4.2.2.2.1. Matthean Redaction

The beatitudes are the first major thought unit in the Sermon on the Mount (5:3-11). They are a unit in themselves and were composed as such. Luke (Q) has it in

---

[441] Betz, *The Sermon on the Mount*, 324.

[442] J. Moffatt, *Love in the New Testament* (London: Hodder and Stoughton, 1932), 42, 72.

[443] Jeremias, *New Testament Theology*, 181.

only four verses (Lk 6:20-23),[444] while Matthew has additional 6 more verses to it (vv4, 5 and vv7-10). That means these verses are distinctively Matthean (M). In this pericope the emphasis on God's fatherhood is very strong, in particular, the seventh beatitude, which is unique to Matthew, as it expressed explicitly on sonship to God.

Within the larger Sermon context, this beatitude of 5:9 corresponds to the section on 'Love for Enemies' (Mt 5:43-48//Lk 6:27-36). The subject of the beatitude has its direct counterpart in the paranesis (Mt 5:9 and Mt 5:44, 45) and both have the same promise of sonship ('sons of God' [5:9b]; 'sons of your Father in heaven' [5:45]). It is interesting to note that this combination of conduct with sonship is found only here in the whole of New Testament. This shows Matthew's strong emphasis on the fatherhood of God.

4.2.2.2.2. Theological Explanation

4.2.2.2.2.1. Peacemaker as Sons of God

The term 'peacemaker' here is the only instance in the whole of the New Testament.[445] However, the noun 'peace' appears many times in both the Old Testament and in the New Testament, and is a key biblical concept.[446] In Septuagint, εἰρήνη is used to translate the Hebrew word *shalom* a term which, like mercy, has a broad range of meanings and can also imply a deep commitment to work of justice.[447] It is this sense of working to establish justice, forgiveness and reconciliation that Matthew seems to emphasize in his Gospel (5:23-24, 44-48; 18:15-18, 21-35). Similar admonition to make peace is also found in wisdom and in rabbinical teachings. For example, *m. Aboth* 1.12 talks about the commands of Hillel to love and pursue peace and love mankind;[448] so also *m. Peah* 1.1 talks about the "deeds of loving-kindness, making peace between a man and his fellow."[449] In each case, concrete steps in inter-human relationships are meant. Several scholars see here social or social-political context as primarily in view. Looking at the level of Jesus, L.J. White sees Jesus as having in mind here primarily the healing of divisions in the community;[450] while for Saldarini,

---

[444] Scholars consider Lukan version of the beatitudes to be original, with the first three verses (Lk 6:20-22) as the core beatitudes; see J. Nolland, *The Gospel of Matthew* (NIGTC; Grand Rapids: Wm B Eerdmans, 2005), 198; G.R. Osborne, *Matthew* (ZECNT; Grand Rapids: Zondervan, 2010), 166.

[445] Elsewhere, this term appears in verb form in a Deutero-Pauline letter, Colossians 1:20, where Paul talks about the cross of Jesus as the peacemaking act through his blood.

[446] For the uses of εἰρήνη in both the Old and New Testament, See J.P. Healey, "Peace," in *ABD* 5 (1992), 206-212.

[447] Healey, "Peace," in *ABD* 5 (1992), 206.

[448] Danby, *Mishnah*, 447.

[449] Danby, *Mishnah*, 11.

[450] L.J. White, "Peacemakers in Matthew's World," in *BT* 23 (1985), 29-34.

looking at the level of Matthew, the Beatitudes including peacemaking reflect the inner attitudes of the Matthean community and the pattern of its deviant behavior, seeking to make the best of its deviant status.[451] Looking Matthew in the context of the Roman Empire, W. Carter sees this as expression of resistance against the promise of the *Pax Romana* as 'God's cosmic peace,' having to do with God's merciful reign.[452]

However, we need to consider this more within the broader literary-theological context of this pericope. Thus looking at this pericope as part of the whole of the Matthean Jesus' Sermon on the Mount, in particular with the following pericope of 'Love for enemies' (Mt 5:43-48), the peacemakers are those who demonstrate love and concern for the enemies. Thus this peacemaking seems to be purely horizontal in emphasis, that is, on human to human relationships. But the next phrase of the same verse makes it more vertical and theocentric. Interestingly, we see the occurrence of the divine passive here in κληθήσονται, where the passive is used in place of the divine name.[453] So the expression of blessedness here is that God blesses those who make peace (μακάριοι οἱ εἰρηνοποιοί). According to Guelich, peacemaking is "the demonstration of God's love through Christ in all its profundity."[454] For him, the peacemakers of 5:9 refer to those who are experiencing the peace of God, thereby becoming his agents in establishing his peace in the world.[455]

Similarly for David L. Turner, "this beatitude is not about being a passively peaceful person but about being an active reconciler of people."[456] In this light the New Living Bible, has the appropriate rendering, "(God blesses) those who work for peace." And, as mentioned above, the blessedness pronounced by Matthean Jesus here to those 'peacemakers' as 'children of God' find its clear connection in Matthew 5:48 (be perfect as your heavenly Father is perfect). Once again Matthean emphasis on the universality of God's fatherhood is very explicit here. Those who make peace (which is of God) are God's children. That means God's children are those who act like God. So for Matthew the deeds of peacemaking simultaneously create sonship to God,[457] which means God's fatherhood covers everyone who engage in peacemaking. It is timeless, vertical, theocentric, universal and inclusive. In this perspective, W. Carter correctly puts forth that peace is "God's cosmic peace in which all things are in just relation with each other and

[451] A.J. Saldarini, "The Gospel of Matthew and Jewish-Christian Conflict," in *Social History of the Matthean Community*, edited by David L. Balch (Minneapolis: Fortress, 1991), 53.

[452] W. Carter, *Matthew and the Margins: A Socio-Political and Religious Reading* (New Delhi: TPI, 2007), 135-136.

[453] Jeremias, *New Testament Theology*, 9.

[454] Guelich, *Sermon on the Mount*, 92.

[455] Guelich, *Sermon on the Mount*, 92.

[456] Turner, *Matthew*, 152.

[457] Minear, *God of the Gospels*, 56.

their creator,"[458] and "peacemakers enact … God's merciful reign, living toward this wholeness and well-being."[459] So Carter's understanding of this expression is inclusive as he talks about peace consisting of all things cosmically in right relation to God.

On the contrary, Nolland understands it in particular and exclusive sense.[460] G.R. Osborne too sees continuity here. In his own words, "Faithful Israel was called 'children of God' in the Old Testament (Deut 14:1; Hos 1:10), and now the new Israel becomes the special children and heirs of God as they become peacemakers in following Christ."[461] David L. Turner sees this sonship idea as linear, horizontal and eschatological sense as he says that those "peacemakers will be recognized as authentic members of God's family when ultimate eschatological *shalom* finally dawns on earth."[462]

4.2.2.2.2.2. Cosmic Sonship

The emphasis here is on the theocentric, inclusive and universal sense. For Matthew to make peace is to be one of God's children now; just as those loving enemies are considered as children of God (cf. 5:45). For Matthew God's children are shaped not by particular nationality but by imitating God.[463] And strikingly similar to this idea is found in the Jewish-Hellenistic literatures, particularly in Philo, who talks about kinship as "not measured only by blood, but by similarity of conduct and pursuit of the same objects."[464] Philo also says that those "who do 'what is pleasing' to nature and what is 'good' are sons of God."[465] We also find the term 'peace' in clear association with God in Philo. While talking about the role of God in his discourse on destruction through human-made war and natural forces at strife in herself, Philo says that God as:

> Peace-maker and peace-keeper, Who destroys faction both in cities and in the various parts of the universe and creates plenty and fertility and abundance of other good things and leaves the havoc of fruits without a single spark to be rekindled.[466]

---

[458] Carter, *Matthew and the Margins*, 135.

[459] Carter, *Matthew and the Margins*, 136.

[460] Nolland, *The Gospel of Matthew*, 205-206.

[461] Osborne, *Matthew*, 169.

[462] Turner, *Matthew*, 153. However, for him (*Matthew*, 152-153) this sonship is basically for believers as he states, "Those who are truly called God's children will bear a filial likeness to their heavenly Father, who treats enemies well (Matt.5:43-48). Their experience of peace with God enables them to seek the cessation of hostilities and the ultimate welfare of the world."

[463] Carter, *Matthew and the Margins*, 136.

[464] *De Virtutibus* 195, in *Philo VIII*, 283-285, trans F.H. Colson and G.H. Whitaker.

[465] *De Specialibus legibus* I. 318, Philo VII, 285, trans F.H. Colson and G.H. Whitaker.

[466] *De Specialibus legibus* 2.192, Philo VII, 427, trans F.H. Colson and G.H. Whitaker.

For Philo, peacemaking is inherently God's, and that for him there is a very thin line between human-human peace and God-human-nature peace. That means Philo's emphasis is on cosmic peace. It seems then that when Matthew is linking 'peacemaking' with God, he is very much closer to Philo, which means to say that Matthew has strong roots in Hellenistic-Judaism in his idea when he talks about peacemakers as God's children. Once again the fatherhood of God as Matthew's central emphasis is clearly seen here. Matthew's emphasis on universality of God's fatherhood is closely related with his emphasis on God as All-seeing Father, again unique in Matthew, to which we now turn.

4.2.2.3. Father Who Sees in Secret (6:1-6)

As a sequel to the teaching on perfection in the preceding pericope Matthean Jesus says:

> Beware of practicing your piety before others in order to be seen by them; for then you have no reward from your Father in heaven. So whenever you give alms, do not sound a trumpet before you, as the hypocrites do in the synagogues and in the streets, so that they may be praised by others. Truly I tell you, they have received their reward. But when you give alms, do not let your left hand know what your right hand is doing, so that your alms may be done in secret; and your Father who sees in secret will reward you. And whenever you pray, do not be like the hypocrites; for they love to stand and pray in the synagogues and at the street corners, so that they may be seen by others. Truly I tell you, they have received their reward. But whenever you pray, go into your room and shut the door and pray to your Father who is in secret; and your Father who sees in secret will reward you.

4.2.2.3.1. Matthean Redaction

This unit, which forms part of the central section of the Sermon on the Mount (6:1-18), is unique to Matthew having no parallels in the Synoptic Gospels. It is interesting to see the occurrence of the expression 'whenever you' (pray, v2), as a plot that culminates in another expression 'and your Father who sees in secret will reward you' (v4). We will see this pattern recurring in the following pericope on prayer (vv5-6) and fasting (vv16-18). According to C.H. Talbert, the whole of this section (6:1-18) is a unity that talks about 'true piety,'[467] with 6:1 as a statement of principle followed by four paragraphs with the same basic arrangement: vv2-4 (on almsgiving); vv5,6 and vv7-15 (on prayer); vv16-18 (on fasting).[468] The expression "Father (in the heavens)" is the guiding word of the whole section (vv

[467] These three acts of almsgiving, prayer and fasting are also typical of Jewish piety.

[468] Talbert, *Reading the Sermon on the Mount,* 102-103.

1, 4, 6, 8, 9, 14, 15, 18). That means it is Matthew who carefully constructed it projecting his convictions and interest about the fatherhood of God.

4.2.2.3.2. Theological Explanation

4.2.2.3.2.1. All-Seeing and All-Knowing Father

The unit begins with a statement of principle, "Beware of practicing your piety before others in order to be seen by them; for then you have no reward from your Father in heaven."[469] The argument involved in this pericope is that piety should be done for God, not for human status before other humans. Otherwise it is a theatre, not worship.[470] This is what, for Matthean Jesus, "the hypocrites do in the synagogue and in the streets, so that they may be praised by others" (6:2).[471] The emphasis on secrecy is underlined by the hyperbolic, "Do not let your left hand know what your right hand is doing" (6:3). The conviction behind such an expression is that the heavenly Father sees perfectly what no one else can see (v4); that he is 'in the secret' and that he sees all that goes on 'in the secret' (6:4 cf. vv 6, 18). There is no exact parallel to this kind of theology elsewhere in the New Testament.[472] So here Matthew is talking about a God who is in secret seeing everything (vv 4, 6, 18) and knows everything (v8). The teachings employ doctrines and concepts rarely attested elsewhere in the New Testament. From where did Matthew have this concept of God?

While the emphasis on secrecy in almsgiving (as ethical virtue) is found in rabbinic literatures,[473] but the concept of an all seeing God is found mostly in the Greek religious traditions. The concept of an 'all-seeing, all-hearing god' goes back to Homer.[474] In the Homeric work *Odyssey* the sun-god Helios is called 'all-seeing' or the 'eye of righteousness.'[475] For Hesiod Zeus is the champion of justice;

---

[469] In the rabbinic literatures, the rabbis sometimes criticized some Pharisees in ways similar to Matthew's depiction of them. The Babylonian Talmud *b. Sotah* 22b describes seven types of Pharisees, one of which is the 'shoulder Pharisee' who packs his good works on his shoulder to be seen by others. See C. A. Evans, *Matthew*, 139.

[470] Talbert, *Reading the Sermon on the Mount*, 103-104.

[471] The 'hypocrites' here has the meaning of 'play-actor.' See *BAGD*, 845.

[472] Though in the Old Testament there are instances of an 'all-seeing' God (Ps 33:13-14; 113:5-6; 138:6).

[473] For example, the Mishnah *m. Shekalim* 5:6 talks about two chambers in the temple, one of which is called the chamber of secrets, into which "the devout used to put their gifts in secret and the poor of good family received support therefrom in secret" (See Danby, *Mishnah*, 158); Similarly in the Jerusalem Talmud in the sayings and proverb of the rabbis there is a clear saying about Rabbi Eliazar exalting secret giving: "who gives charity in secret is greater than Moses. See *The Talmud of Jerusalem* (New York: The Wisdom Library, 1956), 95.

[474] For Homer Zeus, Helios, and other gods 'sees everything and hears everything' (*Iliad* 3. 104, 278).

[475] Homer, *Odyssey* 11. 102.

his eyes sees everything and notice everything.[476] Xenophanes too describes an all-seeing God as he writes that God "sees as a whole, thinks as a whole, hears as a whole."[477] There are other instances of Hellenistic writings that are replete with hymns praising the sovereignty and universality of god or gods in similar expression to this verse in Matthew. An *Orphic hymn* expressing the sovereignty of sun-god Helios goes thus: "To Helios (Sun), Fumigation from Frankincense and manna. Hear, golden Titan, whose eternal eye with matchless sight illumines all the sky ...."[478]

The idea of God's omniscience is also closely related with this All-seeing God in Greek philosophical traditions. The Greek philosophers connected the all-knowing God with theorizing about prayer (and righteousness). In the Pseudo-Platonic dialogue *Alcibiades*, entitled '*On Prayer*' there is mentioned of a Socrates' safe prayer, "King Zeus, give unto us what is good, whether we pray or not; but what is grievous, even if we pray for it, do thou avert."[479] Diogenes Laertius also said about prayer that praying makes sense only if one prays for the truly good things.[480] Epictetus also says regarding the omniscience of God that "it is impossible for a man to conceal from Him, not merely his actions, but even his purposes and his thoughts."[481]

It is striking to see that similar to the Greek philosophical discourses Matthean Jesus is bringing in the idea of an all-seeing and all-knowing Father in the context of religious activities, of almsgiving (6:1-4) and prayer (6:5-8). Of course in Jewish wisdom (e.g., Job 28) and hymnic traditions (e.g., Ps 139:3-4) the idea of the omniscience of God is found,[482] but the idea of All-seeing and All-knowing Father of Matthew in the context of religious discourse (Sermon on the Mount) is unique to Matthew in the whole of New Testament, but quite in the line with the Greek-philosophical discourse on all-seeing and all-knowing God.

The theme of secrecy continues in the next pericope as Matthean Jesus talks about prayer in verses 5 and 6. In this pericope the idea of secrecy is once again come into the fore particularly in the metaphorical expression 'go into your room

---

[476] M.P. Nilsson, *Greek Piety*, 34.

[477] Xenophanes B24, cited in Werner Jaeger, *The Theology of the Early Greek Philosophers* (Oxford: Clarendon Press, 1947), 44.

[478] *Orphic Hymn* 8 to Helios, trans Taylor (Greek hymns c. 3rd B.C.E. to 2nd C.E.), *http://www.theoi.com/Titan/HeliosGod.html*; accessed on 14 April, 2013.

[479] See *Alcibiades* II.143, in Plato, *Charmides, Alcibiates* I and II, *Hipparchus*, the Lovers, *Theages, Minos, Epinomis*, 245, trans W. R. M. Lamb (Cambridge; Mass: Harvard University Press, 1979).

[480] According to him, the question about what is the truly good should be foremost on their minds. The 'good' means the same as the 'just,' that is, the just distribution of the good; see *Diogenes* VI.42, in *Diogenes Laertius* II, 45.

[481] *Discourses* II.14.11, in *Epictetus* I, 309.

[482] So also *Exodus Rabbah* 14:15 clearly says that 'before a person speaks, God knows what is in that person's heart.' See Talbert, *Reading the Sermon on the Mount*, 110.

(ταμεῖόν).' Looking with sociological lens C. Osiek argues that such a statement reflects an urban housing context and intending a literal secrecy but not solitude.[483] J.H. Neyrey examines this unit as a whole (6:1-18) in the context of honor and shame and talks about practicing piety for the sake of God (patron) alone, that is, to honor God in secret.[484] D.A. Hagner explains this as an inner room which, being secret or hidden place, is often used as a store room.[485] Osborne too thinks this as a small storage closet and the most private part of the home that provides "total privacy to commune with the Father apart from outside distractions."[486] For W. Carter, since prayer usually happens in the inner room or storeroom but not in the public places, so for him "naming the place says little about the types of houses in which the members of the audience live, but much more about being out of the public gaze and space, and in the presence of God."[487] As most of the scholars commented, this expression has more to do with being in God's presence, so it points to one's heart which is the inmost being and which matters more than the speculation on literal location.

However, the emphasis on the idea of literal 'place' also matter here as this idea is expressed in relation to practice of religious piety for publicity or showiness. The idea behind this command to go to one's inner room (ταμεῖόν) thus become clearer in the next phrase, as the thought goes on explaining that the Father is in the secret (τῷ πατρί σου τῷ ἐν τῷ κρυπτῷ, v6b) and he sees in secret (ὁ βλέπων ἐν τῷ κρυπτῷ, v6c). The development of the phrase 'in secret' is striking here. First, the Father dwells 'in the secret' and then he sees what is done 'in secret.' On explaining this dominant motif that recurs in verses 4, 6 and 18, Paul Ellingworth suggests that 'place' is understood in verses 6 and 18 so that the understanding is that "God is in the same secret place in which people should pray or give alms, so that he sees what they do."[488]

Once again we see Matthew's strong emphasis on God's fatherhood here. God is an all-seeing Father who demands purity of motives, as he sees all that occurs even in the innermost or secret place. Before him nothing is hidden including one's heart and attitudes. He is the 'eye of righteousness' and that "the only alms he rewards are alms of which the giver is unconscious."[489] It is God who

[483] C. Osiek, "'When You Pray, Go into Your ταμεῖόν' (Matthew 6:6): But Why," in *CBQ* 71 (2009), 723.

[484] J. H. Neyrey, *Render to God: New Testament Understanding of the Divine* (Minneapolis: Fortress, 2004), 65-66.

[485] D.A. Hagner, *Matthew 1-13* (WBC 33A; Dallas: Word, 1993), 142.

[486] Osborne, *Matthew*, 225.

[487] Carter, *Matthew and the Margins*, 162.

[488] P. Ellingworth, "'In Secret?' (Matthew 6.4, 6, 18)," in *BT* 40 (1989), 446-447.

[489] Paul S. Minear, *The God of the Gospels: A Theological Workbook* (Atlanta: John Knox Press, 1988), 31.

alone can distinguish between altruism and egoism.[490] Thus doing religious piety (almsgiving and praying) without any ulterior motive, that is, without expecting any rewards, is what is expected from a God who is all-seeing Father,[491] which is again quite in line with the element of surprise on the part of the righteous in the parable of the judgments (25:31-46), which is another unique parable of Matthew.

The repeated expressions ἐν τῷ κρυπτῷ ('in the secret') also goes along well with the idea of justice and fair dealing - for the receiver to avoid shame and the giver to avoid self promotion (v2). Several Jewish and Hellenistic texts too have similar demands. The principle to give the poor alms secretly in order not to shame them is advocated by R. Yannai, who once said, "It is better you had given him nothing than that you gave him something and put him to shame."[492] Greco-Roman writers too see religious piety as opposed to showiness and presumptuousness.[493] Seneca once said:

> It is the intention that exalts small gifts, gives luster to those that are mean, and discredits those that are great and considered of value ... Good men, therefore, are pleasing to the gods with an offering of meal and gruel; the bad, on the other hand, do not escape impiety although they dye the altars with streams of blood.[494]

Here the emphasis of Seneca is on the purity of motives in relating to God. For Matthew, similar to such Greco-Roman and Hellenistic idea, God sees all, including what is going on in the secret. This is closely related with his emphasis on cosmic Father as seen in the previous pericope. It seems then that the Greek-Hellenistic theology has strong influence on the theology of God in Matthew, particularly the idea of an all-seeing Father. Just as the sun-god Helios of the Greeks, God is for Matthew an all-seeing and all-knowing. He is the revealer of righteousness. Such an image of God is portrayed here.

---

[490] Minear, *The God of the Gospels*, 31; on the idea of selfless giving and the heart of God, see also Miroslav Volf, "Being as God Is: Trinity and Generosity," in *God's Life in Trinity*, edited by Miroslav Volf and Michael Welker (Minneapolis: Fortress Press, 2006), 3-12.

[491] Otherwise giving alms or praying or fasting with the motive of selfish gain (e.g., expecting reward from God or gaining praise from fellow beings) can be nothing more than what Socratic tradition called a commercial transactions-like 'asking and giving' (and expecting in return). In the Socratic dialogue with *Euthyphro* (*Euthyphro* 14.c.d.e, in *Plato* I, trans H. N. Fowler [Cambridge; M.A: Harvard University Press, 1914], 55) there is a rhetorical question as regard to prayer: 'Is then prayer asking [things] from the gods?' If so then 'holiness would be a kind of business transactions between gods and humans.' In this case there is no element of sacrifice on the part of the giver.

[492] C.G. Montefiore, *Rabbinic Literature and Gospel Teachings*, 112, citing *Chagigah* 5a.

[493] Cicero, a Stoic philosopher also said, "No audience for virtue (is) higher than the conscience."See Cicero, *Tusculanarum quaestionum libri quinque* 2.26.

[494] *De Beneficiis* 1.6.2-3 in Seneca, *Moral Essays* III, 25.

The emphasis on an all-seeing and all knowing God implies a God who is transcendent yet immanent; we will find that very emphasis explained cogently as we turn to a pericope that Matthew shares with Luke, that is the Lord's Prayer.

4.2.2.4. Heavenly Father (6:9-13)

In the context of a series of teaching on religiosity and prayer Matthean Jesus sets forth a short prayer (6:9-13) as a model to be followed ('Pray then in this way'):

> Our Father in heaven,.
> Hallowed be your name. Your kingdom come.
> Your will be done, on earth as it is in heaven.
> Give us this day our daily bread.
> And forgive us our debts, as we also have forgiven our debtors.
> And do not bring us to the time of trial, but rescue us from the evil one.

4.2.2.4.1. Matthean Redaction

This prayer of Jesus is recorded both in Matthew and Luke, so the sources is Q and from the view of redaction criticism Luke seems to have preserved an earlier form of the prayer as modifications and expansions are more likely than omission.[495] So Matthew has the model prayer (or 'the Lord's Prayer') retained in a more developed form than Luke (Lk 11:1-4). Matthew's form contains seven petitions compared to Luke's five. The first two petitions are in verbatim agreement. Matthew's fourth petition is in close agreement with the Lukan form except only for Luke's present imperative δίδου (Lk 11:3) for Matthew's aorist δὸς (Mt 6:11) and Luke's 'for each day,' (καθ' ἡμέραν) for Matthew's simple 'today' (σήμερον). Mathew's fifth petition is basically the same as in Luke except for his use of 'our debts' (τὰ ὀφειλήματα, Mt 6:12), where Luke has 'our sins' (τὰς ἁμαρτίας, Lk 11:4). Matthew's sixth petition is in verbatim agreement with Luke's fifth.

We see that Matthew has expanded this prayer with his theological perspective in mind. The prayer itself begin with (a) a typically Matthean formula as the invocation - "our Father in heaven"(v9b), which is followed by (b) three God-centered petitions, all of which employ 'divine passives,' thus referring to the agency of God in the fulfillment of the petition.[496] The third petition is Matthean with additional phrase "on earth as in heaven" (v10c) thus heightening his emphasis on God's glory and sovereignty. (c) The last four petitions involve inclusive ('us') petitions.

---

[495] Jeremias, *New Testament Theology* , 196; On observing the differences Hagner (*Matthew 1-13*, 145) is of the opinion that the prayer was handed down in slightly differing versions in churches of different geographical regions.

[496] Hagner, *Matthew 1-13*, 145.

4.2.2.4.2. Theological Explanation

4.2.2.4.2.1. Transcendent-Immanent Father

The invocation 'Our Father in heaven' is a typical Matthean expression and is loaded with theological significance. Juxtaposed in this address are the contrasting phrases, 'our Father,' pointing to the intimate relationship between God and his children, and 'in heaven,' pointing to his transcendent nature. Underlying the simple Πάτερ is the probable Aramaic original *Abba* (Mk 14:36), an affectionate and familial term which, according to Jeremias, began with Jesus, as a unique way of addressing God and that it has to do with his special consciousness of sonship to God.[497] Some noted scholars, however, are of the view that *Abba* in prayer is not unique to Jesus but conventional Jewish customary prayer of addressing God as 'our Father.'[498] While all the strata of the Gospel tradition (Mark, Q, M and L) agree that Jesus addressed God as Father in prayer,[499] but the very phrase 'in heaven' occurring along with the address 'Father' or 'Our Father' in prayer is found only in Matthew among the Synoptic Gospels. This is where our interest lies. Since the expression 'in heaven' is seen quite in opposition to 'our Father' several Matthean scholars see here Jesus' balancing portrayal of God, that is, expressing God's transcendence and immanence in complementary fashion.[500] However, some scholars understand that 'in heaven' has nothing to do with God's transcendence but instead the limitlessness of God,[501] or simply to contrast God with earthly fathers.[502] A comparison with Luke may help us in answering our query why Matthew alone retains this very expression of Jesus:

Mt 6:9b - Our Father in heaven ....
Lk 11:2 - Father ....

It is seen that Matthew has the added expression 'in heaven' to the simple Lukan Jesus' invocation 'Father.' And it is seen that 'Father in heaven' is one of Matthew's favorites. Yet on a closer look at its surrounding milieu reveal that this expression in not unique to Matthean Jesus. There are striking parallels to this invocation in the prayers of contemporary Jewish rabbis. In a number of rabbinic texts God is addressed with the title 'our Father in heaven.' Most of these expressions are found in the context of prayer in the aftermath of the destruction

---

497 Jeremias, *Prayer of Jesus*, 57; Jeremias, *New Testament Theology*, 67.

498 For argument towards this see, J.H. Charlesworth, *Jesus Within Judaism*, 134; G. Vermes, *Jesus the Jew*, 210-212.

499 For details of the distribution in all the five strata: Mark, Q, M. L and John, see Jeremias, *Prayer of Jesus*, 54.

500 Hagner, *Matthew 1-13*, 101, 148; Nolland, *The Gospel of Matthew*, 286; Osborne, *Matthew*, 227-228.

501 Plummer, *Matthew*, 97; E. Lohmeyer, *The Lord's Prayer*, 60.

502 Luz, *Matthew 1-7*, 377.

of the fall of Jerusalem Temple in 70 C.E. In several rabbinic texts, the writers associate the title with the destruction of Jerusalem or place it on the lips of rabbis whose lives are caught up in its aftermath. As such a passage in *Mishnah* (*m. Sotah* 9.15) talks about the laments of Phineas ben Jair thus:

> When the Temple was destroyed the Associates and the freemen were put to shame and walked with covered head, and the men of good works waxed feeble ... On whom can we stay ourselves? – on our Father in heaven.[503]

The next paragraph of the same passage similarly describes the laments of R. Eliezer ben Hyrcanus over the pathetic situation of life after the fall of the Jerusalem Temple. His account of the woes goes thus:

> Since the day that the Temple was destroyed the Sages began to be like school-teachers, and the school-teachers like synagogue-servants, and the synagogue-servants like the people of the land; and the people of the land waxed feeble, and there was none to seek [compassion for them]. On whom can we stay ourselves? – on our Father in heaven (*Sotah* 9.15).[504]

At the end of *m. Yoma*, which largely describes rituals of atonement which could no longer be enacted after the fall of the Temple, the authors cite a blessing of R. Akiba, who said:

> Blessed are ye, O Israel. Before whom are ye made clean and who makes clean? Your Father in heaven as it is written, *And I will sprinkle clean water upon you and you shall be clean.*[505]

The above instances show that the devastation by Roman army in 70 C.E. and its aftermath have contributed to increasing the importance of 'Father' in Jewish prayer in which the expression "Father in heaven" is found. Is Matthew following the same Jewish linguistic expression which became important in the synagogue particularly in the aftermath of Rome's destruction of Jerusalem and its Temple? Definitely Matthean Community suffered the same consequences with their fellow Jewish nations.[506] And since they are experiencing the same pain and suffering along with their fellow Jews, they seem to have the same convictions – affirming the fatherhood of God in prayer in dire straits.[507] That logically means

[503] Danby, *The Mishnah*, 306.

[504] Danby, *The Mishnah*, 306.

[505] Danby, *The Mishnah*, 172.

[506] S. Brown, *The Origins of Christianity: A Historical Introduction to the New Testament* (revised edition; Oxford: Oxford University Press, 1993), 118.

[507] Thus B. Chilton ("God as 'Father' in the Targumim, in Non-Canonical Literatures of Early Judaism and Primitive Christianity, and in Matthew," in *The Pseudepigrapha and Early Biblical*

that Matthew is responding to the same socio-political realities (Roman Imperial context) when he talks about God as specifically the heavenly Father.[508]

Following the invocation ("our Father in heaven") we have two God-oriented petitions in verse 9c ("Hallowed be your name") and 10 ("Your kingdom come. Your will be done, on earth as it is in heaven"). It has striking parallels to the Jewish prayer the *Qaddish*:

> Magnified and *sanctified* be his great *name* in the world which he hath created according to his will. May he establish his *kingdom* during your life and during your days, and during the life of all the house of Israel, even speedily and at near time, and say ye, Amen.[509] (italics added)

It is seen that the two petitions of the *Qaddish* corresponds to the first two petitions of the Lord's Prayer: the petition that the name of God be hallowed (or sanctified) and the petition that his kingdom come. The main difference is that whereas the petitions of the *Qaddish* are in the third person, those of the Matthean Lord's Prayer are in the second person. Here lies the very theological emphasis of Matthew. For him the expression 'in heaven' while seemingly acknowledging God as transcendent but, as the very address 'our Father' shows, God is very much near and down-to-earth. That is why Matthean Jesus teaches his disciples to speak directly to God their Father (in second person).

This God-oriented petition is that the sacredness of God's name be magnified in every area of life. God's name tells who he is at the core of his being. God's name represents his person and character,[510] so referring to the God's name points to his specific personal identity as made known in his deeds and self-revelation. To sanctify his name will involve fulfillment of his commands in conscious obedience.[511] The very next petition is again another God-oriented petition, "Your kingdom come" (v10a). Here Matthew parallels *Qaddish* prayer as seen above. It is said that for the Jews any prayer that fails to ask for the kingdom is not a true prayer.[512] So this Matthean Lord's prayer asks for the present kingdom

---

Interpretation, edited by J.H. Charlesworth and C.A. Evans [Sheffield: JSOT Press, 1993], 166 sees the expression quite conventional. So for him it means if within Judaism God was addressed as 'heavenly Father' for the purpose of prayer, especially as a resort in difficult times, so also Matthew and his community.

508 Carter (*Matthew and the Margins*, 2) reminds us that the tension within (Matthean community versus synagogue) was not Matthew's only point of reference, the difficulties of life in the Roman Empire must be factored in also. That is, Matthean community also resists the values, commitments, and agendas of the Roman Empire.

509 *The Authorized Daily Prayer Book of the United Hebrew Congregations*, 86.

510 *BAGD*, 712.

511 Nolland, *The Gospel of Matthew*, 287.

512 Luz, *Matthew 1-7*, 379.

to manifest itself in new ways, but especially asks that God end this present order and bring the kingdom in fullness.[513]

The third petition in verse 10b ("Your will be done, on earth as it is in heaven") is unique to Matthew. This God-oriented prayer sums up the other two petitions. All these three petitions have to do with God's character, reign and will on earth, that is, universally. For Matthew, God exercises an absolute claim upon the lives of all. Thus, the most important thing in life is that God's name be honoured and hallowed (v9). This hallowing of God's name, for Matthew, is carried out when (his kingdom comes and when) his will is done (v10). "To hallow him is to ascribe to him alone the kingdom, the power, and the glory."[514] By beginning and ending with him, the prayer expresses faith that all things begin and end with him. Thus this arrangement of three 'your' petitions projects Matthew's portrayal of God's fatherhood - the Father's holiness which is the source of their holiness. Thus once again we see his emphasis on God's fatherhood and sovereignty, that is, God being Father is supreme in everything, hence the petition "Your will be done."

However, this projection of God as 'heavenly' and so giving his due respect in acknowledging his holiness and splendor does not mean that he remains aloof from his children. God is at the same time 'our Father' because he has come near to his children by his grace, establishing an intimate relationship and community. God is an active God, who provides many things for his children including material things (v11). The petition in verse 11 thus talks about God's fatherly concern for his creation, as the very petition is for the provision of daily bread which is based on trust in the Father's providential care: "Give us this day our daily bread" (ἐπιούσιον δὸς ἡμῖν σήμερον).

A close look at its parallel in Luke (Q 11:3) shows that Matthew has slight changes in the expression 'this day' (ἡμῖν σήμερον) against Luke 'each day' (ἡμῖν τὸ καθ' ἡμέραν): "Give us each day our daily bread." The basic meaning is almost the same. God, in his fatherly kindness, is concerned for the provisions of the material needs.[515] In this direction some noted New Testament scholars see in this particular prayer, in the very expression ἐπιούσιος, an allusion to Exodus, where the Israelites' experiences the daily provision of manna from heaven "and gather enough for that day" (Ex 16:4).[516] Thus, the prayer for bread asks that God act in care for his people as he did in the Exodus. As provider of daily needs God is very much near and present. The same idea is seen in another pericope that Matthew

[513] Osborne, *Matthew*, 228.

[514] Minear, *God of the Gospels*, 43.

[515] For detail discussions on various meanings behind the expression 'daily' (*epiousios*) see *BAGD*, 296-297; see also the discussion on the same in Luke 11:3 in chapter three above.

[516] See Carter, *Matthew and the Margins*, 167; J.D. Crossan, *The Greatest Prayer: Rediscovering the Revolutionary Message of the Lord's Prayer* (London: SPCK, 2011), 138; C.A. Evans, *Matthew*, 147.

shares with Luke (so Q), but with some marked redactional emphasis of Matthew, to which we now turn.

4.2.2.5. Heavenly Father Who Knows All (6:24-33)

It is noteworthy that in the teaching of Matthean Jesus, there is a specific emphasis on God's fatherhood in relation to creation. In this pericope Matthean Jesus repeatedly reassures of God's special care for his creatures thus:

> Therefore I tell you, do not worry about your life, what you will eat or what you will drink, or about your body, what you will wear. Is not life more than food, and the body more than clothing? Look at the birds of the air; they neither sow nor reap nor gather into barns, and yet your heavenly Father feeds them. Are you not of more value than they? And can any of you by worrying add a single hour to your span of life? And why do you worry about clothing? Consider the lilies of the field, how they grow; they neither toil nor spin, yet I tell you, even Solomon in all his glory was not clothed like one of these. But if God so clothes the grass of the field, which is alive today and tomorrow is thrown into the oven, will he not much more clothe you– you of little faith? Therefore do not worry, saying, 'What will we eat?' or 'What will we drink?' or 'What will we wear?' For it is the Gentiles who strive for all these things; and indeed your heavenly Father knows that you need all these things. But strive first for the kingdom of God and his righteousness, and all these things will be given to you as well.

4.2.2.5.1. Matthean Redaction

The text comes from Q. But we see redactions of Matthew in some typical Matthean expressions, τὰ πετεινὰ τοῦ οὐρανοῦ, ὁ πατὴρ ὑμῶν ὁ οὐράνιος, αὐτῶν (v26); ὁ οὐράνιος (v32); καὶ τὴν δικαιοσύνην (v33). It is seen that while the term 'birds' (τὰ πετεινὰ, v26) may be available from his source Q, but Matthew has the more inclusive expressions in 'birds of the air' instead of 'ravens' in Q (=Lk 12:24). Matthew has changed the expression from 'God' to 'heavenly Father' in the parallel verse (6:26//Lk 12:24), in keeping with his theological emphasis on the fatherhood of God. Of course, the next occurrences of 'Father' is the same with Luke (6:32//Lk 12:30), except that Matthew has added with his favourite expression 'heavenly' again in line with his theological emphasis. The expression καὶ τὴν δικαιοσύνην αὐτοῦ in verse 33 is also added expression in Matthew. The expressions like τὰ πετεινὰ τοῦ οὐρανοῦ (6:26) and κρίνα τοῦ ἀγροῦ (6:28) are of course typical Old Testament phrases.[517]

---

[517] The former occurs some 34 times in LXX, while the latter are found in 2 Kings 19:26 and Jer 12:4; See, U. Luz, *Matthew 1-7: A Commentary* trans. by W.C. Linss (Minneapolis: Fortress, 1989), 401.

4.2.2.5.2. Theological Explanation

4.2.2.5.2.1. The Heavenly Father Who Cares

This pericope centers on the theme of worry, which is clearly evident in the rhetorical question posed by Matthean Jesus at verse 25: "Is not life more than food, and the body more than clothing?" Scholars see this argument in the manner of rabbinic debate: an argument from the major to the minor (or its reverse, for the minor to the major).[518] That is, if God has given life (the major), then does it not follow that he will provide that which is needed to sustain life (the minor)? So in this very rhetoric of Matthean Jesus the implication is precisely to do with the fatherhood of God: it is the 'heavenly Father' (v26) who takes care of all. The Fatherhood of God is clearly linked to providence here. Once God takes care of the 'higher,' of life and body; surely he will take care also for the 'smaller,' food and clothing.

The argument continues with vivid illustrations from rural sceneries: "Look at the birds of the air … Consider the lilies of the field" (vv26-28). The idea of God as creator and provider is clearly seen in the wisdom literatures of the Old Testament (e.g., Ps 104; 147:9; Job 53:11). The rabbinic and Stoics literatures too have such idea expressed. Rabbi Simeon ben Eleazar is remembered to have argued similarly, even if his main argument was different: "Hast thou ever seen a wild animal or a bird practicing their craft? Yet they have their sustenance without care" (*m. Kiddushin* 4:14).[519] Similarly, the Stoic writer Epictetus talks about God's providential care thus:

> Consider what it would be for us to have to take thought not for merely ourselves, but also for our sheep and our ass, how they are to be clothed and shod, how they are to find food and drink. But just as soldiers appear before their general, all ready for service, shod, clothed and armed ….[520]

Discourse on the providence of God is not new to Matthew and Luke. It has its roots in Old Testament and also has strong affinity with the surrounding religious and philosophical milieus, yet it is Matthew alone who dares to speak of God in a human term: "your heavenly Father feeds them" (v26); "your heavenly Father knows that you need all these things" (v32). In other words, it is Matthew who blended the very transcendent God or rather the idea of a cosmic fatherhood with day-to-day personal expressions in '(your) heavenly Father.'[521]

---

[518] R.J. Dillon, "Ravens, Lilies, and the Kingdom of God (Matt 6:25-33/Luke 12:22-31)," in *CBQ* 53 (1991), 612-613.

[519] Danby, *The Mishnah*, 329.

[520] *Discourses* 1.16.3-5, *Epictetus* I, 109.

[521] See H.D. Betz, *Essays on the Sermon on the Mount* (Philadelphia: Fortress, 1985), 120; but he attribute this idea to a pre-Matthean redactor and opines that the ethics in this pericope of the

4.2.2.5.2.2. God's Fatherhood and Nature

Here Matthean Jesus while bringing the illustration from nature (birds, lilies) deliberately linked it with human activities, of sowing and harvesting (v26), of toiling and spinning (v28). U. Luz would paraphrase this illustration in this way, "In distinction from you, the birds do not sow and harvest; how much more will then God care for you who do work?"[522] That means, for Luz, the illustration presupposes that humankind work. However, the focus is not on the human labor but rather the argument here, which involves the world of human toils and activities, heightens the strong emphasis on the fatherhood of God. The nonworking creatures (birds and lilies) are testimony to God's concern.[523] The emphasis of Matthew here is on God's fatherhood which is seen in the gifts of nature. Thus we see the concentration of God's fatherly nature in creation.

The futility and the limitation of human worry is continued in the following verses (30-33). The expression that recurs throughout this pericope is of course 'worry' (vv25, 27, 28, 31, and 34) and the argument seems to revolve around two structures that set up opposite each other: the human world of cares and the world of birds and flowers, where care is absent but life goes on.[524] This is heightened not only by the targeted argument in verse 30 ("If God so clothes the grass of the field, which is alive today and tomorrow is thrown into the oven, will he not much more clothe you - you of little faith?"[525]) but also by the concluding exhortative expression in verse 34. C.H. Talbert sees the whole of this pericope as to do with insiders, that is, disciples. For him this text "is designed to serve as catalyst for the formation of the character of disciples in the direction of trust in God's providential goodness by enabling them to see a different kind of world."[526] While the subject of 'worry and anxiety' is present as the recurring argument shows, but underlying this pericope is Matthean Jesus' projection of the 'heavenly Father' who cares for all, not only the world of human but also of nature, of birds, lilies and grass. Put it bluntly, for Matthew God's fatherhood is seen in the gifts of nature. Thus in terms of his providence, God's fatherhood is universal.

It is interesting to notice in this pericope rich expressions of nature and economy in relation to the fatherhood of God: the expressions like 'birds of the air' (v26), 'lilies' (v28) and 'grass of the field' (v30) vividly illustrates the open air and wild nature; while expressions like sowing and reaping (v26), toiling

---

Sermon on the Mount is at home in the context of Jewish piety and theology (Betz, *Essays on the Sermon on the Mount*, 123).

522 Luz, *Matthew 1-7*, 405; see also Bultmann, "μεριμνάω," in *TDNT* IV, 592.

523 Luz, *Matthew 1-7*, 405.

524 Talbert, *Reading the Sermon on the Mount*, 129.

525 Jesus calls his disciples as 'those having little faith,' a favorite redactional emphasis of Matthew in keeping with his theme of discipleship.

526 Talbert, *Reading the Sermon on the Mount*, 129-130.

and spinning (v28) illustrates human economy. While the Psalmist in the Old Testament said of the birds that they had their food from God (Ps 147:9), but here we see them bringing closer into the human family, as Matthean Jesus says "your heavenly Father feeds them" (v26). As such we notice here that the life of nature has spoken in a very strong way the character of God, of God's delight in beauty and God's love and care.

The same projection of a down-to-earth God who is interested in the day-to-day activities of humankind is clearly seen in another pericope that Matthew shares with Luke (so Q) to which we now turn.

4.2.2.6. Good Things for the Children (7:9-11)

In the context of teaching on persistence in asking (7:7-11) Matthew has again put forth the idea of God's fatherhood to the fore as Matthean Jesus compares the goodness of God to the attitude of a human father:

> Is there anyone among you who, if your child asks for bread, will give a stone? Or if the child asks for a fish, will give a snake? If you then, who are evil, know how to give good gifts to your children, how much more will your Father in heaven give good things to those who ask him!

4.2.2.6.1. Matthean Redaction

This pericope, which is a self-contained unit, has its parallel in Luke 11:9-13. Most of the expressions in verses 7-10 are in verbatim agreement with Luke except this verse (v11) where we see two very important differences with Luke as Matthew has 'good things' instead of Luke 'Holy Spirit,' and a more intimate and closer expression of God as 'your Father' instead of simply 'the heavenly Father' in Luke.

4.2.2.6.2. Theological Explanation

4.2.2.6.2.1. God as Provider and Nourisher

The focus of this pericope is once again on the nature of God. Matthean Jesus invites his disciples to rely upon the faithfulness of their heavenly Father. The threefold invitation and promise of verse 7, emphasized in verse 8, have as their main point the disciples may confidently trust God. It points to the basic principle of God's comprehensive and faithful care of the disciples. Following the instruction on asking, searching and knocking (vv7-8), Matthean Jesus put forth two rhetorical questions in the following pericope (vv9-10): "Is there anyone among you who, if your child asks for bread, will give a stone? Or if the child asks for a fish, will give a snake?" The Lukan parallel reads egg/scorpion (Lk 11:12), but the logic is the same. A loaf of bread is a necessity for life; a stone is worthless. No father would give his child a stone instead of the requested loaf of bread and no father would give a snake instead of the requested fish. The reasoning is that "a human being is one who is good to one's children."[527] With this reasoning, Matthean Jesus drives home his point in verse 11: "If you then, who are evil, know how to give good gifts to your children, how much more will your Father in heaven give good things to those who ask him!"

The structure of argument is, similar to that found in 6:24-33, from the minor (evil human fathers who give good gifts to their children) to the major (the heavenly Father who gives good gifts to his children). So in this very rhetoric of Matthean Jesus the implication is again to do with the fatherhood of God: it is the 'heavenly Father' (v11) who takes care of even the physical and material needs of his children. The Fatherhood of God is unmistakably linked to providence here. The 'good things' (ἀγαθὰ) certainly points to the ongoing needs of the disciples – the material aspect (cf. 6: 24-33), thus the focus is on the providing Father. It is he who provides the material blessings of the present. God is much more ready to give 'good things' to his own than the earthly fathers. Thus Matthew here presents a very "human and immediate picture of God."[528] It is here that we see a heavenly Father very much linked with the day-to-day lives of humankind here on earth.

4.2.2.6.2.2. Heavenly Father with a Human Heart

While the idea of a sky-god or Father God is present in almost all the ancient religions, but in most cases God is understood as a high-god who stays aloof and the people in antiquity were living in utter fear and respect of him.[529] In the Old Testament such idea of God is seen in the emphasis on the holiness of God so much so that even addressing God is also done by way of circumlocution.[530] The book of Isaiah is a classic example where the prophet talks about the terrifying "otherness of God" in chapter 6.[531] Even in first century Judaism God is addressed in numerous substitutes or circumlocutions, and which means that God is aloof and distant.[532] In ancient Greek religions too God as Father is mainly understood in this sense of fathering or begetting.[533] He is considered as the foremost and the supreme deity,[534] hence an All-Father, who is just a high-god, aloof without any

---

527 Betz, *Sermon on the Mount*, 505.

528 J.R. Donahue, "A Neglected Factor in the Theology of Mark," in *JBL* 101 (1982), 567.

529 W.B. Selbie, *The Fatherhood of God* (London: Duckworth, 1936), 27.

530 E. Jacob (*Theology of the Old Testament* [London: Hodder & Stoughton, 1958], 89) observed that God is called 'Holy One of Israel' for more than 60 times.

531 John N. Oswalt, *The Book of Isaiah Chapters 1-39* (NICOT; Grand Rapids: Wm B Eerdmans, 1986), 33.

532 M.M Thompson, *The Promise of the Father: Jesus and God in the New Testament*, 66.

533 C.H. Moore, *The Religious Thought of the Greeks: From Homer to the Triumph of Christianity* (Cambridge: Harvard University Press, 1916), 18; G. Murray, *Five Stages of Greek Religion* (Oxford: Clarendon Press, 1925), 25.

534 Martin P. Nilsson, *A History of Greek Religion*, 145.

concern for the welfare of his offspring. If at all he is called Father it has to do with his paternal power and despotic nature[535] but nothing to do with the practical relations with his children. But here in Matthew, in stark contrast to such a nature, we see a personal approachable God who is addressed as 'our Father' (cf. 6:9) and who is projected as very much attentive and active in the affairs of humankind in their day-to-day lives (7:11). Unlike the Greek idea of relationship with deity based on begetting or birth, Matthean idea of the fatherhood of God has to do with his loving care and concern. In the projection of Matthew God is interested in the very life and activities of humankind on earth. For Matthew, God is a living, loving and a personal Father. This very idea is all the more strengthened by the use of 'good things,' which means, material needs. The transcendent God (heavenly Father) is at the same time a down-to-earth Father for Matthew. Thus, God is expressed uniquely in "a mythical-personal manner."[536] This is where we see unique Matthean emphasis on the fatherhood of God. Such a picture of God as a compassionate and humane Father is also evident in some of the unique parables of Matthew to which we now turn.

4.2.3. Fatherhood of God in Matthean Community Discourse

4.2.3.1. Heavenly Father and τῶν μικρῶν τούτων (18:10-14)

Set within a context centering on the church Matthean Jesus speaks to his disciples (18:1) concerning care for God's little ones:

> Take care that you do not despise one of these little ones; for, I tell you, in heaven their angels continually see the face of my Father in heaven. What do you think? If a shepherd has a hundred sheep, and one of them has gone astray, does he not leave the ninety-nine on the mountains and go in search of the one that went astray? And if he finds it, truly I tell you, he rejoices over it more than over the ninety-nine that never went astray. So it is not the will of your Father in heaven that one of these little ones should be lost.

4.2.3.1.1. Matthean Redaction

As part of the community discourse (ch 18) this pericope is centered on community life. Since the parable proper in this pericope (about the lost sheep, vv12,13)

---

[535] In the writings of Homer Zeus' despotic nature is seen in that upon Zeus arrival on Olympus, "the whole company of gods rose from their chairs in deference to their Father. There was not one that dared to keep his seat as he approached; they all stood up to greet him" (*Iliad* I.533-535, trans E.V. Rieu, 37).

[536] Betz (*Essays on the Sermon on the Mount*, 120) attributes the whole of the Sermon on the Mount to a pre-synoptic author, and so as regard to this idea of God he remarks that "the SM is not afraid to speak of God in a mythical-personal manner, in contrast to the Hellenistic tendency to depersonalize the deity."

has its parallel in Luke (15:3-7), it is assumed that Matthew draws from Q, but verses 10 and 14 are unique to Matthew, which means that it is drawn from his special source (M). It is striking to see the pairing of 'little ones' with 'my Father in heaven' in verse 10, and the same 'little ones' with 'your Father in heaven' in verse 14. This is a deliberate Matthean arrangement keeping his emphasis on the fatherhood of God. Unlike in Luke (so Q), which is set within a context in which Jesus makes response to the criticism of the Pharisees and scribes that he receives sinners and eats with them (Lk 15:1-2),[537] Matthew's version is set within a context in which Jesus speaks to his disciples (18:1) concerning care for God's 'little ones' (18:6,10,14). But the main focus of Matthew lies in the culminating expression, "So it is not the will of your Father in heaven that one of these little ones should be lost" (18:14). Here Matthew's focus is on the fatherhood of God, God does not will even the loss of a little one (18:14). The compassionate nature of God is thus clearly brought out.

4.2.3.1.2. Theological Explanation

4.2.3.1.2.1. The Father's Concern for the Little Ones

As seen above this pericope makes an important contribution to the community discourse (ch 18), which is centered on community life. To emphasize the value of "these little ones," Matthean Jesus makes the remarkable claim that "in heaven their angels continually see the face of my Father in heaven" (v10). The focus here is on the 'little ones,' which is taken up from verse 6. Matthew in no way assigns who these little ones are. We see Matthew using the same term in 10:42 and similar language in 11:25 ('infants'). So in this context when Matthew is talking about church discipline, it is easy to see them as the disciples (v6). Of course Matthew's focus is more on those who are weak and vulnerable. Children, babes and little ones are members of the community who appear in the world's eyes as those of little social standing. They are the poor, meek and persecuted of the beatitudes (5:3-12) to whom it is given to posses the Kingdom of the heavens. The little ones of 10:42 and the little ones of 18:10 are believers with whom Matthean Jesus especially identifies. They are disciples and members of the community.[538] The term 'little ones' here "expresses the vulnerability of disciples in their difficult, against-the-grain existence centered on Jesus."[539] As such it highlights the disciples' vulnerability and marginality.[540]

---

[537] So Luke (so Q) stresses is on God who rejoices over the repentance of a sinner who needs it (Lk 15:7).

[538] A.J. Hultgren, *The Parables of Jesus: A Commentary* (Grand Rapids: Wm B. Eerdmans, 2000), 54; M. Hannan, *The Nature and Demands of the Sovereign Rule of God*, 158.

[539] Carter, *Matthew and the Margins*, 364.

[540] Carter, *Matthew and the Margins*, 365.

4.2.3.1.2.2. Angel of the All-Seeing Father

The reason for respecting all fellow believers and treating them well is because "in heaven their angels continually see the face of my Father." The language here speaks of a present beholding in God's presence. Thus the literal sense seems to be very strong here as several scholars[541] understand that Matthew is here adopting the traditional Jewish beliefs in guardian angels as found in Old Testament (e.g. Job 33:23; Ps 34:7; 91:11) and other Jewish literatures. For example, the book of *Jubilees* talks about "the angels of the presence"[542] being created on the first day of creation. The book of Tobit talks about the protection that the angel Raphael provided to young Tobias, "I am Raphael, one of the seven angles who stand ready and enter before the glory of the Lord" (12:15). Thus some scholars understand this expression of Matthew as individual guardian angels as expressed in the book of Tobit. Witherington comments that these little ones are so important that they have the top angels representing them in heaven, who have direct access to the face of God.[543] However, Hagner[544] and France[545] understand this in a general way that the expression is not about individual guardian angels but angelic representations of the 'little ones' as a group before the throne of God. While for D. A. Carson these are not angels but the departed spirits after death that sees the Father's face.[546]

Even in today's world people believe in the reality of guardian angels and celestial beings. For a certain noted psychic and medium by name Kyle Gray these guardian angels are divine beings of God, and as extensions of God's love they flow and move with humankind.[547] It seems Matthew too employs this expression in order to heighten his emphasis on the care and compassion of God. Matthew wanted to convey that through these angels, the community is within Gods' care. For him, to look into the interests of 'these little ones' just like any other in the community, as "each follower is special to God, and there is no place for disdain on the part of anyone."[548] So by adding this very enigmatic verse Matthew wanted

---

[541] See D.C. Allison, *Studies in Matthew* (Grand Rapids, Michigan: Baker Academics, 2005), 48, n. 22; E. Koskenniemi, "Forgotten Guardians and Matthew 18:10," in *TynBul* 61 (2010), 119-129; Evans, *Matthew*, 332.

[542] *Jubilees* 2:2, trans O.S. Wintermute, in *OTP* II, 55.

[543] B. Witherington III, *Matthew* (SHBC; Macon; GA: Smyth & Helwys, 2006), 348.

[544] D.A. Hagner, *Matthew 14-28* (WBC 33B; Texas: Word Books, 1995), 527.

[545] R.T. France, *The Gospel of Matthew* (NICNT; Grand Rapids: Wm B. Eerdmans, 2007), 686-687.

[546] D.A. Carson, "Matthew," in *The Expositor's Bible Commentary* vol 8 (Grand Rapids: Zondervan, 1984), 401.

[547] Reported in *The Times of India* (Sunday Times), May 12, 2013 under the caption, "Angels talk to me."

[548] Osborne, *Matthew*, 681.

to project that God is a compassionate Father, who cares for all, more so for the least and the lost.

4.2.3.1.2.3. A Compassionate Shepherd

In the following verses (vv12-13), the parable proper on the lost sheep, which he shares with Luke, the focus is once again on the compassionate nature of God. And verse 14 is the application: just as a shepherd does for the safety of each and every sheep, so God does for each and every one irrespective of their status. This parable is reminiscent of a passage in Ezekiel where God is portrayed as a good shepherd (Ezek 34:11-16), part of which reads, "For thus says the Lord GOD: I myself will search for my sheep, and will seek them out. As shepherds seek out their flocks when they are among their scattered sheep, so I will seek out my sheep ... I will seek the lost, and I will bring back the strayed ...." Here God describes himself as the good shepherd. He rescues the sheep from all places where "they have been scattered on a day of cloud and thick darkness" (v12) and leads the flock to where there are good pastures (v14). The same idea of a good shepherd is found here in Matthew.

In verse 13 the word μᾶλλον ('more than') indicates God rejoices over the returned sheep 'more than' those who remained in the fold. The parable ends with a moving statement unique to Matthew: "So it is not the will of your Father in heaven that one of these little ones should be lost" (v14). God, the Father in heaven, is the compassionate shepherd shepherding the flock and searching persistently for straying ones. For Matthew, God is portrayed as the seeking shepherd. God prefers the least important sheep to the most important. He searches for the lost sheep, finds it, and rejoices over its recovery. Thus the parable implicitly defines the extent of God's care and the sufficiency of his knowledge.[549] While the imagery of God as shepherd is not unique to Matthew, yet his redactional emphasis of 'the little ones' at the beginning and end of the parable shows his theological emphasis that God loves all, that God is a compassionate God, who cares for the least and the lost. The whole pericope has thus centered on the compassion and mercy of God. Similar emphasis on God's unconditional love and mercy and so God's fatherhood is seen in another parable unique to Matthew to which we now turn.

4.2.3.2. Forgiveness from Heart (18:23-35)

This parable appears only in the Gospel of Matthew. It is located at the close of a chapter (18:1-35) which is usually classified as one of the five major discourse sections of Matthew (along with chapters 5-7, 10, 13 and 24-25). The chapter consists primarily of teachings of Jesus concerning the relationship of Jesus' disciples to one another. At the level of the Gospel, it is devoted for the most part to ecclesiastical discipline.[550] Just prior to the parable Peter asks the question how

---

549 Minear, *The God of the Gospels*, 46.

550 Hultrgen, *The Parables of Jesus*, 22.

often he should forgive his brother or sister, suggesting that seven times might suffice (18:21). In response to which comes this parable where Matthean Jesus tells about a king and his hugely indebted slave (vv23-35):

> For this reason the kingdom of heaven may be compared to a king who wished to settle accounts with his slaves. When he began the reckoning, one who owed him ten thousand talents was brought to him; and, as he could not pay, his lord ordered him to be sold, together with his wife and children and all his possessions, and payment to be made. So the slave fell on his knees before him, saying, 'Have patience with me, and I will pay you everything.' And out of pity for him, the lord of that slave released him and forgave him the debt. But that same slave, as he went out, came upon one of his fellow slaves who owned a hundred denarii; and seizing him by the throat, he said, 'Pay what you owe.' Then his fellow slave fell down and pleaded with him, 'have patience with me, and I will pay you.' But he refused; then he went and threw him into prison until he would pay the debt. When his fellow slaves saw what had happened, they were greatly distressed, and they went and reported to their lord all that has taken place. Then his lord summoned him and said to him, 'You wicked slave! I forgave you all that debt because you pleaded with me. Should you not have had mercy on your fellow slave?' And in anger his lord handed him over to be tortured until he would pay his entire debt. So my heavenly Father will also do to every one of you, if you do not forgive your brother or sister from your heart.

4.2.3.2.1. Matthean Redaction

While Matthean redaction is clearly seen not only at the very beginning and ending verses with his favorite expressions, 'the kingdom of heaven may be compared to' (v23a), and 'heavenly Father'(v35), but also on the overall focus of the parable, that is, the compassionate nature of God. In other words, the parable is founded on the compassion that flows from God, which means the emphasis is again on the fatherhood of God.

4.2.3.2.2. Theological Explanation

4.2.3.2.2.1. God as Forgiving and Compassionate King

The parable begins with typical Matthean formula 'therefore' (διὰ τοῦτο cf. 13:24, 31, 33, 45, 47; 20:1; 22:2; 25:1). This expression is usually used in Matthew to introduce a dominical pronouncement within a discourse in order to elaborate a point (6:25; 12:31; 13:52; 21:43; 23:34; 24:44). So that means it has to do with the theme of forgiveness as a kingdom characteristics.[551] The expression ὡμοιώθη

[551] Hultgren, *The Parables of Jesus*, 23.

is also found only in Matthew in the introduction of parables (13:24 and 22:2) and it leads the reader to connect the king with God to whom the kingdom belongs.[552]

As the parable says 'a king (βασιλεύς) wished to settle accounts with his slaves' (δοῦλοι). The term 'king' as referring to God is again found only in Matthew eight times, out of which seven occurrences are in parables.[553] Interestingly, the term 'lord' (ὁ κυρίος) too occurs five times in this parable thus heightening the sovereign nature of God, the 'Lord' of all. And as the parable follows we will see the term 'Father in heaven' occurs in the culminating verse (v35). That means to say that the occurrence of three theocentric terms 'king,' 'lord' and 'Father' in the same pericope is a deliberate Matthean arrangement in line with his emphasis on the centrality of God's fatherhood.

The parable goes on saying that one of the slaves owed the king ten thousand talents (v24), and the textual notes of the NRSV say that "a talent was worth more than fifteen years' wages of a laborer." Several scholars believe that Matthew is behind this exaggerated figure, and that Jesus originally had a lower figure.[554] Of course, elsewhere in Jewish literature the mention of the same figure is seen. According to Josephus, the Romans exacted ten thousand talents from the Jews after Pompey's conquest of Palestine (63 B.C.E.).[555] Carter sees socio-political reality here saying that "the figure evoke Rome's action and reflects proverbial notions of the wealth of kings and of oppressive taxation."[556] In verses 24 and 25 we see the king ordered one of his debtors (slaves) to pay back his huge dues owed to him. The brutal nature is clearly seen in verse 25. The king was compelled to confiscate all his debtor's belongings including his wife and children (v25). We see a similar illustration in Philo describing the inhuman treatment of some debtors by a certain tax collector:

> When some of his debtors whose default was clearly due to poverty took flight in fear of the fatal consequences of his vengeance, he carried off by force their womenfolk and children and parents and their other relatives and beat and subjected them to every kind of outrage and contumely in order to make then either tell him the whereabouts of the fugitives or discharge his debt themselves.[557]

---

[552] D.A. Carson, "The OMOIOS Word-Group as Introduction to Some Matthean Parables," in *NTS* 31 (1985), 278.

[553] Mt 18:23; 22:1-14 [x4]; 25:31-46 [x2].

[554] Jeremias, *The Parables of Jesus* (2nd revised edition; New York: Scribner's, 1972), 30; M.C. De Boer, "Ten Thousand Talents? Matthew's Interpretation and Redaction of the Parable of the Unforgiving Servant (Matt 18:23-35)," in *CBQ* 50 (1988), 229; W.D. Davies and D.C. Allison, *The Gospel according to Saint Matthew* II (ICC; Edinburgh: T&T Clark, 1991), 796.

[555] Josephus, *Antiquities*14.78.

[556] Carter, *Matthew and the Margins*, 372.

[557] *De Specialibus legibus* 3:159, Philo VII, 575.

The similarity of this illustration in Philo's account with that of Matthean parable is striking and it may perhaps throw light on the sociological reality of the time, the exploitation of the poor and debt manipulation. As such Luise Schottroff too sees vital truth behind this parable as a whole. For her, this parable presumes two fundamental situations in the ancient financial economy: the brutality of the collection of taxes and of debts.[558] But the main point of Matthew seems to be theological rather than sociological, that is, the magnitude of the debt on the part of the slave as well as forgiveness on the part of the king. Thus the vivid description of the brutal actions of the king (v25) and the subsequent plea on the part of the slave (v26) heightens the enormity of the debt again, only to be culminated in the act of forgiveness on the part of the king (v27). That is, projecting the magnanimous heart (forgiving) of the king. The occurrence of the very expression σπλαγχνισθεὶς is noteworthy here. The term σπλαγχνίζομαι is used in Matthew and the Gospels mostly in reference to the divine compassion that is revealed in Jesus (cf. 9:36; 14:14).[559]

In verses 28-30, it is seen that a significant amount of debt is not forgiven. According to J.W. Betlyon, a denarius was a silver coin worth one day's wages for a common laborer.[560] So that means the amount of hundred denarii represents a hundred days of earnings by a common laborer, which is a significant amount. Now we are compelled to compare the slave with the king with whom he had encountered similar experience as seen in the preceding verses. It is seen that the debts of the slave, which he owed to the king (ten thousand talents, v24) is much more greater than what his fellow slave owe him (hundred denarii, v28), but the way he treats his debtor (fellow slave) seems to be much more brutal than what the king did to him, "seizing him by the throat" and insisting to pay (v28).[561] Once again this hyperbolic expression also heightens Matthean emphasis on the theme of forgiveness: the unforgiving slave does not do for the other slave what the king has already done for him. He hypocritically accepts mercy but is not willing to grant it to another and hence the consequences.

The parable ends with the punishment being meted out by the king to the former slave (vv31-34), and a moving expression of Matthean Jesus culminates it (v35).[562] It is seen that the story which began with the king's compassion ends

---

[558] Luise Schottroff, *The Parables of Jesus* (trans Linda M. Maloney; Minneapolis: Fortress Press, 2006), 198.

[559] Cf. Helmut Koester, "σπλάγχνον," in *TDNT* VII, 553-55.

[560] John W. Betlyon, "Coinage," in *ABD* I, 1086.

[561] The imagery of seizing a debtor by the throat is found also in *m. Baba Batra* 10:8, See Danby, *Mishnah*, 382.

[562] The imperative on the forgiveness of fellow human beings is also found in *Mishnah*: "For transgressions that are between man and God the day of Atonement effects atonement, but for transgressions that are between man and his fellow the Day of Atonement effects atonement only if he has appeased his fellow" (*m. Yoma* 8:9, See Danby, *Mishnah*, 172).

with his harsh judgment against the slave who did not act compassionately. It is heightened by the apparently threatening expression of the concluding verse, which seems to be the application of the parable, "So my heavenly Father will also do to every one of you, if you do not forgive your brother or sister from your heart" (v35). Some see apparent contradictions here, as it is seen that the unforgiving slave is punished (vv31-34) quite contrary to the idea of unlimited forgiveness stressed in verse 21 and 22!

In dealing with such apparent discrepancy in this parable L. Schottroff suggests a non-allegorical approach, saying that the king in the parable and his actions are not an image of God. She suggests a different rendering to the crucial expression 'so' (οὕτως) in verse 35 as 'How is this, then, to be compared to the kingdom of God?' so that the application will be that 'God is not like this king' or 'God is not so.'[563] De Boer finds strong Matthean redactional activities in verse 35, and sees this expression in line with ecclesiastical instruction of vv15-20. Thus, for him 'brothers and sisters' in verse 35 are the fellow insiders of verse 21.[564] That means for him this parable is presented in exclusive Christian (Matthean) community. But elsewhere in Matthew, the expressions 'brothers and sisters' are used in inclusive universal sense. Matthew 12:50 stressed that '(my) brother and sister' are those who do the will of '(my) Father in heaven.'

C. G. Montefiore, who sees the moral of this parable as thoroughly Rabbinic, observes nothing new to this kind of apparent discrepancy. He takes an example in the reply of R. Yose, who was once asked for an explanation of the apparent discrepancy between Deuteronomy 10:17 on the idea of impartiality of God and Numbers 6:26, on the idea of favoritism, to which, according to Montefiore, the rabbi simply give his explanation in the form of a parable. The parable goes like this:

> A man borrows money from another, and in the king's presence swears by the life of the king that he will repay by a certain date. When he cannot pay, he asks the kings' forgiveness, who replies, The insult to me is forgiven you; now go and ask your neighbor for *his* forgiveness. God forgives sin against himself; but the injured neighbor's forgiveness must be sought as well.[565]

Like the parable of the unforgiving slave here in Matthew, this cited parable also talks about genuineness (to keep one's promise). But there is a slight difference. In this rabbinic story the king is not involved as the actual lender but stands as a witness before two persons. But in Matthew, as seen above, the king is very much involved in the actual business right from the very beginning. He lends and asks for settling accounts with his slaves (vv23-27). But in the second scene Matthean

[563] Schottroff, *The Parables of Jesus*, 202-203.

[564] De Boer, "Ten Thousand Talents? Matthew's Interpretation and Redaction of the Parable," 220.

[565] C. G. Montefiore, *Rabbinic Literature and Gospel Teachings*, 269.

parable reminisces the rabbinic parable clearly: the issue involved between the two slaves as lender-borrowers was brought to the notice of the king (v31) and the king acts a judge (vv32-34). And the message of both the parable is obviously the same – it has to do with a generous and a forgiving heart. The presupposition of it all, however, is the message of God's compassion and mercy. That means that the fatherhood of God is the underpinning of this parable of Matthew.

4.2.3.2.2.2. God's Unconditional Love

Whether this parable comes from the lips of Jesus or not does not matter to us; rather our interest is what Matthew wanted to convey. The hearer and reader are reminded again and again about the fatherhood of God, that God in his fatherly nature deals with his children by grace in a way that surpasses all human calculations of compassion or mercy. The first slave requests the king to be compassionate toward him and his family; he asks for more time (v26). The king subsequently cancels the slave's entire debt (v27). Compassion (v27) and mercy (v33) are extended beyond what anyone could expect.[566] So beyond this apparently contradictory expression – the idea of a vengeful Father! – in verse 35, lies the central emphasis of Matthew, that is, the idea of a compassionate and forgiving Father quite in line with his emphasis elsewhere (e.g., 5:48; 18:10-14). In this perspective Anders Nygren's comment is to the point:

> The feature of the Divine Agape that is most prominent here is its boundless and its unconditional character. But if God's love and His will to forgive is boundless and unconditional, it demands of those who receive its forgiveness that their love and forgiveness shall likewise be boundless and unconditional.[567]

The same emphasis on the goodness and compassionate nature of God is seen in another unique parable in Matthew to which we now turn.

4.2.3.3. Generous Father (20:1-16)

Set within the Judean ministry (19:1-20:34) prior to Jesus' entry into Jerusalem (21:1), Matthean Jesus tells a parable concerning the recruitment of laborers by a landowner (lit. 'householder') for his vineyard. The parable, which is introduced right at the beginning as a parable of the kingdom of heaven (v1) talks about the recruitment of laborers throughout a day:

> For the kingdom of heaven is like a landowner who went out early in the morning to hire laborers for his vineyard. After agreeing with the laborers for the usual daily wage, he sent them into his vineyard. When he went out about nine o' clock, he saw others standing idle in

---

[566] Hultgren, *The Parables of Jesus*, 30.

[567] A. Nygren, *Agape and Eros* (trans Philip M. S. Watson; New York: Harper & Row, 1969), 91.

> the market place; and he said to them, 'You also go into the vineyard, and I will pay you whatever is right.' So they went. When he went out about noon and about three o'clock, he did the same. And about five o'clock he went out and found others standing around; and he said to them, 'Why are you standing here idle all day?' They said to him, 'Because no one has hired us,' He said to them, 'You also go into the vineyard.' When evening came, the owner of the vineyard said to his manager, 'Call the laborers and give them their pay, beginning with the last and then going to the first.' When those hired about five o'clock came, each of them received the usual daily wage. Now when the first came, they thought they would receive more; but each of them also received the usual daily wage. And when they receive it, they grumbled against the landowner, saying 'These last worked only one hour, and you have made them equal to us who have borne the burden of the day and the scorching heat.' But he replied to one of them, 'Friend, I am doing you no wrong; did you not agree with me for the usual daily wage? Take what belong to you and go; I choose to give to this last the same as I give to you. Am I not allowed to do what I choose with what belongs to me? Or are you envious because I am generous?' So the last will be first, and the first will be last.'

4.2.3.3.1 Matthean Redaction

This parable is found only in Matthew and so that means it comes from his special material (M). Matthean characteristics in this parable are his typical introductory formula, 'the kingdom of heaven is like' (v1); the idea of 'householder cum vineyard owner' (cf. the idea of 'householder cum farm-owner' in 13: 24-30); the expression of role reversal at the end (v16 cf. 19:30). This parable centers on God's reversal of human concepts of reward on the basis of God's grace rather than human effort (vv15-16). This clearly indicates his theological emphasis, that is, on the nature of God.

4.2.3.3.2 Theological Explanation

4.2.3.3.2.1. God as Gracious Householder-Employer

Right at the very beginning this pericope is introduced as a parable of the kingdom of God (20:1) For Matthew, here the mention of householder (οἰκοδεσπότης) and the vineyard seems to have an Old Testament allusion echoing Israel as God's vineyard and the owner represents God (cf. Isa 5:1-7; Jer 12:10; Mt 21:28, 33-41).[568] The use of the 'master' or 'lord' for the landowner in verse 8 (ὁ κύριος τοῦ ἀμπελῶνος) heightens the allusion to God. So the landowner who goes out to hire laborers is a metaphor for God. Elsewhere in Jewish literatures we find

[568] Hultgren, *The Parables of Jesus*, 36; Turner, *Matthew*, 480; Osborne, *Matthew*, 728.

similar parables where the metaphorical representation of God as employer (a king) is seen. A parable told by a certain Rabbi Zeira tells of a king who hired many workers, and he noticed that one was especially skillful. He asked the man to accompany him as he walked out. At the end of the day he paid him the same amount as he paid the other workers. The workers grumbled, and the story continues:

> We have been working hard all the day, and this one who only laboured two hours receives as much salary as we do. "It is," answered the king, "because he has done more in two hours than you in the entire day."[569]

Like the parable of Matthew (20:1-16), this parable speaks of equal pay for all, regardless of the hours worked. But there is a major difference between them. In this story the one who receives pay equal to all the rest is given such because he has "done more in two hours" than those who worked "the entire day." That is, the payment is made on the efficiency and merit basis. But in this parable of Matthean Jesus, those who receive pay equal to all the rest are recipients of the extreme generosity of a very unusual employer; there is no hint that they performed as much work as or more than the others. As such this parable can rightly be understood in line with Matthean theological emphasis on the universality of God's fatherhood.

Several scholars have interpreted this parable using historical-critical method. Using form-critical analysis, C.H. Dodd finds the meaning of the story not within the parameters of the narrative, but outside in "the facts of the ministry of Jesus."[570] The 'facts' he has in view is seen his interpretation:

> The divine generosity was specifically exhibited in the calling of publicans and sinners, who had no merit before God. The Kingdom of God is like that. Such is Jesus' retort to the complaints of the legally minded who cavilled at Him as the friend of publicans and sinners.[571]

It is seen that in his interpretation C.H. Dodd identified the generous vineyard owner as 'God;' the last recruited group of workers as 'publicans and sinners;' the workers who were recruited first and who complained are the 'legally minded' Scribes and Pharisees. In the same vein, Jeremias calls this parable as 'the parable of the Good Employer,' told by Jesus "for the vindication of the gospel against its critics."[572] Jeremias sees the emphasis, not on the call to the vineyard, but on the reckoning at the end of the day (20:8-15). That means for him, this

---

569 *Y.Ber.*2:3c; quoted from *The Jerusalem Talmud: Berakhoth*, trans Moses Schwab (New York: Hermon Press, 1969), 51.

570 C.H. Dodd, *The Parables of the Kingdom* (London: Nisbet, 1936), 95.

571 Dodd, *The Parables of the Kingdom*, 95.

572 Jeremias, *The Parables of Jesus*, 38, 136.

parable is eschatological in nature. The employer is generous. He finds the key in verse 15 as he says:

> The parable is clearly addressed to those who resembled the murmurers, those who criticized and opposed the good news, Pharisees for example. Jesus was minded to show them how unjustified, hateful, loveless and unmerciful was their criticism. Such, said he, is God's goodness, and since God is so good, so too am I. He vindicates the gospel against its critics.[573]

It is seen that for Jeremias the main focus of this parable is on the nature of God. For him, this parable is not about vineyard workers at all. The same line of interpretation is followed by Robert H. Stein, who sees in this parable "a description of the gracious character of God as portrayed by the owner of the vineyard."[574] L. Schottroff finds dual focus of this parable in the goodness of God and the behavior of human beings toward one another.[575] For her, this parable intends to speak of the goodness of God. However, for her, "the goodness of God is not depicted as unconnected with anything else; rather its consequences for the life of human beings in community are immediately brought out, as the scene of the grumbling long-shift worker shows."[576] Using structuralist approach with an existential interpretation Dan O. Via finds ironic purpose in this parable. But the conclusion seems to be almost the same with the historical-critical interpreters, that this parable conveys double-edged meaning: God is gracious beyond normal human expectations, even to those who are considered unworthy, and it is a shame that some find fault with that.[577]

However, some recent scholars have a diametrically opposite approach to this eschatological and somewhat allegorical interpretation. For example, W. Herzog attempts to read the parable from the perspective of the peasant farmer who has lost his land to the elite landowner-cum-vineyard owner who turned the peasant farmer land into a vineyard.[578] For him, the employer in the parable is a wealthy man who exploited those whom he hired. He "takes advantage of an unemployed workforce to meet his harvesting needs by offering them work without a wage agreement."[579] Herzog thus exposed the landowner as an elitist oppressor of landless, powerless, day-to-day laborers and have persuasively

---

[573] Jeremias, *The Parables of Jesus*, 38.

[574] R.H. Stein, *An Introduction to the Parables of Jesus* (Philadelphia: Westminster Press, 1981), 127.

[575] L. Schottroff, "Human Solidarity and the goodness of God," 135.

[576] L. Schottroff, "Human Solidarity and the goodness of God," 137.

[577] Dan O. Via, *The Parables: Their Literary and Existential Dimension* (Philadelphia: Fortress, 1967), 152.

[578] William R. Herzog II, *Parables as Subversive Speech: Jesus as Pedagogue of the Oppressed* (Louisville: Westminster/John Knox Press, 1994), 85.

[579] W. Herzog, *Parables as Subversive Speech*, 86.

shifted attention away from seeing a generous God in the landowner-vineyard owner.[580] In similar perspective, V. George Shillington suggests removal of all the embellishments of Matthew and read the parable non-allegorically. He sees implicit in the parable proper (20:1b-15) the core issue of keeping the Sabbath, as he writes, "the meaning of the Jewish Sabbath, while not explicit in the texture of the parable of the workers and non-workers, hovers in the background."[581]

4.2.3.3.2.2. God's Incredible Love

The nature of this parable is such that it has generated rich and polyvalent interpretations. And as we have seen above, most of the interpretations are at the level of Jesus, focusing on Jesus and his actual audiences. However, for us, whether this parable comes from the lips of Jesus or not, does not matter much, our interest is rather at the level of Matthew and our main concern is why Matthew alone retains this very parable and what Matthew wanted to convey. That can be answered when we see this parable in the light of the narrative of the whole Gospel, as part of the broader theme.[582] And it is seen that his emphasis on the generous nature of God is immense in this very parable and which goes in tandem with his emphasis on God as an impartial and compassionate Father elsewhere. From verses 11-14, the inference is that God's gracious generosity vastly exceeds human merit-based expectations. In verse 14 Matthean Jesus says, "Take what belongs to you and go; I choose to give to this last the same as I give to you." The implication is that the landowner (God) is sovereign over his domain and has the moral right to do as he 'wants' (with his money). The next expression (v15) is more powerful, "Am I not allowed to do what I choose with what belongs to me? Or are you envious because I am generous?" These are rhetorical expressions containing very profound theology having to do with the sovereignty of God and W. Harnish has correctly noted that the whole of this pericope centers on this verse as the culmination.[583] In this parable, for reasons known only to himself, the owner of the vineyard (God) wants to be specially generous to the last group

[580] Herzog thus argues, "If the owner is speaking to former free peasants who have been forced into working as day laborers, his claim to the land is akin to rubbing salt in their wounds. How has he gained what belongs to him? ... Their relationship is not as brothers but as exploiter and exploited. The day laborers have no ground on which to stand ... Any vestige of the debt code has been obliterated by his covetous greed ... As pedagogue of the oppressed, Jesus would have facilitated their interaction with his codification, posing problem after problem to break their adhesion to the oppressor, to constantly unveil reality. See W. Herzog, *Parables as Subversive Speech*, 95.

[581] V. G. Shillington, "Saving Life and Keeping Sabbath (Matt. 20:1b-15)," in *Jesus and His Parables: Interpreting the Parables of Jesus Today*, edited by V.G. Shillington (Edinburgh: T&T Clark, 1997), 98.

[582] For details on holistic analysis as part of the redaction criticism, see G.R. Osborne, "Redaction Criticism," in *DJG*, 665-666.

[583] W. Harnish, "The metaphorical Process in Matthew 20:1-15," in *Society of Biblical Literature Seminar Papers* 1977, edited by P.J. Achtemeier (Missoula: Scholars Press, 1977), 241-42.

of workers. The other workers have no right to complain, since they received a normal wage (v11). If the owner (God) wants to show mercy to one group, that is perfectly all right. He has every power and authority to do according to his wish. In this light Jeremias calls this a parable of mercy and grace,[584] and the message is that it is not one's worthiness or amount of service that determines one's reward but rather the grace and will of God. The rhetorical question (v15) "Or are you envious (πονηρός) because I am generous (ἀγαθός)?" contains another very profound theological concept for Matthew. It is striking to see that these two words πονηρός and ἀγαθός are occurring together again in an earlier pericope on loving one's enemies (5:43-48) where Matthean Jesus is talking about God's nature (of compassion and love) as sun. The principle here is "equal pay for unequal work"[585] This is exactly what the Matthean Jesus expresses in the Sermon on the Mount on the indiscriminate goodness of God, that is, the heavenly Father "makes his sun rise on the evil and on the good" (5:45). Thus, there is a strong connection between these two pericope for Matthew. The general background in both cases is God's 'unmotivated love;'[586] that the incredible love of God is central to both this parable and the said pericope (5:43-48). Both have to do with the nature of God: God's love and care is available to all equally. That logically heightens Matthew core emphasis on the fatherhood of God. For him God is generous. God is impartial. This is the theology of Matthew. Such a God is strongly portrayed by Matthew and it is striking to see that both passages are found only in Matthew.

4.2.4. Fatherhood of God in Matthean Eschatological Discourse

4.2.4.1. Father's Just Reward (25:31-46)

As a culminating pericope of the last discourse of Matthean Jesus and a sequel to the Parable of the Talents (25:14-30), Matthew has the discourse ends fittingly in a great judgment scene:

> When the Son of Man comes in his glory, and all the angels with him, then he will sit on the throne of his glory. All the nations will be gathered before him, and he will separate people one from another as a shepherd separates the sheep from the goats, and he will put the sheep at his right hand and the goats at the left. Then the king will say to those at his right hand, 'Come, you that are blessed by my Father, inherit the kingdom prepared for you from the foundation of the world; for I was hungry and you gave me food, I was thirsty and you gave me something to drink, I was a stranger and you welcomed me, I was naked and you gave me clothing, I was sick and you took care of me, I was in prison and you visited me.' Then the righteous

[584] Jeremias, *The Parables of Jesus*, 139.

[585] A. Nygren, *Agape and Eros*, 86.

[586] A. Nygren, *Agape and Eros*, 86.

will answer him, 'Lord, when was it that we saw you hungry and gave you food, or thirsty and gave you something to drink? And when was it that we saw you a stranger and welcomed you, or naked and gave you clothing? And when was it that we saw you sick or in prison and visited you?' And the king will answer them, 'Truly I tell you, just as you did it to one of the least of these who are members of my family, you did it to me.' Then he will say to those at his left hand, 'You that are accursed, depart from me into the eternal fire prepared for the devil and his angels; for I was hungry and you gave me no food, I was thirsty and you gave me nothing to drink, I was a stranger and you did not welcome me, naked and you did not give me clothing, sick and in prison and you did not visit me.' Then they also will answer, 'Lord, when was it that we saw you hungry or thirsty or a stranger or naked or sick or in prison, and did not take care of you?' Then he will answer them, 'Truly I tell you, just as you did not do it to one of the least of these, you did not do it to me.' And these will go away into eternal punishment, but the righteous into eternal life.

4.2.4.1.1. Matthean Redaction

This unit is actually an apocalyptic discourse and is unique to Matthew. It is located within the context of Matthew chapter 24-25, which is called Eschatological or Apocalyptic Discourse, as the culminating pericope.[587] The discourse of these two chapters is the last of the five discourses of Matthean Jesus. It is addressed to Jesus' disciples for Matthew.

4.2.4.1.2. Theological Explanation

Several writers have stressed that historical and sociological factors are at work wherever apocalyptic language becomes prominent. In periods of historical crisis and trauma and in periods of a marked sense of alienation from the outside world, Jewish and early Christian writers turned to apocalyptic.[588] It is not a surprise then that the destruction of Jerusalem Temple in 70 C.E. and its aftermath produced a variety of literary responses in the form of apocalyptic literatures, e.g., 2 Baruch,

---

[587] This final discourse contains a number of smaller units: the Prediction of the Destruction of Jerusalem (24:1-2), Sayings on Signs before the End (24:3-8), Persecution (24:9-14), the Desolating Sacrilege (24:15-22), Warnings against false Prophets (24:23-28), the Coming of the Son of Man (24:29-31), the Saying about the Fig Tree (24:32-36), the Saying about the Flood and the Exhortation to Watchfulness (24:36-44), the Parable of the Faithful and Wise Servant (24:45-51), the Parable of the Ten Maidens (25:1-13), and the Parable of the Talents (25:14-30).

[588] P.D. Hanson, "Apocalypticism," in *Interpreter's Dictionary of the Bible*, edited by K. Crim (Supplementary volume; Nashville: Abingdon Press, 1976), 30; G.W. Nickelsberg, "Social Aspects of Palestinian Jewish Apocalypticism," in *Apocalypticism in the Mediterranean World and the Near East*, edited by D. Hellholm (Tubingen, 1983), 645.

4 Ezra and Apocalypse of Abraham.[589] Matthew 25:31-46 comes from a similar social setting and was intended to function similarly for the first recipients of the Gospel.[590] That means the relationship between Matthew 25 and other Jewish apocalyptic writings which were also written towards the end of the first century strengthen considerably the interpretation of Matthew's final judgment scene. In the aftermath of the destruction of Jerusalem temple apocalyptic writers announced that on the last day God would judge the nations on the basis of their treatment of his people. This is a prominent theme in 4 Ezra, as Ezra contrasts 'the desolation of Zion' with 'the wealth of those who lived in Babylon' (3:2). In chapter 13, Ezra repeatedly assured that the nations will not escape God's judgment; they will be punished for their ungodliness and wickedness:

> And he, my Son, will reprove the assembled nations for their ungodliness (this was symbolized by the storm), and will reproach them to their face with their evil thoughts and with the torments with which they are to be tortured (which were symbolized by the flames); and he will destroy them without effort by the law (which was symbolized by the fire).[591]

This theme is explicit in a judgment scene in 4 Ezra 7. Suddenly at the last judgment the nations are confronted with God's people whom they have denied and failed to serve and they are judged on that basis:

> Then the Most High will say to the nations that have been raised for the dead, 'Look now, and understand whom you have denied, whom you have not served, whose commandments you have despised! Look on this side and on that; here are delight and rest, and there are fire and torments![592]

This passage is quite similar to Matthew 25. It is seen that the judgment of the nations is on the basis of the nation's treatment of God's people. This passage intends to reassure the victim's group which perceives itself to be God's people. This judgment theme is also seen in I Enoch. In this composite works of apocalyptic genre, [593] we see strikingly similar themes to our Matthean pericope. In I Enoch chapter 62, the high and mighty ones of the earth are told:

---

[589] See Philip F. Esler, "Rome in Apocalyptic and Rabbinic Literature," in *The Gospel of Matthew in Its Roman Imperial Context*, 20.

[590] See A.J. Saldarini, "The Gospel of Matthew and the Jewish-Christian Conflict," in *Social History of the Matthean Community*, edited by D. Balch (Minneapolis: Fortress Press, 1991," 39.

[591] 4 Ezra 13:37-38, trans B.M. Metzger, in J.H. Charlesworth, *OTP* vol I, 552.

[592] 4 Ezra 7:37-38, trans B.M. Metzger, in J.H. Charlesworth, *OTP* vol I, 538.

[593] The composite nature of its date of composition, mostly dating back to the inter-testamental era, is explained in E. Isaac, "I (Ethiopic Apocalypse of) Enoch," in J.H. Charlesworth, *OTP* vol I, 6-7.

> On the day of judgment, all the kings, the governors, the high officials, and the landlords shall see and recognize him – how he sits on the throne of his glory, and righteousness is judged before him ... shall fall down before him on their faces, and worship and raise their hopes in that Son of Man; they shall beg and plead for mercy at his feet. But the Lord of the Spirits himself will cause them to be frantic, so that they shall rush and depart from his presence ... So he will deliver them to the angels for punishments in order that vengeance shall be executed on them – oppressors of his children and his elect ones. It shall become quite a scene for my righteous and elect ones. They shall rejoice over ....[594]

Here it is seen that the judgment is on the basis of the nations' treatment of God's children and his elect ones. Quite similar to this scene is seen in the unique Matthean pericope (25:31-46) of Matthean Jesus' apocalyptic discourse. The unit opens with a scene of the last judgment. The Son of man is seated on his glorious throne and "all the angels" are present (v31). Thus recalling I Enoch 62 and other apocalyptic texts in this scene the Son of man is seated upon a throne.[595] Gathered before the Son of man will be "all the nations" (v32). This is the same phrase we encounter at the close of the Gospel in 28:19.[596]

As just mentioned several redactional phrases and motifs in this passage and its central thrust are all strongly reminiscent of passages in apocalyptic writings such as 4 Ezra and I Enoch. This leads us to see Matthew in the same socio-political realities as that of these apocalyptic literatures. Interestingly, the idea of God's fatherhood occurs here, in which theme lies a crucial glue to the setting of Matthean community. That is in verse 34, "Come, you that are blessed by my Father, inherit the kingdom prepared for you from the foundation of the world." In other words, implicit in the very expression of 'my Father,' which has to do with identity in expressing hope and solace, we find Matthean emphasis on the fatherhood of God. It means that the fatherhood of God here has more to do with broader context and setting of the Matthean community and the struggles that

---

[594] I Enoch 62:3-12, trans E. Isaac, in J.H. Charlesworth, *OTP* vol I, 43.

[595] See alsol Enoch 61:8; 69:29; cf. Dan 7:13-14. According to David L. Turner (*Matthew*, 610) this very pericope is a commentary on the realization of Daniel 7:13-27.

[596] The meaning of this phrase πάντα τὰ ἔθνη – the designation of those gathered before the Son of man – is disputed. There has been a good deal of discussion as to whether the term ἔθνη means 'nations' (including Jewish people) or 'Gentiles.' The term 'nations' (including Jewish people) is favored by several scholars including E. Schweitzer, *The Goodnews according to Matthew* (London: SPCK, 1980), 478; F. W. Beare, *The Gospel according to Matthew: A Commentary* (Oxford: Basil Blackwell, 1981), 493; J. R. Donahue, "The 'Parable' of the Sheep and the Goats: A Challenge to Christian Ethics," in *TS* 47 [1986], 14-16; Hagner, *Matthew 14-28*, 742-743) but several other favor 'Gentiles' including T.W. Manson, *Sayings of Jesus*, 250; Jeremias, *The Parables of Jesus*, 209; Stanton, *A Gospel for a New People*, 212-214.

gave rise to the writing of the Gospel, which will be dealt in the next chapter. That sociological aspect of the fatherhood of God apart, Matthew has also in mind in this discourse the care and nurture of his community.[597] In caring for fellow Matthean community members one is caring for Christ (25:40). Thus in the theme of compassion the emphasis on the fatherhood of God is clear in Matthew. This emphasis on the compassion of God and so God's fatherhood reached its climax in his account of the passion narrative. It is to which we now turn.

4.2.5. Fatherhood of God in Matthean Passion Narrative

4.2.5.1. Submission to Father's Will (26:36-42)

At the height of the Matthean passion narrative, just after the Passover meal (26:17-29), Matthean Jesus along with his disciples went out to the Mount of Olives (v30), to a place called Gethsemane and there he prays:

> "My Father, if it is possible, let this cup pass from me; yet not what I want but what you want." Then he came to the disciples and found them sleeping; and he said to Peter, "So, could you not stay awake with me one hour? Stay awake and pray that you may not come into the time of trial; the spirit indeed is willing, but the flesh is weak." Again he went away for the second time and prayed, "My Father, if this cannot pass unless I drink it, your will be done."

4.2.5.1.1. Matthean Redaction

Although, Matthew's passion narrative follows Mark's account, Matthew makes several changes, including this pericope, in order to heighten his theological-christological focus. While Matthew is following Mark's structure (26:36-46//Mk 14:32-42), but a close observation reveals that there is a subtle shift of emphasis in Matthew's account. While Mark stresses Jesus' triple return to the disciples (Mk 14:37, 40, 41) but he records only two times of Jesus going off to pray (Mk 14:35, 39). Matthew retains the same triple return of Jesus to the disciple (40, 43, 45) but he records, unlike in Mark, three instances of Jesus going off to pray (26:39, 42, 44). It shows that Matthew's focus is more on the action of Jesus – the three occasions Jesus goes off to pray to his Father. And for Frank J. Matera, this is because Matthew wanted to project Jesus' prayer as a model for the Church.[598]

Another changes made by Matthew is seen in the content of the second prayer (26:42//Mk 14:39). While Mark records that Jesus "went away and prayed, saying the same words" (Mk 14:39), Matthew has added the content of the prayer in the lips of Jesus, "My Father, if this cannot pass unless I drink it, your will be

[597] Matthew's focus in this perspective is consistently argued by Stanton; see Stanton, *A Gospel for A New People*, 221-230.

[598] Matera, *Passion Narratives and Gospel Theologies*, 95.

done" (26:42). This is Matthew's deliberate addition keeping his theological focus on God's fatherhood.

4.2.5.1.2. Theological Explanation

4.2.5.1.2.1. Fatherhood of God in Prayer

The core expression in this episode is the prayer of Jesus which is recorded in all Synoptic Gospels (Mark 14:32-42; Mt 26:36-46; Lk 22:40-46). While it is Mark alone who retains this very Aramaic term *Abba*, but a close observation reveals that the prayer of Jesus is more developed in Matthew than in Mark. Particularly, the very first prayer of Jesus in Matthew's version is embedded in language which is even more attentive to God's will than that found in Mark:[599] "My Father, if it is possible, let this cup pass from me; yet not what I want but what you want"(Mt 26:39), instead of "Abba, Father, for you all things are possible; remove this cup from me; yet, not what I want, but what you want" (Mk 14:36).

At the level of Jesus, this prayer shows the depth of his relationship with God. And Matthew, by retaining this very intimate way of addressing God as "My Father" (26:39// Mk 14:36), affirms Jesus' special sense of sonship to God.[600] Some noted scholars while acknowledging the expression as expression of personal relationship but not considered as unique to Jesus.[601] According to Bruce Chilton, since within early Judaism, God was known as 'Father' for the purposes of prayer, especially in difficult circumstances, Jesus too in similar manner is seen here addressing God fervently and intimately in his time of greatest need.[602] In the same vein C. H. Charlesworth too observes that in true Jewish manner, Jesus affirmed God as Father in disheartening times, trusting in the "one who always hears the prayers of those who turn to him with a pure heart."[603] Surely for Matthean community such an affirmation of God's fatherhood in difficult circumstances brought tremendous solace to the shattered community.

The vocative "My Father" here in prayer (vv39, 42) rather than the simple "Father" as in 11:25-26, further emphasizes that it is the relationship between Father and Son is here being tested and reaffirmed.[604] The expression "My Father" is Jesus' personal equivalent of the "Our Father" which he taught his disciples to use corporately in 6:9. Thus for Matthew, this prayer of Jesus (vv39, 42) is the logical outcome of his intimate relationship with the Father (11:27). The prayer

[599] Matera, *Passion Narratives and Gospel Theologies*, 96.

[600] In this direction, one of the most influential contributions has been that of J. Jeremias. For him (*The Prayer of Jesus*, 57) *Abba* expression is unique to Jesus, and that it has to do with his special consciousness of sonship.

[601] G. Vermes, *Jesus the Jew*, 210-211; C.A. Evans, *Matthew*, 435.

[602] B.D. Chilton, "God as 'Father' in the Targumim, in Non-Canonical Literatures,"166.

[603] J.H. Charlesworth, "Jewish Prayers in the Time of Jesus," in *The Lord's Prayer: Perspectives for Reclaiming Christian Prayer*, edited by D.L. Migliore (Grand Rapids: Wm B Eerdmans, 1993), 37.

[604] France, *The Gospel of Matthew*, 1004.

of Matthean Jesus here at Gethsemane is also the outcome of his teaching in the Sermon on the Mount. He does not pray in order to be seen (6:5-6). He does not pray by heaping up empty phrases (6:7-8). He prays just as he taught his disciples; he seeks God's kingdom and God's will (6:10).[605]

4.2.5.1.2.2. The Father's Plan

The use of εἰ (condition of fact) for "if possible" stresses the fact that God could do so, but the end of the prayer shows it is not his will. In other words, Matthean Jesus expresses his wish to avoid the agonies of the cross, yet he realizes that the Father's plan takes priority over his wishes; the Father's will must be done (6:10; 26:53-54). Though he is the Son of God, he does not use his power and authority to escape the cup and the suffering but yields to the will of his Father. In other words, in the projection of Matthew, Jesus shows that he is the Son of God not by saving himself but by his obedient trust in the Father.[606] Matthean Jesus thus asks his Father to remove the cup from him (v39). The cup here refers to Jesus' imminent suffering, which includes the denial, betrayal, shame, rejection and subsequent death by crucifixion.[607] When the mother of the sons of Zebedee ask him for the seats of their sons at his right and his left (20:20-21), Jesus answers, "Are you able to drink the cup that I am about to drink (20:22)?" In this pericope also the two sons of Zebedee appear again (26:37) and Jesus prays for removing the cup (26:39). Thus the imagery here points to the suffering. According to C.A. Evans, this expression echoes the idea of the "cup of wrath" of Isaiah (e.g., Isa 51.17, 22). He thus finds here an element of divine wrath in Jesus' suffering.[608] However, R.E. Brown wishes to separate the ideas of suffering and of judgment, and sees the former as the primary focus here.[609] In this moment of sorrow (26:37), Jesus would avoid the suffering, provided it accorded with God's will ("yet not what I want, but what you want," vv39, 42). Thus the fact that the cup of suffering is pictured as being given to Jesus by his Father (who is thus able also to remove it) strikingly expresses the conviction which underlies Matthew's narrative of the passion that God controls the whole process culminating in Jesus' death.

4.2.5.2. Trusting in the Father's Protective Care (26:47-56)

At the arrest of Jesus subsequent to the episode of Gethsemane prayer, when the disciples frantically resists with swords, Matthew has put in the lips of Jesus, projecting his utmost command of the situation:

---

605 Matera, *Passion Narratives and Gospel Theologies*, 97.

606 Matera, *Passion Narratives and Gospel Theologies*, 82.

607 P.S. Minear, *The God of the Gospels*, 110; see also Carter, *Matthew and the Margins*, 510.

608 C.A. Evans, *Matthew*, 435.

609 R.E. Brown, *The Death of the Messiah: From Gethsemane to the Grave: A Commentary on the Passion Narratives in the Four Gospels* (London: Chapman, 1994), 168-70.

> Put your sword back into its place; for all who take the sword will perish by the sword. Do you think that I cannot appeal to my Father, and he will at once send me more than twelve legions of angels? (vv52, 53)

4.2.5.2.1. Matthean Redaction

While Matthew is following Mark as regard to this episode of the arrest of Jesus (26:47-56//Mk 14:43-52), but Matthew has some additional expressions keeping his theological perspective in mind. It is seen in the unique words in the lips of Jesus, in response to the frantic resistance of one of his disciples, who cut off the ear of the high priest's slave (27:51//Mk14:47). Matthew is projecting here the absolute serenity of the Father's Son vis-à-vis the insecure and frantic disciples (vv52, 53). Jesus, in absolute command of the situation, ordered his disciples to put down the sword and then expresses his oneness and faithfulness with God ('my Father,' v53) and finally as fulfillment of scriptures (v54), another prominent Matthean theme, which is closely related with his theological emphasis. All these are deliberate Matthean arrangement keeping his focus on the centrality of the fatherhood of God.

4.2.5.2.2. Theological Explanation

4.2.5.2.2.1. Divine Plan: The Father in Control

While our main focus on this pericope is again around the expression of 'my Father' at this stage of Matthean passion narrative, but viewing this in the light of the whole chapter is ideal to see his theological emphasis. As the narrative unfolds, it is clear that one who suffers is the all-knowing Son of God. At the outset of the passion Jesus announces that he will be crucified (26:2). When preparing for the Passover meal, Matthean Jesus says that his time has come (26:18). At the Passover meal Jesus not only discloses his betrayal, he identifies who the betrayer is (26:25). When he is about to be arrested, Jesus gives Judas permission to do his work (26:50). And now in this very pericope when one of his disciples tries to defend him, Matthean Jesus responds, "Put your sword back in its place; for all who take the sword will perish by the sword" (v52). This is the first of the three verses (vv52-54), of which there is no equivalent in his source Mark and Q. However, there is a strikingly similar tradition found in literatures of early Judaism, particularly as regard to the request of holding back one's sword. As such the exact expression 'put your sword back in its place' is found in an episode in *Joseph and Asenath* 29:4, where Levi prevents Benjamin from slaying the wounded son of Pharaoh: "And now, put your sword back into its place, and come, help me, and we will heal him of his wound."[610] What is more striking is the similarity of its context, in *Joseph and Asenath* the preceding verse deals with the subject of non-retaliation, "it does not befit a man who worship God to repay evil for

[610] Trans C. Burchard in J. H. Charlesworth, *The OTP II*, 246.

evil" (29:3), which idea is again found in the teaching of Matthean Jesus, in the fifth and sixth antithesis on retaliation and loving of enemies (5:38-48) of the Sermon on the Mount.[611] This helps us to see that there is a clear link between this pericope of the Matthean passion narrative and his version of Jesus' Sermon on the Mount. Here in this episode of the passion scene, as a large crowd with swords and clubs surrounds Jesus and his disciples (v47), the expression of Matthean Jesus implies that "one is not to use the sword against an enemy who comes well armed and threatens life."[612] Here we are reminded of the words of Matthean Jesus to love one's enemies, in imitation of the heavenly Father, who "makes his sun rise on the evil and on the good" (5:45). Thus here in this verse (v52), in the context of the arrest of Jesus, the verb to 'put back one's sword' has to do with the way of peace, of non resistance and love of enemies. That is exactly what Matthean Jesus taught in the Sermon on the Mount (cf. 5:38-48). And true to his words Matthean Jesus remains faithful to God's will even to death.[613] Thus here the expression of 'putting one's sword back' has to do with living in accord with the Father's will, which is all the more clearer in the expression of the following verse (v53): "Do you think that I cannot appeal to my Father, and he will at once send me more than twelve legions of angels?"

This expression is again unique to Matthew. In the Old Testament and other Jewish literatures angels are often depicted with military functions and fought for human beings. In 2 Kings 6:15-17 when the king of Aram sent a great army with horses and chariots to capture Elisha, God sent a greater number of army in support of Elisha in answer to his prayer. Similarly in 2 *Baruch* 63:5-11, Sennacherib's army was destroyed by angels sent by God in answer to Hezekiah's prayer. So also in 2 Maccabees 3:26, angels prevent one Heliodorus, an agent of the king, from entering and looting the temple. It is in the light of these traditions that Matthean Jesus' question would have been understood.

Here by this very expression Matthew demonstrates that Jesus trusts the Father's ability to protect him. And here the verse says that Jesus could call on "more than twelve legions of angels" for himself. But he does not do so. Here the reference to 'legions' could evoke the parallel image of the massive Roman forces.[614] However for Matthew, Jesus does not need them at this time, for his Father's will is that he faces the cross and become the sacrifice for sins.[615] And as the following verse reveals ("But how then would the scriptures be fulfilled, which say it must happen in this way?" v54), not only is the Son in charge, it is

---

[611] Nolland (*The Gospel of Matthew*, 1112) believes that both Matthew 26:52 and *Joseph and Asenath* 29:4 come from some common tradition.

[612] Nolland, *The Gospel of Matthew*, 1112.

[613] Mt 27:46-50 cf. 26:39, 42.

[614] D.J. Weaver, "Thus You Will Know them by their Fruits," in *The Gospel of Matthew In Its Roman Imperial Context*, 109.

[615] G. Osborne, *Matthew*, 985.

his Father, and these events are to fulfill Scripture. While the language of divine necessity (δεῖ γενέσθαι) is found in the passion predictions (16:21//Mk 8:31) and governs all the passion events. However, the occurrence of the term δεῖ and 'Father' in the same pericope is a deliberate Matthean scheme in line with his emphasis on the fatherhood of God. Jesus, being the Son to the Father, continues to exude peace and love of the Father. As Jesus struggles in prayer in Gethsemane, he addresses God as "my Father" (26:39, 42); as a true Son, he does so in order obediently to represent the will of the Father in the course of his own life (26:36-46). He must die (cf. 16:21). He has submitted to the Father's will, which means that he will face the humiliation of death on the cross (27:32-37). He refuses to use his power but takes the way of non-retaliation and remains faithful to God's will even to death (27:50). Thus Jesus is portrayed as one who discloses the Father's love (5:43-48). That means for Matthew Jesus embodied the love of God. God's fatherhood is manifested in the suffering of the Father's Son.

4.2.6. Summary

Our main argument throughout this chapter has been that the theme of the fatherhood of God dominates or rather dictates the entire narratives and discourses of Matthew, thus showing the centrality of God in Matthean theology. Right from the infancy narratives, Matthew gives strong emphasis on the fatherhood of God. This is clearly seen in his projection of divine intervention and care right from the conception, naming and upbringing of Jesus (1:18-2:15). At the very beginning Matthew explicitly projected Jesus' messianic lineage (1:1 cf. 2:15). This Matthean emphasis on the sonship of Jesus to God is heightened by the many unique occurrences of the address 'my Father' on the lips of Matthean Jesus. However, it is seen that in this aspect of the fatherhood of God, that is, God's fatherhood in the sense of exclusive Father/Son relationships, Matthew is following his source Mark, as we find the same strong emphasis in all the three Gospels (e.g., Mt 26:39; Mk 14:36; Lk 22:42). Such instances project the unanimity of the Synoptic Gospels in portraying filial relationship between God and Jesus, and thereby pointing to the centrality of God's fatherhood in Synoptic Gospels.

As regard to his emphasis on the idea of God's fatherhood in relation with the disciples, as is evident in the 'your Father'/ 'our Father' occurrences in the Sermon on the Mount, it is seen that Matthew shares the idea of God's fatherhood with Luke (thus Q), especially in relation to God's providence.[616] But Matthew has some unique emphasis on the idea of God's fatherhood that has universal and inclusive significance. For Matthew God is portrayed as cosmic Father. This unique emphasis on cosmic fatherhood of God is clearly seen in the beatitudes of Matthean Jesus as he talks about peacemakers as God's children (5:9). The same idea is seen in 5:45, where the term 'heavenly Father' (for God) is used in the context of teaching on loving of enemies (5:43-48). Particularly, it is in this very

[616] E.g. Mt 6:6-13//Lk 11:2-4; Mt 6:24-33//Lk12:22-32; Mt 7:9-11//Lk 11:11-13.

pericope that the term 'heavenly Father' occurs along with a unique expression, "for he makes his sun rise on the evil and on good, and sends rain on the righteous and on the unrighteous" (5:45b). This projection of the universal benevolence of the heavenly Father is similar to Greek concept of cosmic fatherhood of God - the universality of God. The reference to the sun and the rain (natural phenomena) in Matthew makes that clear. Since such an idea of God as cosmic Father is seen only in Hellenistic literatures, Matthew's expression here in 5:45 seems to have assimilated such ideas in his theology of God.

Matthew also uniquely portrays God as an all-seeing and all-knowing Father. We see this idea of a God who sees in secret only in Matthew. While the idea of an omniscient God is also found in the Old Testament especially in the great hymns like Psalms 139 and Job 28, but again the closest parallel of Matthew seems to be found in the ancient Greek religious discourse where the deity Helios, the sun-god is described as 'all-seeing eye' or 'eye of righteousness.' In Matthew 5:45, as seen above, Matthew uniquely portrays God as impartial as sun and here again in 6:1-18 the picture is of a God who sees all and knows all and so both are closely connected. The latter notion of an all-seeing God has again having closest parallels in the Greek hymns attributing such expression of omniscience to their sun-god. Matthew seems incorporating such a notion here. Such a portrayal of an all-seeing and all-knowing Father is also related with justice and righteousness in Matthew. For Matthew, God is a God of justice. God is the good God who demands good, who sees all that occurs in secret, that is, in the very heart of the person. That is why Matthean Jesus admonishes that one's almsgiving should be in absolute secrecy so much so that even one's left hand should not let one's right hand know what is doing (6:3). As such in this hyperbolic-figurative demand we see Matthean concept of God. For him, God is the revealer of righteousness. Before him nothing is hidden including one's heart and attitudes. The only alms he rewards are alms of which the giver is unconscious. Such an attitude is what is expected from a God who is all-seeing God, quite in line with the element of surprise on the part of the righteous in the parable of the judgments (25:31-46), again unique to Matthew. For Matthew God is a God of justice. He is the revealer of righteousness.

God as 'Father in heaven,' which is distinctively Matthean, also highlights God's sovereignty, that is, one who transcends all that is on earth. However, he is at the same time pictured as a very personal God, 'our Father,' who is concerned for the needs of his children, being attentive even to physical needs (7:11 cf. 6: 24-33). Such a compassionate down-to-earth God is also seen in other parables of Matthean Jesus. In the parable of the lost sheep the very enigmatic expression of the "little ones' angels seeing God always" (18:10) project God as a compassionate God, in whose sight these little ones are special. This becomes clearer in the core parable of the lost sheep. The same emphasis on the justice, goodness, and compassionate nature of God is also seen in other parables of Matthean Jesus.

Thus the parable in 18:21-35 depicts God as God of mercy and God of justice. So also the parable in 20:1-16 depicts the generous goodness of God. It is striking to see that this unique Matthean parable (20:1-16) goes along well with earlier unique Matthean discourse on loving one's enemies (5:43-48), where Matthean Jesus is talking about a God who "makes the sun rise on the evil and on the good, and sends rain on the righteous and on the unrighteous" (5:45). Thus there seems to be a very strong link between these two pericope for Matthew. The incredible mercy of God is central to both. Both have to do with the love of God. For Matthew God's grace is available to all equally and universally. For him God is generous. God is genuinely impartial. In this case, God's fatherhood has universal and inclusive significance for Matthew. The passion narrative too has exceptional emphasis on the fatherhood of God. Matthew's passion narrative is profoundly theological, stressing that Jesus is the all-knowing and all-powerful Son of God even in the midst of suffering and humiliation. Right at the account of the arrest of Jesus, the evangelist demonstrates Jesus trusting in the protective care of his Father (26:53). Being the Son of the Father, he continues to exude peace and love of the Father even at the passion (26:52). For Matthew, the cross is the embodiment of Matthean Jesus' own teaching on God's love and peace. Fatherhood of God is thus seen as one of the overarching theological emphases of Matthew.

Concluding Remarks

This chapter provides us with theological explanations of the fatherhood of God in Matthew. As such we have seen the expositions on how Matthew has given a central emphasis on the idea of God's fatherhood throughout his narratives and discourses. The next chapter will see the why and what of the fatherhood of God in Matthew basing on the very distinct emphasis of Matthew on the theme of God's fatherhood. Thus attempt will be made to put forth the fatherhood of God as the hub of Matthean theology and also place it within the context of the Synoptic Gospels.

Chapter 5

Fatherhood of God: The Hub of Matthean Theology

Introduction

We have observed in the previous chapter how Matthew has given a central emphasis on the idea of God's fatherhood throughout his narratives and discourses, and in this chapter our aim is to explain the why and the what of the fatherhood of God in Matthew basing on the very centrality and distinct emphasis of Matthew on the theme of God's fatherhood. Thus attempt will be made to show that for Matthew the theme of God's fatherhood is the fulcrum in which all other themes are connected. We will also place the idea of the fatherhood of God within the context of the Synoptic Gospels so as to draw attention to the theology of the Synoptic Gospels in general.

However, before delving into the discussion on the place and significance of the theme of God's fatherhood in Matthean theology and the Synoptic Gospels it is necessary to review and assess how the question of God is addressed or placed in New Testament theology. This will help us to put things in perspective as it is to this broad New Testament theology that Matthew and the Synoptic Gospels contribute as a part. Thus in this section as we review the New Testament theology works we will examine how scholars addressed the question of God in relation to the central theological emphasis of the New Testament.

5.1. God Discourse in New Testament Theology

It is a fact that God does not get any extended forefront discussion in the New Testament, in spite of the fact that God is the primary force behind every narrative of the New Testament.[617] The whole of the New Testament writings presupposes

[617] Hurtado, *God in New Testament Theology*, 26.

God. It was N.T. Wright who put this issue into perspectives as he observes in his 1992 work on New Testament studies:

> The question of God, though conspicuous by its absence from the great majority of books about the New Testament, is in fact the question which lies at the root of most if not all of the issues which are more frequently discussed.[618]

In the decades following N.T. Wright's work some prominent New Testament scholars notably J.D.G. Dunn and L.W. Hurtado, bring up the same question of God to the forefront discussion in New Testament studies. Dunn, in his recent work on New Testament Theology (2009), talks about bringing God to proper place in New Testament theology. He affirms that God is "the foundation in which everything else is built, the first principle from which everything else follows."[619] Accordingly, he has devoted a full chapter on 'theology of God' where he talks about the inherited theology, that is, beliefs from the Old Testament and Jewish tradition, and Christology.[620] He addresses the inseparable relationship between God and Jesus as "the challenge of making sense of Jesus (Christology) in relation to *theo-logy*."[621] Similarly, L.W. Hurtado's 2010 monograph has titled *God in New Testament Theology* and brings the same issue to the fore as he argues:

> "God" does not receive extended foreground discussion anywhere in the New Testament, and yet the entire body of NT writings presupposes and reflects beliefs about who "God" is and what "God" has done, and these beliefs are arguably central and critical in every one of these writings.[622]

As both N.T. Wright and Hurtado correctly observed, 'God' has been a rarely discussed subject in New Testament studies in spite of the fact that the core subject matter or foundation of New Testament theology is God. Since New Testament theology is part of biblical theology[623] we will first look at the broader category – Biblical theology as regard to how the theme of God is placed. More so, the Old Testament is the fundamental factor in the shaping of New Testament theology,[624] as Dunn appropriately puts, "No NT theology can ignore the OT or

---

[618] N.T. Wright, *The New Testament and the People of God*, 471.

[619] Dunn, *New Testament Theology: An Introduction*, 41.

[620] Dunn, *New Testament Theology: An Introduction*, 43-69.

[621] Dunn, *New Testament Theology: An Introduction*, 43.

[622] Hurtado, *God in New Testament Theology*, 26.

[623] Dunn, *New Testament Theology: An Introduction*, 42.

[624] The unity of both Old and New Testament is strongly affirmed by F. Watson, who even laments that the fragmentation of the studies of Old Testament theology, New Testament theology and Systematic theology to the detriment of each of the three enterprises. See F. Watson, *Text and Truth: Redefining Biblical Theology* (Grand Rapids; Michigan: Wm B. Eerdmans, 1997), 185.

the profundity of its influence on the NT."[625] We will thus look at some of the prominent biblical scholars who have dealt with the biblical theology and talked about its unifying themes.

5.1.1. God in Biblical Theology

One of the pioneer Old Testament theologians who talk about the centre[626] of biblical theology is W. Eichrodt. He argued that the Old Testament did provide its own centre and scheme of organization. He, however, argued that the organization must not be dictated by dogmatic scheme.[627] For him, the arrangement must spring from the Old Testament material itself. As such he finds a double organizing principle given by the Old Testament's own dialectic and "speaks of a revelation of the God of the People, who in his rule proves himself to be the God of the World and the God of the Individual."[628] From this followed his scheme: God and People; God and World; God and Man.[629] But he combined with this a unitary principle – the covenant (between God and his people). Thus for him the covenant concept is the overarching theme.[630] He finds this covenant theme as the integrating centre of the Bible. He rightly points out that "*that which binds together indivisibly the two realms of the Old and New Testaments – different in externals though they may be – is the irruption of the kingship of God into this world and its establishment here*. This is the unitive fact because it rests on the action of one and the same God in each case."[631] G. von Rad is another noted Old Testament theologian who stood for overarching theological unity of Old and New Testaments. In his two volume work on Old Testament theology he talks about the theological witnesses and an account built upon God's action in history. In the first volume he presents the theology of the Hexateuch, with

---

[625] Dunn, *New Testament Theology: An Introduction*, 24.

[626] Writing several decades after Eichrodt, J. Barr's (*The Concept of Biblical Theology: An Old Testament Perspective* [Minneapolis: Fortress Press, 1999], 343) observation on the scholarship's search for the centre of biblical theology is instructive at this point: "To sum up the question of the 'centre,' it seems to me that the discussion of it has not been a vain waste of breath, as some have thought, and that valuable results have emerged from it ... It is not a matter of reaching a definitive answer, but rather of weighing possibilities for the expression of structure. Whether writers of Theologies define a 'centre' or not, they will very likely have to work with some idea of one (or more?), as a simple necessity for the organization of their work."

[627] W. Eichrodt, *Theology of the Old Testament* I (trans J.A. Baker; Philadelphia: Westminster Press, 1961), 32-33.

[628] Eichrodt, *Theology of the Old Testament* I, 33.

[629] The first category forms the substance of his first volume; the second and third categories form the substance of his second one - *Theology of the Old Testament* II (trans J.A. Baker; London: SCM Press, 1967).

[630] This is the main concentration of his entire first volume work. However for him, it is essentially the covenant with Moses on Sinai. See Eichrodt, *Theology of the Old Testament* I, 36.

[631] Eichrodt, *Theology of the Old Testament* I, 26.

salvation-history as the central theme, which he finds pictured in the ancient confessional summaries.[632] Thus he found in Deuteronomy 26:5-9 recapitulation of the history of God's mighty works in the form of creeds, "A wandering Aramean was my ancestor; he went down into Egypt ... the Lord brought us out of Egypt with a mighty hand and an outstretched arm ... and he brought us into this place ...." Rad finds the starting point of Old Testament theology in such confessional statements. In his own words:

> If there is any truth in the recognition that the whole of the Hexateuch is built upon a very few ancient creedal statements which became constitutive for the Israel of all ages, then this is so important that a theology of the Old Testament would practically have to start out from this fact.[633]

In his second volume he presents the theology of the prophetic traditions, and these again follow the sequence of the various prophets and the traditions attached to them. The whole is preceded by a brief historical sketch of Yahwism and followed by a discussion of relations with the New Testament, in which a very considerable emphasis is laid upon typology.[634] He maintains the unity of the Testaments by way of salvation-historical theology of the 'mighty acts of God.'[635] That means for him the subject of Old Testament theology or rather biblical theology is emphatically about God.

A clear voice on theocentric emphasis has gained ascendancy with the revival of holistic approach, so biblical theology approach, in the 1990s, with the work of Brevard Childs, who stood for unity and continuity and talks about the overarching theological theme of the Bible as a whole in its final canonical form. For him, the Old Testament Israel's *Heilsgeschichte* and the New Testament's witness to God's redemption through Jesus Christ are the key canonical categories for constructing a biblical theology.[636] He put forth that "what binds the testaments indissolubly together is their witness to the selfsame divine reality, to the subject matter, which undergirds both collections, and ... points beyond itself to the reality of God."[637] Accordingly, while discussing the topic of God under the title 'the identity of God,' Childs stressed the continuity of the New Testament with

---

[632] G. von Rad, *Old Testament Theology* I (London: SCM Press, 1975), 122-123.

[633] G. von Rad, *Old Testament Theology* I, vi.

[634] G. von Rad, *Old Testament Theology* II (London: SCM Press, 1975), 364-365.

[635] Thus for him the Christian theological dimension is central to his conception of Old Testament theology. In fact in his third section 'The Old Testament and the New,' a section is devoted under the subtitle 'The Old Testament saving event in the light of the New Testament fulfilment.' See G. von Rad, *Old Testament Theology* II, 357-387.

[636] B. Childs, *Biblical Theology of the Old and New Testaments: Theological Reflection on the Christian Bible* (London: SCM Press, 1992), 92-93.

[637] Childs, *Biblical Theology of the Old and New Testaments*, 721.

the Old Testament. For him the concept of God is not unique to Jesus, whether it is the use of God as 'Father' in the discourses or addressing God in prayer. Rather, for him the Jesus of the Synoptic Gospels is firmly rooted in the Jewish background.[638] For him "the two testaments which comprise Christian scripture together bear witness to the unity of God's identity."[639] That "the Old Testament bears the same witness as does the New to the unity of God's righteousness and mercy which God made known in history with Israel."[640] Thus we see that efforts to find central motif in Old Testament theology beginning with Eichrodt, finds its culmination in Childs, who stressed the continuity of the New Testament with the Old Testament. He categorically stated that both the Testaments witness to the same God. In other words, he finds God and his character and purposes as the central theme of biblical theology.

Childs' argument is carried forward by current New Testament scholar Scott J. Hafemann, who stood for a central unifying theme in biblical theology, by viewing both the Old and New Testaments holistically. According to him "God's relationship with his people within the salvation history recounted in Scripture is the subject matter of 'biblical *theology*.'"[641] Referring to the many texts on the idea of God's fatherhood and sonship of God's people (Isa 9:6-7; Mt 6:9-10; Gal 1:4; Eph 4:6; Phil 4:20; I Thess 1:3; 3:11, 13; Rev 1:6), coupled with the idea of God's love (Deut 7:8;10;18; I Kings 10:9; Ps 33:5; 147:8; Jer 31:3; Jn 3:16; Eph 2:4; 5:2; I Jn 4:10,19) and love for God (Deut 6:4; Lev 19:18; Mk 12:29-31) Hafemann finds the covenant relationship as the heart of both the Testaments.[642] He shows this idea by a threefold covenant structure of past, present and future of the covenant as:

> God's acts as 'King' and 'Father' bring about a response of childlike dependence from the people of his 'kingdom.' Moreover, God's provisions in the past provide the foundation for trusting his promises for the future. This active reliance on God's promises takes the form of obedience to the King's commands as the organic expression of trust in his sovereignty and love.[643]

He thus finds that the theme of covenant relationship as more of providing "the structure that serves to integrate the interrelated themes developed

---

[638] Childs, *Biblical Theology of the Old and New Testaments*, 361.

[639] Childs, *Biblical Theology of the Old and New Testaments*, 372.

[640] Childs, *Biblical Theology of the Old and New Testaments*, 373-374.

[641] Scott J. Hafemann, "The Covenant Relationship," in *Central Themes in Biblical Theology: Mapping Unity in Diversity*, edited by Scott J. Hafemann and Paul R. House (Grand Rapids: Baker Academic, 2007), 21.

[642] Hafemann, "The Covenant Relationship," in *Central Themes in Biblical Theology*, 32-33.

[643] Hafemann, "The Covenant Relationship," in *Central Themes in Biblical Theology*, 35.

throughout the history of redemption delineated in the Scriptures."[644] It is also the argument of Rolf Rendtorff and John Walton. Rendtorff sees 'covenant' as "the most comprehensive and the most theologically weighty term for God's attention to humans in the Hebrew Bible."[645] So also for Walton "both the Old and New Testament weave their theology on the loom of history with the thread of the covenant."[646]

5.1.2. God in New Testament Theology

Coming to the New Testament theology scenario, a defining moment in the issue of central emphasis began with the work of Rudolf Bultmann. His monumental work is a watershed on the subject of New Testament Theology.[647] He is noted for his existential interpretation of the New Testament in ignoring the historical Jesus a part in the New Testament theology. This is clearly stated right at the very beginning of his work:

> *The message of Jesus* is a presupposition for the theology of the New Testament rather than a part of that theology itself."[648]

He then goes on saying:

> Christian faith did not exist until there was a Christian kerygma; i.e., a kerygma proclaiming Jesus Christ – specifically Jesus Christ the Crucified and Risen One – to be God's eschatological act of salvation. He was first so proclaimed in the kerygma of the earliest Church, not in the message of the historical Jesus, even though that Church frequently introduced into its account of Jesus' message, motifs of its own proclamation. Thus, theological thinking – the theology of the New Testament – begins with the kerygma of the earliest Church and not before.[649]

---

[644] The covenant relationship provides, for him, a major theme among many other interlinking themes. In his words, "Like the hub and rim of a wheel respectively, the old (establishment) and new (restoration and consummation) covenants define and hold together the different 'spokes' of divine revelation manifested in the words and deeds of redemptive history. In so doing, the covenant becomes the interpretative lens for seeing clearly the conceptual and historical unity of the Bible in the midst of its diversity." See Hafemann, "The Covenant Relationship," in *Central Themes in Biblical Theology*, 23.

[645] R. Rendtorff, *The Canonical Hebrew Bible: A Theology of the Old Testament* (Tools for Biblical Study 7; Leiden: Deo Publishing, 2005), 433; See also R. Rendtorff, *Canon and Theology: Overtures to an Old Testament Theology*, translated and edited by Margaret Kohl (Edinburgh: T&T Clark,1994), 196-206.

[646] John H. Walton, *Covenant, God's Purpose, God's Plan* (Grand Rapids: Zondervan, 1994), 10.

[647] R. Bultmann, *Theology of the New Testament* (complete in one volume; Trans. by Kendrick Grobel; New York: Charles Scribner's Sons, 1955).

[648] Bultmann, *Theology of the New Testament*, 3.

[649] Bultmann, *Theology of the New Testament*, 3.

This is how Bultmann evaded the significance of the Old Testament and Jesus' tradition and clearly placed the accent on anthropology (human) rather than theology (God) in keeping with his existential interpretation.[650] Since for him the thrust of the New Testament is essentially anthropological (self-understanding), he did not see God as the primary horizon of the New Testament. Such a view is clear from the very content of his two volume works on New Testament theology. In his first volume a very small amount of space is devoted to 'Jesus' idea of God,' as part of 'The message of Jesus,'[651] compared to the exhaustive treatment on the christological theme, 'the kerygma of the earliest Church,' 'the kerygma of the Hellenistic Church' and 'Pauline anthropology' (man prior to the revelation of faith, man under faith).[652] While the entire second volume is devoted to Christology of John and ecclesiology of the later New Testament writings, that is, regarding the development of the church order and doctrine.[653] Thus for him the existential reality and so communion seems to be the overarching theme of the New Testament.

Unlike the contentions of Bultmann, who sees theological thinking in the post Easter kerygma, what we need to keep in mind is that the New Testament theology is a part of biblical theology,[654] and which means that theology precedes Christology. This is where we see weakness of Bultmann theology.

In the decades post Bultmann's work, several New Testament theology works dealt with the question of a 'centre' of the New Testament, which was more or less motivated by Bultmann's trend. It is seen that most of the scholars fall in line with Bultmann's christocentric focus. So in true Bultmannian mould Kasemann follows the discontinuity model in his view of a New Testament theology. He thus talks about earthly Jesus as "a presupposition and not a constitutive part of the New Testament theology."[655] He also argued that the fragmentary nature of the New Testament data makes any attempt to unify the diverse theologies impossible.[656] He holds that New Testament theology has to do with early Christian kerygma which is defined by the Christ event on the Cross.[657]As such he sees the person

[650] His indifference in historical Jesus is clear spelled out in his work *Jesus and the Word*, trans Louise Pettibone Smith and Erminie Huntress Lantero (New York: Scribner, 1958), 8.

[651] R. Bultmann, *Theology of the New Testament* I (Trans Kendrick Grobel; New York: Charles Scribner's Sons, 1954), 22-25. For him (*Theology of the New Testament* I, 23) Jesus' idea of God does not essentially differ from that of the Old Testament and of Judaism.'

[652] Almost the whole of the work of the first volume is devoted to these three chapters; see Bultmann, *Theology of the New Testament* I, 33-345.

[653] *Theology of the New Testament* II (Trans Kendrick Grobel; New York: Charles Scribner's Sons, 1955).

[654] Dunn, *New Testament theology*, 42.

[655] E. Kasemann, "The Problem of a New Testament Theology," in *NTS* 19 (1973), 244.

[656] Kasemann, "The Problem of a New Testament Theology," 242.

[657] Kasemann, "The Problem of a New Testament Theology," 244.

and work of Christ as the sole matter of New Testament theology and totally subsumed the theme of God under Christology. The same idea is seen in the work of Alan Richardson (1958) who structured his New Testament theology according to the categories of dogmatic (kerygmatic) studies. Quite in line with Bultmann's discontinuity mode, his work begins with the theme 'Faith and Hearing,' and categorically states:

> There is nothing in the OT which exactly corresponds to the concept of faith ... the NT faith becomes primarily faith in Jesus Christ, who is himself both the object and the giver of the faith of his disciples. It was Jesus himself who taught his disciples the cardinal necessity of faith.[658]

As stated, Richardson organized his theology of the New Testament along dogmatic lines and subsumed theology under Christology. The whole of his New Testament theology is an exhaustive treatment on the person and work of Christ to the total neglect of theology proper, concerning who God is and what God has done. The subject of God (theology) is dealt indirectly while dealing with the work of Christ (Christology).[659] Unlike Richardson who outlines his work in purely dogmatic lines, Conzelmann (1969) takes a chronological (historical) approach. The subject of God appears in his treatment on the Synoptic tradition (kerygma) with the theme 'The Idea of God.'[660] He talks about the designations of God in the Synoptic Gospels with the term 'God,' 'Father,' 'King,' and 'Lord' as the major designation of God.[661] Yet, as in the work of Bultmann, the christological tone dominates the whole work (the Kerygma of the Primitive Community and the Hellenistic Community; the Theology of Paul; the Development after Paul; and John).[662] Even within the Synoptic kerygma, Christology (the Son, the Son of God, The Messiah, Son of David, the Son of Man, the miracles of Jesus, the messianic Secret) dominates the theological discussion.[663] True to his christological tenor he argued that "the miracles said to have been performed by Jesus are also a factor of christology."[664]

---

[658] Alan Richardson, *An Introduction to the Theology of the New Testament*, 19-20.

[659] Thus Leander Keck criticism is to the point, "The Jesus who teaches everything Richardson attributes to him has been pasted together with New Testament texts; he is not a flesh and blood, first century, north Palestinian, Aramaic-speaking Jew. [Richardson's] Jesus is a Christian theologian, probably an Anglican." See L. Keck, "Problems of a New Testament Theology: A Critique of Alan Richardson's *An Introduction to the Theology of the New Testament*," in *NovT* 7 (1964-65), 237.

[660] Conzelmann, *An Outline of the Theology of the New Testament*, 99-106.

[661] Conzelmann, *An Outline of the Theology of the New Testament*, 100-101.

[662] These are the sectional headings that Conzelmann employs to structure his material; see Conzelmann, *An Outline of the Theology of the New Testament*, 29-358.

[663] Conzelmann, *An Outline of the Theology of the New Testament*, 127-140.

[664] Conzelmann, *An Outline of the Theology of the New Testament*, 137.

New Testament theology continued in Bultmannian trend of christological discussions, and dominated the New Testament theology works and writings in the decades to come. However, J. Jeremias' work is an exception. Unlike Bultmann and Kasemann, Jeremias gives much importance to the teaching of historical Jesus. Accordingly, his main emphasis is that God is the Father of Jesus, and that Jesus always called God *Abba* Father.[665] He argued that Jesus' address to God as *Abba* is unique to Jesus, the *ipsissima vox jesu.*[666] Under the section on 'being a child' he also talks about the fatherhood of God in exclusive sense, that is, in relation with Jesus' sonship to God.[667]

The work of W.G. Kummel (1974) shows God-discussion (theology) subsumed under Christology. He recognizes Christology (Jesus Christ) as the unifying theme of the whole of New Testament theology. While dealing with this central motif of the New Testament theology Kummel notes that "the concern about a theology of the New Testament found itself from the outset confronted with the problem of diversity and unity in the New Testament."[668] With great perception he suggests "that the presentation and arrangement of a 'theology of the New Testament' can come about only as a *result* of work with the diverse forms of the New Testament proclamation."[669] For him, no predetermined center can ever function as an organizing principle for the presentation of a New Testament theology. His assumption is that the center of the New Testament is found in the message and figure of Jesus as recorded in the Synoptic Gospels, and also the proclamation of the primitive community and the first theological reflection on this proclamation by Paul.[670] On the basis of these three blocks Kummel suggests that the following twofold aspect about Jesus Christ constitutes the center of the New Testament: "God has caused his salvation promised for the end of the world to begin in Jesus Christ, and that in this Christ-event God has encountered us and intends to encounter us as the Father who seeks to rescue us from imprisonment in the world and to make us free for active love."[671] Kummel thus recognizes in Jesus Christ the center of the New Testament and talks about God but only in relation to Jesus' proclamation.

The christological focus is again prominent in L. Goppelt's two volume work. The first volume carries the subtitle "The Ministry of Jesus In Its Theological Significance." Following salvation-history approach, Goppelt pointed out the

---

[665] Jeremias, *New Testament Theology* I, 61-68.

[666] Jeremias, *New Testament Theology* I, 171-203.

[667] Jeremias, *New Testament Theology* I, 171-203.

[668] Kummel, *The Theology of the New Testament*, 15.

[669] Kummel, *The Theology of the New Testament*, 17.

[670] Kummel, *The Theology of the New Testament*, 324.

[671] Kummel, *The Theology of the New Testament*, 332.

Easter kerygma as the starting point of New Testament theology.[672] However, for him the foundation of New Testament theology was the reporting of the earthly activity of Jesus, so that New Testament theology, on the basis of its own structure, has to ask for the earthly Jesus.[673] His first volume is completely devoted to Jesus' earthly ministry; the second volume takes up the Christology of the early church, Pauline Christology, theology of post-Pauline writings and Johannine Christology.[674] The second volume has chapter two devoted completely to Christology – The Son of God and the *Kyrios* Christology.[675] Thus the theme of God (theology) is completely subsumed under Christology. The same idea is seen in G.E. Ladd's work, as he too considers the Christ event, the person and work of Jesus Christ, as the central theme of the New Testament theology.[676]

Ladd puts the New Testament writings in the manner of historical development namely Synoptic Gospels, the Fourth Gospel, the Primitive Church, Paul and the General Epistles. In his treatment of the Synoptic Gospels in part one, Ladd provides a thematic cross-section having devoted eight chapters on the aspects of the kingdom as preached by Jesus, and five chapters with aspects of christological concepts.[677] He believes that "there is great richness in the variety of New Testament theology which must not be sacrificed."[678] He has pointed out several theological-christological motifs (e.g., the kingdom of God in Synoptics; eternal life in John; justification and the life in Christ in Paul) as diverse themes that converge into the one great salvific event - the person and work of Jesus Christ, as the central theme of the New Testament theology.[679] The theme of God is covered under the rubric 'the God of the Kingdom' and discussed the theme of God as 'The Seeking God,' 'The Inviting God,' 'The Fatherly God' and 'The Judging God.'[680] Ladd's view of salvation history is made up of a series of events in which God revealed himself as nowhere else. For him the New Testament theology "consists primarily of the recital of what God has done in

---

[672] Goppelt, *Theology of the New Testament I*, 5.

[673] Goppelt, *Theology of the New Testament* I, 7.

[674] L. Goppelt, *Theology of the New Testament* II*: The Variety and Unity of the Apostolic Witness to Christ* (trans John E. Alsup and edited by Jurgen Roloff; Grand Rapids: William B. Eerdmans, 1982).

[675] Goppelt, *Theology of the New Testament* II, 65-106.

[676] Ladd, *A Theology of the New Testament*, 33.

[677] Ladd, *A Theology of the New Testament* , 34-210.

[678] Ladd, *A Theology of the New Testament*, 33.

[679] Ladd, *A Theology of the New Testament*, 33.

[680] Ladd, *A Theology of the New Testament*, 81-90.

Jesus of Nazareth."[681] Thus in Ladd's work the theme of God also finds a place in theological discussion.[682]

Similar idea is seen in the work of D. Guthrie, for whom the key figure in New Testament is Jesus Christ. He asserts, "NT theology is essentially theology about Christ. It is for this reason that Christology comes to be the primary doctrine to be considered."[683] Of course he acknowledged God as the basic doctrine[684] and finds a place for the theme of God in his thematic treatment. The first chapter of his work is devoted to the theme of God as Creator, Father, King and the attributes of God.[685] He points out that the idea of the fatherhood of God, being the most characteristic of New Testament teaching, is seen in three ways - as Father of Jesus, of the disciples and of all creation.[686] For him fatherhood is seen as "inherent in the nature of God."[687] Thus, Guthrie's work shows that God and Jesus are equally significant and that both need to be given due attention in New Testament theology. J.D.G. Dunn's 1977 work dealt with one of the central questions of principle in New Testament theology. He starts from a theological problem: "*Is there a final expression of Christian truth whose meaning is unequivocal?*"[688] By emphatically drawing attention to the issue of diversity he deals with the problem of variety both thematically and in a section dealing with the early history of Christianity. He concludes that the only unifying factor between all different writings and layers of tradition is the conviction of "the unity between the historical Jesus and the exalted Christ. That is to say, the conviction that wandering charismatic preacher from Nazareth had ministered, died and been raised from the dead to bring God and man finally together, the recognition that the divine power through which they now worshipped and were encountered and accepted by God was one and the same person, Jesus, the man, the Christ, the Son of God, the Lord, the life-giving Spirit."[689]

---

[681] Ladd, *A Theology of the New Testament*, 28.

[682] Ladd views both Old and New Testaments holistically and argues, "Biblical theology is *theology*: it is primarily a story about God and his concern for men" (Ladd, *A Theology of the New Testament*, 26). For him, "the bond that unites the Old and the New Testaments is this sense of the divine activity in history" (Ladd, *A Theology of the New Testament*, 26). Thus we see that theocentric focus is implicit in his projection of "the divine activity in history" as the unifying theme of the New Testament.

[683] Guthrie, *New Testament Theology*, 54.

[684] For him, "NT theology begins with some tremendous assumptions – that God exists." See Guthrie, *New Testament Theology*, 75, cf. 73.

[685] Guthrie, *New Testament Theology*, 75-115.

[686] Guthrie, *New Testament Theology*, 80-81.

[687] Guthrie, *New Testament Theology*, 83.

[688] Dunn, *Unity and Diversity in the New Testament*, 2.

[689] Dunn, *Unity and Diversity in the New Testament*, 369.

Dunn's work is thus a radical departure from Bultmannian Christ-centered discontinuity approach to God-centered continuity approach. This anti-Bultmann stance is all the more evident in his recent New Testament theology work, as one of his main findings is given in a rhetorical fashion thus, "On the question *whether the mission and message of Jesus himself is part of NT theology*, the answer has had to be *an unequivocal Yes*."[690] Dunn thus sets the tone on the theme of unity, continuity and so theocentric perspective in New Testament theology.

The work of G.F. Hasel (1978) is more of methodology in New Testament theology as he dealt with its basic issues.[691] However, he identified specific problem areas including the center, unity in diversity, and New Testament theology in relation to Old Testament. Noting the theocentric character of the Bible he affirmed God as the center of the Old Testament and Jesus Christ as the center of the New Testament.[692] He thus upholds the Old Testament-New Testament continuity in New Testament theology and hence he views the theme of God and Christ dynamically.[693]

5.1.3. Theocentric Perspective in New Testament Theology

In the 1990s the New Testament theology took a definite shift towards clear-cut theocentric focus. It is seen in the work of G.B. Caird, who stresses the theological unity of the New Testament.[694] This theocentric emphasis is clear as the main body of his work begins with the chapter titled 'the divine plan' and acknowledged God as the primary force behind every narrative of the New Testament. In his words, "The New Testament is from beginning to an end a book about God."[695] Keeping his theocentric perspective in mind he attempts to bring the New Testament authors together in conversation with one another with his "Conference Table Approach."[696] Caird proceeds thematically, and the New Testament authors are put to speak with their own voices to various aspects of the works of God.[697] At the very beginning Caird clearly stated that the purpose of the New Testament theology, being a historical discipline, is descriptive.[698] He holds out for the theological unity of the New Testament. The model is given by

---

690 Dunn, *New Testament Theology: An Introduction*, 156.

691 G.F. Hasel, *New Testament Theology: Basic Issues in the Current Debate* (Michigan: Wm B. Eerdmans, 1978).

692 Hasel, *New Testament Theology: Basic Issues in the Current Debate*, 216.

693 Hasel, *New Testament Theology: Basic Issues in the Current Debate*, 219.

694 G.B. Caird, *New Testament Theology* (Completed and edited by L.D. Hurst; Oxford: Clarendon, 1994).

695 Caird, *New Testament Theology*, 31.

696 Caird, *New Testament Theology*, 18.

697 For him salvation is the overarching theme of the New Testament. Indeed, six of the eight chapters that comprise the body of the book are essentially about salvation.

698 Caird, *New Testament Theology*, 1.

the New Testament itself in the form of the Jerusalem council,[699] in which there was presumably unity without homogeneity, as Caird puts, "Whatever measure of agreement they achieved there was some outstanding differences of opinion, about which they agreed to differ. Peter and Paul were to go their own separate ways. But they could do this without any sense of radical division, because they had recognized that the same God was at work both in Peter's mission to the Jews and in Paul's mission to the Gentiles."[700] The question is not whether the New Testament texts "all say the same thing, but whether they all witness to the same Jesus and through him to the many splendoured wisdom of the one God."[701] Thus, for Caird the unity of the New Testament is finally a question about the unity of God.

The question of God comes to the fore in I. H. Marshall's work, with unity in diversity stands at the center of his work.[702] He structured with an author-by-author approach reflecting his conviction that if there is to be a synthetic New Testament theology, "it must begin with seeing each writer in his own terms."[703] The investigation of the individual witnesses of the New Testament does not proceed chronologically but, by and large, according to modern canonical groupings (Synoptic and Acts, Pauline corpus, Johannine literatures, the rest of the New Testament). The historical Jesus, however, is not set aside, arguing that New Testament theology must include "jesusology as well as christology."[704] Adopting J.C. Beker's pattern of analysis for Pauline thought, Marshall argues that the core of the New Testament is its message of redemption. He pointed out four noticeable stages to what he called the 'religion of redemption' common to all the New Testament writings: the situation of human need understood as sin that places sinners under divine judgment; the saving act by God that is accomplished through Jesus Christ; the new life for those who show faith in God and Jesus Christ; and the act of God to bring his redemptive action to consummation with the parousia of Christ.[705] For him, in addition to the main theme of redemption, all the New Testament writers share the same larger framework of thought, which is fundamentally Jewish in shape. The basic importance of the Old Testament is presupposed, as are the doctrine of creation and the theological significance of history.[706]

---

[699] Caird, *New Testament Theology*, 23-24.

[700] Caird, *New Testament Theology*, 24.

[701] Caird, *New Testament Theology*, 24.

[702] As the title shows, *New Testament Theology: Many Witnesses, One Gospel.*

[703] Marshall, *New Testament Theology: Many Witnesses, One Gospel*, 726.

[704] Marshall, *New Testament Theology: Many Witnesses, One Gospel*, 46.

[705] Marshall, *New Testament Theology: Many Witness, One Gospel*, 717-718.

[706] Marshall, *New Testament Theology: Many Witnesses, One Gospel*, 718.

For him there is unity amidst diversity among the New Testament writings. There is "a harmony between the different writers."[707] They all "bear testimony to what is palpably the same complex reality."[708] Moreover, "there is a significant core of agreement and identity within the theologies of the individual constituents of the New Testament"[709] with the "saving act by God that is accomplished through Jesus Christ"[710]as the main theme. For him while the redemption is accomplished in Christ "God is the principal actor and Jesus is primarily obedient to God. It is the God of Israel who performs the redemptive act in Christ, who acts as his agent or instrument.[711]" Referring to the unity among the New Testament writers Marshall remarked that "the God who saves in Matthew and Luke-Acts is the same God of Israel as in Paul."[712] Thus Marshall puts emphasis on God's significance along with Jesus.' Following canonical approach F. Thielman's work examines the major theological themes of the three parts of the New Testament Canon: Gospels and Acts; Pauline Letters; and Non-Pauline Letters plus the book of Revelation. He maintains that the writings of the New Testament converge on six theological themes that bind the entire New Testament together: 'The Convergence of the Human Problem and God's Answer to It in Jesus,' 'Faith as Response to God's Gracious Initiative,' 'The Spirit as the Eschatological Presence of God,' 'The Church as the People of God,' 'The Consummation of All Things,' and 'The Centrality of Christ to the Theological Vision of the New Testament.'[713] Thielman thus votes for Jesus Christ as the foundation of New Testament theology.

Another work on exploring diversity and unity is F.J. Matera, who votes for God and Christ as the central emphasis of New Testament theology. At the very introduction of his work he talks about engaging in New Testament theology that helps wrestle with the unity of God's revelation in Christ.[714] According to him "the unity of New Testament theology is a diverse unity: a unity that expresses itself in a multiplicity of ways because no one way can fully capture the mystery that is God in Christ."[715] According to him the central motif of the New Testament theology is salvation. In his words, "New Testament theology begins with soteriology. Apart from soteriology, there would be no need for Christology, ecclesiology, Christian ethics, or eschatology. The experience of the salvation God has accomplished

[707] Marshall, *New Testament Theology: Many Witnesses, One Gospel*, 483.

[708] Marshall, *New Testament Theology: Many Witnesses, One Gospel*, 726.

[709] Marshall, *New Testament Theology: Many Witnesses, One Gospel*, 717.

[710] Marshall, *New Testament Theology: Many Witnesses, One Gospel*, 717.

[711] Marshall, *New Testament Theology: Many Witnesses, One Gospel*, 727.

[712] Marshall, *New Testament Theology: Many Witnesses, One Gospel*, 729.

[713] These are the sectional headings that Thielman employs to structure his material; See F. Thielman, *Theology of the New Testament: A Canonical and Synthetic Approach* (Grand Rapids: Zondervan, 2005), 681-725.

[714] Matera, *New Testament Theology: Exploring Diversity and Unity*, xxx-xxxi.

[715] Matera, *New Testament Theology: Exploring Diversity and Unity*, 480.

in and through Christ, determines how the New Testament writers understand Christ, the Church, the moral life, and the hope of the sanctified."[716]
Another recent work on New Testament theology is by Udo Schnelle who treats New Testament theology as meaning-formation, as he puts:

> A theology of the New Testament is charged with the task of *comprehensively discerning and describing the construction of this world of meaning.* The beginning point must be Jesus of Nazareth, whose ministry and preaching constructed a symbolic universe that evoked other meaning-formations both before and after Easter. All New Testament authors used these meaning-formations as their fundamental reference point.[717]

Accordingly, he structured his work in a chronological development of the New Testament writings; first delineating Jesus' own thought world, then to early Christianity, Paul, Gospels, Deutero-Pauline letters, Catholic epistles, Johannine writings and Revelation. In all these chapters he presented the thought world of each author comprehensively by dividing into thematic sectors: Theology, Christology, Pneumatology, Soteriology, Anthropology, Ethics, Ecclesiology, Eschatology, and Historical-theological standpoint. He treats theological emphasis of each of the New Testament writers separately and gives the theme of God (theology) a forefront discussion in each of the New Testament writings, by putting the theme of 'theology' in the forefront of his thematic subdivisions. Schnelle sees clear theocentric emphasis as he talks about God as the one who acts in history. For him "continuity with Israel plays a central role in his concept of God."[718] He sees "unity between God and Jesus, a unity that is not first created by the resurrection, but is foundational from the very beginning."[719]

Thomas R. Schreiner's *New Testament Theology: Magnifying God in Christ* (2008) is one of the most recent works which focuses on the theme of God in New Testament theology. At the very preface section while dealing with 'the Question of a Center' for New Testament theology, Schreiner categorically states that the subject matter of New Testament theology is God himself and that the New Testament is fundamentally God-centered.[720] Accordingly, a chapter is devoted with the title "the centrality of God in New Testament theology."[721] He correctly positioned that "the centrality of God in Christ is the foundational theme for the

---

[716] Matera, *New Testament Theology: Exploring Diversity and Unity*, 479.

[717] U. Schnelle, *Theology of the New Testament*, 57.

[718] Schnelle, *Theology of the New Testament*, 430.

[719] Schnelle, *Theology of the New Testament*, 431.

[720] Schreiner, *New Testament Theology*, 13.

[721] Schreiner, *New Testament Theology*, 119-167.

narrative unfolded in the NT."[722] He explains this inseparable relationship of God (theology) and Christ (Christology) thus:

> The coming of Christ does not diminish the centrality of God but rather enhances it. Christ does not summon attention to himself so that God is pushed off center stage. God receives praise, glory, and honor for the ministry, death, and resurrection of Christ. God planned, after all, that Christ would come and accomplish redemption for his people.[723]

In this he has covered the treatments on the centrality of God in the Synoptic Gospels, John, Pauline letters, Hebrews, James, I Peter, 2 Peter and Jude, I John and Revelation. While treating God in the Synoptic Gospels he affirms the continuity with the Old Testament view of God and deals with the God of the Kingdom, God's Sovereignty, God's mercy, God's glory, God as Father, Jesus' unique relationship with God, the Father's Authority, the goodness of the Father thus highlighting the centrality of God. L.W. Hurtado's work *God in the New Testament Theology* (2010) deals with the discourse about 'God' in the New Testament with a holistic approach. As mentioned earlier, at the very beginning of his introduction chapter[724] he elaborated about how God has been an infrequently discussed subject in the whole of New Testament studies. He then goes on dealing with the particularity of the deity discourses in the New Testament, emphasizing also of the exclusivity of earliest Christian worship; the consequences for 'God' of the New Testament emphasis on Jesus; the place of the Spirit in New Testament God-discourse and the issue of the unity and diversity in New Testament God-discourse.[725]

The above assessment shows that most of the New Testament theology works in the post-Bultmannian era till the 1980s followed something roughly like Bultmann's general approach, highlighting the significance of Christ-experience. An indication of this is the widespread discussion of the question of a 'center' of the New Testament. This arose indeed from the dissatisfaction with Bultmann's identification of Christ-experience (existential, human's self-understanding) as the centre, to the neglect of the historical Jesus in New Testament theology. He deliberately evaded the significance of the Old Testament in New Testament theology. Yet this is the trend that we see in most of the New Testament theology works till the 1980s, having subsumed most of the discussion on God under Christology, that is, from the lens of Christ Jesus. This tendency is also reflected in the work of D.M. Baillie, a contemporary of Bultmann and a systematic theologian, who, while dealing with 'Christology and the nature of God' said, "if we have not

[722] Schreiner, *New Testament Theology*, 119.

[723] Schreiner, *New Testament Theology*, 120.

[724] Hurtado, *God in the New Testament Theology*, 1.

[725] Hurtado, *God in the New Testament Theology*, 1-113.

a sound Christology, we cannot have a sound theology either."[726] But the reverse is true. A sound Christology needs a sound theology. It is seen that all the key claims about Jesus directly or indirectly implicate God. For example, even the miracles of Jesus are expressed as God's power. Hence God (theology) should be at the forefront in any theological discussion. In fact the whole of the Christological question is a question about God and that the significance of Jesus must not dethrone God. This is the direction we see in the New Testament theology works of the 1990s and onward, as New Testament theologians increasingly affirm the continuity, the inseparability of the Old from the New, and seeing God as the basic foundation of the New Testament thinking and theology.

Some recent New Testament theology works, however, are not in the same tone. George Strecker's work, for example, continues in somewhat Bultmannian vein with an explicit focus upon the existential-experiential aspect;[727] that for him the 'Christ-event' stands in discontinuity to Old Testament traditions.[728] Moreover, he rejects the assumption of a theological unity in the New Testament.[729] So also Philip F. Esler's work (2005) is another example of recent work on Bultmannian vein with an explicit focus upon the subjective, experiential aspect having identified 'communion and community' as the overarching theological theme of New Testament. Esler stated his intention of writing New Testament theology "to promote a specifically Christian rationale for reading the New Testament that is related to its role in speaking of God's ongoing relationship with human beings and with the cosmos."[730] Thus the whole of his descriptive, historical investigations is "set within a theologically and socially constructed framework of persons in communion."[731] These are the two sides of Esler's proposal: on the one hand, there is the adamant commitment to the historical-critical and social-scientific enterprise, but, on the other hand, there is the attempt to develop a theological account of personhood. Thus, his theological discourse is subjective, existential. As such he talks about overarching theological emphasis as God for us, that is, "God's way of being in relationship with us – which is God's personhood – is a perfect expression of God's being as God."[732]

---

[726] D.M. Baillie, *God was in Christ: An Essay on Incarnation and Atonement* (London: Faber and Faber Limited, 1948), 65.

[727] G. Strecker, *Theology of the New Testament* (edited by F.W. Horn; trans E. Boring; Louisville: Westminster John Knox Press, 2000), 2.

[728] Strecker, *Theology of the New Testament*, 9.

[729] Strecker, *Theology of the New Testament*, 2-3.

[730] P.F. Esler, *New Testament Theology: Communion and Community* (Minneapolis: Fortress Press, 2005), 1.

[731] Esler, *New Testament Theology: Communion and Community*, 276.

[732] Esler, *New Testament Theology: Communion and Community*, 65.

5.1.4. Fatherhood of God – Core Motif in New Testament Theology

As we have seen in the analysis above the question of God and so theocentric thinking has gained ascendancy in New Testament theology particularly in the 1990s and onward. Contrary to the Bultmannian idea of anthropological-existential emphasis, there is a strong current in seeing the theocentric nature of the New Testament theology. God, being acknowledged as the primary force behind every narratives of the New Testament, is increasingly recognized as the center of New Testament theology.[733] In fact God is acknowledged as forming "the warp with many other themes forming the weft in the tapestry being woven by the NT writers."[734] Pressing in this direction Dunn argues:

> It is imperative that a NT theology tackle this subject and make explicit the inexplicit; otherwise the rationale underpinning so many other beliefs and practices will have been lost to view. Without an appreciation of the axiom, the consequent propositions will lack persuasiveness. Without an awareness of the foundation, the logic of the superstructures will be unclear, and the superstructures will seem all the less secure.[735]

It is with this perspective that scholars begin to put things in perspective and affirm the centrality of God in the New Testament theology. As seen above Schreiner noted the character and purpose of God's sovereignty, mercy, glory and fatherhood as the foundational theme particularly in the Gospels.[736] Watson too noted the God-Jesus correlation, so fatherhood-sonship relationship, as the heart of the Gospel narratives.[737] So also Dunn sees theocentric nature of New Testament theology by noting the language of God being saturated throughout the New Testament writings. He even noted the expression of the idea of God as Father, particularly in the letter openings (e.g., Rom 1:1; I Cor 1:1; 2 Cor 1:2) and the same expressed in the various doxologies that appear in the letters (e.g., Rom 1:25; 2 Cor 1:3; Eph 1:3; 1 Pet 1:3).[738] Moreover, the theme of God's fatherhood is clearly understood in what is considered as the central categories of several New Testament theology works: Christology, salvation-history, covenant, kingdom of God, etc. In all these themes biblical scholars have identified and understood God as the subject, the doer of the action and which means that

---

[733] Caird, *New Testament Theology*, 31; Schreiner, *New Testament Theology*, 13; Dunn, *New Testament Theology: An Introduction*, 22, 24; Hurtado, *God in New Testament Theology*, 26.

[734] Dunn, *New Testament Theology: An Introduction*, 41.

[735] Dunn, *New Testament Theology: An Introduction*, 42.

[736] Thomas R. Schreiner, *New Testament Theology: Magnifying God in Christ A Summary of New Testament Theology* (Grand Rapids; Michigan: Baker Academic, 2010), 39-46.

[737] F. Watson, *Text and Truth: Redefining Biblical Theology* (Grand Rapids: Wm B. Eerdmans, 1997), 83.

[738] Dunn, *New Testament Theology: An Introduction*, 41.

the theme of the fatherhood of God is central. This is also reflected in some of the perceived Christ-centered New Testament theology works, notably Ladd and Guthrie, who have devoted significantly to the idea of God's fatherhood, in spite of their "pronounced Christocentricity."[739] So also in the biblical theology works, in the work of Hafemann, for example, the covenant relationship is projected as the overarching theme of both Old and New Testaments. In all these the idea of God's fatherhood looms large. That means the idea of the fatherhood of God seems to provide the overarching theme or structure that serves to integrate the interrelated themes developed in the Bible. We will show this as we turn to the next section on Matthean theology.

5.2. Fatherhood of God: The Fulcrum of Matthean Theology

5.2.1. Fatherhood of God and Christology

The centrality of the theme of God's fatherhood is seen in the fact that Matthew has prominently projected the sonship of Jesus in his Gospel much more than his Synoptic counterparts. In several instances the christological expression is seen as Matthean redactional works (1:23; 2:15; 14:33; 16:16; 26:63; 27:40, 43). Such instances of strong christological content in Matthew led several scholars to see Matthew from the christological lens, thus find no place for God in their christology-dictated works on Matthew. Till the 1990s most scholars see Matthew from the lens of Christology, arguing that the identity of Jesus as the Son of God (Christology) as the foremost theme of Matthew. Beginning with J. D. Kingsbury,[740] who finds the 'Son of God' as the key Christological title in Matthew, several scholars affirm the same. According to D. Hagner, "Matthew's doctrine of Jesus as the Christ is fundamentally important to every theological emphasis in the Gospel, for it is the identity of Jesus that determines such things as fulfillment, authoritative exposition of the law, discipleship, ecclesiology, and eschatology."[741] D. Senior and R.T. France too assert that each and every aspect of the Gospel of Matthew relates to the theme of Christology.[742] So also U. Luz, who has brought out some of the most exhaustive work on Matthew in the recent decades,[743] views Christology as the overarching theme in Matthew. In his 1995 monograph, following literary narrative approach, he views Matthew with christological lens

---

[739] For this expression see Hurtado, *God in New Testament Theology*, 2.

[740] *Matthew: Structure, Christology, Kingdom*, 41. In his later work (*Matthew As Story*, 10-11), he argues the same using narrative criticism.

[741] Hagner, *Matthew 1-13*, lxi.

[742] D. Senior, *What Are They Saying About Matthew*, 74; D. Senior, *The Gospel of Matthew*, 53; R.T. France, *Matthew - Evangelist and Teacher*, 279-317.

[743] His exhaustive commentary series on Matthew includes *Matthew 1-7: A Commentary*, trans W. Linss (Minneapolis: Augsburg, 1989); *Matthew 8-20*, trans J.E. Couch (Hermenia Series; Minneapolis: Fortress, 2001); *Matthew 21-28*, trans J.E. Couch (Hermenia Series; Minneapolis: Fortress, 2005).

as he clearly noted right at the introduction that "the entire Gospel is bracketed by the fundamental Christological motif of 'God with us' (Immanuel) in 1:23 and 28:20."[744] Another more recent work on Matthew is by R. Schnackenburg,[745] who subsumed the theme of God under Christology, so much so that even the pericope of 'Jesus walking on the water' (14:22-33), in which the very expression 'Son of God' occurs, is termed as 'Christophany.'[746] With the influence of literary critical methods there is a growing awareness in Matthean studies to attend to the structure and flow of the narrative to discern the theology and intent of the text. Thus in some recent works we see addition to this approach the insights that the allusions and actions of Matthean Jesus also communicate his messianic claims. There are some scholars who argue that Matthew projects Jesus as Wisdom[747] and Jesus as a new Moses,[748] thus compliment the Son of God[749] Christology in Matthew. The above survey reveals, for most Matthean scholars, Christology is the overarching theological emphasis of Matthew and it drives and informs all other theological categories.

While the prominence of Jesus (and so Christology) is obvious in Matthew as in the rest of the New Testament writings, yet our point is that the prominence of Jesus is always expressed with reference to God,[750] and that this emphasis on Christology must not dethrone the place of God. Christology and theology are inseparably related. A very careful observation reveals that in all the christological expressions of Matthew, Jesus' significance is articulated always with reference to God. For example, even in the very expression 'Son of God,' which is the most prominent christological expression of Matthew, the prominence of the Son (Jesus) is always expressed with reference to God. Thus we see how intimately the

---

[744] Luz, *The Theology of Matthew*, 4.

[745] Schnackenburg, *The Gospel of Matthew*.

[746] Schnackenburg, *The Gospel of Matthew*, 143-145.

[747] C. Deutsch, "Wisdom in Matthew: Transformation of a Symbol," in *Nov T* 32 (1990), 13-47; of course pioneering work in this perspective is seen in the work of M. J. Suggs, *Wisdom, Christology, and Law in Matthew's Gospel* (Cambridge: Harvard University, 1970).

[748] D.C. Allison, *The New Moses: A Matthean Typology* (Minneapolis: Fortress Press, 1993).

[749] Very recently some Matthean scholars are seeing even in the expression the Son of God anti-imperial tones R.L. Mowery ("Son of God in Roman Imperial Titles and Matthew," in *Bib* 83 [2002], 100-110), noting these several unique occurrences of the term θεοῦ υἱὸς in Matthew, sees anti-imperial overtones. He establishes that a number of Roman emperors were denoted as θεοῦ υἱὸς. He argues that since in three clear instances of θεοῦ υἱὸς in Matthew derive from the hand of the evangelist himself, as he introduced the phrase into his Markan source in both 14:33 and 27:43, while in 27:54 he has inverted the original υἱὸς θεοῦ (Mk15:39). He argues that this formula would have evoked Roman imperial usage for his (Matthew's) community, and would have demonstrated that Jesus and not the emperor is in fact the Son of God. See also similar idea, W. Carter, "Matthean Christology in Roman Imperial key: Matthew 1.1," in *The Gospel of Matthew In Its Roman Imperial Context*, 143-165.

[750] For a detail discussion in this perspective, see Hurtado, *God in New Testament Theology*, 53-64.

sonship of Jesus is related with the fatherhood of God. In other words, in all the christological discussion of Matthew the idea of God's fatherhood is intimately present. Right at the infancy narrative, Matthew presents Jesus as fulfilling both Isaiah 7:14 in Matthew 1:23 ("'Look, the virgin shall conceive and bear a son, and they shall name him Emmanuel,' which means, 'God is with us'") and Hosea 11:1 in Matthew 2:15 ("out of Egypt I called my son"). This is to show that Jesus the Son brings the presence of God to immediate reality (cf. 11:27; 18:20; 28:18-20).[751] As the narratives furthers in Matthew we see this inseparable relationship between Christology and the fatherhood of God theme. It is seen that Jesus' identity is very much defined through his connection with Father. Jesus is the one about whom the voice from heaven speaks: "This is my Son, the Beloved, with whom I am well pleased" (3:17). Jesus is the one who has intimate relationship with the Father, such that he makes the bold claim for himself that "no one knows the Son except the Father, and no one knows the Father except the Son and anyone to whom the Son chooses to reveal him" (11:27).

Clearly the identity of Jesus (Sonship) is always defined with reference to the Father (Fatherhood of God). The term 'Son of God' which occurs several times in Matthew heightens his emphasis on God's fatherhood. In the pericope of Jesus' walking on the water (14:22-33//Mk 6:45-52), it is Matthew alone who has added the confession of the disciples, "Truly you are the Son of God" (14:33). Again it is Matthew alone who added the very expression "the Son of the living God" (16:16) to his source Mark, where Peter confesses simply saying "Your are the Christ" (Mk 8:29). So also in 26:63, it is Matthew alone who has the more articulated expression "I adjure you by the living God, tell us if you are the Christ, the Son of God," against his source Mark's expression "Are you the Christ, the Son of the Blessed" (Mk 14:61). At the passion narratives, again it is Matthew alone having the expression on the lips of the bystanders (27:40) and religious leaders confessing of Jesus as the Son of God (27:43 cf. Mk 15:32).

Thus in all these unique occasions in Matthew, in the very identity of Jesus as the Son of God, the fatherhood of God holds the overarching and crucial place.[752] It is seen that the sonship or sonhood of Jesus is inseparably connected with God's fatherhood in Matthew. And that as often as Matthew project the theme of the Son of God the more the centrality of God's fatherhood is heightened.

---

[751] See Dunn, *New Testament Theology: An Introduction*, 60; In expressing 'christology as an aspect of theology,' Dunn termed Matthew 1:23 and 28:18 as 'christo-theological words' which form an inclusio and bracketed the whole Gospel; see J.D.G. Dunn, *The Christ and the Spirit I: Christology* (Grand Rapids; Michigan: Wm. B. Eerdmans, 1998), 382-383.

[752] Hurtado, *God in New Testament Theology*, 53.

5.2.2. The Fatherhood of God and the Social Setting of Matthean Community

Even the life situation of Matthean community is closely connected with the theme of the fatherhood of God. A crucial clue to the setting of Matthean community seems to be present in the prominent Matthean expression 'Father in heaven.' Not only does Matthew prefer to call God as Father the most, but his usage also stands out by regularly connecting God as Father with the idea of heaven. It is Matthew alone who consistently gives emphasis in expressing God as Father in heaven or heavenly Father.[753] The expression 'Father in heaven' occurs nowhere else in the New Testament, except once in Mark 11:25 as ὁ πατὴρ ὑμῶν ὁ ἐν τοῖς οὐρανοῖς which parallels Matthew 6:14 (ὑμῖν ὁ πατὴρ ὑμῶν ὁ οὐράνιος). This makes us to ask the question: What is the context that contributes to the increasing importance of 'heavenly Father' as a designation for God in Matthean community? In order to answer this question we need to consider the setting (*sitz im leben*) of Matthew and his community.

5.2.2.1. The *Sitz im Leben* of Matthean Community

The inquiry into Matthew's setting and community in the light of early Jewish-Christian relations is very complicated. It is mainly because of the mixed messages found throughout the Gospel of Matthew. There are strong themes in Matthew which stand in tension with one another: Jewish particularism[754] juxtaposed with Gentile-including universalism[755] and a stress on the continuing validity of the Law (5:17) combined with a harsh critique of Pharisaic Judaism (23:1-36). Clearly, Matthew is the most 'Jewish' of the Gospels, yet at the same time it provides the strongest condemnations of Judaism and the most straight-forward claims about mission to the Gentiles.[756]

As a result of these mixed messages, there have been several varied positions in the history of interpretation. Because of its Jewish features many scholars maintain that Matthew's community is still tied to synagogue, despite growing tensions.[757]

---

[753] This expression is found 20 times in Matthew - 5:16, 45, 48; 6:1, 9, 14, 26, 32; 7:11, 21c; 10:32, 33; 12:50; 15:13; 16:17; 18:10c, 14, 19, 35; 23:9.

[754] We have in Matthew the particularism that limits Jesus and his disciples' ministry to Israel (10:5-6, 23 cf.15:24), plus the generally Jewish tone of the Gospel with its stresses on the abiding validity of the Law (5:17-18), the necessity of righteousness, the exhortation to accept the teaching authority of the scribes and Pharisees (23:2-3) and the fulfilment of messianic prophecy in the formula quotations.

[755] We have the explicit idea of universalism (e.g., 2:1-12; 4:14-16), the condemnation of the Jewish nation and the subsequent transference of the kingdom motif to a new community (20:1-16; 21:41-43; ch 23), and various other inclusive tones (e.g., 5:44-45; 12:11-12).

[756] E.g. 2:1; 4:15-16; 5:14; 8:11-12; 10:18; 12:18-21; 24:14; 28:18-20.

[757] J.A. Overman, *Matthew's Gospel and Formative Judaism* (Minneapolis: Fortress Press, 1990), 157-158; Saldarini, "The Gospel of Matthew and the Jewish-Christian Conflict," 38-61.

However, there are some who argues that Matthew and his community is already detached from Judaism as a separate entity.[758] In the recent debate, several scholars such as G. Stanton, S. Brown, D. Hagner and J. Riches argue for a mediating position.[759] The nature of the Gospel of Matthew is such that it continues to generate debate on this issue of whether Matthew and his community are inside or outside of Judaism or somewhere in between.

However, it is not a place here to arbitrate this debate, as our interest is on the theme of God's fatherhood. The focus of this section is to see how a recognition of Matthew's fatherhood of God theme relates to the life situation of Matthew and his community, the original hearers. This leads us to broaden our focus by orienting ourselves to the world of Matthew, which involves recognition of religious, political and social dynamics. This has been the major focus of Matthean scholarship in the 1990s and onward. Several scholars deal with the social setting of the Matthean community.[760] Viewing Matthew in the wider world of Roman Empire, W. Carter reminds us that the tension within (Matthean community versus synagogue) was not Matthew's only point of reference, but the difficulties of life in the Roman Empire must be factored in also.[761] Thus the fatherhood of God idea in Matthew can also be understood in the context of Roman Empire, the ultimate socio-political power and force in the region of the time. This is heightened by the consistent uses of the kingdom language throughout the narratives and discourses of Matthew. The kingdom of heaven which is also one of Matthew's recurring themes is seen in close relation with the theme of God's fatherhood.

---

[758] W.D. Davies, *The Setting of the Sermon on the Mount* (Cambridge: Cambridge University Press, 1966), 286, 290-315; J.P. Meier, *The Vision of Matthew: Christ, Church and Morality in the First Gospel* (New York: Paulist Press, 1979), 17-25.

[759] G. Stanton, *A Gospel for a New People: Studies in Matthew* (Edinburgh: T & T Clark, 1992), 124, 280-281; D. Hagner, *Matthew 1-13*, lxxi; S. Brown, *The Origins of Christianity*, 118-121; John Riches, *Matthew* (Sheffield: Sheffield Academic Press, 1996), 44, 52-60; C.A. Evans, *Matthew*, 6-7.

[760] For example, Overman (*Matthew's Gospel and Formative Judaism*) and Saldarini (*The Gospel of Matthew and the Jewish-Christian Conflict*) argue that Matthean and his community is still within Judaism; while Stanton (*A Gospel for a New People: Studies in Matthew*) sees the issue as complicated in that Matthew may have been writing for a number of communities struggling with self-definition in the aftermath of the Jewish War.

[761] W. Carter, "Matthews's Gospel: Jewish Christianity, Christian Judaism, or Neither?" in M. Jackson-McCabe (ed.), *Jewish Christianity Reconsidered: Rethinking Ancient Groups and Texts* (Minneapolis: Fortress Press, 2007), 155-179; Carter, *Matthew and the Margins*, 2. See also Overman, *Matthew's Gospel and Formative Judaism*, 155.

5.2.3. The Fatherhood of God and the Kingdom of Heaven

A theme that is so intimately linked with the theme of God's fatherhood in Matthew is the theme of the kingdom of heaven.[762] The importance of the theme of 'kingdom' for Matthew is obvious from the fact that the 'kingdom' and its related expressions occur the most in Matthew among the Gospels. The word 'kingdom' is found fifty-five times in Matthew, with a wide variety of phrases, including 'kingdom of heaven' (32 times), 'kingdom of God' (4 times), and several other references such as 'his' or 'your' kingdom.[763] Kingsbury found the central emphasis of Matthew in the phrase "the gospel of the kingdom" occurring at important structural seams of Matthew (4:23; 9:35; 24:14).[764]

Most of the studies on the kingdom of God in Matthew revolve around the theological point that 'kingdom of heaven' is simply a circumlocution for 'kingdom of God' that Matthew used for the sake of his readers' conscience.[765] However, such argument is weakened by the fact that Matthew employs the term 'God' 51 times, including 4 times in the phrase 'kingdom of God.' It seems Matthew deliberately used the very expression 'kingdom of heaven' in many instances rather than the 'kingdom of God.'[766] According to W.D. Davies and D.C. Allison Matthew's use of the phrase 'kingdom of heaven' is simply a stylistic variation similar to the use of 'kingdom,' 'kingdom of the Father,' and 'kingdom of God' to refer to the same reality.[767] However, this view fails to explain why it is Matthew alone uses this term 'kingdom of heaven.' Some scholars have argued that expression 'kingdom of heaven' and 'kingdom of God' are not the same in Matthew. M. Pamment argues that 'kingdom of heaven' refers to a totally future reality while 'kingdom of God' denotes God's sovereignty which can be experienced in the present.[768] However, this argument finds contradiction within

[762] In fact the relation between the two is so close that T.W. Manson (*The Teaching of Jesus* [Cambridge: Cambridge University Press, 1955], 163) would go even to the extent of saying that "the Kingship and the Fatherhood are one and the same thing looked at from different points of view." He draws this conclusion because he understands the kingdom of God in its essence is the reign of God, the personal relationship between the sovereign God and the individual. Thus, for him, there is no point in asking whether the kingdom is present or future, just as there is no point in asking whether the fatherhood of God is present or future. See Manson, *The Teaching of Jesus*, 135.

[763] See Kohlenberger, *The Exhaustive Concordance*, 141-142.

[764] Kingsbury, *Matthew: Structure, Christology, and Kingdom*, 128.

[765] A.W. Argyle, *The Gospel According to Matthew* (Cambridge: Cambridge University Press, 1963), 10; D.A Hagner, *Matthew 1-13*, 47-48; Kingsbury, *Matthew: Structure, Christology, Kingdom*, 134; U. Luz, *Matthew 1-7*, 167. See also B.M. Metzger, *The New Testament: Its Background and Content* (Nashville: Abingdon Press, 1983, 2nd edition), 147. n. 5.

[766] This is also the view of R. Foster, "Why on Earth Use 'Kingdom of Heaven'? Matthew's Terminology Revisited," in *NTS* 48 (2002), 488.

[767] Davies and Allison, *A Critical and Exegetical Commentary on the Gospel of Matthew* I, 392.

[768] M. Pamment, "The Kingdom of Heaven According to the First Gospel," in *NTS* 27 (1981), 211-232.

Matthean text itself in several instances. A clear contradiction to this view is seen in Matthew 11:12, which apparently talks about the kingdom of heaven as a present reality, as when Matthean Jesus says "From the days of John the Baptist until now the kingdom of heaven has suffered violence, and the violence take it by force." So also in Matthew 19:23 and 24, the phrase 'kingdom of heaven' and 'kingdom of God' occur as parallel sentences - as Matthean Jesus speaks to his disciples about the rich young man's status in gaining eternal life (19:16-22) - and so seems to indicate that these two phrases represent the same reality.[769] Moreover, in the parable discourse of Matthew 13, in which the expressing kingdom of heaven occurs, the idea of present reality is also found especially in the parable of the mustard seed (vv31-32), which imply the growth of the kingdom of heaven from small beginnings.[770] Another scholar who sees the difference between the two expressions is R. Gundry. For him the term 'kingdom of heaven' stresses the sovereignty of God. He also thinks that this expression highlights Jesus' co-ruling with the Father.[771] However, it is difficult to comprehend how 'kingdom of heaven' communicates that God reigns more clearly than the 'kingdom of God.' Both the expressions communicate that God reigns over a kingdom. Thus, the use of the 'kingdom of heaven' must function in the Gospel of Matthew as more than simply a different symbol of God's rule. In addition, Matthew may have used the term 'kingdom of heaven' to convey Jesus' co-ruling with the Father, but at other times he quotes Jesus as referring solely to 'my Father's kingdom' (e.g., 26:29). Of course, our point here is to show how closely the kingdom of heaven is related to our theme of the fatherhood of God in Matthew.

This leads us to the point that in Matthew God's fatherhood is inseparably connected with God as Lord (κυρίος) and King (βασιλεὺς).

5.2.3.1. Father and Lord

In Matthew the term κυρίος used for God also occurs in close connection with the fatherhood of God. It is clearly seen in the Matthean infancy narratives which has six unique occurrences of the term 'Lord' for God (1:20, 22, 24; 2:13, 15, 19). It seems to be a deliberate Matthean design projecting God's purposes and activity. Particularly the presence of the term 'Lord' in the formula in 2:15 is noteworthy, for this formula introduces a scriptural quotation ("Out of Egypt I have called my son") which identifies the divine speaker ('I') as the Son's parent. Though the term 'Father' is not used by Matthew at this stage of his narrative (infancy narratives), the idea of God's fatherhood is implicit in the pericope. As Robert Mowery has clearly pointed out that it has to do with deliberate Matthean design. That the presence

---

[769] Pamment argue that verse 23 pertains to the future and verse 24 to the present pursuit of righteousness.

[770] D.C. Duling, "Kingdom of God/Kingdom of heaven," in *ABD* IV, 57.

[771] R. Gundry, *A Commentary on His Literary and Theological Art* (Grand Rapids: Eerdmans, 1982), 43.

of 'Lord' rather than 'Father' here in 2:15 accords with four Matthean patterns: the frequent use of 'Lord' in Matthew 1-2, the association of the Scriptures with the Lord rather than the Father, the absence of references to the Father prior to the Sermon on the Mount, and the presence of such references only in words of Jesus.[772] Another instance where 'Father' and 'Lord' are closely linked is found in 11:25, which of course parallels Luke 10:21 (so Q). The terms 'Father' and 'Lord (of heaven and earth)' come in the same breath when Jesus is talking about the 'gracious will' of God. Such pairing is typical of Jewish-Hellenistic tradition of prayers (e.g., 3 Macc 6:2-3, 5-8). According to D' Angelo, this very expression "exhibits God's will and providence as the governor of history."[773] The linking of 'Father' and 'Lord' here has more to do with sovereignty of God having authority over all things, while this expression may also give the idea of God as the creator and sustainer of the universe. That means, for Matthew, the Father (God), who is 'Lord of heaven and earth' is the creator of all, that is, universe.[774] The same pairing of Lord and Father occurs again in a unique Matthean parable (18:23-35). The term 'Lord' (ὁ κυρίος) occurs five times in this parable thus heightening the sovereign nature of God as Father. And as the parable follows we will see the term 'Father in heaven' occur in the culminating verse. Interestingly, the term 'king' as referring to God too occurs at the very beginning of this parable (18:23). That means to say that the occurrence of three terms 'king,' 'lord' and 'Father' in the same pericope is a deliberate Matthean arrangement, with the theme of God's fatherhood as the fulcrum.

5.2.3.2. Father and King

In Matthew God's fatherhood is inseparably connected with the idea of God as King (βασιλεὺς).[775] This idea of God as King is rooted in the Old Testament. The New Testament writers appealed to the Psalms and other Old Testament writings as a source for the knowledge of God when the need arose in addressing the concerns of theology and Christology.[776] The idea of the lordship or kingship of God is very clear in Psalms 100:3 "Know that the LORD is God." Here in this Psalm the subject of the sentence is the name Yahweh. There are other instances in the Old Testament where the idea of God as King is clear. In 1 Chronicles 29:11, David acknowledges God saying, "Yours, O LORD, are the greatness, the power, the glory, the victory, and the majesty; for all that is in the heavens and on

[772] R.L. Mowery, "From Lord to Father in Matthew 1-7," in *CBQ* 59 (1997), 644.

[773] D'Angelo, "Theology in Mark and Q: *Abba* and 'Father' in Context," 167.

[774] J. Pennington (*Heaven and Earth in the Gospel of Matthew* [Grand Rapids: Baker Academic, 2007], 334) expressed this as a monotheistic cosmological duality.

[775] Of course this close connection of Father and kingdom is also seen in Q tradition (=Lk 6:46; 11:2; 12:30) and Luke's special tradition (Lk 12:32; 22:29).

[776] James Luther Mays, 'The God Who Reigns: The Book of Psalms,' in A. Andrew Das and F. J. Matera (eds.), *The Forgotten God: Perspectives in Biblical Theology*, 30.

the earth is yours; yours is the kingdom, O LORD, and you are exalted as head above all." Here it is seen that the use of the title 'Lord' is applied to God which is in harmony with the idea of God's kingship. That means to say that the κύριος (Hebrew *ʾăḏōnāy*) is, in fact, a substitute expression, replacing the proper name of Israel's God Yahweh.[777] Interestingly, it is only in Matthew among the Synoptic Gospels that we see the idea of God as King. The term 'king' is used for God in eight instances: once in the Sermon on the Mount (5:35) and the rest of the seven occurrences are found in the parables in the later discourses of Matthew.[778]

However, our interest is in the very close relationship of God as Father and King in Matthew. The unity of God as Father and King is very clear when Matthean Jesus prays, "Our Father in heaven ... Your kingdom come" (6:9).[779] God as Father and Ruler is explicitly clear here. Close link between God as Father and King is also found in the rabbinic literatures. In a text that is attributed to rabbi Akiba, he prayed, "Our Father, our King! [Thou art our Father, and] we have no King but Thee. Our Father, our King for thine own sake have compassion upon us! (*b. Ta'anit* 25b)"[780] Joseph Heinemann sees relationship between references to God's kingship in Jewish prayer and emperor worship.[781] For him then the expression also carries anti-imperial sentiments and reflections when the Jews pray, "our Father, our King, we have no king but you." The strikingly similar expression in Matthean Lord's Prayer can also be understood in the same socio-political reality.

It is striking to see that the term '(heavenly) Father' and 'kingdom' have significant overlap in Matthew's narrative. In three instances unique to Matthew (so M) we find clear point of contact between these two phrases, as illustrated below:

> 13:43 - Then the righteous will shine like the sun in the kingdom of their Father.
>
> 18:23-35 - For this reason the kingdom of heaven may be compared to a king who wished to settle accounts with his slaves ... So my heavenly Father will also do to every one of you, if you do not forgive your brother or sister from your heart.

---

[777] N. Richardson, *God in the New Testament* (London: Epworth Press, 1999), 11.

[778] Mt 18:23; 22:1-14 [x4]; 25:31-46 [x2].

[779] The message here is more of theocentric and present rather than eschatological and future for Matthew, that the kingdom of God as God's (fatherly) rule of grace at the present. This idea of the present action of God is also seen in another pericope in the Matthean Jesus' Sermon on the Mount (6:23-33).

[780] For detail reference of God as Father and King in Jewish literatures, see Moore, *Judaism* II, 209-210.

[781] Joseph Heinemann, *Prayer in the Talmud: Forms and Patterns* (SJ 9; Berlin: de Gruyter, 1977), 94-96.

25:34 - Then the king will say to those at his right hand, 'Come, you that are blessed by my Father, inherit the kingdom prepared for you from the foundation of the world ....'

In three instances in Matthew, which has parallels in Luke (Q), we find points of contact between these two phrases:

Mt 6:9b-10: *Our* Father *in heaven* ... Your kingdom come.

Lk11:2 - Father, hallowed be your name. Your kingdom come.

Mt 6:32, 33 - For it is the Gentiles who strive for all these things; and indeed your *heavenly* Father knows that you need all these things. But strive first for the kingdom of God and his righteousness, and all these things will be given to you as well.

Lk 12:30, 31- For it is the nations of the world that strive after all these things, and your Father knows that you need them. Instead, strive for his kingdom, and these things will be given to you as well.

Mt 7:21 - Not everyone who says to me, 'Lord, Lord,' will enter the *kingdom of heaven*, but only the one who does the will of *my Father in heaven.*

Lk 6:46 - Why do you call me 'Lord, Lord,' and do not do what I tell you?

While in one instance which Matthew shares with both Mark and Luke (so Mark) the Father and kingdom occurs in the same breath:

Mt 26:29 - I tell you, I will never again drink of this fruit of the vine until that day when I drink it new with you in *my Father's* kingdom.

Mk 14:25 - Truly I tell you, I will never again drink of the fruit of the vine until that day when I drink it new in the kingdom of God.

Lk 22:18 - For I tell you that from now on I will not drink of the fruit of the vine until the kingdom of God comes.

It is striking to see that in all the passages cited above the expressions 'in heaven,' 'heavenly,' 'kingdom of heaven' or 'Father's kingdom' are all redactional emphasis of Matthew. In these redaction activities of Matthew we see the expressions 'Father' and 'kingdom' are connected by the word 'heaven' (οὐρανοῖς).[782] This close connection between '(heavenly) Father' and 'kingdom (of heaven)' provides a crucial clue to Matthew's theological point. As we have seen above that in the contemporary Jewish thought both Father and King are intimately connected,

[782] As Matthew emphasizes that God's kingdom is a heavenly one, so too it is appropriate for him to emphasize that God the Father is likewise in heaven.

and that Father in heaven likely serves the same purpose that kingdom of heaven does for Matthew.

5.2.4. The Significance of 'Heaven' or 'In Heaven' in Matthew

Matthew uses the word 'heaven' a total of 82 times, including 32 occurrences as part of the phrase – kingdom of heaven, it occurs only 18 times in Mark, while Luke uses 34 times.[783] But the phrase 'kingdom of heaven' is not at all found in both Mark and Luke. As shown above, one of the key passages to understand the significance of this expression is found in Matthew's version of the Lord's Prayer (6:9-11), where we see the occurrence of both the term '(our) Father in heaven' and '(your) kingdom' in the same breath. As seen in our previous chapter, Matthean commentators explain that the 'in heaven' occurrence along with 'our Father' is a combination of God's transcendence and intimacy. For example, Hagner expresses that the Father in heaven "combines the personal, or immanent, element of fatherhood with the transcendental element of God's otherness, 'in heaven.'"[784] For him, the 'heaven' element and the 'Father' element are complementary aspects.[785] However, some scholars understand that the 'in heaven' has nothing to do with God's transcendence but instead the limitlessness of God,[786] or simply to contrast God with earthly fathers.[787]

H.D. Betz understands the heavenly aspect in yet a different way. He argues that the kingdom of heaven is the main theological idea of the Sermon on the Mount and that the rule of this kingdom is expressed through the idea of a cosmic Father. For him the heavenly fatherhood of God in the Sermon expresses both God's cosmic character as it relates to the *creatio continua* and his special relationship with the disciples.[788] This is how Betz sees the close connection between the kingdom of heaven and the Father in heaven. Robert Foster too sees the close link between the theme of the Fatherhood of God and the kingdom of heaven in Matthew.[789] Since the theme of 'heaven' occurs the most in the chapters 5-7, he argues that "the heavenly language guides the whole structure of the sermon."[790] For him, together with kingdom of heaven, Father in heaven serves an

---

783 See H. Bietenhard, "Heaven," in *NIDNTT* II, 192.

784 Hagner, *Matthew 1-13*, 101.

785 Hagner, *Matthew 1-13*, 148.

786 A. Plummer, *An Exegetical Commentary on the Gospel According to Saint Matthew* (Grand Rapids: Wm B. Eerdmans, 1953), 97; E. Lohmeyer, *The Lord's Prayer* (London: Collins, 1965), 60.

787 Luz, Matthew 1-7, 377.

788 H.D. Betz, "Cosmogony and Ethics in the Sermon on the Mount," in Betz, *Essays on the Sermon on the Mount*, 120.

789 R. Foster, "Why on Earth Use 'Kingdom of Heaven'?"487-499.

790 R. Foster, "Why on Earth Use 'Kingdom of Heaven'?" 499.

important rhetorical and social purpose.[791] From these scholars view it is clear that the expression 'kingdom of heaven' and the 'fatherhood of God' are inseparably related, and that the expression 'kingdom of heaven' can be understood only in relation with the theme of God's fatherhood in Matthew.

Apart from Robert Foster, who gives us a hint on how Father in heaven functions in Matthew, there is no comprehensive examination of why the emphasis of 'Father in heaven' in Matthew and what it means and functions in Matthew. At this juncture we are compelled to examine the religious context of Matthew, the rabbinic Judaism, where the very idea of heavenly Father and kingdom of heaven is widespread.[792] There are striking parallels to the Matthean expression 'Father in heaven' or 'heavenly Father' both in discourses and prayers of contemporary Jewish rabbis.

5.2.4.1. 'Father in Heaven' or 'Heavenly Father' in Matthew and Rabbinic Judaism

The connection of the notion of 'heaven' specifically with God as Father apparently developed in the first century C.E.[793] and become especially prominent in mainstream rabbinic usage.[794] In fact, no occurrences of the expression 'heavenly Father' or 'Father in heaven' are found in the Old Testament or in the Apocrypha or pre-Christian Apocalyptic or Pseudepigraphal literature.[795] Even in the New Testament, apart from Matthew, there is only once that this expression occurs, that is, in Mark 11:25 (ὁ πατὴρ ὑμῶν ὁ ἐν τοῖς οὐρανοῖς), which parallels Matthew 6:14 (ὁ πατὴρ ὑμῶν ὁ οὐράνιος).[796] However, the Matthean contemporary rabbinic and Targumic literatures are replete with this expression 'Father in heaven.' Both in the rabbinic literature and the Targums, when God is referred to

[791] That is, to encourage the disciples in their allegiance to Jesus while undermining the temptation to revert or convert to formative Judaism; R. Foster, "Why on Earth Use 'Kingdom of Heaven?'" 499.

[792] And for D. Angelo ('*Abba* and "Father,"' 611-630) such interpretation of God as heavenly Father firmly situates Matthew's community in the context of Rabbinic prayer language.

[793] G. Dalman, *The Words of Jesus* (Edinburgh: T&T Clark, 1909), 186.

[794] E.g., *m. Sota* 9:15; *m. Yoma* 8:9; *Sifre Deuteronomy* 48. For fuller lists, see Dalman, *Words*, 186-189; Moore, *Judaism* II, 201-211.

[795] However, the address of God as 'Father' was widespread and conventional, see Schrenk, "God as Father in Judaism," in *TDNT* V, 978-98; B. Chilton, "God as 'Father'" in *The Pseudepigrapha and Early Biblical Interpretation*, 151-169. In fact Chilton goes to the extent of saying, "Matthew's Jesus does not say anything radically new about God in calling him 'Father.' See Chilton, "God as 'Father'" in *The Pseudepigrapha and Early Biblical Interpretation*, 169.

[796] However, the originality of Mark 11:25 is in question. For details in favor of this argument, see J. Pennington, Heaven *and Earth in the Gospel of Matthew*, 71. n. 12. The other occurrence is Luke 11:13 (ὁ πατὴρ [ὁ] ἐξ οὐρανοῦ) which seemingly parallels Matthew 7:11(ὁ πατὴρ ὑμῶν ὁ ἐν τοῖς οὐρανοῖς). However this originality is again doubtful; see J. Pennington, *Heaven and Earth in the Gospel of Matthew*, 72. n. 14.

as Father it is most often with the added description "in heaven."[797] The Targum of *Pseudo-Jonathan* to Leviticus 22:28 says: "My people, children of Israel, as our Father is merciful in heaven so shall you be merciful on earth."[798] This reading is quite similar to a saying of Matthean Jesus: "Be perfect as your heavenly Father is perfect (Mt 5:48)." It is also noteworthy that in both the Targums and the rabbinic literatures, the expression 'Father in heaven' is always prefaced with a personal pronoun, 'our' ('my,' 'your,' or 'his') Father in heaven' but never as 'the Father in heaven.'[799] Surely there seems to be a definite meaning and purpose for adding the words 'in heaven' to the 'Father.'

Some scholars have made passing suggestions as regard to this addition '(who is) in heaven.' For example, according to Gustaf Dalman, in the very expression 'heavenly Father,' God is conceived as the counterpart of the 'earthly Father.'[800] So also G. F. Moore explains that in the addition 'of heaven' to 'Father,' there is no suggestion of remoteness, but instead "they remove the ambiguity of the bare word 'Father' by thus distinguishing between God and an earthly father."[801] He particularly finds this explicit heavenly versus earthly father contrast in a rabbinic text of *Sifre Deuteronomy* 48 which says that a wise son not only makes 'his earthly father' glad, but also 'his heavenly Father.'[802] Similarly for Schrenk, the expression 'Father in heaven' does not communicate transcendence as distance but instead expresses the sovereignty or limitlessness of God. But for him, nearness is also emphasized by the addition of the pronominal adjectives like 'our,' 'your, 'my, or 'his,' to the phrase 'heavenly Father.'[803] Referring to the phrase 'heaven' as the common shared theme, Schrenk goes on stating that heaven "is continually used to proclaim, not rigid transcendence and other worldliness, but final orientation from the heavenly sphere, the direction of earth by the reality which is above earth, the correspondence of the heavenly and the earthly."[804] Similarly, J.T. Pennington too finds the expression 'Father in heaven' as part of Matthew's heaven and earth discourse.[805] D. Crossan, in his exposition on the Lord's Prayer, too finds the axis of the prayer in the expression 'on earth as it is in heaven' (6:10c). Referring to the key expression of the Prayer in verse 10c he remarks, "That centrally key phrase insists on mutuality and reciprocity, on an interaction between the heavenly

[797] For details references in rabbinic literatures see, Dalman, *Words*, 184-194; Moore, *Judaism* II (Cambridge: Harvard University Press, 1927), 201-211.

[798] Quoted in C.A. Evans, *Ancient Texts for New Testament Studies: A Guide to the Background Literature* (Peabody; Massachusetts: Hendrickson Publishers, 2005), 188.

[799] Moore, *Judaism* II, 204.

[800] Dalman, *Words,* 186.

[801] Moore, *Judaism* II, 205.

[802] Dalman, *Words*, 186.

[803] Schrenk, "God as Father in Judaism," in *TDNT* V, 986.

[804] Schrenk, "God as Father in Judaism," in *TDNT* V, 986.

[805] Pennington, *Heaven and Earth in the Gospel of Matthew*, see especially 236-251.

'Your' of God's name, kingdom, and will and the earthly 'Our' of bread, debt, and temptation."[806]

However, with all these views the query of what exactly is the context of this emphasis '(Our) Father in heaven' and what it means and functions in Matthew remains unanswered.

As we carefully observe the occurrences of the expression 'Father in heaven' in rabbinic literatures, particularly in the *Mishnah*, it is seen that most of the expressions occur in prayers and lament after the destruction of Jerusalem temple (70 C.E.). A text from *Mishnah* clearly reveals this:

> R. Phineas b. Jair says: When the Temple was destroyed the Associates and the freemen were put to shame and walked with covered head, and the men of good works waxed feeble ... On whom can we stay ourselves? – on our Father in heaven.[807]

As seen above, the expression 'Father in heaven' is found in the context of prayer in the aftermath of the destruction of Jerusalem temple. Thus the expression emphasizes that "what is in heaven can now serve as a true substitute for what is destroyed on earth [i.e., the Temple]."[808] In other words, the destruction of the temple by Rome in 70 C.E. and its aftermath have contributed to increasing the importance of 'heavenly Father' in Jewish prayer. The whole lives of the Jews were centered on the temple of Jerusalem. But now the temple is in ruins and the very identity of Jewishness is at stake.[809] It made both persecution and forgiveness acute issues.[810] In such a context we see the rabbis lamenting by calling God not only as 'Father,' but specifically as 'heavenly Father.'[811] Thus this expression would certainly provide consolation as the persecuted look to their Father in the heavenly world.

The same can be said of Matthew and his community, whose Jesus not only prays 'our Father in heaven' (6: 9), but also categorically rejects the earthly father by saying not to call anyone as "your father on earth, for you have one

[806] J.D. Crossan, *The Greatest Prayer: Rediscovering the Revolutionary Message of the Lord's Prayer* (London: SPCK, 2011), 49.

[807] See Danby, *The Mishnah*, 306.

[808] Schrenk, "God as Father in Judaism," in *TDNT* V, 980. In n. 215, he also cites a certain rabbi Cadoq (c. 70 C.E.) who prays, "My Father who art in heaven, Thou hast destroyed thy city and burnt thy temple and remainst untroubled and calm."

[809] Sandgren, Leo D. *Vines Intertwined: A History of Jews and Christians from the Babylonian Exile to the Advent of Israel* (Peabody: Hendrickson Publishers, 2010), 258.

[810] As rabbis, notably Johannan ben Zakkai, believed that it was because of Israel's sins that God allowed the temple to be destroyed. See Philip F. Esler, "Rome in Apocalyptic and Rabbinic Literature," in *The Gospel of Matthew in its Roman Imperial Context*, 29.

[811] The language suggests the juxtaposition of the two authorities - heavenly Father / God versus Emperor on earth / Rome. It was particularly appropriate as a title by which the persecuted could invoke God's power, or the repentant God's forgiveness (D'Angleo, "Abba and 'Father,'" 622).

Father – the one in heaven". (23:9).[812] This means that both Matthean community and other Jewish communities were engaging with the same political realities, languishing under the ultimate power and force in the region, the Roman Empire. The Roman Empire flourished under the sovereign power and authority of the Emperor, whose relation with his subject functions under the title as *Pater Patriae*. It is to this we now turn.

5.2.4.2. Fatherhood of God in Matthew and Roman Emperor as *Pater Patriae*

Undoubtedly the Roman Empire under the authority of the Emperor was the one fact that loomed largest on the horizons of early Christianity and Judaism.[813] And as we have seen earlier that father-figure became an important part of the image of the political leader, especially with Caesar and Augustus. More so, the imperial fatherhood was very much at force beginning with the reign of Augustus. He was called the savior and founder of Roman peace (*Pax Romana*), and conferred the title *Pater Patriae* ('Father of Your Country' or Father of the Fatherland) in 2 B.C.E.[814] The title *Pater Patriae* was earned by benefactions and military victories. According to Suetonius, Vespasian too adopted the title 'Father of the Fatherland' but very late in his life.[815] The Greco-Roman literatures portray Roman emperors as the elect mediators of the gods. Roman coins portrayed them as good father, patron and rulers of the whole world.[816]

The *Pax Romana*, a term used to designate Roman political rule beginning with the reign of Caesar Augustus, reflects both imperial ideal and propaganda toward its own citizens and its imperial holdings. Thus on Roman imperial theology, J.D. Crossan's statement is to the point, "Rome spoke of itself in transcendental terms as an empire divinely mandated to rule without limits of time or place. It did not simply proclaim dominion around the Mediterranean Sea. It announced world conquest, global rule, and eternal sovereignty."[817] In the centuries following Augustus, this ideal of imperial peace remained intact even as the empire grew. Most important for understanding how the imperial peace was understood by Augustus were his own words published in the *Res Gestai Divi Augusti* ('the Accomplishments of Divine Augustus'). In this propaganda work the life and deeds of the Emperor Augustus as a father-figure of the whole empire

[812] Matthew also has Jesus lays claims to all authority on heaven and earth (28:18 cf. 23:9).

[813] D'Angelo, "Abba and 'Father,'" 623.

[814] Augustus 58 in *Suetonius: The Twelve Caesars*, 83; *Roman Civilization Sourcebook II: The Empire,* 8.

[815] Vespasian 12 in *Suetonius: The Twelve Caesars*, 281.

[816] W. Carter (*Matthew and Empire: Initial Explorations* [Harrisburg; PA: Trinity Press International, 2001], 20-29) offers several examples.

[817] Crossan, *God and Empire: Jesus Against Rome, Then and Now* (New York: Harper One, 2007), 15.

(*Pater Patriae*) is extolled in a comprehensive way.[818] The very beginning of this work goes: "The accomplishments of the deified Augustus by which he brought the whole world under the empire of the Roman people ...."[819] It is followed by the account of his own achievements in 35 sections.[820] Talking about his powerful and merciful nature, the third section begins, "I waged many wars throughout the whole world by land and by sea, both civil and foreign, and when victorious I spared all citizens who sought pardon."[821] From such works the emperors were projected as being powerful, affectionate, compassionate Father for the whole empire. However, in the works of some Roman authors we see this idea of Roman Peace (*Pax Romana*) in a totally different light. For example, Epictetus notes the incongruities between the Roman ideal and reality, as he talks about audacious and resisting persecution, "O Caesar, what do I have to suffer under your peaceful rule?"[822] Thus, what could be hailed by Romans at home as an empire of strength and peace was characterized otherwise by many of its subjects, having experienced oppression and taxation, both during Augustus reign and his successors' reign.[823] This clearly reveals the severity and harsh reality under the Roman Empire. There is no doubt that under such rule the early Christian communities, including Matthean community, experienced the same harsh realities.[824] In such a context the Roman imperial fatherhood might too have informed and shaped Matthean idea of God's fatherhood, as he retells and reinterprets the teaching of Jesus. Matthew in several texts posits God's sovereignty over against earthly authority:

---

[818] "*Res Gestai Divi Augusti* 1-35," in *Roman Civilization*, 9-19.

[819] "*Res Gestai Divi Augusti* 1-35," in *Roman Civilization*, 9.

[820] "*Res Gestai Divi Augusti* 1-35," in *Roman Civilization*, 9-19.

[821] "*Res Gestai Divi Augusti* 1-35," in *Roman Civilization*, 10.

[822] *Discourses* 3.22.55, *Epictetus* II, 149.

[823] J.E. Bowley, "Pax Romana," in *DNTB*, 773. We also see in another discourse of Epictetus (*Discourses* 1.9.3-7, *Epictetus* I, 65) talking about resorting to God thus expresses the reality of the imperial fatherhood: "Why should not such a man called himself a citizen of the universe? Why should he not call himself a son of God? And why shall he fear anything that happens among men? What! Shall kinship with Caesar or any other of them that have great power at Rome be sufficient to enable men to live securely, proof against contempt, and in fear of nothing whatsoever, but to have God as our maker, and father, and guardians, shall this not suffice to deliver us from grief and fears?" The expression is taken to be a counterpart to the earthly situation; thus in political bondage an antithesis and consolation is sought by looking to God as maker and Father of the universe (cf. Mt 11:25). So for Epictetus the fatherhood of God here has to do with socio-political situation, an antithesis to imperial fatherhood.

[824] The Roman armies (so Roman Rule) came to Jewish territory in 4 B.C.E., in 66 C.E. and finally in 132 C.E.; See J.D. Crossan, *God and Empire*, 109. And J. Riches ("Introduction," in *The Gospel of Matthew In Its Roman Imperial Context*, edited by J. Riches and David C. Sim [London: T&T Clark, 2005], 1-8) talks about the harsh treatment and public humiliation of the Jews under the Roman rule. So also for Carter ("Matthew Negotiates the Roman Empire," in *In the Shadow of Empire*, 136), Matthew's Gospel "offers Jesus' followers various strategies for negotiating the elite-dominated socio-political Roman imperial order."

it is (not the emperor but) God who is the Father in heaven (e.g., 6:9; 23:9) and also the 'Lord of heaven and earth' (11:25).[825] Thus Matthew's 'heavenly Father' also seems to reflect the anti-imperial context. Interestingly, in several instances in Matthew God as 'heavenly Father' occurs in the same pericope where the slurring references to Gentiles (ἐθνικοί) are also found. In some way this may also reflect anti-imperial sentiments of Matthew and his community. The Gentiles appear as example of how not to act: "When you are praying do not heap up empty phrases as the Gentiles do ... for your Father knows what you need before you ask him" (6:7-8). The Gentiles again appear as materialist, who seek all the material things (food, drinking and clothing) while "your heavenly Father knows that you need all these things" (6:32). The Gentiles are again cited as negative example of doing motivated services, in greetings only their brothers and sisters, that culminates in the commands of Matthean Jesus to be perfect "as your heavenly Father is perfect" (5:47-48). The term 'Gentile' is again combined, in an excommunication formula, with the hated 'tax collector,' who contracted with the Roman authorities to gather taxes, at a profit to himself (18:17). The culminating verses (18:19, 20) of the pericope has again the expression 'Father in heaven.' That means, for Matthew the expression 'Father in heaven' is a socio-political expression, and that by the very expression 'Father in heaven' or 'heavenly Father,' Matthew and his community counter Roman Empire with its *pater* emperor as inferior and ultimately subservient to God's fatherhood.

Thus for Matthew, the theme of God's fatherhood, particularly when used with the expression 'in heaven,' emphasizes the uniqueness and universal sovereignty of God in the Roman Imperial context. In other words, the expression 'Father in heaven' or 'heavenly Father' acts as an antitype to the imperial fatherhood. Thus, invoking the heavenly Father brought tremendous solace and comfort to Matthean community, as it asserts that their identity, affirmation and goal were in heaven and not on earth. So for Matthew the theme of God's fatherhood serves to legitimate and encourage Matthean community that they are the true people of God.[826]

Thus we see that the some of the occurrences of 'Father' language in Matthew are imperial-motivated (and so has to do with anti-imperial rhetoric), in which case fatherhood of God has strong social implications for his community as seen above, but there are also other 'Father' usage and fatherhood idea in Matthew which has more to do with theological and philosophical meaning and significance. That means within Matthew itself there are different aspects of the fatherhood of God. It is to these that we now turn.

---

[825] Carter, *Matthew and the Empire*, 63.

[826] This is also the point of John Riches (*Matthew*, 66-67) who argues that "whether or not Matthew was writing from inside or outside the Jewish community, he was engaged in consolidating and legitimising his community." See also J. Riches, *The Gospel of Matthew In Its Roman Imperial Context*, 1.

5.2.5. Fatherhood of God in Relation to Creation and Nature in Matthew

5.2.5.1. Cosmic Fatherhood

One of Matthew's unique expressions in relation to the fatherhood of God is seen in the prayer "Our Father in heaven" (6:9). In this expression God is affirmed as transcendent ('Father in heaven)') but at the same time affirmed as immanent ('Our Father'). In this perspective both G.F. Moore[827] and Schrenk[828] noted how often the 'Father in heaven' phrases are found in conjunction with mention of the earth. And for Schrenk, it is the heaven - which controls the earth, seen in the expression ὄνομά, βασιλεία and θέλημά of the Father (6:9-10), saying that "what is perfect in heaven is to be actualized on earth as the kingdom of God."[829] So also for Pennington Father in heaven is part of Matthew's overarching heaven and earth discourse,[830] which, in his view, is in continuity with the dualistic worldview of the Old Testament and Judaism.[831] Crossan too finds this Matthean version of the Lord's Prayer in the manner of biblical poetic parallelism between divinity and humanity, with the phrase 'as in heaven so on earth' (6:10c) as the hinge of the prayer. For him, the first half, the divine aspect 'Your' name, kingdom and will, is paralleled by the other half, the earthly aspect 'Our' bread, debts and temptation.[832] However, a close observation of Matthean occurrences of the fatherhood idea in relation to the cosmos reveals that Matthew's idea is closer to the Hellenistic idea of cosmic fatherhood.

The pericope of 5:13-16, where we see the occurrence of the term 'Father' for God for the first time, as Matthean Jesus tells ethical maxims on salt and light, uses several key cosmological terms including heaven, earth, and world. Of course the maxim on salt is found in both Mark (9:49, 50) [833] and Luke (14:34, 35); and so also the maxim on light in Luke (Lk 11:33). But it is Matthew who brought the two saying together to link with his favourite expression 'Father in heaven.' Because of its wide usage in the ancient world,[834] it is difficult to interpret the image of salt here, but it can be understood figuratively. Thus the point here is actions that are of benefit to the world, for example, 'peacemaking' (5:9).[835] Interestingly, it is in Philo that we see the expression 'salts of friendship,' that is,

---

827 Moore, *Judaism* II, 205.

828 Schrenk, "God as Father in Judaism," in *TDNT* V, 980.

829 Schrenk, "God as Father in Judaism," in *TDNT* V, 987.

830 Pennington, *Heaven and Earth in the Gospel of Matthew*, 238-251.

831 Pennington, *Heaven and Earth in the Gospel of Matthew*, 193.

832 J.D. Crossan, *The Greatest Prayer*, 48-49.

833 Mark links 'salt' with 'peace.'

834 Davies and Allison, *Matthew* I, 472-473.

835 Hagner, *Matthew 1-13*, 99; Nolland, *Matthew*, 212; Turner, *Matthew*, 155.

salt linking with friendship.[836] It makes perfect sense when we see these maxims in line with its preceding pericope, the Matthean beatitudes (5:3-12) and the culminating pericope of the same discourse, 'loving of one's enemies' (5:43-48):

> 5:9 - Blessed are the peacemakers, for they will be called children of God.
>
> 5:13-16 - You are the salt of the earth ... the light of the world ... so that they may see your good works and give glory to your Father in heaven.
>
> 5:44, 45 - Love your enemies ... so that you may be children of your Father in heaven.

For Matthew to make peace is to be one of God's children now (5:9); and those loving enemies are considered as children of God (cf. 5:45). That means for Matthew God's children are shaped by imitating God (5:9).[837] God's children are those who act like God. So for Matthew the fatherhood of God covers everyone who engage in peacemaking. In this case Matthew is closer to the Hellenistic idea, especially Philo, who not only likened salt with friendship, as seen above, but also talks about peace with nature as synonymous with peace with God.[838] Again in another situation Philo also talks about God as "peace-maker and peace-keeper, who ... creates plenty of fertility and abundance of other good things and leaves the havoc of fruits without a single spark to be rekindled."[839] So there is a strong emphasis on fatherhood of God as cosmic in both Philo and Matthew, as they link peacemaking, nature, and God together.

Interestingly, the pericope on 'ethical maxims' (5:13-16) culminates in the expression on giving glory to "(your) Father in heaven" are replete with cosmological terms, 'salt' (ἅλας), 'earth' (γῆς), 'light' (φῶς), and 'world' (κόσμος). Hence, we see the very close connection between the fatherhood of God and earth. Matthew's emphasis here has to do with God as cosmic Father, that is, universality of God's fatherhood, which covers both the world of humanity and the world of nature. For Matthew, Jesus' disciples are to be of benefit to the world like salt.[840] The implication is that in becoming the salt of the earth, one makes peace to all creation (cosmos), and in these good works, the heavenly Father is glorified (5:16). So a kind of organic unity of God-human-nature is seen here.

---

836 See, *Somniis* 2.210 in Philo V, 537.

837 Carter, *Matthew and the Margins*, 136.

838 *De Specialibus Legibus* I.318, Philo VII, 285. Elsewhere Philo also talks about kinship as "not measured only by blood, but by similarity of conduct and pursuit of the same objects." See *De Virtutibus* 195, in Philo VIII, 283-285.

839 *De Specialibus legibus* 2.192, Philo VII, 427.

840 C.A. Evans, *Matthew*, 111.

It is complemented by the words of Matthean Jesus on love of enemies and pray for the persecutors, to become the children of heavenly Father, who "makes his sun rise on the evil and on the good and sends rain on the righteous and the unrighteous" (5:44, 45). When we put this along with the seventh beatitude of Matthean Jesus (5:9), the emphasis of Matthew on the universality of God's fatherhood is very clear. Just as those who make peace (which is of God) are God's children, so also those who love enemies are children of the heavenly Father, whose indiscriminate goodness and love is for all (as sun and rain). Thus, this very expression of Matthean Jesus here in verse 44 and 45 speaks about the universality of God's fatherhood. Several scholars see in this expression the potential universal fatherhood of God but not actual fatherhood.[841] Whether it talks about potential or actual fatherhood our point is that Matthew consistently connects the theme of God's fatherhood with creation and nature. This is evident in a unique expression of Matthew found in 5:45, where we see Matthew describing God's beneficence as sun and rain (creation), which gives the idea that God's fatherhood is cosmic or universal. This is observable in the following:

> But I say to you, Love your enemies and pray for those who persecute you, so that you may be children of your Father in heaven; for he makes his sun rise on the evil and on the good, and sends rain on the righteous and on the unrighteous. (5:44-45)

In explaining this very expression, some scholars reject the idea of God's fatherhood in creation. J. Moffat categorically states that "no NT book connects the divine Fatherhood with creation."[842] For Moffat the sun and rain is rather God's goodness in the outward blessings of nature and has nothing to do with God's fatherhood, which is in the gift of God's personal care and kingdom.[843] Similarly, G.E. Ladd too argues that "the goodness of God in sending rain to all men, good and evil alike, is not to be confused with the divine Fatherhood."[844] Further as regard to Matthean Jesus' saying on God's providence (6:26), he argues, "it is not as Father that God cares for the birds, and it is not as Father that God bestows his creaturely blessings on those who are not his children. The fatherhood of God belongs to those who have responded to the divine seeking-love and have submitted themselves to God's kingdom."[845] The contention of both the scholars is that God is not depicted as universal Father at all in Matthew and the New Testament; God's fatherhood has to do only with personal relationship.

[841] Argyle, *God in the New Testament*, 65-66; N. Richardson, *God in the New Testament* (London: Epworth Press, 1999), 21.

[842] J. Moffat, *Love in the New Testament* (London: Hodder and Stoughton, 1932), 72.

[843] Moffat, *Love in the New Testament*, 73.

[844] G.E. Ladd, *The Presence of the Future: The Eschatology of Biblical Realism* (Grand Rapids; Michigan: Wm B. Eerdmans, 1996), 181.

[845] Ladd, *The Presence of the Future: The Eschatology of Biblical Realism*, 181.

But the concentration of God's fatherly nature in creation and nature is unmistakable in this expression (5:45). Moreover, when we see this expression along with his emphasis elsewhere (e.g., 5:9), the emphasis of Matthew on the universality of God's fatherhood is crystal clear. Those who love enemies are children of the heavenly Father, whose indiscriminate goodness and love is for all (as sun and rain). This idea of cosmic fatherhood is at home in Greek-Hellenistic thought. This leads us to the immanent earthly aspect of the fatherhood of God.

5.2.5.2. Ecological Aspect of the Fatherhood of God in Matthew

The expression in 5:45 is unique to Matthew in the whole of New Testament, so there is very strong possibility of Matthean colouring here. And as we have argued in the previous chapter, there are striking similarities to this idea in Greek and Hellenistic writings. God linked to sun and rains are found in Greco-Roman as well as Hellenistic writings. In *Odes of Solomon* there is a hymn that describes God's activities in relation to creation: "And the Lord (is) like the sun upon the face of the land."[846] Similarly, in Greek religion rain comes from Zeus, the weather-god.[847] Zeus is the giver and God of fruitfulness.[848] In the writings of Aeschylus too, the inseparable relationship between God and nature is vividly illustrated. For him, it is God Zeus who gives rain and thus nourishes the earth.[849] Quite in line with such Greek and Hellenistic idea, Matthew connects God as Father with creation. Thus there is strong emphasis of God's fatherhood in relation to creation in Matthew. For him, God is very much part of the earth, who fosters the earth (5:45). Thus we find in Matthew that God is organically related with earth and humanity. There is thus a strong ecological implication of the Fatherhood of God in Matthew.

This very idea of the fatherhood of God, of cosmic fatherhood, seems to have a strong Hellenistic influence.[850] As he reinterprets the teaching of Jesus,

---

[846] *Odes of Solomon* 11.13, trans J. H. Charlesworth, in Charlesworth, *OTP* II, 745.

[847] Such belief in a personal belief in God's fatherhood is replete in the literatures of Greco-Roman and Hellenistic literatures. For example, Marcus Aurelius 5.7 in M. A. Antoninus (*Emperor of Rome*, 105, trans C.R. Haines [Cambridge: Harvard University Press, 1919]) talks about "a prayer of the Athenians: Rain, Rain, O dear Zeus, upon the corn-land of the Athenians and their meads. Either pray not at all, or in the simple and frank fashion."

[848] M.P. Nilsson, *A History of Greek Religion*, 121.

[849] M.P. Nilsson, *A History of Greek Religion*, 122.

[850] At the time when Christianity appeared, that is, during the Hellenistic period, there was a constant interchange of ideas between various systems; see, L. Bouyer, *The Invisible Father: Approaches to the Mystery of the Divinity* (Edinburgh: T&T Clark, 1999), 188; Delbert Burkett, *An Introduction to the New Testament and the Origins of Christianity* (Cambridge: Cambridge University Press, 2002), 72-74. For a detail treatment on interaction between Judaism and Hellenism, see M. Hengel, *The Hellenization of Judea in the First Century after Christ* (London: SCM Press, 1989), especially 49-50.

Matthew drew from the rich Greek-Hellenistic traditions and thus blended together with his Jewish tradition.[851]

In this regard Matthew is quite closer to the cosmological fatherhood idea of Plato. Plato, in his cosmological elaboration of the Father idea in *Timaeus* 28c, emphasizes the creator relationship of the 'universal Father' to the entire cosmos. He speaks of God as 'fatherly' in his generative powers and contrasted passive, 'maternal' matter with the active and creative male principle.[852] That means, the idea of fatherhood is connected with the mother metaphor. As such in Plato's understanding, God's fatherhood has strong feminine aspect as it covers the whole cosmos. This idea can help explain the notion of the fatherhood of God in Matthew. As we have highlighted above, Matthew too projects God as cosmic Father. And perhaps this can also help us explain that the fatherhood of God in Matthew is non-patriarchal in nature, as it has more do to with care, closeness and compassion. Just as in the Greek-oriental tradition, where both paternal and maternal traits are combined in the All-Father, Matthew too projects in similar way, highlighting the fatherhood of God in close relation to earth and nature. As Matthew connects the heavenly Father with sun and rain (5:45) the idea of God's fatherhood is that of nourishment and sustenance of the earth. As Matthew projects God addressing in an inclusive manner 'Our Father' (6:9) the idea of God as universal Father is heightened. More so by the reference to earth (6:10c) and bread (6:11) in the prayer makes it more feminine and ecological, as food is grown on earth.[853] The prayer of Matthean Jesus embraces the whole of creation. It is again Matthean Jesus who talks about heavenly Father as provider of good things (7:11). Thus the imagery is again of a parent – both father and mother, the nurturer of all life, with the equally strong motherly and fatherly nature, which offers a protective umbrella under which basic necessities of life are shared so that all the children may decently live. Thus the fatherhood of God and motherhood idea are inseparably related in Matthew.

5.2.6. The All-Seeing Father

The unique emphasis on cosmic Father is also heightened by his emphasis on the idea of an all-seeing Father, again unique to Matthew (6:1-18). God is explicitly described as '(your) Father who sees in secret' (6:4, 6, 18) and 'who is in secret' (v18). Thus the teaching of Matthean Jesus is that the disciples should give alms or prays or fast so that God sees everything they do (vv 4, 6, 18) and knows

[851] This is also the point of S. Brown (*The Origins of Christianity*, 33) as he observes, "The age in which the New Testament books were written was marked by a unique cultural interaction between Hellenism and Judaism, which is expressed in the variety of sources used by the New Testament writers."

[852] *Timaeus* 50d-51a, *Plato* IX, 117-119.

[853] M.J. Joseph, *The Eco-Vision of the Earth Community: Biblical and Theological Perspectives* (Bangalore: BTESSC/SATHRI, 2008), 42-43.

everything (v8). The idea of all-seeing and all-knowing Father is found only here and there is no exact parallel to this kind of theology elsewhere in the New Testament.[854] From where did Matthew have this concept of God? The concept of an all seeing God is found mostly in the Greek religious traditions. For the *Iliad* of Homer the god Zeus and Helios "sees everything and hears everything."[855] So also in *Odyssey* the sun-god Helios is called "all-seeing" or the "eye of righteousness."[856] Similarly for Hesiod, Zeus is the champion of justice; his eyes see everything and notice everything.[857] That means Zeus is depicted as very much earth-bound. The teaching on giving alms in secret is found in rabbinic Judaism,[858] but again the idea that God knows what is done in secret have striking parallels in Greek writings. Epictetus says that "God himself is present within you, seeing and hearing everything."[859] He also says "that there is God, and that he provides for the universe, and that it is impossible for a man to conceal from Him, not merely his actions, but even his purposes and his thoughts."[860] Quite in line with such Greek-philosophical discourse on all-seeing and all-knowing God, Matthean Jesus is bringing in the idea of an all-seeing and all-knowing Father in the context of religious activities, of almsgiving (6:1-4) and prayer (6:5-8). It seems then that this all-seeing Father is again closely related with Matthean unique idea of a cosmic Father. Matthew seems to have transferred the nature of Zeus to the heavenly Father as he reinterprets the tradition of Jesus. Just as Zeus is earth-bound so also Matthean heavenly Father is. He is omnipresent and omniscient, and interested in the activities of humanity. As Father and judge it is he who also rewards and blesses those who are righteous at heart. Thus we find that the fatherhood of God is a central theme in Matthew and that all other themes are connected to it.

5.2.7. Fatherhood of God and Theology of the Synoptic Gospels

While the idea of the fatherhood of God is the most prominent in Matthew among the Synoptic Gospels, yet as we have argued in chapter three, the usage of 'Father' for God and the idea of God's fatherhood is also present in Mark and Luke (Q). That simply means, 'Father' is seen to be used by all the Synoptic authors as an appropriate address for God. Mark has 4 instances of 'Father' usage for God (8:38; 11:25; 13:32; 14:36), among which the expression '*Abba*' (Mk 14:36) is the only instances of the occurrences of Aramaic prayer supposed to be uttered by

---

[854] Though in the Old Testament there are instances of an 'all-seeing' God (Ps. 33:13-15; 113:5-6; 138:6).

[855] Homer, *Iliad* 3.104, 278.

[856] Homer, *Odyssey* 11. 102.

[857] M.P. Nilsson, *Greek Piety*, 34.

[858] E.g., *m. Shekalim* 5.6; *b. Baba Batra* 9b.

[859] *Discourses* 2.8.14 in Epictetus I, 263.

[860] *Discourses* 2.14.11 in Epictetus I, 309.

Jesus. Likewise, the 'Father' usage for God too occurs 17 times in Luke.[861] We will turn to Mark and Q and see their theology in regard to the fatherhood of God.

5.2.8. Theology of Q

5.2.8.1. Fatherhood of God and Providence

The theme of God's fatherhood in relation to providence in nature is seen in both Matthew and Luke. Both Matthew and Luke bring in the theme of God's fatherhood when they talk about God's care for the 'birds of the air' and the 'lilies of the field' (Mt 6:25-33//Lk 12:22-32). So also the saying about the Father who concerns for even the insignificant creatures, that not even a sparrow falls to the ground without the knowledge and will of the Father is found in both of them (Mt 10:29-31//Lk 12:6-7). Similarly, we also see the saying on God as Father who provides physical and material needs of humanity (Mt 7:7-11//Lk 11:9-13). While the Old Testament and Judaism talks about God as other than this world, as its maker, completely aloof and separated from the world, the best example of which is the book of Isaiah where we see God depicted.as holy and totally transcendent,[862] but here in Q we see the idea of God's fatherhood in close connection with creation. That is, a God who is very much part of the earth, who fosters and gives food and nourishment (Mt 6:11//Lk 11:3; Mt 7:11//Lk 11:13).

Looking at the level of Jesus, Schrenk finds in the pericope where heavenly Father in relation to providence occurs as more to do with discipleship than fatherhood of God. In his words, "the concern in Jesus' preaching of fatherhood is always to instruct the disciples about the βασιλεία. The reference to creation is always related closely to a reference to the rule of the commanding and gracious God whom Jesus declares in His call to repentance and in His message."[863] As such in the pericope of Matthew 6:24-33, Schrenk finds the key in verse 33, of seeking kingdom and righteousness; and in Matthew 10:29-33, on discipleship and eschatological hope in the midst of impending persecutions.[864] However, both Matthew and Luke (Q) consistently relate the theme of God's fatherhood in relation to nature and creation. Of course this Q idea has strong affinity with Stoic theology, as in the Stoic teaching God's fatherhood is seen in the gifts of nature.[865]

So there seems to have strong interaction with Greek-Hellenistic thought. Hence, we see the clear emphasis on the theme of fatherhood of God in the theology of Matthew and Luke (so Q).

---

[861] 2:49; 6:36; 9:26; 10:21-22 [x5]; 11:2, 13; 12:30, 32; 22:29, 42; 23:34, 46; 24:49.

[862] On numerous occasions in Isaiah, God is expressed as 'the Holy one of Israel.'See John N. Oswalt, *The Book of Isaiah 1-39* (NICOT; Grand Rapids: Wm B. Eerdmans, 1986), 33.

[863] Schrenk, "God as Father in Judaism," in *TDNT* V, 990-991.

[864] Schrenk, "God as Father in Judaism," in *TDNT* V, 990-991.

[865] E.g. Epictetus, *Discourse* 1.9.3-7; 16.3-5.

Again Q does have theological images drawn from nature; particularly noteworthy is the two clear instances of female imagery for God in both Matthew and Luke. In the first instance God is imaged as a baker woman:

> And again he said, "To what should I compare the kingdom of God? It is like yeast that a woman took and mixed in with three measures of flour until all of it was leavened."(Lk 13:20, 21//Mt 13:33)

In the second instance God is depicted as a (mother) hen gathering her brood (Lk 13:34-35//Mt 23:37-39). This "scriptural picture of divine protection"[866] forms the lament reflecting Jesus' own ministry:

> Jerusalem, Jerusalem, the city that kills the prophets and stones those who are sent to it! How often have I desired to gather your children together as a hen gathers her brood under her wings, and you were not willing! (Lk 13:34//Mt 23:27)

Here Q Jesus expresses in a clear feminine image and it depicts God's compassion at work in Jesus' ministry. Looking at the level of Jesus, Mollenkott explains:

> When Jesus used the image of the hen and her chicks, he was speaking from the point of view of a being outside of human history (that is, speaking as God's wisdom), and was expressing unconditional love toward those who were in the process of rejecting him and that eternal One who sent him.[867]

There is no doubt that this feminine (fostering) element of God's nature is quite in line with Q Jesus discourse on the fatherhood of God seen in the gifts of nature.

5.2.9. Fatherhood of God in the Synoptic Gospels

As mentioned above the idea of the fatherhood of God is found in Mark, the main source of both Matthew and Luke. When we explore the content and the occurrences of the term 'Father' for God in all the three Gospels together, they occur in similar contexts.

---

[866] David Tiede, *Luke* (Minneapolis: Augsburg, 1988), 259, cf. Deut 32:10-14; Isa 40:31.

[867] V.R. Mollenkott, *The Divine Feminine: The Biblical Imagery of God as Female* (New York: Crossroad, 1984), 93.

5.2.9.1. Fatherhood of God and Prayer

5.2.9.1.1. Father of the Son[868]

While it is interesting to see that all the three Synoptic authors recorded Jesus' prayer addressing God as his own Father in Gethsemane:

> Mk 14:36 - Abba, Father, for you all things are possible; remove this cup from me; yet, not what I want, but what you want.
>
> Mt 26:39 - My Father, if it is possible, let this cup pass from me; yet not what I want but what you want.
>
> Lk 22:42 - Father, if you are willing, remove this cup from me; yet, not my will but yours be done.

So we see here that all three Synoptic writers retain the word of Jesus addressing God as Father in difficult circumstances.[869] The implication is that all the Synoptic writers affirm God as Father, "one who always hears the prayers of those who turn to him with a pure heart."[870] Thus for Synoptic Jesus the fatherhood of God is a profound spiritual experience and a burning conviction, linked especially with the practice of prayer.[871] It is no mere metaphysical relationship, but, as T.W. Manson rightly puts, "a moral tie, a fatherly love and care on the one side, and a filial devotion and obedience on the other."[872] The relation between God and Jesus was a personal one. God was his Father and he was God's Son. He loved his Father and his Father loved him. He realized his entire dependence on his Father. He thus gladly submitted himself to his Father (Mk 14:36//Mt 26:39//Lk 22:42). Such a strong Father-Son correlation or rather a strong filial relationship between God as Father and Jesus as Son is portrayed by all the Synoptic evangelists.

---

[868] J. Moltmann ("The Motherly Father. Is Trinitarian Patripassianism Replacing Theological Patriarchalism?" in *God as Father?* [eds. Johannes-Baptist Metz and Edward Schillebeecks; New York: T & T Clark, 1981], 51), describes this close filial relationship as the 'Father of the Son,' where "the Father is passionately involved in what happens to the Son; if the Son suffers, the father suffers with him. The Son is dependent on him, but he is also dependent on the Son, since they are one in their love. Thus neither can exist without the other."

[869] As J.H. Charlesworth (*Jesus Within Judaism*, 134) correctly puts, "There is not a world of difference between 'our Father' and 'Father;' both expressions evoke a loving and intimate God!"

[870] J.H. Charlesworth, "Jewish Prayers in the Time of Jesus," in *The Lord's Prayer: Perspectives for Reclaiming Christian Prayer*, 37.

[871] Since most of the 'Father' usage occur in Mark in the context of prayer (e.g., 11:22-25; 14:36) Mary D' Angelo ("Theology in Mark and Q: Abba and 'Father' in Context," 160) is of the view that the spiritual experience of the community is the most important context of Mark. However Matthew and Luke too have the same occurrences of 'Father' for God in prayer contexts (e.g., Mt 6: 9-14//Lk 11: 2-4; Mt 11: 25-27//Lk 10: 21-22; Mt 26: 39, 42//Lk 22: 42), so the same can be said even for Matthew and Luke.

[872] T.W. Manson, *The Teaching of Jesus*, 91.

This is supplemented by the fact that in all the three Gospels we see the occurrences of the word ἀγαπητός referring to Jesus. When Jesus was baptized there was a voice from heaven that greeted him as "my Son, the Beloved" (Mk 1:11//Mt 3:17//Lk 3:22), an experience repeated at the Transfiguration episode (Mk 9:7//Mt 17:5 // Lk 9:35), and it occurs again in a parable which surely speaks about God's beloved Son (Mk 12:6//Mt 21:37//Lk 20:13). The Evangelists leave us in no doubt about the love of the Father for God's beloved Son. It is supplemented by the frequent occurrences of the Father/Son correlation in the major strata of Jesus' traditions (Mark and Q). In a discourse on discipleship found in all the Synoptic Gospels (Mk 8:34-9:1//Mt 16:24-28//Lk 9:23-27), we see the occurrences of Jesus saying God as his Father:

> Mt 16:27 - For the Son of Man is to come with his angels in the glory of his Father,
>
> Mk 8:38 - When he comes in the glory of his Father ....
>
> Lk 9:26 - When he comes in the glory of the Father ....

Again in the eschatological discourse of Jesus, found in Mark and Matthew (so Markan source), we see the occurrences of Father/Son correlation:

> Mk 13:32 - But about that day or hour no one knows, neither the angels in heaven, nor the Son, but only the Father.
>
> Mt 24:36 - But about that day and hour no one knows, neither the angels of heaven, nor the Son, but only the Father.

So also in Q, in the context of discipleship and mission discourse (Mt 9:35-11:30// Lk 9:51-10:24) we see Jesus thanking his Father in prayer (Mt 11:25-27// Lk10:21-22). He prays:

I thank you, Father, Lord of heaven and earth, because you have hidden these things from the wise and the intelligent and have revealed them to infants; yes, Father, for such was your gracious will. All things have been handed over to me by my Father; and no one knows the Son[873] except the Father, and no one knows the Father[874] except the Son and anyone to whom the Son chooses to reveal him (Mt 11:25-27).

Such instances show the unanimity of the Synoptic Gospels in portraying filial relationship between God and Jesus, and thereby pointing to the strong emphasis on the fatherhood of God in the Synoptic Gospels and so in the theology of the Evangelists.

[873] 'who the Son is' (Lk 10:22).

[874] 'who the Father is' (Lk 10:22).

5.2.9.1.2. Fatherhood of God and Forgiveness

It is also striking to see that in all the Synoptic Gospels we see 'Father' or 'heavenly Father' is linked with teaching on forgiveness. Commenting on the withered fig tree just after the cleansing of the temple in Jerusalem, Markan Jesus tells his disciples that they should forgive others when praying:

> Mk 11:25 - Whenever you stand praying, forgive, if you have anything against anyone; so that your Father in heaven may also forgive you your trespasses.

Though in a different context Mathew and Luke have the same theme of fatherhood of God in the context of teaching on forgiveness and prayer:

> Mt 6:9-15 - Our Father in heaven ... forgive us our debts ... For if you forgive others their trespasses, your heavenly Father will also forgive you; but if you do not forgive others, neither will your Father forgive your trespasses.

> Lk 11:2-4 - Father, hallowed be your name ... forgive us our sins ....

Thus in all the Synoptics the emphasis is that God as Father relates reciprocally to others in forgiveness.[875] Not only in prayer but also in the other teachings of Synoptic Jesus we see the idea of a forgiving God. All the Synoptic Gospels tell that around Jesus the tax-collectors and the sinners gathered. He ate with them (Mk 2:15//Mt 9:10//Lk 5:29), so that he was called the friend of publicans and sinners (Mt 11:19; Lk 7:34). He said that he had come to call, not the righteous, but sinners to repentance (Mk 2:17//Mt 9:13//Lk 5:32). He said that "it is not the will of your Father in heaven that one of these little ones should be lost" (Mt 18:14), and that there was joy in heaven over one sinner who repents (Lk 15:7, 10). The emphasis of the Synoptic Jesus is a compassionate, forgiving and seeking Father, who cares for the least and the lost. So we find here the idea of a forgiving Father in the teaching of Synoptic Jesus, which is quite in line with the notion of love and compassion as one of the central ingredients of the Father image of Synoptic Jesus (cf. Lk 6:27-36; Mt 5:43-48).

5.2.9.2. Loving and Compassionate Father

The central characteristic of the fatherhood of God is love. The love of God is implied throughout the Synoptic Gospels. Not only that it is implied in the very intimate and familial language 'Father' in addressing God, but that in the very activities of Jesus, found in all the Synoptic Gospels, the fatherhood of God is

[875] For D' Angelo ("Theology in Mark and Q: Abba and 'Father' in Context," 161) 'Father' in Mark evokes God as the refuge of the persecuted and the giver of forgiveness.

revealed, as Argyle rightly puts, "Jesus revealed God's love less by words than by deeds of compassion and forgiveness."[876]

The Synoptic Jesus believed his ministry of preaching and healing to be a special 'time' (Mk 1:15), in which the kingdom of God was not merely at hand but even, in some sense, actually present (Mt 12:28//Lk 11:20 cf. Lk 17:21).[877] In other words, there is a direct connection between the miracles Jesus performed and his proclamation of the coming of God's kingdom in all the three Gospels. The exorcisms of the demoniac (e.g., Mk 1:21-27//Lk 4:33-35), the healing of the sick (e.g., Mk 2:1-12//Mt 9:2-8//Lk 5:17-26), the stilling of the storm (Mk 4:35-41//Mt 8:23-27// Lk 8: 22-25), all these activities bear evidence to the rule of God (Mk 3:23-30//Mt 12:25-27//Lk 11:17-23). The miracles, which are called δυνάμεις ('works of power'),[878] were the eruption of divine power into the human situation for help and healing (Mk 5:30//Lk 8:46). Jesus was moved with compassion, either for the crowds or for the sufferer.[879] It is σπλαγχνίζομαι which is the strongest word in Greek for the experience of pity and compassion. Σπλαγχνα describes the pity and compassion which moves a person to the depths of his or her being. The miracles are the sign of power and compassion in the heart of Jesus, and therefore in the heart of God. They are the sign that the power of God is used in compassion, and that the compassion is backed by power. In the miracles we see the power and the compassion of God combine to deal with the human situation.[880]

In a pericope found in all the Synoptic Gospels, 'the cleansing of a leper' (Mk 1:40-45//Mt 8:1-4//Lk 5:12-16), the compassion and love of God is highlighted and understood in the very action of Jesus, though the expression 'moved with pity' is found only in Mark:

> Mk 1:41: Moved with pity, Jesus stretched out his hand and touched him, and said to him, "I do choose. Be made clean!"
>
> Mt 8:3: He stretched out his hand and touched him, saying, "I do choose. Be made clean!" Immediately his leprosy was cleansed.
>
> Lk 5:13: Then Jesus stretched out his hand, touched him, and said, "I do choose. Be made clean." Immediately the leprosy left him.

---

[876] Argyle, *God in the New Testament*, 77.

[877] Jesus did not consider his healing ministry to be on par with the activity of other miracle workers, of which he was quite aware (cf. Mt 12:27//Lk 11:17-23). The Synoptic Jesus believed that his own authority to be rooted in his mission from God. See S. Brown, *The Origins of Christianity*, 60-61.

[878] Mt 11:20-23; 13:54-58; Mk 6:2, 5; Lk 10:13; 19:370.

[879] Mt 9:36; 14:14; 15:32; 20:34; Mk 1:41; 6:34; 8:2; Lk 7:13.

[880] Barclay, *The Mind of Jesus*, 88.

As such the healing miracles of Jesus are the revelation of God's power and compassion; they are the sign that God cares. In the action of Synoptic Jesus we see the power and the pity of God combine to deal with the human situation. Thus God's fatherhood is strongly implied in this pericope. The same is true in the nature miracles.

In one of the nature miracles of Jesus recorded in all the Synoptic Gospels, 'the stilling of the storm' (Mk 4:35-41//Mt 8:23-27//Lk 8: 22-25), we see the demonstration of God's authority and love in the very deeds of Jesus. All these reveal the idea of God's fatherhood in all the three Gospels. While redaction critics find different emphasis of each of the evangelist in this pericope, as the details of the episode are seen reversed particularly in Matthew when compared with Mark. In Mark Jesus brought the storm to silence first and then rebukes his panicky disciples. In Matthew this scene is reverse. The explanation is given that Matthew focus more on discipleship while Mark focus on the actual act of stilling the storm by displaying the power of God.[881] Yet equal emphasis on the theological-christological aspect is also seen in all the three Gospels:

> Mk 4:39-41 - He woke up and rebuked the wind, and said to the sea, "Peace! Be still!" Then the wind ceased, and there was a dead calm. He said to them, "Why are you afraid? Have you still no faith?" And they were filled with great awe and said to one another, "Who then is this, that even the wind and the sea obey him?"
>
> Mt 8:26-27 - And he said to them, "Why are you afraid, you of little faith?" Then he got up and rebuked the winds and the sea; and there was a dead calm. They were amazed, saying, "What sort of man is this, that even the winds and the sea obey him?"
>
> Lk 8:24-25 - They went to him and woke him up, shouting, "Master, Master, we are perishing!" And he woke up and rebuked the wind and the raging waves; they ceased, and there was a calm. He said to them, "Where is your faith?" They were afraid and amazed, and said to one another, "Who then is this, that he commands even the winds and the water, and they obey him?"

In this miracle of stilling of the storm we see demonstrated the power and the compassion of God exercised in love for disciples. In the midst of a terrifying upheaval, Jesus the very Son of God ('Who then is this') brought peace and comfort to the fearful disciples. Thus the fatherhood of God is implicit in this episode. So also in the feeding miracles found in all Synoptics the same emphasis on the love and compassion of God is seen. While the explicit expression ἐσπλαγχνίσθη is found only in Mark (6:34) and Matthew (14:14) but in all the Synoptic Gospels

[881] G. Bornkamm, "The Stilling of the Storm in Mathew," in *Tradition and Interpretation in Matthew*, 55.

God's compassion is implicit in the very activities of Jesus, that is, feeding the multitudes (Mk 6:34-44//Mt 14:14-21//Lk 9:11-17). In this very pericope fatherhood of God is clearly seen in the caring, selfless and compassionate deeds of Jesus.

Thus in the Synoptic miracle stories we see demonstrated the power and compassion of God exercised in love for humanity. In all the 'deeds of power' of Jesus, highlighted in all the Gospels, we see the love of God at work. In the depiction of the Synoptic Gospels, as Jesus brings healing of the diseases, restore the chaos of the unruly seas and feed the multitudes, they manifest the fatherly rule of grace, that is, God's rule for the benefit of humanity. Thus love and compassion of God, so God's fatherhood, is once again central even in the miracles of Jesus in the Synoptic Gospels. The emphasis on the love and compassion of God is all the more evident as all three has the shepherd-sheep imagery. Mark has this idea expressed in miracle of feeding the multitudes (Mk 6:34-44):

> Mk 6:34 - As he went ashore, he saw a great crowd; and he had compassion for them, because they were like sheep without a shepherd; and he began to teach them many things.

The shepherd and sheep imagery is occurring in Luke and Matthew in discourse context:

> Lk 15:3-7: Which one of you, having a hundred sheep and losing one of them, does not leave the ninety-nine in the wilderness and go after the one that is lost until he finds it? When he has found it, he lays it on his shoulders and rejoices. And when he comes home, he calls together his friends and neighbors, saying to them, 'Rejoice with me, for I have found my sheep that was lost.' Just so, I tell you, there will be more joy in heaven over one sinner who repents than over ninety-nine righteous persons who need no repentance.
>
> Mt 18:10-14: What do you think? If a shepherd has a hundred sheep, and one of them has gone astray, does he not leave the ninety-nine on the mountains and go in search of the one that went astray? And if he finds it, truly I tell you, he rejoices over it more than over the ninety-nine that never went astray. So it is not the will of your Father in heaven that one of these little ones should be lost.

Luke may have preserved its original setting in Jesus' welcome to outcasts and sinners (15:1-2), as Matthew has this illustration in a discourse on church context (18:1-20). Nevertheless, echoing Ezekiel (34:11-16) and Isaiah (40:11), it clearly depicts God's compassion at work in Jesus' ministry. In other words, the shepherd-sheep imagery found in all the Synoptic Gospels heighten the caring and compassionate nature of God, which means that the theme of the fatherhood of God is found in all the Synoptic Gospels.

5.2.9.3. The Death of Jesus and the Fatherhood of God

As seen in all the Synoptic passion accounts, the love of God and so the fatherhood of God is revealed ultimately in the death of Jesus (Mk 15:22-37//Mt 27:33-50//Lk 23:33-46). The cross revealed the love of God for humankind, which is a pardoning and redeeming love.[882] While the explicit words of Jesus' trust in the Father at the dying moment is found only in Luke (Lk 23:46), yet the very presence of the ejaculatory words of Jesus on the cross "My God, My God, why have you forsaken me?" in Mark (15:34) and Matthew (27:46) too imply that God was present for him even then. It indicates Jesus' continued sense of intimate and mutually responsible relationship with God.[883] He experienced forsakenness (Mk 15:34//Mt 27:46) but does not cease to trust God.[884] Earlier to this episode the Gethsemane prayer projects that it was the will of the Father that Jesus experience the cup (Mk 14:36//Mt 26:39//Lk 22:42). As Father, God has placed this cup before Jesus. So God wills Jesus' death.[885] According to A.J. Appasamy, one of the pioneer Indian theologians, Jesus has his own will but devotes it entirely to that of the Father. In his own words, "the doing of the Father's will was of the essence of His oneness with the Father."[886] It is implicit in a saying of the Synoptic Jesus in the context of teaching his disciples on his approaching death:

> That the Son of Man must undergo great suffering, and be rejected by the elders, the chief priests, and the scribes, and be killed, and after three days rise again (Mk 8:31//Mt 16:21//Lk 9:22).

Here his (Jesus) impending death is revealed as a divine necessity (δεῖ). And with this declaration, he goes on expounding the idea of self-giving or self sacrifice for others sake:

> For those who want to save their life will lose it, and those who lose their life for my sake, and for the sake of the gospel, will save it (Mk 8:35//Mt 10:39//Lk 17:33).[887]

Even the expressions of mocking on the lips of the religious leaders - "he saved others; he cannot save himself" (Mk 15:31//Mt 27:42//Lk 23:35) - contain

---

[882] Argyle, *God in the New Testament*, 77.

[883] For more on this topic, see R.E.O. White, "That 'Cry of dereliction' ...?" in *ExpT* 113 (2002), 188-189.

[884] Thus for R. Bauckham (*Jesus and the God of Israel: God Crucified and Other Studies on the New Testament's Christology of Divine Identity* (Grand Rapids: Wm B. Eerdmans, 2008], 258) "the address to 'my God' ensures that the cry is not one of despair but of faith, even thought the faith is under severe assault."

[885] Minear, *God of the Gospels*, 110.

[886] See A.J. Appasamy, *The Gospel and India's Heritage* (London: SPCK, 1942), 37.

[887] This self-giving idea is most explicit in John (12:24): "Very truly, I tell you, unless a grain of wheat falls into the earth and dies, it remains just a single grain; but if it dies, it bears much fruit."

the ironic truth: Jesus is indeed the savior.[888] He was the complete expression of the Father. Through him God spoke and acted. The word 'save' recalls the occasions when Jesus did save others by his powerful deeds (e.g., Mk 1:41//Mt 8:3//Lk 5:13; Mk 5:26//Mt 8:26//Lk 8:24). Thus when one met him one was met – and saved - by God.[889] And now in his self-giving sacrifice on the cross, he redeems the world, thus the fatherhood of God is fully revealed on the cross (Mk 15:37//Mt 27:50//Lk 23:46). As a result of his death, the temple curtain is torn from top to bottom (Mk 15:38//Mt 27:51//Lk 23:45) and the centurion confesses that Jesus was the Son of God (Mk 15:39//Mt 27:54). There were two curtains in the temple: one separated the holy of holies from the holy place (Ex 26:31-35) while the other hung at the entrance of the temple (Ex 26:37). The Synoptic Evangelists do not specify which curtain was torn. Probably it was the curtain which shut off the Holy of Holies in the temple.[890] That curtain served to conceal God's glory: "and the curtain shall separate for you the holy place from the most holy" (Ex 26:33).[891] Thus the rending of the curtain is the symbolic statement of the fact that by the death of Jesus, God's glory shines forth to all humanity, Gentile as well as Jew.[892] Jesus came to humanity with an invitation to approach the Father to whose presence there were no barriers any more. Fittingly, the Synoptic Evangelists projected a Gentile (Roman) centurion confessing Jesus as the Son of God. The universality of God's fatherhood is clearly seen here. For the Synoptic evangelists, the death of Jesus was the full disclosure of the fatherhood of God, his heart of love and compassion. As J. Moltmann puts:

> On Golgotha the eternal being of God is made known. God is love. Love is susceptible to suffering. Love's susceptibility to suffering finds its fulfillment in self-sacrifice … In suffering he displays his compassion. 'He covers all suffering with his own immeasurable suffering.'[893]

The death of Jesus is the crown and center of his whole life for he who thus preaches and acts fulfills on the cross the truth of fatherhood.[894] Thus the love of God is the overarching theological emphasis of the Synoptic Gospels. The whole

---

[888] Jesus cannot save himself; only God can save him. If he tries to save himself, he will lose his life (Mk 8:35 // Mt 16:25 // Lk 9:24).

[889] J.A.T. Robinson, *Honest to God* (40th anniversary edition; Louisville: Westminster John Knox, 2002), 71.

[890] However, commentators are divided on the question of which curtain is meant, with some favoring the inner and others the outer. The evidence does not allow us to determine which veil is meant. For discussion of the temple curtain, see J. Nolland, *The Gospel of Matthew*, 1211-1213.

[891] Into the Holy of Holies only the High Priest could enter, and that too only one day. The one day on which he could enter was the Day of Atonement.

[892] Matera, *Passion Narratives and Gospel Theologies*, 47.

[893] Moltmann, "The Motherly Father. Is Trinitarian Patripassianism Replacing Theological Partriarchalism?" 54.

[894] Schrenk, "God as Father in Judaism," in *TDNT* V, 995.

narratives in the Gospels talk about the activity of the Father of the Son, that is, God's active works in his redeeming love that work out through his Son.

5.2.10. Summary

The goal of this chapter has been to show the meaning and function of the fatherhood of God theme in Matthew. Prior to dealing with place and significance of the theme of God's fatherhood in Matthew and the Synoptic Gospels, we have also shown how Old Testament and New Testament theologians addressed the question of God in relation to the central theological emphasis of the New Testament. And we have shown that scholars are increasingly discovering the centrality of God in New Testament theology. That theocentric thinking and emphasis help heightens our argument and forwarding of the theme of God's fatherhood as the core motif in New Testament theology. This broad focus and perspective is substantiated by our specific argument on the theme of God's fatherhood as the key theme and so the hub of Matthean theology. As seen above when Matthew discussed about the sonship of Jesus (christology) the fatherhood of God appears prominently. Again the fatherhood of God theme holds the key to understand the life situation of Matthew and his community (*Sitz im leben*); while the theme of the kingdom of God too is inseparably related to the fatherhood of God. Both the term 'Lord' or 'King' occur in Matthew in close connection with the theme of the fatherhood of God. We have also seen that fatherhood of God in Matthew has both sociological and theological implications. That means to say that there are different aspects of the fatherhood of God, as both socio-political realities of the time and strong theological-philosophical environment shaped Matthew's theme of the fatherhood of God. In this regard the recurrence of the expression 'heavenly Father' or 'Father in heaven,' which are mostly redactional emphasis of Matthew, is striking. It has strong sociological significance. As Matthew and his community use the expression 'Father in heaven' or 'heavenly Father,' they subvert earthly fatherhood, and thereby positing an alternative, true Father in heaven, instead of the emperor on the earth (Roman Emperor). Matthew's meaning and usage of the fatherhood of God is thus to strengthen and legitimate his community, to encourage them that they are the true people of God. Matthew finds that comfort in the heavenly Father. In other words, Matthean community is defined by relationship to the heavenly Father. However, this heavenly Father, for Matthew's community, is an all-embracing and approachable "Our Father," whose nature is more of care and concern. This leads us to the theological-philosophical aspect of the fatherhood of God in Matthew.

The theological-philosophical significance of God's fatherhood in Matthew lies in his very unique idea of cosmic fatherhood. The key expression is again found in the Sermon on the Mount, Mathew's first discourse, where we see in several instances the concentration of God's fatherly care in creation and nature (e.g., 5:45; 6:9-11). Thus, the idea of God's fatherhood in Matthew is seen in the immanence and practical nature of God, but not as transcendent and domineering nature, as seen mostly in the Old Testament. This idea comes from Matthew's Greek-Hellenistic background. As he reinterprets the teaching of Jesus, Matthew drew from the rich Greek-Hellenistic traditions and thus blended together with his Jewish tradition.

Apart from the unique Matthean cosmic fatherhood idea, there are fatherhood elements common with Mark and Luke. Several characteristics of God's fatherhood idea in Matthew are in common with his Synoptic counterparts - Mark and Luke. All three of them project the fatherhood idea as reciprocal filial Father-Son correlation, fatherhood and forgiveness, fatherhood as love and compassion. The presence of such common fatherhood elements show that God's fatherhood is emphasized in all the Synoptic Gospels.

Concluding Remarks

With this we will now turn to the relevance chapter and see how this fatherhood of God idea so prominently and centrally placed in the Gospel of Matthew can be utilized for doing theology in a religiously pluralistic context of India. In other words, we will see the relevance of Matthean theology for and in understanding God in Indian multi religious traditions.

Chapter 6

Fatherhood of God: A Reconceptualization in Indian Thinking, Theology and Christian Witness

Introduction

We have discussed in the previous chapter that the theme of the fatherhood of God is the fulcrum of Matthean theology. Keeping this perspective in mind the aim of this chapter is to explore how the very idea of God's fatherhood can be utilized for doing theology in a religiously pluralistic context of India. But before delving into this implication part of the fatherhood of God in Indian religious traditions, we will address the issues that the feminist theologians raise concerning the use of Father for God, their criticism of the idea of the Fatherhood of God. Basing on our Matthean study above we will also show whether or not Matthew's idea of the fatherhood of God is patriarchal or sexist, as raised by the contemporary feminist theologians.

6.1. The Fatherhood of God in the Context of Feminist Theological Movement

6.1.1. Feminist Critique of the Fatherhood of God

Feminist theologians find the language of God in the biblical traditions, specifically the projection of God as Father, problematic. Mary Daley, for example, in her work *Beyond God the Father* has provided us with the key to open the door and gives access to the protests of feminist theologians against 'God the Father' with the radical dictum, "If God is male, then the male is God."[895] Viewing the Bible with sexist lens she thus protests against the God of the patriarchal system and

[895] M. Daly, *Beyond God the Father*, 19.

the andocentric aspects of biblical religion. According to her the image of God as the patriarchal Father confirmed the status quo, of the patriarchal society which legitimizes the domination of men over women. God, for her, is the absolutely transcendent, almighty, and self-sufficient ruler of the universe, whose authority is reduplicated in the hierarchical structures of society, men on top and women on the bottom. This is why women have been prevented from finding full meaning for themselves personally, physically, and sexually.[896]

Daly believes this fatherhood of God has been confirmed and reinforced by the man Jesus of Nazareth, the Son of God. Daly, then, is concerned not only with the father-image that is evoked by her protest, but also with the implicit or explicit man-ness of Father and Son, in other words, with male images of God.[897] The same voice of protest is seen in Daphne Hampson, who voices not only against male conceptualization of God (as Father)[898] but also in the designation of God as the Father of the central figure of its faith, Jesus of Nazareth.[899] Karen Bloomquist too talks about the theological necessity of depatriarchalizing God with the expression, "Let God be God."[900] She argues:

> If God is symbolized as "Father," God is concretized in terms of the human relationship of father and child. *At the same time*, this human relationship is consecrated into a pattern of the divine-human relationship, thereby giving fatherhood theonomous, sacramental depth. If a segment of reality is used as a symbol for God, that realm is elevated into the realm of the holy ... If we are to speak of the God revealed through the Bible, we cannot avoid using human vehicles, but a more balanced variety of symbols rather than nearly exclusively male ones can help circumvent the tendency to divinize the male at the expense of the female.[901]

Rosemary Radford Ruether too made a revolutionary statement against the patriarchy and hierarchy found in the Bible. She avoids all designations for God that presuppose some sort of hierarchical rule or authority. Instead, she defines God, whom she calls 'God/ess' as 'the Primal matrix' the great womb within all things, gods and humans, sky and earth, human and nonhuman beings are generated.[902] In proposing this she argues that patriarchal language is not a

---

[896] This is the argument throughout her book.

[897] M. Daly, *Beyond God the Father*, 71.

[898] Daphne Hampson, *Theology and Feminism*, 53.

[899] Daphne Hampson, *Theology and Feminism*, 8.

[900] K. Bloomquist, "'Let God be God:' The theological necessity of depatriarchalizing God," in *Our Naming of God*, 45-60.

[901] K. Bloomquist, "Let God be God," 48.

[902] R.R. Ruether, *Sexism and God-Talk: Toward a Feminist Theology With a New Introduction* (Boston: Beacon, 1993), 48-49.

privileged way. Masculine language is on the same level as all human language – inadequate, partial, and not literally true when applied to God. She thus argues that "if all language for God/ess is analogy, if taking a particular human image literally is idolatry, then male language for the divine must lose its privileged place."[903] In the same vein both Elizabeth Johnson[904] and Gail Ramshaw concur that God being beyond human naming, and so beyond gender, we must not privilege language drawn from one human gender.[905]

So the voice of the feminists is that they want to make God inclusive and meaningful to both sexes. So they talk about giving equal emphasis to both male and female image of God as Ruether succinctly argues:

> God is both male and female and neither male nor female. One needs inclusive language for God that draws on the images and experiences of both genders ... Inclusiveness can happen only by naming God/ess in female as well as male metaphors.[906]

Thus she voices for equivalent images for God as male and female, not merely feminine nature within the father (male) nature, but images of male and female as equivalents. For her, "adding an image of God/ess as loving, nurturing mother, mediating the power of the strong, sovereign father, is insufficient."[907] To enhance this argument she cites the parables of Jesus on mustard seed (Mt 13:31-32 and parallels) and yeast (Mt 13:33 and parallels) and see God as farmer and women respectively. Being a biblical scholar herself, Ruether found out that the Hebrew monotheism is neither supporting nor going against the identification of monotheism solely with the male gender, because God is beyond all literal anthropomorphic images.[908] Unlike radical feminists, for example, Mary Daly[909] and Elizabeth A Johnson,[910] who wanted to take biblical imageries in a literal sense, Reuther sees the imageries of God in the Bible as analogies and metaphors, and not move beyond that point.[911] In arguing so she labels that it is idolatrous to take a particular human image for God literally.[912]

---

903 Ruether, *Sexism and God-Talk*, 68-69.

904 Elizabeth A. Johnson, *She Who Is: The Mystery of God in Feminist Theological Discourse* (New York: Crossroad, 1995), 117.

905 Gail Ramshaw, *God Beyond Gender: Feminist Christian God-Language* (Minneapolis: Fortress, 1995), 21.

906 Ruether, *Sexism and God-Talk*, 67.

907 Ruether, *Sexism and God-Talk*, 69.

908 Ruether, *A Reader in Feminist Theology*, 24.

909 Which is obvious in her famous dictum "If God is male then male is God."

910 As Elizabeth A. Johnson (*She Who Is*, 33) also argues that "the problem consists in the fact that these male terms are used exclusively, literally and patriarchally"

911 Ruether, *Sexism and God-Talk*, 67-69.

912 Ruether, *Sexism and God-Talk*, 66, 69.

Ruether's argument is supported by other feminist scholars in Sally McFague and V.R. Mollenkott. According to Mcfague both Father and Mother (for God) as equally metaphorical so they ought to be accorded equal status in religious languages.[913] Mollenkott too finds no problem in retaining the masculinity of God, as she emphasized that God is equally depicted as male and female in the Bible.[914] It is thus seen that recognition of the feminine aspects of God along with masculine aspects is important to the feminists.

6.1.2. Jesus' God Language and Biblical Patterns

It is clearly the case that a central argument against the feminist challenge to language for God as Father is Jesus' own practice of addressing God as Father. Talking about the revelatory status in Jesus' own address of God as Father, Gerhard O. Forde puts:

> First of all, we have to do with revelation in time, through historical particularity. We have to do with a Jew in first-century Palestine who called God his Father and who has invited us to pray on his warrant (in his name) to God as father ... There is no exhaustively necessary reason we can cite to show why Jesus should have used this language. The fact is simply that he did ... and so must we.[915]

The point here is that Jesus' address to God as Father is and should be the norm in the Christian churches. This leads logically to the argument that such address to God is the language of the Bible. In this perspective John Cooper, one of the advocates of the traditional language of Father for God, talks about "biblical patterns" of speech for God. He argues:

> If Scripture is the source and norm for the God-language of the Christian faith, that language will not be gender-inclusive. However, if Christian language must be gender-inclusive, then the doctrine of divine genderlessness is in fact operating at a more basic and determinative level than Scripture.[916]

He thus concludes that "the only reasonable conclusion is that the intended practice of Scripture as a whole is to speak of God as a masculine person."[917] This

913 S. Mcfague, *Metaphorical Theology: Models of God in Religious Language* (Philadelphia: Fortress Press, 1982), 128.

914 V.R. Mollenkott, *The Divine Feminine: The Biblical Imagery of Female* (New York: Crossroads, 1984).

915 Gerhard O. Forde, "Naming the One Who Is above Us," in *Speaking the Christian God: The Holy Trinity and the Challenge of Feminism*, edited by Alvin F. Kimel (Grand Rapids: Eerdmans, 1992), 118.

916 John W. Cooper, *Our Father in Heaven: Christian Faith and Inclusive Language for God* (Grand Rapids; Michigan: Baker Books, 1998), 188.

917 Cooper, *Our Father in Heaven*, 114.

is the pattern which should have primacy for those who make any sort of claim to heed the authority of scripture. In similar vein Claude Geffre says:

> The name "Father" is the one best calculated to manifest the novelty of the God of Jesus, as compared not only with the God of the Greeks but with the God of the Jews ... Compared with the God of Israel the God of Jesus represents a revolution in so far as God is the God of grace before being the God of the law.[918]

One of the well known evangelical writer J.I. Packer, in his influential book *Knowing God* talks about the uniqueness of the fatherhood of God in the New Testament thus:

> For everything that Christ taught, everything that makes the New Testament new, and better than the Old, everything that is distinctively Christian as opposed to merely Jewish, is summed up in the knowledge of the Fatherhood of God. 'Father' is the Christian name of God.[919]

In similar vein John Cooper puts:

> Feminine images for God ... are greater in number and directness in the Old Testament than in the New Testament. In other words, as the Bible progressively reveals God as Father, Son, and Holy Spirit and Jesus as the Messiah, the Son of God, the feminine imagery for God does not increase but recedes into the background.[920]

Thus Cooper calls Father the distinctive New Testament title-name and sees "definitive revelatory status" in the address of God as Father.[921] That means Jesus' use of Father in the Gospels becomes the basis for all subsequent argumentation for holding on to the traditional language.

Dealing with the question of how to speak about God in respect to liturgical language, biblical translation and theological discussion, Francis Martin, a New Testament scholar himself, suggests that masculine language better mediates the biblical understanding of God. He argues that in the Hebrew Bible, the use of masculine forms for God reflects the unique teaching of Israel concerning God as creator. He states, "It is a transcultural fact that as natural images, *male* mediates transcendence and otherness and *female* mediates immanence and closeness."[922] In saying this Martins is in favor of the male language for God, that is, the biblical pattern of God as Father as against the female language and imagery, which he

---

918 Claude Geffre, "'Father' as the Proper Name of God," in *God as Father?*, 44-45.

919 J.I. Packer, *Knowing God* (London: Hodder and Stoughton, 1975), 224.

920 Cooper, *Our Father in Heaven*, 90.

921 Cooper, *Our Father in Heaven*, 105, 110.

922 Francis Martin, *The Feminist Question: Feminist Theology in the Light of Christian Tradition* (Grand Rapids: Wm B. Eerdmans, 1994), 251.

views negatively as a "tendency to pantheism and a loss of the sense of the absolute freedom of God's creative and redemptive action."[923]

It is thus seen that both the feminist and traditionalist camps are equally fortified and the problem persists. In the voice of a well known biblical theologian W. Brueggemann, however, we see a balanced view. He argues:

> Biblical faith is quite uninterested in questions of God's sexuality, masculine or feminine, or even in God's asexuality but is singularly and passionately concerned with God's covenanting and the implication of covenanting for human history. In its singular concern, it is free to use various images to articulate that paradigm of covenanting.[924]

Inferred in this very concise statement is that God's fatherhood has to be accepted as an expression of the activity of God as redemptive and nurturing but not sexist or patriarchal as such. Interestingly, some of the feminist biblical scholars too find non-patriarchal or anti-patriarchal tones within the very use of Father for God, thus toning down the stance on patriarchal or sexist language in God-talk. They argue that Jesus' own understanding of God's fatherhood alleviates the patriarchalism inherent in the term. Thus looking at the level of Jesus, Elisabeth Schussler Fiorenza puts in perspective and moves into (but not beyond and away from) the very locus of biblical revelation itself, which, according to her, critically breaks away from patriarchal religion and culture. Accordingly, for Fiorenza, Jesus redefined the character of God and discipleship in terms of service and self-giving love.[925] She writes about "the *basileia* vision of Jesus as the praxis of inclusive wholeness"[926] and explains the text that supports her argument. For her, "the praxis and vision of Jesus and his movement is best understood as an inner-Jewish renewal movement that presented an *alternative* option to the dominant patriarchal structures rather than an oppositional formation rejecting the values and praxis of Judaism."[927] She thus finds the corrective to patriarchy and hierarchy within Jesus' own use of Father, specifically citing the words of Jesus in Matthew 23:9. She says:

> The new kinship of the discipleship of equals does not admit of "fathers," thereby rejecting the patriarchal power and esteem invested in them ... The "father" God is invoked here, however, not to justify patriarchal structures and relationships in the community of disciples

---

[923] Martin, *The Feminist Question*, 252.

[924] W. Brueggemann, "Israel's Social Criticism and Yahweh's Sexuality," in *JAAR* Supplement 45/3 (September 1977), 739. Similar idea is expressed by Moltmann as he grapples with the name 'Father' for God, "It is not actually intended that God should be sexually determined as male ... God-likeness is expressed in both sexes." See J. Moltmann, "The Motherly Father," 52.

[925] See, Fiorenza, *In Memory of Her*, 34.

[926] Fiorenza, *In Memory of Her*, 118.

[927] Fiorenza, *In Memory of Her*, 107.

> but precisely to reject all such claims, powers and structures ... The address "father" used by Jesus and his disciples has caused many Christian feminists great scandal because the church has not obeyed the command of Jesus "to call no one father, for you have "one father," and because it has resulted in legitimizing ecclesial and societal patriarchy with the "father" name of God, thereby using the name of God in vain.[928]

Stressing further on the strong anti-patriarchal tones seen in the words of Jesus, Fiorenza continues:

> The saying of Jesus uses the "father" name of God not as a legitimization for existing patriarchal power structures in society or church but as a critical subversion of all structure of domination. The "father" God of Jesus makes possible "the sisterhood of men" (in the phrase of Mary Daly) by denying any father, and all patriarchy, its right to existence. Neither the "brothers" nor "the sisters" in the Christian community can claim the "authority of the father" because that would involve claiming authority and power reserved for God alone.[929]

Thus for Fiorenza, by envisioning God as the only Father all disciples are equal as brothers and sisters. Rosemary Radford Ruether agrees with Fiorenza, especially on her reconstruction of the counter-cultural egalitarian vision of the Jesus movement, but stresses even more its links with the Hebraic prophetic tradition. Pointing to the references where Father for God occurs, particularly Matthew 23:1-10, she states that the relationship to God as *Abba* abolishes all hierarchy (dominance-dependence relations) between people within the Jesus' community.[930] That means both Fiorenza and Ruether see anti-patriarchal overtones in the very Jesus' traditions of his use of Father for God.

6.1.3. Summary

In our above analysis of the contemporary feminist challenge we see that the issue on patriarchy or non patriarchy centers mainly on Jesus' own calling of God as *Abba*,[931] that is, at the level of Jesus and his theology.[932] However, as stated at the

---

[928] Fiorenza, *In Memory of Her*, 150-151.

[929] Fiorenza, *In Memory of Her*, 151.

[930] Ruether, *Sexism and God-Talk*, 64-65; the same idea is argued by Brian Wren in his work, *What Language Shall I Borrow? God-Talk in Worship: A Male response to Feminist Theology* (New York: Crossroad, 1991), 186-187.

[931] For details on the *Abba* language in the lips of Jesus and his experience of God, see chapter three.

[932] However, even within the level of Jesus it is not the maleness of father language that is significant, but its familial meaning as language of relationship and intimacy. In other words, the term 'Father' is relational, familial, and intimate. Its function is not to stress God's sex, God's maleness, but

very beginning, our main focus is at the level of the Matthew the Evangelist and his theology. And as we have been arguing, the theme of God's fatherhood is the central emphasis of Matthew, who exhibits a particular fondness for 'Father' over other ways of referring to God.[933] Yet when Matthean Jesus says in prayer "our Father" or when in his teaching talks about God with the expression "Father" or "(your) Father," in all these the expression has more to do with love and relationship, and so the idea of patriarchy does not arise. Moreover, as argued in the previous chapter, Matthew has used several other imageries mostly feminine imageries and experiences towards his emphasis on the fatherhood of God theme – shepherd, householder, parent and mother. This means that in Matthew the fatherhood of God is open to enrichment and completion from other forms of imagery. As seen above, the Gospel of Matthew gives us sufficient indication of this openness to allow us to speak of maternal traits in God. In this perspective we see that there is a strong emphasis on the fatherhood of God in relation to creation and nature in Matthew, that is, on caring, compassion and nurturing aspect of God. God is depicted as organically related with earth and humanity. That means that in Matthew God's fatherhood has to do with the idea of care and nurture but not to do with domineering and sexist idea. That means Matthew's idea of the fatherhood of God is clearly non-patriarchal in nature. While Matthew presented God as Father to his community, as he best understood, in the language of the day, yet when we look at this usage within the overall projection of God's fatherhood theme in Matthew we see that it has more to do with nurturing, caring and compassion.

With this we will now turn to illustrate how the very emphasis on the centrality of the fatherhood of God can be of significance in theologizing in religiously pluralistic India.

6.2. The Fatherhood of God in Hindu Religious Traditions and Scriptures

6.2.1. Introduction

India is a country of many religions. Several religions have their roots in the Indian subcontinent – Hinduism, Jainism, Sikhism and Buddhism. Hinduism is the predominant religion in India. Hinduism is well known for its tolerance. Hindu concept of God is very complicated. Nevertheless there are glimpses of the idea of the fatherhood of God in the manifold religious literatures of Hinduism. While it is explicit in the Vedic prayers and hymns and in the Bhagavad Gita, in the classical and philosophical Hinduism the fatherhood of God idea is implicit

---

God's close immediacy to Jesus and his disciples. They (the disciples) address God in prayer, knowing that he responds. Even noted feminist scholars agree on this. For example, see Elizabeth A. Johnson, *Consider Jesus: Waves of Renewal in Christology* (New York: Crossroad, 1994), 57.

[933] Out of the forty-four occurrences of 'Father' for God in Matthew, a staggering thirty one times that Matthew alone used this term 'Father' for God. On this details, see chapter 4.

in the theistic discourse itself. The idea of God's fatherhood is very clear in the sacred literatures of the primitive stage of Ḥinduism, that is, the four Vedas, and in the later devotional literatures, especially in hymns, prayers and dialogues. It is to these literatures we now turn.

6.2.2. Fatherhood of God in the Vedas

6.2.2.1. *Dyaus Pitar* and the Cosmic Fatherhood

In the primitive Hindu religious traditions there is belief in the person of a supreme heavenly God called *Dyaus Pita*, which means Sky-father. It is said that this deity was actually worshipped as Mother-goddess in the culture of pre-Aryan Indus valley civilization prior to the coming of the Indo-European immigrants between 2000 and 1500 B.C.E.[934] And according to E.O. James "it was from this non-Aryan substratum that the fertility element in Hinduism seems to have been derived."[935] It is seen that even in the Vedic hymns *Dyaus* is almost inalienably paired with a consort *Prithvi*, and together they symbolized the heaven-and-earth couple, that is, the visible world.[936] That means, *Dyaus*, the Father (*Dyaus Pitar*) is seen incomplete without *Prithvi*, the Mother earth.[937] The Father God and Mother Earth are thus inseparably related in ancient Indian worship of God. In fact in the very hymn of *Dyava-Prithvi* we see the concept of the Divine Earth.[938] That means to say that the Hindu Vedic idea of God's fatherhood is basically physical and literal in nature. It is clearly evident in a hymn of the Rig Veda which talks about physical paternity thus:

> The heaven is my parent and progenitor, the navel (of the earth) is my kinsman; the spacious earth is my mother. The womb (of all being) lies between the two ladles, and in it the parent has deposited the germ (of the fruitfulness) of the daughter (Rig Veda I.164.33).[939]

There is a strong feminine and ecological aspect of the fatherhood of God here, as vegetation (rain=seed), and the life which it made possible, was thought

---

[934] See E.O. James, *The Concept of Deity: A Comparative and Historical Study* (London: Hutchinson House, 1950), 52; see also E.O. James, *The Cult of the Mother-Goddess*, 32-33; Louis Bouyer, *The Invisible Father: Approaches to the Mystery of the Divinity* (London: T&T Clark, 1999), 116.

[935] E.O. James, *The Concept of Deity*, 52. James thus concludes that the Indian religion arose out of the dual tradition of the Mother-goddess of West Asia and a highly developed nature worship of cosmic gods of the Indo-European immigrants. See, E.O. James, *The Concept of Deity*, 52-53.

[936] S. Bhattacharji, *The Indian Theogony: A Comparative Study of Indian Mythology from the Vedas to the Puranas* (Cambridge: Cambridge University Press, 1970), 23.

[937] See Rig Veda I.195.2 in *Rg-Veda Samhita* I, trans M.N. Dutt (Delhi: Parimal Publications, 1986), 385 n. 3.

[938] See, S.R.M. Murthy, *Vedic View of the Earth* (New Delhi: D.K. Printworld, 1997), 212.

[939] See *Rg-Veda Samhita* I, trans M.N. Dutt, 413-414.

to have arisen by conception from heaven and earth. Their combination *Dyava Prithvi*, is called the beneficent Father and the Mother of all creatures. In other words, God is clearly depicted as cosmic (Heaven and Earth) parent (father and mother) who preserve the world, as seen in Rig Veda I. 160.1-2:

> Those two, the divine Heaven and Earth, are the diffusers of happiness on all, encouragers of truth, able to sustain the water (of the rains) ... Wide-spreading, vast, unconnected, the father and mother (of all beings), they two preserve the worlds. Resolute, as if (for the good) of embodied (beings), are heaven and earth, and the father has invested everything with (visible) forms.[940]

In the Rig Veda I.159.1-2, the hymn of the Rishi to the deity Heaven and Earth says:

> I glorify with sacred rites the mighty Heaven and Earth ... I propitiate, by my invocations, the mind of the benevolent father, and the great and spontaneous (affection) of the mother (of all beings). The parents, with kindness, have secured, by their excellent protections, the vast and manifold immortality of their progeny.[941]

Thus we see that at the very root of the Father God idea is the cult of the Mother-Goddess.[942] This helps us to explain the feminine aspect of the fatherhood of God. In other words, the very paternal and maternal traits may perhaps reflect the feminine deity of its origin which has to do with both sky (heaven) and earth.[943] It is thus seen that the idea of God as mother is very much present along with the idea of God's fatherhood.

6.2.2.2. God as Father in Invocations

There are explicit references to the idea of God's fatherhood in the ancient Vedic traditions, particularly in invocations. Thus a prayer in the Rig Veda says:

---

940 *Rg-Veda Samhita* I, trans M.N. Dutt, 387.

941 *Rg-Veda Samhita* I, trans M.N. Dutt, 385.

942 As E.O. James observed that the Mother-goddess and "her symbolism unquestionably has been the most persistent feature in the archaeological record of the ancient world." See E.O. James, *The Worship of the Sky-God: A Comparative Study in Semitic and Indo-European Religion* (London: Athlone Press, 1963), 11; Othmar-Keel and C. Uehlinger in their work too observed that the religious symbol systems of the ancient Israel were marked by images of fertility and sexuality and talks about openness to "the buried feminine aspects of the Judeo-Christian image of God," See Othmar Keel and C. Uehlinger, *Gods, Goddess, and Images of God In Ancient Israel* (Edinburgh: T&T Clark, 1998), 409.

943 Almost all the religions of the ancient civilizations – Indians, Egyptians, Canaanite, Israelite-Judean, Persians, Greece, Romans - have strong traditions of the worship of the mother-goddess and earth-mother fertility goddess; See E.O. James, *The Cult of the Mother-Goddess*; P. A. H. De Boer, *Fatherhood and Motherhood in Israelite and Judean Piety* (Leiden: E.J. Brill, 1974).

> Like unto a father to his son, O Agni, be easily accessible unto us; be ever present with us for our well-being.[944]

In *Yajur Veda* similar prayer says:

> O Lord, thou art our Father; do thou instruct us like a father. We offer our salutations to thee. Do thou not destroy us; do thou protect us ever.[945]

In all these instances the addressing of God as Father are quite similar in tone to the Jewish prophets and writers and their community experiences as found in the Jewish literatures and New Testament. Particularly the familial and intimate expression seen in the *Yajur Veda* text, invoking God as "our Father" is quite meaningful and closer to the address of Matthean Jesus in prayer, "Our Father" (Mt 6:9). This means that the invocation of God as Father in prayer is quite at home in Indian religious traditions and so the idea of God's fatherhood is a common thought. It also shows how God-inclined or theocentric Indians are. Such invocation can be a meeting point as expressing what is common to the Gospels and Indian religious traditions.

6.2.3. The Fatherhood of God in the Upanishads

The concept of one reality the Supreme Being called Brahman is well articulated in the Upanishads. The Upanishads are also called Vedanta, which literally means 'the end of the Vedas.' And as mentioned earlier, in the Upanishads the fatherhood of God idea is implicit in the very exposition of the concept of God.

6.2.3.1. Brahman and Isvara

According to Advaita (literally 'non-duality') Vedanta of Sankara,[946] Brahman (God) alone is real and all else including the world is unreal. Brahman is thus infinite, eternal, omnipresent, impersonal, and indescribable (*nirguna* Brahman). Sankara asserts that from the purely philosophical or transcendental point, Brahman cannot be described at all. However, it was Ramanuja, who in his Vishishtadvaita Vedanta, gives more emphasis on the theistic or personal aspect of Brahman called Isvara, who is creator, Lord, and ruler of the world. It is called *saguna* Brahman, a God with attributes and known within human religious experience.[947] Thus for

---

[944] *Rig Veda* I.I.9 in *RG-Veda Samhita* I, trans M.N. Dutt, 3.

[945] *Shukla Yajur Veda Samhita* 37.20, trans Swami Yatiswarananda, *Universal Prayers* (Chennai: Sri Ramakrishna Math, 2001), 19.

[946] For details on the various schools of Vedanta and their theologies, see Klaus K. Klostermaier, *A Survey of Hinduism* (Third Edition; New York: State University of New York Press, 2007), 355-367.

[947] Such interpretation is based on the expositions of the Upanishadic passages, e.g., Maitri Upanishad VI.15, which talks about two forms of Brahman: "There are, verily, two forms of *Brahman*, time and the timeless. That which is prior to the sun is the timeless, without parts. But that which begins with (has a beginning from) the Sun is time, which has parts...." Trans S.

Ramanuja, Isvara is perfect, omniscient, omnipresent, creator of the world, its active ruler and also the eventual destroyer. He is the material and the efficient cause of the world. He is both immanent and transcendent. He is the subject of worship.[948] This distinction between *nirguna* Brahman and *saguna* Brahman helps us to understand how Brahman can be both in the world and beyond it, that is to say, both immanent and transcendent. So in Isvara we find the personal aspect of God in Hinduism, having the attributes such as perfect, omniscient, omnipresent, creator, ruler, and destroyer. This is where the idea of God's fatherhood can be seen. God is not merely impersonal but personal who is engaged in the material world.

6.2.4. Fatherhood of God in Bhagavad Gita[949]

6.2.4.1. God as Cosmic Parent

In Gita we find similar development to that of the Vedas as regard to the fatherhood of God idea. The Gita teaches about the worship of a parent God who is all-loving benevolence for his faithful, and who is both transcendent and personal. The Gita teaches that the world is filled with God. He is present everywhere, sustains everything, great and small. God fills the heavens, the earth and all space. The whole universe lives in Him, but does not exhaust Him; it reveals the glory of God. He is the Lord of the universe. It is the Lord who brings the body to existence and bestows it with life. God is both father and mother. Thus God is addressed as the devotees' real father and mother, as Lord Krishna, expressing his divinity, says:

> I am the father of this universe, the mother, the regulator, the grandfather ... The goal, the nourisher, the lord, the witness, the place of swelling, the refuge, the friend, the source, the end, the place of continuance, the store-house, the eternal seed. I cause heat and light; I cause rain .... (IX.17-19)[950]

From this passage, which affirms the goodness and power of God, we observe that there is a strong parental, rather more feminine aspect of God in Hindu religious traditions. That means the feminine nature of God is deeply

---

Radhakrishnan, in S. Radhakrishnan, *The Principal Upanishads* (London: George Allen & Unwin Ltd, 1953), 828.

[948] On Ramanuja's emphasis on bhakti or devotional aspect, see P.S. Daniel, David C. Scott, G.R. Singh (eds.), *Religious Traditions of India* (Serampore: Indian Theological Library, 1988), 146-149.

[949] Gita is actually a sermon which Krishna delivers to Arjuna on the eve of the battle which is the climax of the Mahabharata.

[950] All texts are from *The Bhagavad Gita*, trans Mohini M. Chatterji (New York: Causeway Books, 1960).

rooted in Indian religions.[951] This is complemented by others passages in the Gita where God is projected as the source of everything[952] and God as immanent.[953]

6.2.4.2. God as Father

In the eleventh chapter of the Gita, in response to an urgent petition from Arjuna, Krishna manifests his form to him. The chapter gives a detailed account of this strange and powerful form and then goes on to describe the effect of the vision on the mind and soul of Arjuna. When Arjuna saw Krishna standing before him in a glorious blaze of light, he realized his own utter insignificance and sinful nature and prayed to Krishna thus:

> Of this universe, animate and inanimate, thou art the father and the object of adoration, the greatest of the great. There is none equal unto thee, how can there be a superior, O Thou with majesty unimagined in the three worlds? Therefore, bowing down, and holding the body so low, thee, O Lord, I pray for grace; forgive, O Lord, as forgives the father the son, the friend the friend, and the lover the beloved (XI. 43, 44).

Gita also talks about realizing God, the creator of the universe as father, as Arjuna exclaims:

> Salutation in the east, and salutation also behind, O thou All; salutation in all directions; thou art of infinite valor and immeasurable power; thou pervades all things and hence art All (XI. 40).

God's mercy pours upon the world in a ceaseless stream. God is both the end and the means. That means God's fatherhood pervades the universe. It has strong ecological implications, as affirmation of God's fatherhood involves an attitude of friendliness to all creations because, at the root of it and filling it all, is God.[954]

6.2.5. Fatherhood of God in Bhakti Traditions

The idea of the fatherhood of God is also strongly implied in the bhakti doctrine (devotion to God) in the Gita. Bhakti as conceived by the Gita is based on the premise that Krishna, the supreme being, is the Lord, the end and aim of life. That means in Gita we see devotional aspect of Hinduism, having the worship of

---

[951] Pointing to the deep roots of this strong feminine nature of God in Indian soil, Appasamy (*The Gospel and India's Heritage*, 73) envisions, "It is a beautiful way of thinking of the tender, devoted and unselfish love of God ... there is no reason why we should not think of God as Mother. While Jesus does not speak of God as Mother, the doctrine is not in any way opposed to the spirit or the letter of His teaching and life."

[952] e.g., Gita IX. 39-42.

[953] e.g., Gita VII. 7-10.

[954] K.L. Seshagiri Rao, "'Love of God' in the Bhagavadgita," in *The Love of God in the World's Religions* edited by K.L. Seshagiri Rao and Henry O. Thompson (Delhi: ISPCK, 1984), 150.

God in the form of a particular being or person in Krishna. Gita thus talks about God's dwellings in those who worship Krishna with utter devotion (bhakti). Here are some excerpts:

> I am equal to all creatures; there is none hated or beloved by Me. But those who worship Me in love, they are in me and in them I am (IX .29)
>
> Such as one quickly becomes righteous-souled, for he comes to perpetual peace. Swear, O son of Kunti, my devotee never is destroyed (IX. 31).

It is seen that the fatherhood of God idea in Gita, especially as seen in the above verses, is quite in line with the Synoptic idea of filial relationship between Father and Son and by extension to all believers.[955] The idea of impartial nature of God is also seen in both Gita and the Gospels especially Matthew. There are also several instances where the same idea of mutual indwelling is seen in Gita. In these instances Krishna identifies the universal spirit with Himself by using the first person. He speaks to Arjuna as a personal being. He consoles, teaches, assures and loves Arjuna:

> Who sees me everywhere, and sees everything in me, for him I am not lost, nor is he lost for me. Whoever, relying on spiritual one-ness, worships me, who am in all creatures, he, the sage in yoga, in whatever condition existing, is present in me (VI. 30-31).
>
> Knowing me, the Enjoyer of all sacrifice and penance, the Supreme Lord of all worlds and the friend of all creatures, he attains rest (V. 29).

In such passages we discover a distinct personal sphere and a loving relationship between God and his devotee/s. Thus Gita teaches divine concern for humans. Humanity is the object of his constant care. He is friend and savior.

6.2.5.1. God as Merciful Father

The idea of the fatherhood of God is clearly seen in the expression of close relationship between God and his devotee Arjuna, as the latter continues his prayer for the divine grace:

> Therefore, bowing down, and holding the body so low, thee, O Lord, I pray for grace; forgive, O Lord, as forgives the father the son, the friend the friend, and the lover the beloved. (XI. 44)

Similarly a prayer in Mahabharata goes like this:

---

[955] Of course the closest idea is seen in John's Gospel: "Those who love me and keep my word, ad my Father will love them, and we will come to them and make our home with them" (John 14: 23 cf. 15:1-17).

> Save me and protect me always as a father would his own son; protect me, I need your protection; obeisance to you, O pure Lord![956]

So also in the *Naradiya Purana* occurs a prayer:

> Compassionate Lord! The wrong which we did you in the past in pour ignorance, put up with all that and look after us, like a father his sons.[957]

In these instances of prayer of individual the loving relationship between God and the devotees is very clear. In all these prayers the prominence given to parental affection is striking, and it shows the affirmation of God's fatherhood in prayers. Such prayers addressing God for forgiveness and protection are also found in the Jewish literatures (e.g., 4Q372 I) and the Gospels. The concept of grace and mercy of God toward the devotees is strong in these texts, so also the affirmation of God as protector. Thus in all these the idea of God's fatherhood is clear.

6.2.5.2. Compassionate and Benevolent God

The idea of God's fatherhood is also implicit in the idea of *avatara*, particularly the idea of Vishnu incarnate in Krishna, which is explicit in Gita 4.7-8, where Krishna himself reveals to Arjuna about his (divine) intervention into the world to aid humankind:

> O son of Bharata, whenever there is decline of righteousness and uprising of unrighteousness, then I project myself into creation. For the protection of the righteous and the destruction of the evil-doer, and for the proper establishment of the law of righteousness, I appear from age to age (IV. 7-8).

In Hindu tradition God coming to earth is mainly for rescuing and protecting his devotees, in which God's vengeful nature is also seen. Nevertheless, there is also a strong element of God's fatherhood in the sense of his protective nature. It is God who takes the initiative to save his faithful devotees, out of care and concern. This theme of *avatara* is related with the deity Vishnu, the protector and sustainer of the world, a member of the Hindu triad as Brahma, Vishnu and Siva.[958] The deity Vishnu thus possessed traits of benevolent activity towards humankind. And *Bhagavata Purana* talks about the countless incarnations of the

---

[956] *Mahabharata, Santiparva,* ccxc 74-185, trans V. Raghavan, *Prayers, Praises, and Psalms* (Madras: G.A. Natesan and Co, 1938), 107.

[957] *Naradiya Purana* ii.73, trans V. Raghavan, *Prayers, Praises, and Psalms*, 171.

[958] K.W. Morgan (ed.), *The Religion of the Hindus* (New York: The Ronald Press Company, 1953), 53-55.

deity Vishnu, among which ten incarnations are accepted.[959] According to Rudolf Otto Indians consider Christianity "as pretty much identical with their bhakti-religion, and acknowledge Christ as an *avatara*."[960] In saying this he put forth that "India possessed the doctrine of incarnation long before Christianity."[961] A.J. Appasamy, one of the pioneer Indian theologians, also attempted to use the term *avatara*, described in the Gita, for God's incarnation idea in Indian context.[962]

As seen above, Appasamy has pointed out that the idea of the *avatara* is inadequate in the fact that, as seen in the Gospels, God came to redeem the world but Gita talks about the visitation of God on earth time to time to rescue the righteous and for the destruction of the wicked. He also argues that the message of the cross is lacking in Hinduism.[963] In the same vein E.O. James observed that these *avatars* of the Hindu religious traditions for the regeneration and preservation of the world at times of crisis were closer to the renewal of the divine kingship in ancient society than to the idea of incarnation underlying the Christian doctrine of the Word made flesh.[964] However, in the very spirit of the *avataras*, that is, in God's concern, care and protection for his devotees, a clear idea of God's fatherhood is understood.

With the rise of the bhakti movement, the idea of God's abiding presence through grace come to the forefront in the emphasis of the theistic Hindu religious traditions. The bhakti tradition, though has more of centripetal aspects, that is, human's search and longing for God, yet God's searching (centrifugal) is also implicit. It is clearly evident in the expressions and moving confessions of worshippers. For example, in the quoting of Appasamy of the confessions of Hindu Bhakti practitioners, we see clearly the idea of God's fatherhood. A verse of Tukaram, expressing the uttermost expression of the fatherhood of God, says:

> I am a mass of sin; Thou art all purity; Yet Thou must take me as I am and bear my load for me.[965]

Again in the quoting of a penitence of Dadudayal, a 17th century Gujarati poet, we see the idea of God's fatherhood very clearly:

> Before Thee I am guilty in every nerve and vein; a sinner am I every moment; Master, forgive me! Not a single good deed have I done;

---

[959] They are: Fish, Tortoise, Boar, Man-Lion, Dwarf, *Parasurama*, *Rama*, *Balararnu*, *Buddha* and *Kalkin*; See Morgan (ed.), *The Religion of the Hindus*, 55.

[960] R. Otto, *Indian Religion of Grace and Christianity Compared and Contrasted* (New York: The Macmillan Company, 1930), 64.

[961] R. Otto, *Indian Religion of Grace and Christianity Compared and Contrasted*, 105.

[962] Appasamy, *The Gospel and India's Heritage*, 259.

[963] Appasamy, *The Gospel and India's Heritage*, 69.

[964] E.O. James, *The Concept of Deity: A Comparative and Historical Study* (London: Hutchinson's, 1950), 61.

[965] Appasamy, *The Gospel and India's Heritage*, 125.

> no virtue is there in me; no merit is mine. Yet forsake not Thy sinful child, for without Thee where is my refuge? Desire, pride, anger and falsehood have misled me since my birth; O miserable man that I am! Thou only art my help: Father, wash me with the nectar of Thy rich forgiveness and heal the mind that is sore.[966]

In such deep expressions we see affirmations of a Father God who forgives and heals the guilt of sins. It also reveals the profound spirituality of the Hindus, having a real passion for God and trying to understand the depth of God's fatherly concern and love.

6.2.6. Popular Polytheistic Hindu Religious Traditions and One God Idea

In the popular Hindu religious practices and traditions there is a very thin line between monotheism and polytheism. As stated earlier, Hinduism is known for its tolerance. Hinduism absorbs and accommodates all kinds of gods. In fact one can be monotheistic and polytheistic at the same time. It is implicit in the Hindu scriptures. For example, concerning the worship of one in many Rig Veda I.64.46 says:

> They have styled (him, the Sun), Indra, Mitra, Varuna, Agni, and he is the celestial, well-winged Garumat, for learned priests call one by many names as they speak of Agni, Yama, Matariswan.[967]

For a polytheistic Hindu, who is a worshiper of popular gods, there seem to be no real contradiction in affirming the one God while acknowledging several deities. In this regard A. Danielou's observation is to the point:

> In the polytheistic religion each individual worshipper has a chosen deity (*ista-devata*) and does not usually worship other gods in the same way as his own, as the one he feels nearer to himself. Yet he acknowledges other gods. The Hindu, whether he be a worshipper of the Pervader (Vishnu), the Destroyer (Siva), Energy (Shakti), or the Sun (Surya), is always ready to acknowledge the equivalence of these deities as the manifestations of distinct powers springing from an unknowable "Immensity." He knows that ultimate Being or non-Being is ever beyond his grasp, beyond existence, and in no way can be worshipped or prayed to. Since he realizes that other deities are but other aspects of the one he worships, he is basically tolerant and must

[966] A.J. Appasamy, *Temple Bells: Readings from Hindu Religious Literature* (Calcutta: Association Press, 1930), 62-63.

[967] See, *Rg-Veda Samhita* I, trans M.N. Dutt, 417-418.

be ready to accept every form of knowledge or belief as potentially valid.[968]

As seen in the expression above, Hinduism absorbed all kinds of gods, yet at the core the affirmation of the one God is also present. Thus in popular polytheistic Hinduism there is no real contradiction in affirming monotheism while acknowledging plurality of gods (polytheism).

Having seen some of the major aspect of philosophical and popular Hinduism as regard to the theme of God's fatherhood, it is appropriate to consider a bit of Islam. Though it did not originate in India, the sheer number of adherents deserve a brief consideration.

6.3. The Fatherhood of God in Islam

6.3.1. Quran

Islam, being a monotheistic religion, strongly stresses on God oriented life. Its main scripture is Quran, which teaching can be summed up under two basic headings: Oneness of God and brotherhood of humankind. This Islamic concept of divine unity, of God's oneness, of his uniqueness is seen clearly in Quran (*Al-Ikhlas*) 112:1-4:

He is God
The one the most unique,
God the immanently indispensable.
He has begotten no one, and is begotten of none.
There is no one comparable to Him.[969]

In line with this monotheistic affirmation Islam talks about God as God of the entire universe and not of any exclusive tribe, race, people, nation, country or region, as seen in Quran (*Al-Hujurat*) 49:13:

O men, We created you from a male and female, and formed you into nations and tribes that you may recognize each other. He who has more integrity has indeed greater honour with God. Surely God is all-knowing and well-informed.

The recognition of unity of God implies the correlative recognition of the brotherhood and equality of humankind. So the idea of the family of God comes in and hence idea of the fatherhood of God.[970] God's fatherhood is also implicit in

[968] Alain Danielou, *Hindu Polytheism* (London: Routledge & Kegan Paul, 1964), 9.

[969] Verses of the Quran are taken from *Al-Quran: A Contemporary Translation* by Ahmed Ali (Princeton; New Jersey: Princeton University Press, 1984).

[970] Of course in Islam God is never addressed explicitly or described as 'Father.' Unlike the biblical idea of an intimate God, in Islam God is known more in the sense of lordship and aloofness. The clearest example is seen when the Lord's Prayer found in the Gospels (Mt 6:9-15; Lk 2-4) and the opening Surah of the Quran (*Surat Al-Fatihah* 1) is examined side by side. Yet in the

the very emphasis on the loving, merciful and forgiving nature of God in Quran (e.g. *Al-Imran* 3:31; 134-135, etc).[971]

6.3.2. Fatherhood of God in Sufism

In the Islamic mystic and devotional traditions the idea of God's fatherhood is clearly understood in its strong emphasis on universal brotherhood of humankind. It is said that in the prophetic tradition *Hadith* the prophet talks about all humanity as belonging to God's family.[972] In one of the sayings of the latter Sufi saints Rumi we see the same emphasis:

> We are all children of God and His infants
> As the Prophet had said, All belong to his family
> ...
> All are in His family
> And for them He is the best provider
> There is only one God, the God of all people and all religion.
> All of mankind belongs to God's family.[973]

If all humankind belongs to God's family, then it implies that all human beings are children of the one Father. The emphasis on the universal fatherhood of God is thus seen in Islam, particularly in Sufi mystic traditions.

6.3.3. Summary

We observe that while Hindu concept of God is very complicated, yet there are glimpses of the idea of God's fatherhood in the manifold religious literatures of Hinduism. While it is explicit in the primitive Vedic prayers and hymns and in the Bhagavad Gita, in the classical and philosophical Hinduism this fatherhood of God idea is implicit in the theistic discourse itself. Interestingly, as in Matthew and the Synoptic Gospels, it is seen that Hindu scriptures has strong emphasis on invocations of God as Father in prayer and religious discourses. So also the idea of God as cosmic parent or cosmic Father and the resultant feminine and ecological implications of God's fatherhood in Hindu religious traditions has strong similarities with Matthean idea of God's fatherhood with strong maternal traits. As regard to Islam, in its emphasis on the oneness of God and brotherhood of humankind the fatherhood of God idea is understood.

---

very affirmation of the one God one can find Muslim and Christian hope of mutual prayer. For details on this idea see, Kenneth Cragg (*Alive to God: Muslim and Christian Prayer* (London: Oxford University Press, 1970), 1-55, 18.

[971] For details on the idea of God's love in Quran, see also Shaykh Abdullah Nuraddin Durkee, "The Love of Allah or: He Loves Them and They Love Him," in *The Love of God in the World's Religions*, 53-114.

[972] Sadia Dehlvi, *Sufism: The Heart of Islam* (Noida: HarperCollins Publishers India, 2010), 22.

[973] Sadia Dehlvi, *Sufism: The Heart of Islam*, 22-23.

Having seen the idea of God's fatherhood in major religious traditions of India, we now turn to the Ao Naga religious traditions and consider the theme of God's fatherhood.

6.4. The Fatherhood of God in the Ao Naga Religious Traditions

Like in any traditional tribal society, religion permeates all aspects of life in Ao Naga tribal society. The religion is basically a community religion. For them religious belief and action are inseparable. Religion is seen in performing observances of rituals and ceremonies.[974] The Ao religion has no written scriptures. The religious beliefs and principles carry on in the oral traditions and rituals. The Aos have a strong belief in the existence of a Supreme Being called *Tsungrem*, who is acknowledged as the creator of the universe. And yet like other animistic religions of the world, the Aos believe in the existence of deities and spirits, as J.P. Mills, a British civil officer and ethnographer writing in the 1920s, talks about the Ao religion:

> It is the *tsungrem* who play [*sic*] an important part in human life. On their goodwill largely depend a man's health and happiness. They are everywhere – in the village, in the fields, in the jungle, by streams, in trees, and, most favourite haunt of all, in the huge boulders which are so numerous in the Ao country.[975]

The same is observed by B.B. Gosh, editor, *Nagaland Gazetteer* (1979), who describes *Tsungrem* as "a consolidated form of several deities pertaining to household, jungle, mountain, aerial, etc."[976] He thus sees Aos' religious practices as polytheistic.

6.4.1. *Tsungrem* – The One and Many

As mentioned above, the Ao religion is not merely belief in spirits and deities but there is a strong belief in the existence of a Supreme Being called *Tsungrem*, who is mostly understood as a male deity. *Tsungrem* literally means 'divine hidden,' which is a combination of two words '*tsung*' (divine or supernatural) and '*arem*' (concealment or hidden).[977] According to O. Alem, one of the pioneers Ao Naga tribal theologians, *Tsungrem* literally means 'concealed Chief,' a supreme God who is transcendent, and who cannot be seen with human naked eyes and as

[974] On this idea, see also Wati Longchar, *The Traditional Tribal Worldview and Modernity* (Jorhat: Eastern Theological College, 1995), 6.

[975] J. P. Mills, *The Ao Nagas* (London: Macmillan, 1926; 2nd edition by Oxford University Press, 1973), 216.

[976] B. B. Gosh, *Nagaland District Gazetteers: Mokokchung District* (Dimapur: Sethi Press, 1979), 55. n.1.

[977] O. Alem Ao, *Tsungremology: Ao Naga Christian Theology* (Mokokchung: Clark Theological College, 1994), 26.

Chief, *Tsungrem* is the owner of the whole universe by whose power everything exists.[978] *Tsungrem* is mostly known as *Lungkitsungba*, or *Lijab*a or *Meyutsungba*. These names given to the supreme God do not represent three different gods but functional names for the one God.[979] B.B. Gosh describes the three main deities in the religion of the Aos thus:

> Their pantheon known as Tsungrem is constituted of the following: (1) Lijaba – Potentate of terrestrial sphere, who is also the creator of heaven and earth. (2) Mojing – Deity of world hereafter. (3) – Lungkitsungba – Dispenser of justice, and is said to be standing right at the gate of the world-hereafter. Curiously this deity in Ao conception has his presence symbolized in any rocky eminence.[980]

However, for Bendangangshi and Apok there are six deities in Ao religion: *Kotaktsungba* (God of heaven), *Anungtsungba* (God of the sky), *Longkitsungba* (God of huge rock or temple), *Meyutsungba* (Supreme Judge in heaven), *Lijaba* (Creator and sustainer of the universe and mankind), and *Teroktsungba* (God of the sun and the moon and of universe).[981] However, they are quick to add that "even if we use many names of gods sometimes they are addressed as one god and one lord and their names are interchangeably used in different occasions. There is no contradictions in them but have great unity in themselves."[982] Thus, in the observation of Bendangangshi and Apok, the Ao concept of God is a kind of polytheistic monotheism.

It is interesting to see that the stem '*tsung*' in *Tsungrem* and also the '*tsungba*' in the functional names as mentioned above is closely related with meteorological terms *tsungi* (thunderbolt), *tsungpret* (lightening), *tsunglu* (rain), *tsungkum* (seasons/winter). It suggests the Aos' concept of God as revealing through nature, thus shows the inseparable relationship between God and nature in Ao religion. In this perspective, O. Alem remarks that the *tsung* "describes the mundane nature of God whose presence and acts are as real as lightening, thunder, rain and seasons (*tsungkum*)."[983] It is the *tsung* who sends rain, lightning and thunder and regulates the seasons. This is where we see both the transcendent and immanent aspects of God in Ao religion.

---

[978] O. Alem Ao, *Tsungremology*, 28.

[979] O. Alem Ao, *Tsungremology*, 35.

[980] B.B. Gosh, *Nagaland District Gazetteers: Mokokchung District*, 55.

[981] I. Bendangangshi and I.T. Apok Aier, *The Religion of the Ao Nagas* (Guwahati: Sariaghat Press, 1990), 22-24.

[982] Bendangangshi and Apok Aier, *The Religion of the Ao Nagas*, 29.

[983] O. Alem Ao, *Tsungremology*, 28.

6.4.2. *Tsungrem* as both Transcendent and Immanent

Tsungrem, the one supreme God of the Aos is called by many names, among which *Lungkitsungba*, *Meyutsungba* and *Lijaba* are prominently used for God. The function of *Lungkitsungba* and *Meyutsungb*a are almost the same. *Lungkitsungba* is the Ruler, Lord, King or God of cavern or God of huge rock and sometimes his name is used interchangeably with *Meyutsungba*, God of heaven. *Meyutsungba* is worshipped as the entertainer and the Supreme Judge in heaven, who awards every soul according to one's work on earth, whether good or bad. *Lungkitsungb*a is a combination of the term '*Lungki*' (meaning house of stone) and '*Tsung/ba*' means Supreme or Chief. He is the dispenser of justice. The transcendent and all pervading nature of God is expressed through the term *Anungtsungb*a. Just as the sky, covering the whole earth, symbolizes mystery and everlastingness, so does *Tsungrem*, who is known as one who sees all as nothing is hidden from him, just as the sun and the moon cannot be hidden. He is addressed in worship as the God of the sun and the moon which means he is the highest God symbolizing the omnipresent nature.

According to J.P. Mills, referring to the description of E.W. Clark, the first missionary among the Aos, the meaning and function of *Lungkitsungba*, the greatest deity, is that of overseeing the destiny of mankind. Sitting high upon the dome of his dwellings *Lungkitsungba* is said to fix the state or condition of all humankind in this world by pulling to pieces a kind of leaf called *am* and upon each of these pieces he pronounced a fate or destiny.[984] Thus the Aos believe that *Lungkitsungba* is the one who fixes human's destiny through the ritual of *Amsu*.[985] That means in *Lungkitsungba* we see God as omniscient and all-seeing heavenly Father, who sustains and holds life. He is human's last hope and resort in times of trouble. His concern extends to every individual without partiality. He is compassionate and humane. That means he has the heart of human and grants mercy to those who seek his mercy. The Aos called him father, and even grandfather.[986] The Aos' belief in *Lungkitsungba*, the high God has tremendous ethical significance. Because he is all-knowing and all-sustaining God, it is to him that all should pay their due. It is necessary to do right (purity of motives) because from his throne in heaven *Lungkitsungba* sees everything. Thus the function of *Lungkitsungba* expresses the transcendence of God. As *Lungkitsungba* is the name of the God of heaven for the Aos, the heavenly Father is none other than *Lungkitsungba* for the Aos. In fact the first missionary Dr Clark, in consultation with the native converts, used the very name *Lungkitsungba* in the first Ao Christian hymn:

---

[984] See J.P. Mills, *The Ao Nagas*, 225, n. 1.

[985] *Amsu* literally means tearing of leaf. In Aos' traditions, a kind of leaf is used by the medicine man through which he predicts the future.

[986] O. Alem Ao, *Tsungremology*, 49.

> *O! Kodak kubok alee noong aleer Im, temang, keedong, O por, Tsooboo aga temasheeba tamaremba Loongkeezingba Tetsung sotak Kalumangko.*
>
> O! Those living on earth, under heaven Entire village, clan, and people, With fear and awe before the holy and majesty *Lungkitsungba* Worship him by kneeling.[987]

The universality of *Lungkitsungba Tsungrem* is very clear here. A clear idea of the fatherhood of God in literal sense is understood in the interaction of a German Anthropologist by name Christoph Von Furer Haimendorf with a village elder of Merangkong named Sakchimtuba (Tsukjemtuba), while the former was passing through Ao land *en route* to the Konyak land in 1937. The conversation goes:

> 'Why should we not pray to Lunkizungba?' wondered Sakchimtuba. 'Is not he lord over all? Even our life belongs to him.' 'But when you invoke him, does he really help you?' I asked carefully. 'Certainly, Sahib; he sees all and helps everybody. If we ask something of him, we receive it. Of course,' he added with a smile, 'we cannot become rich when we want.' 'You say that Lunkizungba is the lord over all, but in Changtongia the people told me that they prayed to Lichaba at their sacrifices.' 'Oh yes, Lichaba! We, too, give him offerings; he made the earth; but first we always call Lunkizungba, for he was there first. He is the wind, and he made the sky; also the sun and the moon he made - only afterwards Lichaba made the earth. But it was Lunkizungba who made men; therefore we belong to him ....'[988]

It is seen that *Lungkitsungba* is clearly acknowledged as the creator of human being. Though the explicit address of *Lungkitsungba* as Father is not found, yet it is implicit in that he is acknowledged as the creator and as lord of all. God's fatherhood is clear here. But the transcendent and remote nature of God is stronger here. It is to him that people give sacrifice and thereby receive blessings. The response of the Ao elder, as seen in the above conversation ('Even our life belongs to him') expresses the common belief of the Aos. Hence, a clear vertical theocentric idea is seen the religious traditions of the Aos.

---

[987] This is recorded in the work of Rev L. Kijung Ao, *Nokinketer Mongchen* (Gauhati: Christian Literature Centre, 1972), 28. English translation is done by the researcher.

[988] Christoph Von Furer-Haimendorf, *The Naked Nagas: Head-hunters of Assam in Peace and War* (London: Methuen and Co, 1939, Indian reprint, 2004), 60-61.

6.4.3. God-Human-Nature Relationship in Ao Naga Religion

God-human-nature relationship in Ao religious traditions is seen in the worship of the *Lijaba Tsungrem*. The term '*Lijaba*' in *Chungli* dialect[989] literally means 'earth-walker' or '(one who) walks on earth' ('*Li*' means 'earth' and '*jaba*' or '*jajaba*' means 'walk').[990] However, some Ao scholars have a slightly different understanding in that '*Li*' or '*ali*' as refers to earth, while '*cha*' or '*aja*' means to call or caller. And so "*Lichaba*, the one who called the earth to come out is known as the creator of earth."[991] As the above explanations show, *Lijaba* (or *Lichaba*) is closely related with earth. And tradition has it that *Lijaba* walks upon the earth as human do, visiting the Aos from time to time. In the understanding of the Aos God (*Lijaba*) is not only the creator but also as the source of life, nourishment and fertility. This is remembered during the *Moatsu Among* in the spring season every year (April-May), when the sowing of the crops mainly paddy is completed. Every village celebrates for several days in honor of *Lijaba* God who, being the Creator, is the Lord of the earth and so the owner of the land. The very term *Lijaba* itself tells the function of God, as the one who enters or indwells the earth. Just as a seed gets buried beneath the soil soon to be germinated into vital life for the benefit of others, *Lijaba* enters the earth with the seeds and rises again along with the crops. He is the one who gives vegetation in the land and regenerates the earth by entering into the earth every year.[992] That means, for the Aos God and nature are inseparably related. *Lijaba* is not only creator but continue to create in sustaining the earth. He is a co-worker with the earth. That is, he continues to create the earth and thus "the earth continues to supply the necessary fertility to all the vegetation, thereby converting them into food for the animals and human beings."[993] For the Aos *Lijaba* is the provider, always active, giving life and vitality to all creation. He is present everywhere. He indwells in creation. Thus we see strong ecological element in Ao Naga religions traditions.

This strong theological-ecological element in *Lijaba* is evident in another important *Among* called *Lijabamong*, which is observed every year in the mid rainy season (June). Strict observances are held by the people of the whole village in honor of *Lijaba*. On this day no one should disturb the earth. No piercing or spearing or digging on the earth, no cutting of firewood, no pounding of rice, lest earth be disturbed. Even children were not allowed to play with the sand in

---

[989] Several Ao villages speak Chungli (Ao) dialect, which is the common dialect of the Ao literature. The other dialect groups are Mongsen (Ao) and Changki (Ao) dialect speaking group.

[990] See, O. Alem Ao, *Tsungremology*, 59.

[991] N. Talitemjen & A. Lanunungsang, *Naga Society and Culture: A Case Study of the Ao Naga Society and Culture* (Mokokchung: Nagaland University Tribal Research Centre Publications, 2005), 153. n. 2.

[992] O. Alem Ao, *Tsungremology*, 59-60.

[993] O. Alem Ao, *Tsungremology*, 61.

the open places.[994] The logic behind this is that if the earth is disturbed *Lijaba* is disturbed. If the earth is honoured *Lijaba* is honoured. It is *Lijaba* who firmly holds the earth. So *Lijaba* is honoured during this *Among* seeking protection from landslides and so to safeguard crops and paddy cultivation in the hill slopes. Moreover, the earth cannot bear fruit and live in harmony without *Lijaba*. Thus, it is during this *Among* that *Lijaba* is honoured and invoked[995] for protection of their rice-fields from various other natural calamities (e.g., excessive rains, hail storms, drought) so as to have a rich harvest. That means *Lijaba* is organically related with the earth. The Aos consider that the rich harvests, prosperity and wealth are bestowed by *Lijaba Tsungrem*. *Lijaba* thus expresses the immanence of God – one who is very much part of the earth, having concern for his creation. So in the nature of *Lijaba* we see a clear idea of the fatherhood of God in Ao religion.

Another important event of theological significance is *Tsungrem-mong*. This yearly ceremony is observed on the first three days of August. *Tsungrem-mong* literally means 'God's ceremony.'[996] So this ceremony is in honour of *Tsungrem* in general, a thanksgiving ceremony to God just ahead of the harvest time. It is thus held when the rice fields are almost ready for harvest and at the sight of the ripen paddy fields the people rejoice and in turn give thanks for his unspeakable love towards his people. In one of the songs sung during this celebration *Lungkitsungba* is recognized thus:

> *O Amongdangbo; Lungtitsungba Amongdangbo; Surem tasen abener; Shi den chiyonga mongdini.*
>
> Oh! During celebration *Lungkitsungba* celebration Having worn new shawl Let's celebrate and with food and meat.[997]

In this celebration *Lijaba*, the creator of the earth, is also recognized. This is nothing but a thanksgiving ceremony to *Lijaba*, by whose power the earth gives nourishment to all vegetation. Thus in one way this *among* is also an extension of the *Lijaba mong*.

---

[994] N. Talitemjen Jamir, *Asen Sobalibaren* (Mokokchung, 2003), 112.

[995] Of course the idea of placating and appeasing of God is stronger here. A pig was sacrificed and eaten by the village elders and the whole day was observed very strictly and the same observances were at force that evening. Even sexual intercourse was also forbidden that night. People retire to their houses early and late in the night each householder throws an old pot out of his door as an offering to *Lijaba*, asking him to accept it. *Lijaba* comes at night and collect these petty offerings. Should anyone transgress, the wind will wreck his house or flatten his crops. Thus we find the wrathful and arbitrary nature of *Lijaba*.

[996] *Tsungrem-mong* and *Moatsu* are the two prominent ceremonies or festivals as special days of merrymaking, feasting, singing, dancing and drinking in honour of their God. On the occasions of these two festivals the Aos sing all types of songs connected with love, headhunting, goodwill, historical events, etc.

[997] This song is found in Jamir, *Asen Sobalibaren*, 76. English translation is done by the researcher.

The fatherhood of God idea is implicit in a popular Ao-Naga myth, which talks about *Lijaba* coming to the village in disguise as a tattered old man. It is said that while the Aos were living at *Chungliyimti* village, *Lijaba* visited the village in disguise as an old man. He went from door to door requesting for shelter but no one was prepared to entertain him. Some made excuses that the whole family is observing *anembong* (taboo) because of the birthing in their domestic fold. Some made other excuses. None but two orphan sisters, shy in their poverty, invited him to their little hut. The old man assured them not to worry about food. He knew that they had nothing to cook. The old man *Lijaba* blessed them instantly with food both cooked rice and meat in their pot. Next morning *Lijaba*, viewing from the bamboo platform at the back of their hut, enquired the two orphan sisters of the vast rice fields at far distance, and on pointing at their rice field, he blessed them for a rich harvest. Eventually they had a great harvest and prospered and lived happily thereafter. The whole villagers finally realized that the old man who visited them was none other than *Lijaba*.[998]

This myth provides a profound understanding of God in Ao tribal religion. What he did reveals who he is. *Lijaba* is a loving, compassionate and provider parent God. A clear idea of the fatherhood of God is thus seen in the visitation of *Lijaba*.

6.4.4. Significance of Matthean Fatherhood of God for Ao Religion

6.4.4.1. Transcendence of God's Fatherhood in Matthew and in Ao Religion

While we have seen in the Matthean version of the Lord's Prayer (Mt 6:9-13) addressing God as "Our Father" with the added expression "in heaven," which is further supplemented by the transcendental aspect, "Hallowed be your name" (Mt 6:9). Similarly, in Ao Naga religion one of the names in which the transcendent and all pervading nature of God is expressed is *Lungkitsungba* or *Anungtsungba*, the deity supposed to live in heaven. Just as the idea of omniscient and omnipotent God, an all-seeing and all-knowing Father (Mt 6:1-18) is projected in Matthew, so also in Ao religion, *Lungkitsungba* is known as the one who sees all, fixing human's destiny through the ritual of *Amsu*. That means in *Lungkitsungb*a we see God as omniscient and all-seeing heavenly Father, who sustains and holds life. The Aos believe that before the Supreme Being *Lungkitsungba*, it is impossible to hide not merely one's actions but even one's purposes and thoughts. The same idea is found in Matthean idea of an all-seeing Father who demands purity of motives, as he sees all that occurs even in the secret (Mt 6:4, 6, 18).

[998] For details of this myth, see Bendangangshi and Apok Aier, *The Religion of the Ao Nagas*, 26-28.

6.4.4.2. Universality of God's Fatherhood in Matthew and in Ao Religion

The Matthean idea of God as impartial and universal (e.g., Mt 5:45) is also seen in the function of *Anungtsungba*, who is a God of justice and fair dealing. The term *Anungtsungba* itself, expressing the natural phenomena, speaks about the universality of God's fatherhood. It is *Anungtsungba Tsungrem* who sends rain, lightning and thunder and regulates the seasons. This is very much in line with the Matthean understanding of God as Father who makes his sun shine and sends rain on all impartially (5:45), and providing good things (7:11). Thus in both Matthean and Aos' understanding God's presence and acts are as impartial and universal as the sun and the rain. It also means that God is both simultaneously transcendent and immanent, as the very presence of God and his acts are as sure and concrete as the sunshine and the rain.

6.4.4.3. Immanence of God's Fatherhood in Matthew and in Ao Religion

We have seen that in Matthew God's fatherhood is closely related with providence, creation and nature; that he projects a God who is not remote and inaccessible but who participates in the day-to-day activities of humanity (6:10-11, 24-33; 7:9-11). The same aspect of God's fatherhood in Ao Naga religion can be said of the nature of *Lijaba*, the creator of all. As seen above, the very term *Lijaba* is inseparably related with the earth. God and nature are inseparably related for the Aos. *Lijaba* is the one who gives vegetation in the land. He is the source of life, nourishment and fertility. *Lijaba* is not only creator but who continues to create and sustains the earth. That means for the Aos *Lijaba* is the provider, always active, giving life and vitality to all creation. He is present everywhere. So we see that *Lijaba* is organically related with the earth. His goodness and activity is seen in his sending of ideal rain for the cultivation and so providing fertility to the earth for the growth of all vegetable life thereby providing food for both animals and humans. The Aos consider that the rich harvests, prosperity and wealth are bestowal of *Lijaba Tsungrem*. *Lijaba* thus expresses the immanence of God, God as very much part of the earth, being concern for his creation. So in the nature of *Lijaba* we see a clear idea of the fatherhood of God in Ao religion.

6.4.4.4. The Feminine Aspect of the Fatherhood of God in Matthew and Ao Religion

We have seen that in Matthew the idea of God's fatherhood is closely connected with mother earth. (5:45; 6:10c-11; 7:11). Similarly, strong motherly aspects are seen in Ao concept of God *Lijaba*. It is implicit in the function of *Lijaba*, the creator of the earth. As the celebration of *Lijabamong* shows, *Lijaba* continues to create in sustaining the earth. He is a co-worker with the earth.[999] He is the one who gives vegetation in the land and regenerates the earth. That is, he continues to create the earth by giving nourishment and fertility to all the vegetation, thereby converting them into food for the animals and human beings. That means for Aos, *Lijaba* is the provider, always active, giving life and vitality to all creation. He is very much part of the mother earth. For Aos God and nature are inseparably related. So we see strong feminine and earth element in the Ao Naga religious traditions. The very myth of the visitation of *Lijaba* also shows that the nature of his work is motherly. He is not far away, but always near and present. Like a mother he is interested in the affairs of the household. As the myth shows, on seeing the need in the family of the two orphan sisters, even a small bit of food blessed by *Lijaba* increases to plenty. God not only blessed the kitchen but even blessed the rice-field of the two orphan sisters. God is interested in what is happening in every home. He is curious to know about every need of the family. That means Lijaba is seen as motherly or rather as a mother,[1000] having loving, caring and merciful nature. Thus we see that just as in Matthew where the maternal aspect is seen in the very idea of the fatherhood of God so also in Ao religion motherly traits are seen in the nature of *Lijaba*.

6.5. Summary

In sum we observe that in Ao religion the address of God as Father is not explicitly seen, yet it is implicit in the very belief and worship of the deity *Tsungrem*, the Supreme Being. This *Tsungrem* is seen in several functional names, of which *Lungkitsungba* is clearly acknowledged as the creator and lord of all. In this very acknowledgement of *Lungkitsungba* as creator and lord we see the idea of the fatherhood of God. *Lungkitsungba* is omniscient, all-seeing and fixes the destiny of humankind. His concern extends to every individual without partiality. The function of *Lungkitsungba* expresses the transcendence of God. However, the immanence of God is also implicit in *Lijaba Tsungrem*, who is not only the creator but also as the source of life, nourishment and fertility. So in the nature of *Lijaba* we see a clear idea of the fatherhood of God in Ao religion, God as very much part of the earth, having concern for his creation, nurturing and caring as a mother. In the projection of God as transcendent and immanent simultaneously fatherhood of God idea is heightened.

6.6. Fatherhood of God: A Unifying and Revivifying Factor in Religiously Pluralistic India

Indian society is religiously pluralistic. Several religions have their roots in Indian subcontinent: Hinduism, Buddhism, Jainism and Sikhism. Along with these home

[999] For this idea see Wati Longchar, *The Traditional Tribal Worldview and Modernity*, 37-39.

[1000] On the idea of *Lijaba* as Mother, see Takatemjen, *Studies on Theology and Naga Culture* (Mokokchung: Clark Theological College, 1997), 70.

religions Christianity and Islam came as missionary movements and firmly rooted in Indian soil. The tribal and primal religious traditions too need to be recognized in their own right, having unique features expressed through oral traditions and distinctive cultural life. As we have argued throughout that the theme of the fatherhood of God is central to Matthew and the Gospels and so the idea is home to the New Testament Christianity. And as we have explained above the idea of the fatherhood of God is also present in other theistic religions including Hinduism and even tribal religious traditions. This helps us to ponder on the possibility of bringing in the idea of the fatherhood of God and so theocentric idea as a unifying factor in theologizing and Christian witnessing in India.

In this perspective we will look at some of the prominent Indian theologians and secular figures of the 20th century who emphasized on one God and the relational convergence of all religions, keeping the unity in diversity in mind. Already in the early part of the 20th century some leading Indian thinkers and theologians put much stress on the theology of God. Thus on theological-christological relationship, V. Chakkarai observes that "to believe that God is best defined by Christ is not to believe that God is confined to Christ."[1001] Appasamy too in his study of the Fourth Gospel wrote, "Jesus always lived in whole-hearted trust and faith in the Father. He did not consider himself identical with God."[1002] Appasamy brought out the deep devotional and God-centred Indian religious traditions with the Gospels' traditions of the love of God.[1003] He compared and highlighted the deep spirituality of the Hindus, having a real passion for God and trying to understand the depth of God's concern and love with the theme of the love of God as depicted in the Gospels. Dhanjibhai Fakirbhai is another theologian who, following Appasamy, talks about God as love. Robin Boyd gives a succinct summary of Fakirbhai's theology thus: "God can be best described as Love, *prema*. He can indeed be described as *Saccidananda*, but we can go even further and say that he is Love, for love includes and subsumes everything else. Where intellect fails, and can describe God only in negative terms (*neti neti*), Love goes further, for love transcends all other categories, and to call God as love is to go even higher than *nirguna Brahman*."[1004]

Thus we see theologians making effort in presenting the Gospel relevant to the Indian context so as to have meaningful engagement with Indian religious traditions. However, a fuller engagement and theologizing in India in the context of religious pluralism came to the fore in the latter part of the 20th century in Christian thinking. Some prominent theologians emerged talking about the

[1001] V. Chakkarai and A.J. Appasamy, *Jesus the Avatar* (Madras: Christian Literature Society, 1926), 210.

[1002] A.J. Appasamy, *The Johannine Doctrine of Life? A Study of Christian and Indian Thought* (London: SPCK, 1934), 2-3.

[1003] A.J. Appasamy, *Christianity as Bhakti Marga* (Madras: Christian Literature Society, 1926).

[1004] Robin Boyd, *An Introduction to Indian Christian Theology* (Delhi: ISPCK, 1969), 213.

theocentric idea in the context of religious pluralism. It is to these theologians and their thought that we now turn.

6.6.1. S.J. Samartha

Being born and brought up in religiously pluralistic India Samartha is one of the leading exponents of inter-faith dialogue and religious pluralism. One of his main convictions was that of a theocentrism which "grounds cooperation not on expediency, but on theology, providing a vision of participating with all human beings in God's continuing mission in the world."[1005] On his theocentric emphasis in relation to Jesus Christ he stresses:

> The question of God and the question of Jesus are intimately related ... But at the same time, in a religiously plural world, there *can* be and there *are* theologies without reference to Jesus Christ. To ignore or deny this fact is to be insensitive to the faiths of our neighbours. To confuse christology with theology or to seek to displace theology with christology is not only to impoverish Christian theology but also to do grave injustice to the theologies of neighbours of other faiths. A christology which claims that God has revealed God's self in order to redeem humanity *only* in Jesus of Nazareth, and that this revealing and redeeming activity of God has taken place *once-for-all* in the first century, runs the risk of contradicting another strand of Jewish and Christian theology which affirms that God is the God of love and justice as creator, sustainer and redeemer of all creation. If, according to the earliest tradition of the New Testament, Jesus Christ always points to God and is therefore himself theocentric or God-centred, then the only way to be Christ-centred is to be God-centred, but in a religiously plural world to be Christ-centred is not the only way to be God-centred.[1006]

In saying this Samartha calls for putting things into perspective, that is, christology as clearly within theology. He argues why this is so from the perspective of a religiously pluralistic country like India that "it is not the dogmas and doctrines about Christ or the institutions of the Church that have touched the heart and mind of India, but the life and teachings of Jesus of Nazareth, his death and resurrection, the illumination he has brought into the Mystery of God, and the transforming power he has introduced into human life, as he invites all persons to move from self-centredness to God-centredness."[1007] Thus Samartha

---

[1005] S.J. Samartha, "The Cross and the Rainbow," in *The Myth of Christian Uniqueness*, edited by John Hick and Paul F. Knitter (London: SCM Press, 1987), 81.

[1006] S.J. Samartha, *One Christ – Many Religions: Toward a Revised Christology* (New York: Orbis Books, 1991), 105-106.

[1007] Samartha, *One Christ – Many Religions*, 102-103.

takes the historical Jesus seriously and sees Jesus himself as theocentric. While he acknowledged Jesus as central importance to Christian faith and practice, yet he strongly argued for the theocentric nature of the New Testament. He thus warns of the danger of over-emphasis on the prominence of Christ so much so that Christian faith becomes a kind of what he called 'Christo-monism,' which he finds incompatible with the evidence of the New Testament.[1008]

Samartha argues the exclusive claim "that Jesus *is* God has led to a sad impoverishment of the profound depth of Christian faith in God through Christ and has hindered Christians from recognizing new insights in Christology today that are emerging through the leading of the Holy Spirit."[1009] Keeping the pluralistic context in mind Samartha further argued that "God is One not many, that the God of Israel is not the God of the nations but that the God of the nations is also the God of Israel."[1010] Thus in Samartha, we see a clear voice for a God-centred or God-ward emphasis in theological discussion in a religiously pluralistic context like India.[1011]

6.6.2. R. Panikkar

One of the renowned Catholic theologians Raymond Panikkar too gives God a forefront and prominent place in his theological discussions. In one of his earliest works *The Trinity and World Religions*, he talks about the essential oneness of the Father (God) and the Son (Christ).[1012] He also talks about the revelatory experience of historical Jesus calling God as his Father.[1013] He then argues that this very Jesus' calls of God as his Father invites us humanity to do the same by virtue of the divine Spirit that dwells in us humanity.[1014] He categorically argues that "if Jesus as man is God's natural son, then nothing would prevent us too from being the same."[1015] Pointing to the several texts in the Gospels and other New Testament writings that talk about God and human as having the divine nature,

---

[1008] Samartha, *Lordship of Christ*, 12, Samartha, *One Christ – Many Religions*, 136.

[1009] Samartha, *One Christ – Many Religions*, 142.

[1010] Samartha, *One Christ – Many Religions*, 133.

[1011] Of course there are earlier theologians and Christian thinkers who talked about stressing on God in theological discussion in India, most notably A.J. Appasamy, V. Chakkarai and Dhanjibhai Fakirbhai.

[1012] R. Panikkar, *The Trinity And World Religions: Icon-Person-Mystery* (Madras: Christian Literature Society, 1970), 48-49.

[1013] See R. Panikkar, *The Fullness of Man: A Christophany* (trans Alfred DiLascia; Delhi: ISPCK, 2006), 91; He thus categorically states, "without a shadow of a doubt he seems to have had a very intense experience of a divine filiation." See, Panikkar, *The Fullness of Man*, 93.

[1014] Panikkar, *The Fullness of Man*, 92.

[1015] Panikkar, *The Fullness of Man*, 94.

he says that "all these texts speak to us of a real, not just juridical filiation."[1016] He then goes on explaining the great utterance of Jesus[1017] thus:

> There is a definitive "we," an ultimate "we" – I and the Father. There is the Father and the Son, and they are different. The Father is Father and the Son is Son. But the Father is Father because he is the Father of the Son, because it is he who generates. And the Son is Son because he is the Son of the Father who generates him. A father without a son would not be father – a son without a father would not be son. The father is father-of-the-son and the son is son-of-the-father. This paternity and filiation constitute their entire "Being." They are pure relation.[1018]

For Panikkar, the whole universe is involved in this relation and compared this theology of the fatherhood of God of Jesus' traditions[1019] with the great utterance of the Upanishads *Aham Brahmasmi* (I have become the Brahman). He thus stresses that "man's dignity lies precisely in his being conscious of the fact that he and the Father *are* one."[1020]

In his work '*The Unknown Christ of Hinduism*,' Panikkar talks about genuine revelation of God in Hinduism.[1021] For him "Hinduism is the desire for fullness, and that fullness is Christ, hence Hinduism is already pointing towards the same mystery as does Christianity – already contains, indeed, the symbolism of the Christian reality."[1022] Panikkar talks about the living presence of Christ within Hinduism, and which for him implies that "Christ does not belong to Christianity; he belongs to his Father only."[1023] So his emphasis on theocentrism is very clear here. Relating the Advaita of Hinduism and Trinity of the Christianity, he expounds the Brahman-Isvara relationship as analogous to God-Son (Christ) relationship of the Christian Trinity.[1024] Referring to the God-world relationship Panikkar expounds the Brahma Sutra 1.12 which explains that Brahman is the total ultimate cause of the world.[1025] While interpreting this passage Panikkar

---

[1016] Panikkar, *The Fullness of Man*, 95.

[1017] Particularly the utterance of Johannine Jesus, "The Father and I are one" (Jn 10:30).

[1018] Panikkar, *The Fullness of Man*, 111.

[1019] Particularly highlighted in the Gospel of John (e.g., Jn10:30 cf. 10:38; 14:9).

[1020] Panikkar, *The Fullness of Man*, 119.

[1021] See, R. Panikkar, *The Unknown Christ of Hinduism: Towards an Ecumenical Christophany* (Revised and Enlarged Edition; Bangalore: Asian Trading Corporation, 1982), 88.

[1022] Panikkar, *The Unknown Christ of Hinduism*, 90.

[1023] Panikkar, *The Unknown Christ of Hinduism*, 54.

[1024] Panikkar, *The Unknown Christ of Hinduism*, 148.

[1025] Panikkar referring this to *Taittiriya Upanishad* III.I, which reads, "That verily, form which these beings are born, that, by which, when born they live, that into which, when departing, they

says that it is not Brahman but Isvara who is the cause of this world,[1026] though he of course maintained that Isvara, the personal God, is in fact none other than Brahman, but Brahman in the aspect of personal God and creator.[1027] This God-world tension in Isvara is explained by Panikkar that "Isvara is essentially *saguna*, yet somehow claims also to be *nirguna*."[1028] He goes on explaining that Isvara "is not merely *saguna* Brahman, or an emanation of it, or a mere 'modality' of the Godhead. The sutra instead seems to indicate a way to what the Christian tradition calls God the Father through God the Son. It points to an Isvara, who, though being *saguna*, has not ceased to be *nirguna*."[1029] He thus concludes the commentary on the Brahma Sutra 1.12: "*that from which this World comes forth and to which it returns and by which it is sustained, that is Isvara, the Christ*."[1030] Thus for Panikkar, in the very discourse of Brahman-Isvara, a point of convergence is seen in the mystery of the Brahman-Isvara relationship of the Upanishads and that of the Christian God-Son correlation. This is what Panikkar expounds the God-talk in the direction of theology of religious pluralism.

The idea of theocentrism is discussed and promoted not only by theologians; rather, several prominent secular personalities of India, particularly in the 20th century, have adopted this pluralistic approach in order to have inter-religious harmony and peace in the country. Mahatma Gandhi and S. Radhakrishnan are the two foremost personalities who held on to this approach to religions.

6.6.3. Mahatma Gandhi

Being a champion of peace and religious harmony Gandhi accommodated all religions as true, in the sense that their fundamental unity is based on God. Gandhi understood religion as the search for Truth or God through non-violent means. For him, religion "is simply the pursuit of Truth under a different name."[1031] One element of Gandhi's pluralism is theocentrism. He upheld that there is one God, and it is the same God, who is expressed and mediated through the religions, which God himself transcends. Thus for Gandhi, though God is known by countless names, he is one and the same to all. In his own words:

> The Allah of Islam is the same as the God of Christians and Isvara of the Hindus. Even as there are numerous names of God in Hinduism,

---

enter. That, seek to know. That is Brahman." Trans S. Radhakrishnan, in Radhakrishnan, *The Principal Upanishads*, 553.

[1026] Panikkar, *The Unknown Christ of Hinduism*, 152.

[1027] Thus for Panikkar, *Isvara* becomes the link between undifferentiated *Brahman* and the created world. See Panikkar, *The Unknown Christ of Hinduism*, 153-154.

[1028] Panikkar, *The Unknown Christ of Hinduism*, 159.

[1029] Panikkar, *The Unknown Christ of Hinduism*, 159.

[1030] Panikkar, *The Unknown Christ of Hinduism*, 162.

[1031] Rex Ambler, "Gandhi's Concept of Truth," in J. Hick and Lamont C. Hempel (eds.), *Gandhi's Significance for Today* (London: Macmillan, 1989), 102.

> there are many names of God in Islam. The names do not indicate individuality but attributes, and little man has tried in his humble way to describe the Mighty God by giving Him attributes, though indescribable and immeasurable. Living faith in this God means acceptance of the brotherhood of mankind. It also means equal respect to all religions.[1032]

The same understanding of the universality of God is evident in his appreciation of a certain General called Smuts of South Africa, of whom he positively talks about offering "a prayer that goes up to God, not the God of white men, not the God of the negro, not of the Mussalman, not of the Hindu, but the God of all, the God of the Universe."[1033]

Gandhi thus finds a unity underlying all religions in the transcendent which undergirds and is the focus of religions. That means for Gandhi, God is one and religions are different roads converging to the same God. In one of his discourse Gandhi puts:

> God is certainly One. He has no second. He is unfathomable, unknowable and unknown to the vast majority of mankind. He is everywhere. He sees without eyes, and hears without ears. He is formless and indivisible. He is uncreated, has no father, mother, wife and child; and yet He allows Himself to be worshipped as father, mother, wife and child. He allows himself even to be worshipped as stock and stone, although He is none of these things. He is the most elusive ....[1034]

Gandhi's thought was of a kind of "pan-cosmic-pantheistic cum theistic ambivalence in his experience, interpretation and conception of God and His transcendence."[1035] As such true to his Advaitic inclinations, he rejected all sorts of exclusive claims[1036] and preached oneness of God and the doctrine of the universal brotherhood of humanity. Thus expounding the oneness of all humankind in true Advaitic thought, he says:

> I believe in Advaita, I believe in the essential unity of man and for that matter of all that lives.[1037]

[1032] *Harijan*, 12-8-1938, in K.L. Seshagiri Rao, *Mahatma Gandhi and Comparative Religion*, 72.

[1033] *Young India*, 7-1-1926, in *The Collected Works of Mahatma Gandhi*, vol 29 (Ahmadabad: Navajivan Trust, 1968), 361.

[1034] *Young India*, 25-9-1924, in *The Collected Works of Mahatma Gandhi*, vol 25, 178.

[1035] Balwant A.M. Paradkar, "Hindu Interpretation of Christ from Vivekananda to Radhakrishnan," in *IJT* 18 (Jan-Mar 1969), 73.

[1036] As Gandhi categorically asserts, "Revelation is the exclusive property of no nation, no tribe." See *Young India*, 25-9-1924, in *The Collected Works of Mahatma Gandhi*, vol 25, 178.

[1037] *Young India*, 4-12-1924, in *The Collected Works of Mahatma Gandhi*, vol 25, 390.

Being raised in a Vaishnavite family Gandhi, however, is rooted in a strongly devotional and theistic context.[1038] His concept of God is not merely that of an impersonal absolute but also of a personal caring God, in whom he puts his faith and trust, who he prays to and sees acting in his life. In one of his discourses Gandhi talk about God thus:

> He is a personal God to those who need His personal presence. He is embodied to those who need His touch. He is the purest essence. He simply Is to those who have faith. He is all things to all men. He is in us and yet above and beyond us.[1039]

That means for Gandhi, God is both transcendent and immanent. Gandhi's concept of God is very clear here. He views a universal God who is the creator of all, having the characters of infinite love, compassion and forgiving. And in this very explanation we see the idea of the brotherhood of humankind, which logically points to the affirmation of the fatherhood of God. Thus his affirmation of the One God in all religions is worth noting.[1040] As seen above he made no distinction between religions and sees the fundamental unity in all the religions. He recognized the spiritual truths and insights in all religions. It is important that we consider his theocentric view as they are the best solutions for a pluralistic country like India where religious intolerance and extremism are everyday phenomenon.

6.6.4. S. Radhakrishnan

One of the chief exponents of universalism is Radhakrishnan. He advocated the oneness and fellowship of all religions. According to him, "the different religious traditions clothe the one Reality in various images and their visions could embrace and fertilize each other so as to give mankind a many-sided perfection."[1041] He thus talks about the relativity of all revelations. Although, he accepts the possibility of revelation as a source of knowing the ultimate reality, he does not regard any one revelation in any one particular religion to be final.[1042] For him God is a living God who "is essentially self-communicative and is of ungrudging goodness."[1043]

[1038] In fact Margaret Chatterjee commented that this Vaishnava tradition was woven into the warp and woof of Gandhi's religious thought. See Chatterjee, "Gandhi and Christianity," in *Gandhi's Significance for Today*, 162.

[1039] *Young India*, 5-3-1925, in *The Collected Works of Mahatma Gandhi*, vol 26, 224.

[1040] However, some scholars criticize Gandhi's religious thought. For example, A.J. Anandan (*God for All, God for Me: Gandhiji's Religious Dualism* [Bangalore: SAIACS Publications, 1998]) considers his stance on religion as dualistic, especially on seeing his public interactions and private life and convictions inconsistent.

[1041] *Radhakrishnan: Selected Writings on Philosophy, Religion, and Culture*, edited by Robert A. McDermott (New York: Dutton, 1970), 289.

[1042] S. Radhakrishnan, *The Heart of Hindusthan* (Madras: G.A. Natesan & Co, 1936), 102, 104.

[1043] *Radhakrishnan: Selected Writings*, 290.

Upholding the general revelation of God, he argues that "the conception of a unique revelation of a chosen people is contrary to the love and justice of God."[1044] Revelation for him is thus "a universal gift, and not a parochial possession."[1045]

Radhakrishnan commends the idea of the Christ of faith because it perfectly resembles his Vedantic Christ. For him "salvation is mediated through the Eternal Christ, the Word of God, which is not to be confused with the historic Jesus. It is open to those who have not heard him and are yet loyal to the spirit of truth."[1046] He thus attaches greater significance to the inward revelation than the outward, because such a belief would be in congruence with his Advaitic thinking. He argues that a direct contact with the central reality is possible not through any historical revelations, oracles, prayers, etc., but by intuitive experience where the individual becomes the partaker of the divine nature.[1047] This is where his emphasis on universal religion is seen.[1048] He thus talks about universal humanity, universal brotherhood, and by implication the universality of God's fatherhood. His idea of religious pluralism or Universalist approach is summed up in one of his discourse thus:

> If God is love, he cannot be a jealous God. With the jealous God goes the doctrine of the chosen people. If God's light is the light that lighteth every man that he left not Himself without witness, the adherents of religions other than our own are not shut out from the love of God.[1049]

And he concludes, "Mankind stems from one origin from which it has figured out in many forms."[1050]

In this very emphasis on the common origin of all humanity, we see his emphasis on the universality of God.

As we have argued in the previous chapter Matthew talks about the same universality of God idea. There is a strong theocentric-pluralistic tone in the Matthean Jesus' discourse on the Sermon on the Mount, where Matthean Jesus

---

[1044] Radhakrishnan, "My Search for Truth," in Vergilins Fermi (ed.), *Religion in Transition* (London: George Allen & Unwin Ltd., 1937), 18-19.

[1045] Radhakrishnan, *East and West in Religion* (London: George Allen & Unwin, 1933), 38.

[1046] Radhakrishnan, *Recovery of Faith* (London: Allen & Unwin, 1956), 147.

[1047] Radhakrishnan, *Eastern Religions and Western Thought* (London: Oxford University Press, 1939; Second Edition; 1940), 129.

[1048] On this aspect see, *Radhakrishnan: Selected Writings*, 294-296.

[1049] *Radhakrishnan: Selected Writings*, 304. Elsewhere he also commented that "Peace is not the mere absence of war; it is the development of a strong fellow-feeling, an honest appreciation of other people's ideas and values." See *Radhakrishnan: Selected Writings*, 308.

[1050] *Radhakrishnan: Selected Writings*, 308.

talks about the indiscriminate goodness of God (5:45)[1051] and peacemakers as children of God (5:9). That means as Matthean Jesus talks about the universal idea like peacemaking and love and the fatherhood of God in the same breath, we see his clear theocentric emphasis. This theocentric idea is very much the theological emphasis of Matthew. This helps us to understand and put forth that the theme of the fatherhood of God as a common theme, a unifying and revivifying factor in doing theology and in Christian witness today in a religiously pluralistic India.

6.6.5. The Fatherhood of God and Theocentrism[1052]

There is no doubt that today there are various religions other than Christianity and the people of all faiths are now living together in India and almost everywhere. So that means plurality of religions is a reality that we cannot afford to overlook. And as we have seen in the discussion above one thing that is common in all the religions is that of belief in one supreme God. Rooted in the biblical tradition Christianity believes in one God, the Creator of heaven and earth. The one God idea is clearly seen in Matthew in his exposition of the various aspects of the fatherhood of God, especially his unique emphasis on the idea of God, as cosmic Father. The same is seen in Hinduism and Islam[1053] and even in primal religions.

[1051] Mt 5:45-48 gives the idea of God as the 'heavenly Father' whose love and goodness if for all universally.

[1052] Theocentrism is used here to mean that God alone stands at the center and the various religions, including Christianity, represented many ways leading to God (see Veli-Matti Karkkainen, *An Introduction to the Theology of Religions: Biblical, Historical & Contemporary Perspectives* [Illinois: Intervarsity Press, 2003], 25). Theocentrism thus implies affirmation of the plurality of religion and its independent validity. One of the pioneers of the theology of religious pluralism is John Hick. Hick (*God Has Many Names* [Philadelphia: Westminster Press, 1980], 18) talks about the idea of a "Copernican revolution," a paradigm shift in theological thinking "from a Christianity-centered or Jesus-centered model to a God-centered model of the universe of faiths." Thus Hick sees the great world religions as different human responses to the one divine Reality, and logically argues that all revelations are relative, and there is no right to claim one religion as the absolute Truth; See J. Hick, *The Rainbow of Faiths* (London: SCM Press, 1995), ix-x. In the same vein Samartha (*One Christ – Many Religions: Toward a Revised Christology*, 4) too observed that plurality in religions came into existence as a result of response to the Mystery of Ultimate reality in different ways. And as such for him the age-long affirmation of the decisiveness of God's revelation in Jesus Christ and its universal significance is being questioned. Samartha ("Dialogue in a Religiously Plural Society," in *The Multi-Faith Context of India: Resources and Challenges for Christians* edited by I. Selvanayagam [Bangalore: BTTBPSA, 1994], 10) thus further highlighted a convincing argument against the unique claim of Jesus in the Bible: "Although God has disclosed himself in Jesus Christ in a unique and decisive way there is no clue in the Bible that God has stopped to be active in the life and history of other people. He is still active as he was in terms of his omnipresence, logos, Spirit or cosmic Christ." There are also people of other faiths have a high sense of commitment to one God and the welfare of humanity.

[1053] In fact for Kenneth Cragg (*Alive to God: Muslim and Christian Prayer*, 17-19) the very affirmation of the one God, particularly in prayer and worship, is a vibrant aspect, a meeting point of Muslim-Christian unity.

That means to say that God is essentially the focus of human's worship and ritual activities as projected in all religious traditions and scriptures.[1054] And as we have seen above some Indian theologians and thinkers have attempted to hold on to that one God idea as the focus of discussion, engagement and doing theology in the multi-religious context or religiously pluralistic India. This logically implies that the theme of the fatherhood of God can be carried forward in Indian Christian thinking and theology. The idea of the universality of God or the fatherhood of God reinforces the idea of the one God. As we engage in God-talk the fatherhood of God idea is inevitable and clear in the very exposition of the transcendent and immanent aspect of the one God.[1055] Thus the idea of the fatherhood of God and theocentrism are inseparably connected.

It should be recognized that Indian Christian theology or God-talk has already been influenced by the theology of Hinduism.[1056] Already in the 19th century a pioneer Indian theologian Brahmabandhab Upadhyaya attempted to conflate Vedantic terms and Christian vocabularies in his God-talk:

> The Father, Sun, Supreme Lord, unborn, The seedless Seed of the tree of becoming, The cause of all, Creator, Providence, Lord of the Universe.[1057]

The comparison between Christian Trinity and Vedantic *Saccidananda*, initiated by Keshub Chandra Sen in the 19th century was again popularized in the 20th century by Swami Abshiktananda[1058] and Raymond Panikkar.[1059] The Christian mystery is thus at home in Indian religious traditions from the beginning as expounded by Indian theologians notably Panikkar and Samartha. But this is what even Gandhi and Radhakrishnan were talking about. This also means that serious incorporation of the God-talk found in Indian religious traditions becomes very significant and necessary for our own understanding of God.[1060] The God depicted in the Gospel of Matthew and so Christian tradition is that of a Father God who is both transcendent and immanent as we have seen in the

---

[1054] N. Smart, *The Religious Experience of Mankind* (New York: Charles Scribner's Sons, 1984), 16.

[1055] For details on the various absolute terms, epithets and relational terms for God abound in Indian religious traditions ideal for God-talk, see Selvanayagam, "Non-Biblical Resources for Theological Writing in India," in *The Multi-Faith Context*, 25-28.

[1056] Selvanayagam, "Non-Biblical Resources for Theological Writing in India," in *The Multi-Faith Context*, 25.

[1057] Margaret Chatterjee, *The Religious Spectrum: Studies in An Indian Context* (New Delhi: Allied Publishers Private Ltd., 1984), 181.

[1058] For details on the pioneer theologians and their thinking see M. Chatterjee, *Religious Spectrum*, 171-193; on Swami Abhishiktananda, see R.H.S. Boyd, *An Introduction to Indian Christian Theology*, 287-297.

[1059] R. Panikkar, *The Trinity And World Religions.*

[1060] Selvanayagam, "Non-Biblical Resources for Theological Writing in India," in *The Multi-Faith Context*, 25.

previous chapter. Similarly we see in the Indian religious tradition God having the same transcendent and immanent traits. Even in the non-dualistic Advaitic tradition God is understood as both *nirguna* and *saguna* Brahman. And as we have shown the fatherhood of God idea is clearly seen in the Gita. This means that the theme of the fatherhood of God can be a unifying factor in inter-religious dialogue or dialogical process and so doing theology in India. The affirmation that the fatherhood of God means that God is one for all, the source, course and end of all things visible and invisible. This is another way of saying that all are children of God and so the universality of God's fatherhood.

This idea of the universality of God or the fatherhood of God has several implications. It implies unity, love, peace, freedom, socio-economic equality and justice, which ideals are found in all the religious traditions and so are universal. It is to which we now turn.

6.6.5.1. Fatherhood of God in the Context of War and Terrorism

The world is witnessing enormous conflicts today. Countries big or small try to build massive military power, in the name of safeguarding their sovereignty and also economic advantage as they search for the foreign markets for their products to increase their national income and wealth. They steadily enlarge their military influence to gain recognition from the world public for other benefits to satisfy their self-interests. These are the most destructive forces humankind has ever conceived. We can now annihilate people by simply pushing a button.[1061] When this destructive power is unleashed, it causes enormous ecological damage. Where is the solution? The answer is basically found in the religions of the world, including the Bible. We can see the truth of the scriptures; get closer to the core of all religions, to the one God as Father, who is the God of all grace, goodness, love and peace.[1062] Thus there is need of vertical alignment, as Radhakrishnan would talk about personal sanctification in order to conforming to the will of the Supreme, that "the change from self-centredness to God-centeredness brings with it a peace and radiance of living."[1063] This is exactly what Matthean Jesus meant when he says, "Blessed are the pure in heart, for they will see God. Blessed are the peacemakers, for they will be called children of God" (Mt 5:8-9).

The basic affirmation of the fatherhood of God, which is the awareness of the one God and one humanity or theocentric thinking promotes love and unity

---

1061 *Cesim: The Non-Proliferation Monthly* 73 (Dec 2012), *http://www.cesim.fr/observatoire/eng/73/article/7;* accessed on 7 Jan, 2014.

1062 For unity of world's religions on the idea of love, see K.L. Seshagiri Rao and Henry O. Thompson (eds.), *The Love of God in the World's Religions*; Geevarghese Mar Osthathios, *One Religion of Love: Globalization of Divine Love, Personalization of Conviction and Religious Faiths* (Thiruvalla: Christava Sahitya Samithy, 2000); see also Homer A. Jack (ed.), *World Religions and World Peace: The International Inter-Religious Symposium on Peace* (Boston: Beacon Press, 1968).

1063 *Radhakrishnan: Selected Writings*, 301.

within the greater family of humankind. Such knowledge enables to transcend the boundaries of nation, race, religion and all sorts of distinctions that divide humankind. In other words, the affirmation of the universal fatherhood of God unites human with God and trains people to form a united humanity. It gives human a universal consciousness in place of consciousness based on various distinctions. Such theocentric knowledge or the idea of the universal fatherhood of God makes all humanity universal citizens under one God, which is clearly expressed in the Gospel of Matthew.[1064] Such affirmation of the fatherhood of God is the solution to all kinds of conflicts, war and terrorism.

6.6.5.2. Fatherhood of God in the Context of Religious Intolerance and Extremism

Fundamentalism and narrow sectarian conflicts are everyday phenomenon today. Narrow-minded adherents of religion indulge in acts of discrimination, hate and cruelty towards adherents of other religions. Fanatics indulge in acts of religious persecution, torture and even communal riots. These acts defeat the very purpose and destroy the very essence of religions. Is there something more forceful than the spirit of tolerance as Matthean Jesus commanded in the Sermon on the Mount to show love to all so as to "be perfect as your heavenly Father is perfect" (Mt 5:48)? It is a call to be inclusive in one's love. Thus the idea of the universal fatherhood of God seems to be the antidote for religious fundamentalism and extremism. Divine love is to be the key that will unlock the riddle and unite even enemies into human fraternity under one Father.[1065] There is a need for universal religious conviction which should work as force for integration of humankind and should emphasize upon unity of minds with one God. The emphasis on the idea of the fatherhood of God and so theocentric thinking will remove the narrow-mindedness, chauvinism, fanaticism and communalism from society. Holding fast to the idea of the universality of God's fatherhood is the need of the hour. Going back to the idea of one heavenly Father helps all of humanity to live as brothers and sisters. So instead of focusing on the differences in the details we must cling to the unity at its source, that is, basic unity, and thus promote inter-religious brotherhood. That means to say that all religions originated from one God and they also lead to the same goal – God. Thus the emphasis on the universal Fatherhood of God or Father centric theology brings harmony and peace.

[1064] For example, Matthew 23:9 informs us that all "have one Father – the one in heaven." Certain Hellenistic writer Epictetus (*Discourses* I.9.3-7) too talks about humanity as citizen of the universe, as sons of God, the Maker, Father and Guardians of all, of course in the context of Roman imperialism and domination

[1065] Geevarghese Mar Osthathios, *One Religion of Love*, 15.

6.6.5.3. Fatherhood of God in the Context of Economic Exploitation

The feeling of commonness, of brotherhood and the spirit of sharing with others are inseparably related, and is firmly rooted in the idea of the fatherhood of God. In other words, focusing on the fatherhood of God enables us to live us brothers and sisters under a sharing God, creating a sharing world, and sharing the resources of God without destroying them, but producing more, and sharing it with a sense of stewardship out of love.[1066] This is strongly affirmed in Matthew and even in various Indian religious traditions. Both Matthew and Q traditions affirm the goodness of God's creation and rejoice in its beauty (Mt 6:25-33; Lk 12:22-32). It recognizes that God is the source of life for all creation. The heavenly Father's concern is for all people (Mt 5:45). God wants all the good things for his children – the humanity (Mt 7:11). He is the source of all goodness. Hence any attitude towards others must be one of selfless love (Mt 5:48). Creation does not belong to human, but human belongs to creation, and creation is God's. The implication is that since God is the owner and that the earth resources derive their origin from God and they belong to all, no one has the right to exploit and waste the earth's resources. No community or group is excluded in this God's domain. All are to enjoy together in the Father's domain including "the least" (Mt 25:31-46). Thus, acknowledging God as Father, creator and so the owner of everything brings equality, fellowship and freedom, which is solution to all sorts of exploitations and injustices.

6.6.5.4. Fatherhood of God in the Context of Ecological Crisis

The world is experiencing ecological crisis in an unprecedented scale today. The list of environmental problems and crisis that humanity faces today is long and growing: global climate change;[1067] decreasing agricultural yields; increasing water stresses; contamination of air, water and soil; the depletion of many kinds of non-renewable resources; annihilation of many species of plants and animals; increases in extreme weather events; rapid increases in urbanization without corresponding increases in water and sewage infrastructure; destructive mining practices; deforestation; and more. In the light of such grave situation, the affirmation of the fatherhood of God is the need of the hour, especially to address our ecological concern.[1068] In fact the very intimate and intricate relationship and

---

[1066] Geevarghese Mar Osthathios, *One Religion of Love*, 121.

[1067] According to an article reported in *The Times of India*, Bangalore, dated Tuesday, the 14th August, 2012, titled "Arctic sea ice may vanish in 10 years," the polar experts predicted that due to the global warming arctic sea ice will vanish within 10 years as it is melting faster than previously expected. The consequence of losing Arctic's ice coverage, even for only part of the year, could be profound, say the polar experts. Ocean temperature will rise and methane deposits on ocean floor could melt, evaporate and bubble into atmosphere.

[1068] However Gordon D. Kaufman would suggest God, instead of anthropomorphic terms, as Cosmic Serendipitous Creativity to address today's ecological crisis. See Kaufman, "Re-conceiving

interrelatedness is truly part of the message of the religious traditions of the world. The basic biblical affirmation of believing in one God, as Father and Maker of heaven and earth is also true to Islam and even Hinduism. In spite of the many differences Christians and Hindus have a considerable point of affirming together that the present world is created and preserved by God. God's relationship with the world is one of the central concerns of the major religious traditions.

As we have developed, that there is a strong feminine aspect in the idea of God's fatherhood in the various religious traditions. The cosmic fatherhood idea is clearly seen in the Vedic literatures. As we have seen the heavenly Father of Matthew has its Hindu counterpart in *Dyaus Pitar*, the Father God, the transcendent sky Father, who is seen incomplete without the immanent *Prithvi*, the Mother Earth in ancient Indian worship of God.[1069] So also the Gita teaches that the world is filled with God. He is present everywhere, sustains everything, great and small. God fills the heavens, the earth and all space. In the same vein the Aos attach sacred significance to earth and nature. The Aos venerate the nature as it is their life giver in day-to-day life. Today both religious and secular activists working for environmental protection look to these traditions with great respect.[1070]

The fatherhood of God is very significant in inter-religious theological-ecological engagement. The fatherhood of God theme is thus a vital source or basis of inter-religious co-operation in working for a better world. As we have shown there is a strong ecological element in the Matthean theology of the fatherhood of God. In the theology of Matthew the whole created order bears testimony to the goodness of the Creator. While special emphasis is placed on God's care for humanity (Mt 7:7-11), the natural world upon which humankind depends also shares in the divine benevolence (Mt 6:24-32; 10:29-31). Matthean theology presents God in close connection with creation and nature. There is a clear interdependence between humankind and the natural world, because the origin of both is the same – God. Thus the very presence of the idea of God's immanence means that it affirms the interconnectedness of all: God-human-nature. That is, God as organically related with nature. And this very basic awareness of interconnectedness of all things is the solution to all ecological problems.

6.6.5.5. Fatherhood of God in the Context of Social Discrimination

Discrimination based on race, colour, ethnic origin, descent or birth is rampant even today. In spite of the efforts made by several political and social reformers caste-discrimination is prevalent today. Even within the Christian Church the

---

God and Humanity in Light of Today's Ecological Consciousness: A Brief Statement," *www.crosscurrents.org/kaufman.htm*; accessed on Jan 12, 2014.

[1069] See, S.R.M. Murthy, *Vedic View of the Earth* (New Delhi: D.K. Printworld, 1997), 212.

[1070] On this aspect see Wati Longchar, *Returning to Mother Earth: Theology, Christian Witness and Theological Education – An Indigenous Perspective* (Kolkata: PTCA, 2012), 28-30, 96-128.

same drama continues. One of the finest examples of unity in diversity within the Christendom is the existence of the Church of South India, which was formed in 1947. It was a union of churches having diverse customs and practices.[1071] However casteism is a big challenge even within the Church.[1072] Dalits still experience injustice, restrictions, feelings of contempt, isolation and thus suffer a lowered self-esteem, confusion of self-identity, self-hate and the perception of the world as a hostile place. It thus destroys the common identity of a nation. The tribals also undergo similar experience and humiliation. In addition, the tribal communities struggle against land alienation through developmental activities and erosion of their culture and identity.[1073]

We can also categorize sexual minorities, people with different sexual orientation as the victims of discrimination. On December 11, 2013 the Supreme Court dealt a cruel blow to lakhs of people having different sexual orientation.[1074] The verdict was greeted with widespread uproar all over the nation, in support of the people having different sexual orientation. Voices against this verdict are heard from every corner including the prominent current political leaders, saying that this verdict is against basic human rights and personal freedoms. "Love knows no gender" goes one of the placards in the nation-wide protests against Section 377 of Indian Penal Code in solidarity with the sexual minorities.[1075]

The affirmation of common humanity under one God as Father is the answer again. The fatherhood of God implies the inclusion of all humanity irrespective of gender, descent, ethnic, colour or social standing. This idea is clearly seen in the Gospel of Matthew (23:9), which can shatter all sorts of hierarchy and discrimination. All humanity as brothers and sisters are under the same love and compassion of God. Thus when we look to God as our Father and count all humanity as God's children and so as one's brothers and sisters, then our duty to the world is seen in a totally new perspective. It is this realization which can ultimately root out all kinds of discrimination.

6.6.5.6. Fatherhood of God in Inter-Faith Dialogue and Mission

Clinging to the idea of fatherhood of God is the need of the hour. It speaks to us today in all fronts – within the church life, and the church in relation to other

---

[1071] For a detail on the formation of the Church of South India, see J.G. Muthuraj, *"...That They May Also be Sanctified In Truth:" A Response to the CSI Moderator's Paper "Wider Revitalization or Renewal of the Church of South India"* (Delhi: ISPCK, 2012), 38-42.

[1072] See J.G. Muthuraj, "The Bishops And Caste Reforms in The Nineteenth Century Indian Church." A Paper presented to the United Theological College Faculty Research Seminar dated July 26, 2013, 31.

[1073] For details on this aspect, see Wati Longchar, *Returning to Mother Earth*, 204-207.

[1074] *The Times of India*, Thursday, December 12, 2013 gives a comprehensive coverage on this issue. The front page headline goes "SC Makes Homosexuality A Crime Again: Upholds Section 377 Of IPC, Which Prescribes Jail For Life."

[1075] It appeared in the front page of the *Bangalore Times*, Wednesday, December 18, 2013.

faiths and communities, that is, dialogical life. Thus the theme of the universal fatherhood of God should be our slogan in doing mission today. It promotes inter-religious harmony and ultimately a peaceful-coexistence in unity amidst diversity. Putting the particularity and divisive elements and differences aside, the fatherhood of God idea enables us to focus on the commonness of all humanity as brothers and sisters. It is high time that the churches today revive and go back to this very idea of the fatherhood of God. As shown above this very affirmation of the fatherhood of God carries rich implications. Focusing on theocentric or universal approach in theology helps address key challenges to present society. Its affirmation help dissolve the forces that tear the fabric of human society including war and terrorism, religious intolerance, social discrimination, casteism, sexism, socio-economic and political injustice.

6.7. Summary

Our main argument throughout this section has been that that the fatherhood of God can be greatly utilized and put forth as a revivifying force in Indian thinking, theology and Christian witness and mission today. It is seen that in the major theistic religious traditions of India theocentric idea is very strong. And as we have pointed out some Indian theologians and thinkers have attempted to hold on to that one God idea as the focus of discussion, engagement and doing theology in the multi-religious context of India. The idea of the universality of God as Father strengthens the idea of the one God. As we engage in God-discourse the fatherhood of God idea is inevitable and clear in the very exposition of the transcendent and immanent aspect of the one God. Thus the theme of the fatherhood of God can be carried forward in Indian Christian thinking and theologizing. The affirmation of the universality of God's fatherhood means that God is one for all, the source, course and end of all things visible and invisible. This is another way of saying that all are children of God. This universality of God implies compassion, love, non-violence, freedom and justice. Such ideals are found in all religious traditions and so universal. More so in Matthew there is a strong emphasis on the universality of God and the commonness of all human and living beings as children of the same parent (5:45). God is accessible so as to address as 'Our Father.' Thus the theme of the fatherhood of God, which is the core theological emphasis of Matthew, can serve as the bedrock of theologizing and be a unifying factor in doing theology in India, in inter-religious dialogue and relationships.

Concluding Summary

Keeping the Matthean emphasis on the centrality of the fatherhood of God in mind we have been arguing throughout this chapter that the theme of God's fatherhood can be put forth as a unifying force in Indian thinking, theology and witness. At the outset we have dealt on the fatherhood of God in the context of feminist movement. As such we have shown the contentions of several feminist scholars who voiced against male language for God. Some radically opposed the address of God as Father, notably Mary Daley, Daphne Hampson, Karen Bloomquist and Elizabeth Johnson; while some are seen more or less in reformist tone, notably Sally McFague, V.R. Mollenkott, E.S. Fiorenza and R.R. Ruether. We have also examined scholars who stood for status quo, that addressing God as Father as biblical patterns, and thus saw the continuing tension in this regard. We have also highlighted some among the feminist scholars who stood for reformation within the very Father language itself, notably Fiorenza and Ruether. And since our main focus is on Matthew, we have shown that Matthean idea of God as Father has not much to do with patriarchal, domineering sexist language, but rather with care and concern.

We have shown how the theme of God's fatherhood can be of significance in theologizing in religiously pluralistic context of India. As argued, quite similar to Matthean emphasis, Indian religious traditions have an interest in the Father concept of God. The invocation of God as Father in prayer is quite at home in Indian religious traditions. That means that the religious inclination or devotion to one God or theocentric emphasis is deeply ingrained in Indian thinking. Even Islam has strong emphasis on the unity of God, where fatherhood of God idea is implicit. So also in the religion of the Ao Nagas, we have pointed out that in the very belief in the Supreme transcendent God *Lungkitsungba* and the immanent God *Lijaba*, the idea of the fatherhood of God is implicit. More so, the strong God-human-nature organic relationship seen in the worship of *Lijaba* is a strong pointer towards the eco-feminine aspect of God in Ao Naga religion. The implication of Matthean fatherhood of God for Ao Naga religion is thus shown.

We have also highlighted the theme of the fatherhood of God as a unifying and revivifying aspect in religiously pluralistic India. In this perspective we have examined some of the prominent theologians and secular thinkers who are proponents of religious pluralism, namely S.J. Samartha, R. Panikkar, Mahatma Gandhi and S. Radhakrishnan. Having explored these thinkers and theologians, we have established that our idea of the fatherhood of God and theocentrism, as the theologians and secular thinkers pointed to, are inseparably connected. As we engage in God-talk the fatherhood of God idea is inevitable and clear in the very discourse of the one God. Thus the theme of the fatherhood of God can be carried forward in doing theology and mission in India. It is the need of the time to reclaim and reaffirm the fatherhood of God idea in inter-faith dialogue and mission, in the context of terrorism, growing religious intolerance and extremism, economic exploitation, ecological crisis, social discrimination for a peaceful and harmonious society, and to coexist as common humanity.

Chapter 7

Conclusion: The Fatherhood of God in Matthew

This concluding chapter will cover three areas. First we will provide a brief overall summary of the study. Second, we will highlight the distinctive emphasis of the fatherhood of God in Matthew and show its meaning and functions. And finally, we will show how the strong God-focus or the theocentric nature of Matthean theology can be utilized for doing theology from Indian perspective.

7.1. Overall Summary and Conclusions

We have argued at the very beginning of our study that the fatherhood of God, in spite of being the most prominent theme in Matthew, has received the least attention. As such we have stated that the very purpose of this study is to examine the theological significance of the fatherhood of God in Matthew. This theocentric emphasis as seen in Matthew is the right place for doing theology and to relate with various faith traditions of India. The work is carried out by making use of the historical-critical tools, mainly redaction critical approach as the main tool, giving priority to the context of Matthew the Evangelist, examining his life-situation and theological point. Also history of religions perspective has been used, as the first century broader Greco-Roman Mediterranean world and Jewish context was to which Matthew and the Gospel writers belong. The focus has been to examine the theological significance of the theme of God's fatherhood in Matthew, as he reveals it in the structures and composition of the various parts of his text, so as to highlight his contribution to the on-going understanding of God in New Testament theology, and also for doing theology or theologizing in India.

In order to grasp the significance of Matthew's theology of God, our second chapter is entirely devoted to background study focusing on the broader Greco-Roman and Jewish social, religious and political milieus. Looking into the closer circle and immediate context of Matthew, we have also examined the Old Testament and the literatures of early Judaism, that is, the various Jewish and Hellenistic literatures - the Old Testament Apocrypha, the Old Testament Pseudepigrapha, the Dead Sea Scrolls, Josephus, Philo and Rabbinic literatures and found out that they are indispensable as they help us understand and shed light on Matthew and the Synoptic writers' idea of the fatherhood of God. The fatherhood of God is found in almost all the literatures and these explain how pervasive is the idea of God's fatherhood in each of the writings of the Palestinian and Hellenistic Judaism, in which immediate environment Matthew and the Synoptic writers' idea of God's fatherhood seem to have flourished. That means to say that while the idea of God's fatherhood in Matthew has its roots in the Old Testament, yet there is also strong influence from the Hellenistic literatures. A new trajectory on the idea of God's fatherhood in individual sense and so a trend towards universality of God as Father of all, which is so prominent in the theology of Matthew, comes from the Jewish and Hellenistic writings of Sirach (e.g., 23:1, 4) and Wisdom of Solomon (e.g. 2:13-16). So also God's fatherhood in relation to providence, which is so prominent in the theology of Q, has strong influence from Wisdom of Solomon (e.g., 14:3), *Sibylline Oracles* (e.g., 3.50, 604, 278; 5.406, 500) and *The Letter of Aristeas* (e.g., 132, 190). That means to say that the fatherhood of God in relation to nature so clearly expressed in Q is found in these Hellenistic literatures. However, it is Philo where we see strikingly similar to Matthean idea of cosmic fatherhood. Moreover, the presence of feminine traits in the very exposition of God's fatherhood in Matthew is again closer to Plato's cosmological fatherhood idea. In *Timaeus*, Plato talks about fatherhood that covers the entire cosmos and it helps us explain Matthew's unique idea of God as cosmic Father. In other words, Matthew drew eclectically from Platonic and Stoic-Philonic traditions. The Greco-Roman and Jewish-Hellenistic literatures are of immense help for us. It helps us understand early Christianity including Matthew as a religious phenomenon that has synthesized biblical religion and Hellenistic religion and culture. However, the fatherhood of God idea, as seen in the various literatures, is such a composite in nature that it cannot be explained only in theological-philosophical areas of influence. There is strong socio-political aspect embedded in it. The fatherhood idea has strong Greco-Roman socio-political connotations.

We have examined that the father-figure was very strong in the Greco-Roman society, both within the family and in the political sphere. The father-figure became an important part of the image of the political leader, especially with Caesar and Augustus. Thus imperial rule flourished with the idea of *paterfamilias* with the emperor as *Pater Patriae* (emperor as father of the country or empire). Such a context of imperial ideology or theology has permeated the whole of the then Greco-Roman region and surroundings including Matthean community and other Jewish communities as reflected in the literatures of rabbinic Judaism.

Thus, it helps us to inquire how far such a characterization of the Greco-Roman father has informed Matthew's idea of God's fatherhood.

In the third chapter while dealing with Matthew's source Mark and Q, we have shown the very Aramaic expression *Abba* in the lips of Jesus addressing God, found only in Mark, as the epicenter in the exposition of the theological significance of the idea of God's fatherhood. It has generated a lot of debate as to whether it is unique to Jesus or in line with Judaism. While several noted scholars notably G. Vermes and C.H. Charlesworth see nothing unique in this *Abba* expression of Jesus, yet along with several others, notably J.D.G Dunn, N.T. Wright and E. Schillebeeckx, we have established that there is something distinctive about this *Abba* expression. In our examination of the overall theological presentations of Mark, we have argued that Jesus' experience of Sonship to God and the kingdom activities of Markan Jesus are inseparably connected. The strong theological-christological focus of Mark has been highlighted by expounding several miracle-related pericope. Accordingly we have shown that the fatherhood of God in Mark is inseparably related with the miracles of Jesus. Whether it is nature miracles (e.g., 4:35-41; 6:45-51) or healing miracles (e.g., 1:21-28; 5:1-20), the displaying of the power of God is seen as the main focus of Mark, thus pointing to the strong theological-christological interest of Mark. The theological significance is seen in the fact that implicit in the deeds of Jesus demonstrates God's fatherhood, authority and compassion. This emphasis is heightened by a recurring pattern of Mark of the projection of the amazement on the part of the onlookers and crowds at the very end of the pericope (e.g., 1:27; 4:41; 5:20). Moreover, we have shown that for Mark God's rule is manifested in the very speech and action of Jesus. As Markan Jesus utters words of rebuke (e.g., 5:8; 4:39; 1:25), the nature is subdued (e.g., 4:39) or the demon is exorcised (e.g., 1:25; 5:8); this is how, for Mark, the rule of God or the fatherhood of God is very much at force in the very words and actions of Jesus. As such we have shown in Mark that Jesus' deeds of care and compassion as indicative of God's fatherhood.

Our exposition of the idea of God's fatherhood in Luke reveals that the strong filial relationship of God-Son in *Abba* expression of Mark is carried further in Luke in retaining the words of Jesus on mutual knowledge of the Father and the Son (Lk [Q]10:21-22). This fatherhood of God in exclusive sense is supported by a pericope unique to Luke (2:48-49), where Luke again depicted Jesus as one who is uniquely related to God as Son to the Father. Yet we have also shown that there is also a strong emphasis on the theocentric, so universal aspect of the fatherhood of God in Luke. In several instances of Luke, which is also found in Matthew, the author links the kingdom of God with the fatherhood of God (Lk 11:2; 12:22-32). The kingdom of God is seen as-Father's realm of love and care at the present. So a strong theocentric ethics is seen in the theology of Luke (Q). This is supported by Lukan emphasis on God's compassion and mercy. Both in Q (6:32-36) and Lukan special materials (10:30-37; 15:3-32) God's love, mercy and forgiveness is clearly highlighted. Even a parable unique to Luke about a loving father (15:3-32) can be seen in line with Lukan Jesus' teaching on imitating the compassionate Father (6:35-36). In the passion narrative, Luke highlights the universality of God's fatherhood by portraying God as an inclusive Father who shows compassion to all (23:32-43). Luke portrays Jesus as the Father's compassion in action. Thus in the portrayal of Luke God's fatherhood is fully revealed on the cross, in the death of God's Son.

Along with Matthew's Synoptic counterparts we have also examined the idea of God's fatherhood in Pauline writings, the earliest written documents in the New Testament. A very significant point we have examined in Paul's emphasis of God's fatherhood is that he stands with his fellow believers in Christ in referring to God as "our Father." This is the very notion of God's fatherhood that Paul talks about in Romans (8:16-17) and Galatians (4:6). However we have also highlighted the idea of the universality of God's fatherhood in Paul. As such we have shown the presence of the idea of God as Father of all creation (e.g., I Cor 8:6; Rom 1:19-21; Eph 2:11-18).

Thus we have shown that while their God-language and even so the theme of God's fatherhood may be rooted in the Old Testament and Jewish traditions, yet the idea of God's fatherhood portrayed in Mark, Luke and Paul seem to be equally rooted in the filial consciousness of Jesus with God. It is thus seen that while all of them give emphasis on the idea of God's fatherhood but on different aspects of God's fatherhood. While all of them have shown their focus on the relationship between Jesus and God as Son and Father, that is, fatherhood of God understood in the projection of Jesus' relationship to God as Son of the Father, but one aspect of Mark's projection of God's fatherhood is seen in Jesus' Sonship (Son of God) activities, in which the fatherhood of God is strongly implied. While in Luke the theme of the fatherhood of God is seen prominently in the discourse of Lukan Jesus, thereby projecting God as Father, whose care and concern is for all. As in the case of Paul, an exclusive or christological oriented fatherhood of God idea as well as the idea of the universality of God's fatherhood are seen.

In chapter four we have shown how the theme of God's fatherhood dominates or rather dictates the narratives and discourses of Matthew, thus showing the centrality of God in Matthean theology. Matthew's central emphasis on the fatherhood of God is indicated, as our data analysis have shown, by the occurrences of the term 'Father' for God, occurring more than Mark and Luke combined, that is, 44 times against 4 and 17 in Mark and Luke respectively. As our Synoptic parallel analysis have shown, not only that the occurrence are most in Matthean special material (M), but that he also added 'Father' to his sources Mark (20:23//Mk 10:40; 26:42//Mk 14:39) and Q (7:21//Lk 6:46; 18:14//Lk 15:7). Moreover, in some cases Matthew replaced 'God' with 'Father' in his sources Mark (12:50//Mk 3:35; 26:29//Mk 14:25) and Q (6:26//Lk 12:24; 10:29//Lk 12:6; 10:32//Lk 12:8; 10:33//Lk 12:9) thus exhibiting a particular fondness for 'Father' over other ways of referring to God. Not only these statistics but, as our analysis have shown, the theme of God's fatherhood recurs throughout Matthew's carefully arranged narratives and discourses, thus showing the centrality of God in Matthean theology. At the infancy narratives, Matthew has a unique pericope on divine intervention at Jesus' infancy, which projects his strong theocentric emphasis, with special focus on the fatherhood of God (also in line with Matthean unique Son of God idea). Quoting Hosea's theme of God-Israel filial relationship (Hos 11:1 "my son") Matthew brought to focus the activity of God, so the centrality of God in his theological discourse.

The emphasis on the theme of God's fatherhood is strong in Matthean Sermon on the Mount (5-7). It is only in Matthew that we see the description of the heavenly Father who "makes his sun rise on the evil and on the good, and sends rain on the righteous and on the unrighteous" (5:45). The fatherhood of God expressed in creation and nature is unique here in the New Testament. We have also shown that Matthean linking of God and sun are in the manner of Greek-Hellenistic tradition. That means it is Matthew who brought this idea in order to show that God is cosmic Father or God's fatherhood is for all universally.

The idea of all-seeing (6:4, 6[x2],18[x2]) and all-knowing Father (6:8, 32) in the Sermon on the Mount is again unique to Matthew in the whole of the New Testament. This too, in line with his emphasis on cosmic Father, has a strong influence from Greek philosophical discourse on all-seeing and all-knowing God. Just as the Greco-Roman god Zeus and Helios, the sun-god, God is for Matthew an all-seeing and all-knowing Father. This again heightens Matthew's cosmic (peace), universal, inclusive and so theocentric emphasis. Quite in line with this idea, Matthew has another unique pericope that talks about "peacemakers as sons of God" (5:9). This idea is again unique to Matthew among the New Testament writings and found only in Jewish-Hellenistic literature of Philo, who links peacemaking, nature and God together, thus projects a kind of organic unity of God-human-earth. This shows Matthew's Hellenistic influence. Matthew drew for the rich Greek-Hellenistic traditions and blended together with his Jewish traditions.

Apart from the Matthean Sermon discourse, other narratives and discourses also exhibit his central focus on God's fatherhood. So quite in line with his emphasis on God as a caring and attentive Father, a compassionate down-to-earth God is also seen in other parables of Matthean Jesus. In the parable of the lost sheep the very enigmatic expression of the "little ones' angels seeing God always" (18:10) project God as a compassionate God, in whose sight these little ones are special. This becomes clearer in the core parable of the lost sheep. The same emphasis on the justice, goodness, compassionate nature of God is also seen in other parabolic teachings of Matthean Jesus. The parables in 18:21-35 depicts God as God of mercy and God of justice while Matthew 20:1-16 also depicts the generous goodness of God. It is striking to see that this unique Matthean parable goes along well with earlier unique Matthean discourse on loving one's enemies (5:43-48) where Matthean Jesus is talking about a God who "makes his sun rise on the evil and on the good, and sends rain on the righteous and on the unrighteous" (5:45). Thus there is a very strong link between these two pericope for Matthew. The incredible mercy of God is central to both. Both have to do with the love of God. For Matthew God's grace is available to all equally and universally. For him God is generous. God is genuinely impartial. In this case God's fatherhood has universal and inclusive significance for Matthew. The passion narrative too has exceptional emphasis on the fatherhood of God. Matthew's passion narrative is profoundly theological stressing that Jesus is the all-knowing and all-powerful Son of God even in the midst of suffering and humiliation. Right at the account of the arrest of Jesus, Matthew demonstrates Jesus trusting in the protective care of his Father (26:53). Being the Son of the Father, he continues to exude peace and love of the Father even at the hour of his betrayal and arrest (26:52-56). Thus for Matthew the cross is the embodiment of Matthean Jesus' own teaching on God's love and peace. It is clear that the fatherhood of God is the overarching theological emphasis of Matthew.

In the fifth chapter we have shown how the theme of God's fatherhood plays pivotal role in Matthean theology and that various themes are closely connected with this theme including Christology and life-setting. We have thus shown how the socio-political realities and theological-philosophical climate surrounding Matthew help us understand the meaning and significance of God's fatherhood in Matthew. In the sixth chapter we have shown that the fatherhood of God idea so prominently and centrally placed in the Gospel of Matthew can be utilized for doing theology in a religiously pluralistic context of India.

7.2. The Meaning and Significance of God's Fatherhood in Matthew

As we have shown in our studies Matthew has several unique emphases on the theme of the fatherhood of God. And in these distinct nature and characteristics we will also see their functions and significance.

1. *The expression 'Heavenly Father' functions as anti-imperial expression.* At the very beginning we have asked a vital question: Why God as 'Father' attracted so much to Matthew? Our investigations lead us to conclude that Matthew's fascination with the theme of God's fatherhood, particularly the expression 'heavenly Father' or 'Father in heaven' which is seen mostly in Matthean redaction, has strong connection with social and political realities of the time. Showing much affinity with rabbinic Judaism, Matthew is ascribing 'Father' to God alone. So for Matthew, fatherhood of God idea in these instances serves as anti-type to Greco-Roman Emperor (*Pater Patriae*). In other words, the expression 'Father in heaven' is deliberately used by Matthew in the context of oppressive rule and dominance of Rome with the Emperor as Father. So the expression heavenly Father serves as a subversive strategy for Matthew and his community. As Matthew uses this

expression, it subverts earthly fatherhood (Imperial rule) and posits an alternative, true Father in heaven. So one of Matthew's meaning and usage of the fatherhood of God is to consolidate, legitimate and encourage his community that they are the true people of God. Matthew finds that solace in the heavenly Father.

2. *The theme of the fatherhood of God in Matthew is both particular and universal.* We have also asked further important question at the beginning: Is the idea of God's fatherhood in Matthew to do with disciples or with all universally? Whether or not the idea of God's fatherhood in Matthew reflect Jewish notion of God's fatherhood or Greco-Roman and Hellenistic fatherhood idea? Our investigations again lead us to conclude that it is both. As shown in our study above there are composite nature of God's fatherhood reflected in Matthew. The exclusive idea comes from Jesus and so Jewish tradition while the inclusive idea comes from Matthean Hellenistic environment. When it comes to the usage of God's fatherhood in the sense of exclusive Father/Son relationships, Matthew is following his source Mark, as we find the same strong emphasis in all the three Gospels (e.g., Mt 26:39; Mk 14:36; Lk 22:42). As regard to his emphasis on the idea of God's fatherhood in relation with the disciples, as is evident in the 'your Father'/ 'our Father' occurrences in the Sermon on the Mount, it is seen that Matthew shares the idea of God's fatherhood with Luke (thus Q), especially in relation to God's providence (e.g., Mt 6:6-13//Lk 11:2-4; Mt 6:24-33//Lk12:22-32; Mt 7:9-11//Lk 11:11-13).

However, strong theological-philosophical environment shaped Matthew's theme of God's fatherhood. This is clearly seen in a unique idea of universal or cosmic Father in 5:45, coupled with another unique Matthean expression in depicting God as all-seeing (6:4, 6, 18) and all-knowing Father (6:8, 32). It is only in Greek philosophical God-discourses that describes Zeus as cosmic Father. In the work of Greco-Roman writings Zeus is depicted as a weather-god (e.g., Marcus Aurelius 5.7). So also in a Hellenistic literature *Odes of Solomon* (11.13) Helios is depicted as the nourisher of life. Again the closest parallel to Matthew's idea of God as all-seeing and all-knowing Father is found in the ancient Greek religious discourse of Homer who describes the deity Helios, the sun-god as 'all-seeing eye' or 'eye of righteousness' (e.g., *Iliad* 3.104, 278; *Odyssey* 11.102). Matthew thus transferred the function of Zeus and Helios to the heavenly Father. In other words, Matthew incorporated the cosmic Father idea found in Greek literatures in his theology of God.

3. *In Matthew the fatherhood of God idea includes a strong maternal component.* This idea can help explain the notion of the fatherhood of God with motherly (caring and practical) traits in Matthew (5:45; 6:9-13, 24-33; 7:9-11). And this in turn helps us to respond to the feminist challenge, explaining that the fatherhood of God in Matthew is non-patriarchal, non-sexist in nature, as it has more to do with care, closeness and compassion. Just as in the Greek tradition, where both paternal and maternal traits are combined in the All-Father (e.g., Plato, *Timaeus*

28c), Matthew too projects in similar way, highlighting the fatherhood of God in close relation to earth and nature. As Matthew connects the heavenly Father with sun and rain (5:45) the idea of God's fatherhood is that of nourishment and sustenance of the earth. As Matthew projects God addressing in an inclusive manner 'Our Father' (6:9) the idea of God as universal Father is heightened. More so by the very mention of earth (6:10c) and bread (6:11) in the prayer makes the fatherhood of God idea more feminine and ecological. The prayer of Matthean Jesus embraces the whole of creation. It is again Matthean Jesus who talks about heavenly Father as provider of good things (7:11). The imagery is again of a parent – both father and mother, the nurturer of all life, with the equally strong motherly and fatherly nature, which offers a protective umbrella under which basic necessities of life are shared so that all the children may decently live.

4. *Quite in line with this idea of God as cosmic Father, Matthew also talks about cosmic sonship* (5:9). This idea is again unique to Matthew in the New Testament writings and found only in Jewish-Hellenistic literature of Philo, who talks about peacemaking as the criteria of kinship instead of blood relationship (*De Virtutibus* 195). Philo also talks about those who uphold goodness as children of God (*De Specialibus legibus* I.318). In Matthew, just as in Philo, there is a strong emphasis on the fatherhood of God as cosmic, as he links peacemaking, nature and God together. For him God's fatherhood is closely connected with earth. He projects a kind of organic unity of God-human-earth (5:45; 6:9-11; 7:9-11). This very idea of cosmic fatherhood has again a strong Hellenistic influence. As Matthew reinterprets the teaching of Jesus, he draws from the rich Greek and Hellenistic traditions and thus blended together with his Jewish traditions.

7.3. The Meaning and Significance of God's Fatherhood in the Synoptic Gospels

Jesus' unique relationship with God as the Son of the Father: A strong Father-Son correlation or rather a strong filial relationship between God as Father and Jesus as Son is portrayed by all the Synoptic writers. It is seen that all three Synoptic writers recorded Jesus addressing God as Father in prayer (Mk 14:36//Mt 26:39// Lk 22:42). This is supplemented by the fact that in all three of them we see the occurrences of the term ἀγαπητός referring to Jesus. When Jesus was baptized there was a voice from heaven that greeted him as "my Son, the Beloved" (Mk 1:11//Mt 3:17//Lk 3:22), an experience repeated at the Transfiguration episode (Mk 9:7//Mt 17:5 //Lk 9:35), and it occurs again in a parable which surely speaks about God's beloved Son (Mk 12:6//Mt 21:37//Lk 20:13). So also in a discourse on discipleship found in all the Synoptic Gospels we see the occurrences of Jesus claiming God as his Father (Mk 8:38//Mt 16:27//Lk 9:26).

Fatherhood of God and Prayers: In all the Synoptic Gospels we see Jesus affirming God as Father in difficult times. This helps us to understand that, for Synoptic writers, God is an ever-present prayer answering Father (Mk 14:36//Mt

26:39//Lk 22:42). The idea of a forgiving Father is also seen in all the Synoptic Gospels. In the depiction of all the Synoptic Evangelists, God as Father relates reciprocally to other in forgiveness (Mk 11:25//Mt 6:9-15//Lk 11:2-4). Quite in line with the forgiving Father idea is the notion of a loving and compassionate Father seen in all three of them. All the Synoptic writers project God's love being revealed ultimately in the death of Jesus (Mk 15:22-37//Mt 27:33-50// Lk 23:33-46).

7.4. The Centrality of God's Fatherhood in Matthew – A Reorientation in New Testament Theology

As we have shown in our study that the focus on God has always been a vibrant aspect of New Testament theology particularly in the late 1970s and onward. In our assessment of the several New Testament theology works post Bultmann's work we have highlighted the shift in focus from Christocentric to theocentric in the 1990s and onward. We have argued that in most of the central categories identified by scholars in their New Testament theology works, e.g., Christology, Kingdom of God, God is the subject, the doer of the action, so God's fatherhood is clearly understood. Yet the theme of the fatherhood of God has not been pointed out as a specific subject of research. We conclude from our study that the theocentric nature of New Testament theology can be explained more precisely with the motif of the fatherhood of God. This broad focus and perspective is substantiated by our specific argument on the theme of the fatherhood of God as the key theme or the hub of Matthean theology. In this regard we have argued that Christology does not erase God (theology) in Matthew. Rather, it is seen that when Matthew discussed about the sonship of Jesus (Christology) the fatherhood of God appears prominently. In all the christological terms that Matthew employs, whether it is 'Emmanuel' (1:23 cf. 2:15) or 'Son of God' (14:33; 16:16; 26:63; 27:40, 43), Jesus' significance is always articulated with reference to God. Again the fatherhood of God theme holds the key to understand the life situation of Matthew and his community (*Sitz im leben*); while the theme of the kingdom of God too is inseparably related to the theme of the fatherhood of God. Both the term 'Lord' or 'King' occur in Matthew in close connection with the theme of the fatherhood of God (e.g., 6:9-10, 32-33; 7:21; 13:43; 25:34).

7.5. Fatherhood of God in Matthew: A Unifying and Vivifying Factor in a Religiously Pluralistic Context of India

We have also shown in our study that the theocentric thinking or focus on one God has always been a lively features of theologizing, doing mission and Christian witness in multi-faith context of India. In our examination of the various religious traditions we have shown that, like Matthew and the Synoptic Gospels, Indian religious traditions too have a strong interest in the Father concept of God. The invocation of God as Father in prayer is quite at home in Indian religious traditions. Apart from the invocations and prayers, Indian religious traditions too have the idea of God as cosmic Father in the Vedic traditions, the understanding of God as both *nirguna* and *saguna* in the Advaitic traditions of the Upanishads, the idea of God as Father in the Bhagavad Gita and the emphasis on God's love in the later Bhakti traditions. All these reveal that the religious inclination or devotion to one God or theocentric emphasis is deeply ingrained in Indian thinking. Even Islam, which has strong adherents in Indian sub-continent, has strong emphasis on the unity of God, where fatherhood of God idea is implicit. So also in the tribal religious traditions, especially of the Ao Nagas, we have shown that implicit in the belief in the Supreme transcendent God, *Lungkitsungba*, and the immanent God *Lijaba*, the idea of the fatherhood of God is clear. Particularly the organic relationship of God and earth in *Lijaba* is a strong pointer towards the eco-feminine aspect of God, so fatherhood idea in Ao Naga religion. The significance of the idea of God's fatherhood in Matthew for Ao Naga religion is thus shown. Moreover, by pointing to the theocentric focus in the diverse religious traditions of India, we have highlighted that this God-centered Matthean theology is the right place to relate with and doing theology from Indian perspective.

Our argument in this perspective is further substantiated by examining some of the prominent theologians and secular thinkers who are proponents of religious pluralism, namely, S.J. Samartha, R. Panikkar, Mahatma Gandhi and S. Radhakrishnan. Having explored these thinkers and theologians we have established that our idea of the fatherhood of God and theocentrism are inseparably connected. The fatherhood of God idea is evident in the very discourse of the one God. Thus holding on to the idea of one God and so the fatherhood of God theme can be carried forward in Indian Christian thinking, theology and mission. The theme of the fatherhood of God needs to give its due place and attention. It is the need of the time to regain and reaffirm the fatherhood of God, a theme that is so strongly and centrally emphasized in Matthew, in inter-faith dialogue and mission in the context of terrorism, growing religious intolerance and extremism, economic exploitation, ecological crisis, social discrimination for a peaceful and harmonious society, and to coexist as common humanity.

Bibliography

Ancient Texts and Translations

The Ancient Near East: Supplementary Texts and Pictures Relating to the Old Testament. Edited by James B. Pritchard. Princeton: Princeton University Press, 1969.

The Ancient Near Eastern Texts relating to the Old Testament. Edited by James B. Pritchard. 3rd Edition. Princeton: Princeton University Press, 1955.

The Apocrypha and Pseudepigrapha of the Old Testament in English. Edited by R. H. Charles. 2 vols. Oxford: Clarendon Press, 1969.

Aristotle. *Nicomachean Ethics.* Translated by H. Rackham. Cambridge; Mass: Harvard University Press, 1926.

________. *Oeconomica and Magna Moralia.* Translated by G. Cyril Armstrong. Cambridge; Mass: Harvard University Press, 1935.

The Bhagavad Gita. Translated by Mohini M. Chatterji. New York: Causeway Books, 1960.

The Dead Sea Scrolls in English. Translated by G. Vermes. 4th Edition. London: Penguin Books, 1995.

The Dead Sea Scroll. Translated by F.G. Martinez and Eibert J.C. Tigchelaar. 2 vols. Leiden: Brill, 2000.

Diogenes Laertius. *Lives of Eminent Philosophers.* 2 vols. Translated by R. D. Hicks. Cambridge; Mass: Harvard University Press, 1925.

Epictetus. *The Discourses as Reported by Arrian, The Manual and Fragments.* Translated by W.A. Oldfather. 2 vols. Cambridge; Mass: Harvard University Press, 1925-1928.

Greek New Testament. 4th Revised Edition. Edited by Barbara Aland, Kurt Aland, Bruce M. Metzger, et al. Stuttgart: Biblia-Druck, 1994.

The Holy Bible containing Old and New Testaments with the Apocryphal / Deuterocanonical Books. NRSV. Nashville: Thomas Nelson, 1989.

The Holy Bible. New Revised Standard Version. Michigan: Zondervan Bible Publishers, 1990.

Homer. *The Iliad.* Translated by E.V. Rieu. Great Britain: Penguin Books, 1950.

_______. *The Odyssey*. Translated by E.V. Rieu. Great Britain: Penguin Books, 1946.

Josephus: The Complete Works. Translated by W. Whiston. Nashville: Thomas Nelson Publishers, 1998.

Marcus Aurelius Antoninus. *Emperor of Rome*. Translated by C.R. Haines. Cambridge; Mass: Harvard University Press, 1916.

The Mishnah. Translated by H. Danby. London: Oxford University Press, 1933.

The Old Testament Pseudepigrapha. Edited by J.H. Charlesworth. 2 vols. New York: Doubleday, 1983-1985.

Philo. Translated by F.H. Colson and G.H. Whitaker. 12 vols. Cambridge; Mass: Harvard University Press, 1929-62.

Plato. *Charmides, Alcibiates I and II, Hipparchus, the Lovers, Theages, Minos, Epinomis*. Translated by W. R. M. Lamb. Cambridge; Mass: Harvard University Press, 1979.

_______. *Critias, Cleitophon, Menexenus, Epistles*. Translated by R.G. Bury. Cambridge; Mass: Harvard University Press, 1929.

_______. *Laws*. 2 vols. Translated by R.G. Bury. Cambridge; Mass: Harvard University Press, 1926.

_______. *Timaeus, Critias, Cleitophon, Menexenus Epistles*. Translated by R. G. Bury. Cambridge; Mass: Harvard University Press, 1929.

The Principal Upanishads. Translated by S. Radhakrishnan. London: George Allen & Unwin Ltd, 1953.

Plutarch. *Moralia*. Translated by Frank C. Babbitt. 15 vols. Cambridge; Mass: Harvard University Press, 1927-1969.

_______. *Lives*. Translated by B. Perrin. 11 vols. Cambridge; Mass: Harvard University Press, 1914-1926.

Quran: A Contemporary Translation by Ahmed Ali. Princeton; New Jersey: Princeton University Press, 1984.

Res Gestae Divi Augusti. In *Roman Civilization: Sourcebook II: The Empire*. Edited by N. Lewis and M. Reinhold. New York: Harper & Row, 1966.

Rg-Veda Samhita I. Translated by M.N. Dutt. Delhi: Parimal Publications, 1986.

Seneca. *Ad Lucilium Epistulae Morales*. Translated by Richared M. Gummere. 3 vols. Cambridge; Mass: Harvard University Press, 1917-1925.

_______. *Moral Essays*. Translated by John W. Basore. 3 vols. Cambridge; Mass: Harvard University Press, 1928-1935.

Shukla Yajur Veda Samhita. Translated by Swami Yatiswarananda. Chennai: Sri Ramakrishna Math, 2001.

Suetonius. *The Twelve Caesars*. Translated by Robert Graves. Great Britain: Penguin Books, 1957.

Reference Works

Bauer, W., Arndt, W.F., Gingrich, F.W., and Danker, T.W. (ed.). *A Greek-English Lexicon of the New Testament*. Chicago: Chicago University Press, 1979.

Blass, F. and a. Debrunner. *A Greek Grammar of the New Testament and Other Early Christian Literature*. Edited by Robert W. Funk. Chicago: The University of Chicago Press, 1961.

Gospels Parallels: A Synopsis of the First Three Gospels. 4th Revised edition. Edited by Burton H. Throckmorton. Bangalore: TPI, 1998.

Greek-English Edition of the Synopsis Quattuor Evangeliorum with the Text of the Revised Standard Version. Edited by Kurt Aland. Stuttgart: Wurttembergische Biblelanstalt, 1964.

Kohlenberger III, J. R. and J. A. Swanson (ed.). *The Hebrew-English Concordance to the Old Testament*. Grand Rapids: Zondervan, 1998.

________., E.W. Goodrick and J.A. Swanson. *The Exhaustive Concordance to the Greek New Testament*. Grand Rapids: Zondervan Publishing House, 1995.

Liddell, Henry George and Robert Scott. *A Greek-English Lexicon*. 2 vols. Oxford: Clarendon Press, 1925-1940.

McReynolds, P. R. *Word Study Greek-English New Testament with Complete Concordance*. Wheaton, Ill: Tyndale House, 1998.

Spicq, Ceslar. *Theological Lexicon of the New Testament*. Translated and edited by James D. Ernest. Vol 1-3. Peabody; Hendrickson Publishers, 1996.

Trenchard, W.C. *A Concise Dictionary of New Testament Greek*. Cambridge: Cambridge University Press, 2003.

Random House Unabridged Dictionary. Second Edition. New York: Random House, 1993.

Monographs and Commentaries

Albright, W.F. and C.S. Mann. *Matthew: Introduction, Translation and Notes*. The Anchor Bible. New York: Doubleday & Company, 1971.

Allison, D.C. *The New Moses: A Matthean Typology*. Minneapolis: Fortress Press, 1993.

________. *The Sermon on the Mount: Inspiring the Moral Imagination*. New York: Crossroad, 1999.

Ao, L. Kijung. *Nokinketer Mongchen*. Gauhati: Christian Literature Centre, 1972.

Ao, O. Alem. *Tsungremology: Ao Naga Christian Theology*. Mokokchung: CTC, 1994.

Appasamy, A.J, *Christianity as Bhakti Marga*. Madras: Christian Literature Society, 1926.

_______. *Temple Bells: Readings from Hindu Religious Literature*. Calcutta: Association Press, 1930.

_______. *The Johannine Doctrine of Life? A Study of Christian and Indian Thought*. London: SPCK, 1934.

_______. *The Gospel and India's Heritage*. London: SPCK, 1942.

Argyle, A.W. *The Gospel According to Matthew*. Cambridge: Cambridge University Press, 1963.

_______. *God in the New Testament*. London: Hodder & Stoughton, 1965.

Aune, D.E. (ed.). *The Gospel of Matthew In Current Study: Studies In Memory of William G. Thompson, S.J.* Grand Rapids, Michigan: Wm B. Eerdmans, 2001.

Bacon, B.W. *Studies in Matthew*. New York: Hort, 1930.

Bald, H. "Eschatological or Theocentric Ethics? Notes on the Relationship between Eschatology and Ethics in Jesus' Preaching." In *The Kingdom of God*. Edited by Bruce Chilton. London: SPCK, 1984, 133-153.

Baillie, D.M. *God was in Christ: An Essay on Incarnation and Atonement*. London: Faber and Faber Limited, 1948.

Balla, G. *The Four Centuries Between the Testaments*. Vallejo; CA: Bibal Press, 1993.

Barclay, W. *The Mind of Jesus*. London: SCM Press, 1960.

Barr, J. *The Concept of Biblical Theology: An Old Testament Perspective*. Minneapolis: Fortress Press, 1999.

Bartlett, J.R. *Jews in the Hellenistic World: Josephus, Aristeas, The Sibylline Oracles, Eupolemus*. Cambridge: Cambridge University Press, 1985.

Bauckham, R. *Jesus and the God of Israel: God Crucified and Other Studies on the New Testament's Christology of Divine Identity*. Grand Rapids: Wm B. Eerdmans, 2008.

Bendangangshi, I. and I.T. Apok Aier, *The Religion of the Ao Nagas*. Guwahati: Sariaghat Press, 1990.

Bhattacharji, S. *The Indian Theogony: A Comparative Study of Indian Mythology from the Vedas to the Puranas*. Cambridge: Cambridge University Press, 1970.

Best, E. *Mark: The Gospel as Story*. Edinburgh: T&T Clark, 1983.

Betz, H.D. *Essays on the Sermon on the Mount*. Philadelphia: Fortress, 1985.

_______. *The Sermon on the Mount.* Hermenia; Minneapolis: Fortress Press, 1995.

Birnbaum, P. *Daily Prayer Book*. New York: 1977.

Betz, O. *What do we know about Jesus?* London: SCM Press, 1968.

Borg, M.J. *Jesus: Uncovering the Life, Teachings, and Relevance of a Religious Revolutionary*. New York: Harper Collins Publishers, 2006.

Bornkamm, G. "The Stilling of the Storm in Mathew." In G. Bornkamm, G. Barth, H. J. Held, *Tradition and Interpretation in Matthew*. London: SCM Press, 1963, 52-57.

Bouyer, L. *The Invisible Father: Approaches to the Mystery of the Divinity*. Edinburgh: T&T Clark, 1999.

Boyd, Robin. *An Introduction to Indian Christian Theology*. Delhi: ISPCK, 1969.

Brown, R.E. "The Pater Noster as an Eschatological Prayer." In R.E. Brown, *New Testament Essays*. Milwaukee: Bruce Publishing Company, 1965, 217-253.

_______. *The Birth of the Messiah: A Commentary on the Infancy Narratives in the Gospels of Matthew and Luke*. New York: Doubleday, 1993.

_______. *The Death of the Messiah: From Gethsemane to the Grave: A Commentary on the Passion Narratives in the Four Gospels*. London: Chapman, 1994.

Bruce, A.B. "The Synoptic Gospels." In *The Expositor's Greek Testament* vol I. Edited by W. Robertson Nicoll. New York: George H. Horan, 1912, 36-43, 61-340.

Brueggemann, W., George W. Stroup (eds). *Many Voices One God: Being Faithful in a Pluralistic World*. Louisville; Westminster John Knox Press, 1998.

Bultmann, R. *Theology of the New Testament*. 2 vols. Trans Kendrick Grobel. New York: Charles Scribner's Sons, 1954-1955.

_______. *Jesus and the Word*. Translated by Louise Pettibone Smith and Erminie Huntress Lantero. New York: Scribner, 1958.

_______. *History of Synoptic Tradition*. New York: Harper and Row, 1976.

Burkett, D. *An Introduction to the New Testament and the Origins of Christianity*. Cambridge: Cambridge University Press, 2002.

Caird, G.B. *New Testament Theology*. Completed and edited by L.D. Hurst. Oxford: Clarendon, 1994.

Carr, Anne., Elisabeth Schussler Fiorenza (ed.). *Motherhood: Experience, Institution, Theology*. Edinburgh: T&T Clark, 1989.

Carter, W. *Matthew and the Empire: Initial Explorations*. Harrisburg: Trinity Press International, 2001.

_______. "Matthean Christology in Roman Imperial Key: Matthew 1.1." In *The Gospel of Matthew In Its Roman Imperial Context*. Edited by John K. Riches and David C. Sim. London: T&T Clark, 2005, 143-165.

_______. *Mathew and the Margins: A Sociopolitical and Religious Reading*. New Delhi: Theological Publications of India, 2007.

Catchpole, D.R. *The Quest for Q*. Edinburgh: T&T Clark, 1993.

Chakkarai, V. and A.J. Appasamy, *Jesus the Avatar*. Madras: Christian Literature Society, 1926.

Charlesworth, J. H. *The Old Testament Pseudepigrapha and the New Testament.* Cambridge: Cambridge University Press, 1985.

_______. *Jesus Within Judaism: New Light from Exciting Archaeological Discoveries*. London: SPCK, 1990.

Charlesworth, M.P. *The Roman Empire*. London: Oxford University Press, 1961.

Chatterjee, M. *The Religious Spectrum: Studies in An Indian Context.* New Delhi: Allied Publishers Private Ltd., 1984.

Chen, Diane G. *God as Father in Luke-Acts*. SBL 92. Bern/Frankfurt: Peter Lang, 2006.

Childs, B. *Biblical Theology of the Old and New Testaments: Theological Reflection on the Christian Bible*. London: SCM Press Ltd., 1992.

Chilton, B. "God as 'Father' in the Targumim, in Non-Canonical Literatures of Early Judaism and Primitive Christianity, and in Matthew." In *The Pseudepigrapha and Early Biblical Interpretation*. Edited by J.H. Charlesworth and C.A. Evans. Sheffield: JSOT Press, 1993, 151-169.

Cohen, A. *Everyman's Talmud.* London: J.M. Dent & Sons Ltd., 1961.

Collins, J.J. *The Sibylline Oracles of Egyptian Judaism*. SBL Dissertation Series 13. Missoula: Montana University Press, 1972.

Conzelmann, H. *An Outline of the Theology of the New Testament.* New York: Harpers & Row, 1969.

_______. *Jesus*. Philadelphia: Fortress Press, 1973.

Cooper, John W. *Our Father in Heaven: Christian Faith and Inclusive Language for God.* Grand Rapids; Michigan: Baker Books, 1998.

Cragg, Kenneth. *Alive to God: Muslim and Christian Prayer*. London: Oxford University Press, 1970.

Crosby, Michael H. *Thy Will be Done: Praying the Our Father as Subversive Activity*. Maryknoll: Orbis Books, 1977.

Crossan. J.D. *God and Empire: Jesus Against Rome, Then and Now*. New York: Harper One, 2007.

_______. *The Greatest Prayer: Rediscovering the Revolutionary Message of the Lord's Prayer*. London: SPCK, 2011.

Cullmann, O. *Prayer in the New Testament*. London: SCM Press, 1995.

Dalman, G. *The Words of Jesus*. Edinburgh: T&T Clark, 1909.

Daly, M. *Beyond God the Father: Toward a Philosophy of Women's Liberation*. Boston: Beacon, 1973.

Daniel, P.S., David C. Scott, G.R. Singh (eds.). *Religious Traditions of India*. Serampore: Indian Theological Library, 1988.

Danielou, Alan. *Hindu Polytheism*. London: Routledge & Kegan Paul, 1964.

Das, A. Andrew and F. J. Matera (ed.). *The Forgotten God: Perspectives in Biblical Theology*. Louisville: Westminster John Knox Press, 2002.

Davies, W.D. *The Setting of the Sermon on the Mount.* Cambridge: Cambridge University Press, 1966.

Davies, W.D., D.C. Allison. *The Gospel according to St. Matthew*. ICC. 3 vols. Edinburgh: T&T Clark, 1987-1991.

De Boer, P. A. H. *Fatherhood and Motherhood in Israelite and Judean Piety*. Leiden: E.J. Brill, 1974.

De Jonge, Marinus. *God's Final Envoy: Early Christology and Jesus' Own View of His Mission*. Grand Rapids; Michigan: William B. Eerdmans, 1998.

Dehlvi, Sadia. *Sufism: The Heart of Islam*. Noida: Harper Collins Publishers India, 2010.

Dodd, C.H. *The Parables of the Kingdom*. London: Nisbet, 1936.

Donaldson, T.L. *Jesus on the Mountain: A Study of Matthean Theology*. JSNT Supplement 8; Sheffield: JSOT Press, 1985.

Dunn, J.D.G. *Jesus and the Spirit: A Study of the Religious and Charismatic Experience of Jesus and the First Christians as Reflected in the New Testament*. Philadelphia: Westminster Press, 1975.

_______. *Unity and Diversity in the New Testament: An Inquiry into the Character of Earliest Christianity*. London: SCM Press, 1977.

_______. *The Christ and the Spirit I: Christology*. Grand Rapids; Michigan: Wm. B. Eerdmans, 1998.

_______. *The Theology of Paul the Apostle*. Grand Rapids: Wm B Eerdmans, 2006.

_______. and J. W. Rogerson (eds.). *The Eerdmans Commentary of the Bible*. Grand Rapids: Eerdmans, 2003.

_______. *New Testament Theology: An Introduction*. Nashville: Abingdon Press, 2009.

Eichrodt, W. *Theology of the Old Testament* I. Trans. J.A. Baker. Philadelphia: Westminster Press, 1961.

_________. *Theology of the Old Testament* II. Trans. J.A. Baker; London: SCM Press, 1967.

Engnell, I. *Studies in Divine Kingship in the Ancient Near East*. Oxford: Blackwell, 1967.

Evans, C.A. *Ancient Texts for New Testament Studies: A Guide to the Background Literature*. Peabody: Hendrickson Publishers, 2005.

_________. *Matthew*. NCBC. New York: Cambridge University Press, 2012.

Esler, Philip F. "Rome in Apocalyptic and Rabbinic Literature." In *The Gospel of Matthew In Its Roman Imperial Context*. Edited by J.K. Riches and Davis C. Sim. London: T&T Clark, 2005, 9-33.

_______. *New Testament Theology: Communion and Community*. Minneapolis: Fortress Press, 2005.

Fiorenza, E.S. *In Memory of Her: A Feminist Theological Reconstruction of Christian Origins*. New York: Crossroad, 1983.

Fitzmer, J.A. *The Gospel according to Luke X-XXIV.* AB28a; New York: Doubleday, 1985.

Fowler, R.M. *Loaves and Loaves.* California: Scholars Press, 1981.

France, R.T. *Matthew - Evangelist and Teacher.* Exeter: The Paternoster Press, 1989.

_______. *The Gospel of Mark.* NIGTC. Grand Rapids: Wm B Eerdmans, 2002.

Fuller, R.H. *A Critical Introduction to the New Testament.* Letchworth: The Garden City Press, 1971.

Gandhi, Mahatma. *The Collected Works of Mahatma Gandhi.* Vols 1-100. Ahmedabad: Navajivan Trust, 1958-1994.

Geffre, Claude. "'Father' as the Proper Name of God." In *God as Father?* Edited by Johannes-Baptist Metz and Edward Schillebeecks. New York: T & T Clark, 1981, 43-50.

Goppelt, L. *Theology of the New Testament I: The Ministry of Jesus In Its Theological Significance.* Translated by John E. Alsup and edited by Jurgen Roloff. Grand Rapids: William B. Eerdmans, 1981.

_______. *Theology of the New Testament II: The Variety and Unity of the Apostolic Witness to Christ.* Translated by John E. Alsup and edited by Jurgen Roloff. Grand Rapids: William B. Eerdmans, 1982.

Gort, Jerald., Hendrik Vroom, Rein Fernhout, et al. *Dialogue and Syncretism: An Interdisciplinary Approach.* Grand Rapids; Michigan: Wm B Eerdmans1989.

Gosh, B.B. *Nagaland District Gazetteers: Mokokchung District.* Dimapur: Sethi Press, 1979.

Goulder, M.D. *Midrash and Lection in Matthew.* London: SPCK, 1974.

Grant, F.C. *Hellenistic Religions: The Age of Syncretism.* New York: The Bobbs-Merrill Company, 1953.

Grant, R.M. *The Early Christian Doctrine of God.* Charlottesville: University Press of Virginia, 1966.

_______. *Gods and the One God: Christian Theology in the Greco-Roman World.* London: SPCK, 1986.

Grentz, E. "God in the New Testament." In *Our Naming of God.* Edited by Carl E. Braaten. Minneapolis: Fortress, 1989, 75-90.

Guelich, R.A. *The Sermon on the Mount: A Foundation for Understanding.* Waco: Word Books, 1982.

Gundry, R.H. *The Use of Old Testament in St. Matthew's Gospel.* Leiden: Brill, 1967.

_______. *A Commentary on His Literary and Theological Art.* Grand Rapids: Eerdmans, 1982.

Guthrie, D. *New Testament Theology.* London: Inter-Varsity Press, 1981.

Hafemann, Scott J. "The Covenant Relationship." In *Central Themes in Biblical Theology: Mapping Unity in Diversity*. Edited by Scott J. Hafemann and Paul R. House. Grand Rapids: Baker Academic, 2007, 20-65.

Hagner, D.A. *Matthew 1-13, 14-28.* Word Biblical Commentary; Texas: Word Books, 1993, 1995.

Hamerton-Kelly, R. *God the Father: Theology and Patriarchy in the Teaching of Jesus*. Philadelphia: Fortress Press, 1979.

_______."God the Father in the Bible and in the Experience of Jesus: The State of the Question." In *God as Father?* Edited by Johannes-Baptist Metz and Edward Schillebeecks. New York: T & T Clark, 1981, 95-102.

Hampson, D. *Theology and Feminism*. Oxford: Basil Blackwell, 1990.

Hannan, M. *The Nature and Demands of the Sovereign Rule of God in the Gospel of Matthew*. New York: T & T Clark, 2006.

Hare, D.R.A. *Matthew Interpretation: A Biblical Commentary for Teaching and Preaching*. Louisville: John Knox Press, 1993.

Hare, D.A. *Mark*. Louisville: Westminster John Knox Press, 1996.

Harnish, W. "The Metaphorical Process in Matthew 20:1-15." In *SBL Seminar Papers 1977*. Edited by P.J. Achtemeier. Missoula, MT: Scholars Press, 1977, 241-42.

Harris, Erdman. *God's Image and Man's Imagination*. New York: Charles Scribner's Sons, 1959.

Harris, Murray J. *Jesus as God: The New Testament Use of Theos in Reference to Jesus*. Grand Rapids; Michigan: Baker Book House, 1992.

Hasel, G. *New Testament Theology: Basic Issues in the Current Debate*. Grand Rapids: Wm B. Eerdmans, 1987.

Hendricks, H. *The Miracle Stories of the Synoptic Gospels*. San Francisco: Harper and Row, 1987.

Heinemann, J. *Prayer in the Talmud: Forms and Patterns*. Berlin: de Gruyter, 1977.

Hengel, M. *Judaism and Hellenism: Studies in their Encounter in Palestine during the Early Hellenistic Period*. Philadelphia: Fortress, 1974.

_______. *The Son of God*. Philadelphia: Fortress Press, 1976.

_______. *The Hellenization of Judea in the First Century after Christ*. London: SCM Press, 1989.

Herbert-Brown, Geraldine. *Ovid and The Fasti: A Historical Study*. Oxford: Clarendon Press, 1994.

Hick, John. *God Has Many Names*. Philadelphia: Westminster Press, 1982.

_______. and Paul F. Knitter. *The Myth of Christian Uniqueness*. London: SCM Press, 1987.

_______. and Lamont C. Hempel (ed.). *Gandhi's Significance for Today*. London: Macmillan, 1989.

_______. *The Rainbow of Faiths*. London: SCM Press, 1995.

Hill, D. *The Gospel of Matthew*. London: Oliphants, 1972.

Horsley, R.A. (ed.). *In The Shadow of Empire: Reclaiming the Bible as a History of Faithful Resistance*. Louisville: Westminster John Knox Press, 2008.

Howell, D. *Matthew's Inclusive Story: A Study in the Narrative Rhetoric of the First Gospel*. JSNT Supplement Series 42; Sheffield: Sheffield Academic Press, 1990.

Hultgren, A.J. "The Bread Petition of the Lord's Prayer." In *Christ and His Communities: Essays in Honor of Rignald H. Fuller*. Edited by A.J. Hultgren and Barbara Hall. Cincinnati: Forward Movement, 1990, 41-54.

Hultgren, A.J. *The Parables of Jesus: A Commentary*. Grand Rapids: Eerdmans: 2002.

Hurtado, L.W. *How on Earth Did Jesus Become a God: Historical Questions about Earliest Devotion to Jesus*. Grand Rapids; Michigan: Wm B. Eerdmans, 2005.

_______. *God in New Testament Theology*. Nashville: Abingdon Press, 2010.

Hus, Alain. *Greek and Roman Religion*. Translated by S. J. Tester. New York: Hawthorn Books, 1962.

Jack, Homer A. (ed.). *World Religions and World Peace: The International Inter-Religious Symposium on Peace*. Boston: Beacon Press, 1968.

Jaeger, W. *The Theology of the Early Greek Philosophers*. Oxford: Clarendon Press, 1947.

James, E.O. *The Concept of Deity: A Comparative and Historical Study*. London: Hutchinson House, 1950.

_______. *The Cult of the Mother-Goddess, An Archaeological and Documentary Study*. London: Thames and Hudson, 1959.

_______. *The Worship of the Sky-God: A Comparative Study in Semitic and Indo-European Religion*. London: Athlone Press, 1963.

Jeremias, J. *The Eucharistic Words of Jesus*. Translated by N. Perrin. London: SCM Press, 1966.

_______. *The Prayer of Jesus*. London: SCM Press, 1967.

_______. *New Testament Theology* I. London: SCM Press, 1971.

_______. *Jesus and the Message of the New Testament*. Edited by K.C. Hanson. Minneapolis: Fortress Press, 2002.

Johnson, Elizabeth A. *Consider Jesus: Waves of Renewal in Christology*. New York: Crossroad, 1994.

_______. *She Who Is: The Mystery of God in Feminist Theological Discourse*. New York: Crossroad, 1995.

Joseph, M.J. *The Eco-Vision of the Earth Community: Biblical and Theological Perspectives*. Bangalore: BTESSC/SATHRI, 2008.

Kaiser, O. *The Old Testament Apocrypha: An Introduction*. Peabody: Hendrickson Publishers, 2004.

Karkkainen, Veli-Matti. *An Introduction to the Theology of Religions: Biblical, Historical & Contemporary Perspectives*. Illinois: Intervarsity Press, 2003.

Kaufman. G. D. *God the Problem*. Cambridge; MA: Harvard University Press, 1973.

________. *God, Mystery, Diversity: Christian Theology in a Pluralistic World*. Minneapolis: Fortress Press, 1996.

Kaufman, W. *Religions in Four Dimensions: Existential, Aesthetic, Historical, Comparative*. New York: Reader's Digest Press, 1976.

Kawlni, R. C. *Lord God Most High My Savior: Theocentricity in Lukan Theology: An Exploration into the Portrayals of God in Luke-Acts*. Delhi: ISPCK, 2009.

Keel, O. and C. Uehlinger. *Gods, Goddess, and Images of God In Ancient Israel*. Edinburgh: T&T Clark, 1998.

Keener, C. S. *A Commentary on the Gospel of Matthew*. Grand Rapids: WmB Eerdmans, 1999.

Kilpatrick, G. D. *The Origins of the Gospel According to St. Matthew*. Oxford: Clarendon, 1946.

Kingsbury, J.D. *Matthew: Structure, Christology, Kingdom*. Philadelphia: Fortress Press, 1975.

________. *Jesus Christ in Matthew, Mark, and Luke: The New Testament Witness for Preaching*. Philadelphia: Fortress, 1981.

________. *The Christology of Mark's Gospel*. Philadelphia: Fortress, 1983.

________. *Matthew As Story*. Philadelphia: Fortress Press, 1988.

Klostermaier, Klaus K. *A Survey of Hinduism*. Third Edition; New York: State University of New York Press, 2007.

Koester, H. *Introduction to the New Testament: History, Culture, and Religion of the Hellenistic Age*. 2 vols. New York: Philadelphia, 1982.

Kummel, W.G. *The Theology of the New Testament*. London: SCM Press, 1974.

Lacey, W.K. "Patria Potestas." In *The Family in Ancient Rome: New Perspectives*. Edited by B. Rawson. London: Routledge, 1992, 121-144.

Ladd, G.E. *A Theology of the New Testament*. London: Lutterworth Press, 1974.

________. *The Presence of the Future: The Eschatology of Biblical Realism*. Grand Rapids; Michigan: Wm B. Eerdmans, 1996.

Layton, Bentley. *The Gnostic Scriptures: A New Translation with Annotations and Introduction*. New York: Doubleday, 1987.

Lerner, Gerda. *The Creation of Patriarchy*. New York: Cambridge University Press, 1986.

Lewis, Alan. E (ed.). *The Motherhood of God*. Edinburgh: The Saint Andrew Press, 1984.

Lincoln, Andrew T. and A.J.M. Wedderburn. *The Theology of the Later Pauline Letters*. Cambridge: Cambridge University Press, 1993.

Lohmeyer, E. *The Lord's Prayer*. London: Collins, 1965.

Longchar, Wati. *The Traditional Tribal Worldview and Modernity*. Jorhat: Eastern Theological College, 1995.

_______. "Myth: A Source for Conceptualizing Tribal Theology." In *An Exploration of Tribal Theology*. Jorhat: Eastern Theological College, 1997, 78-95.

_______. *Returning to Mother Earth: Theology, Christian Witness and Theological Education – An Indigenous Perspective*. Kolkata: PTCA, 2012.

Luz, U. *Matthew 1-7: A Commentary*. Translated by W. Linss. Minneapolis: Augsburg, 1989.

_______. *The Theology of Matthew*. Cambridge: Cambridge University Press, 1995.

_______. *Matthew 8-20*. Translated by J.E. Couch. Hermenia Series; Minneapolis: Fortress, 2001.

_______. *Matthew 21-28*. Translated by J.E. Couch. Hermenia Series; Minneapolis: Fortress, 2005.

_______. *Studies in Matthew*. Grand Rapids; Michigan; Wm B. Eerdmans, 2005.

Macquarie, J. *God-talk: An Examination of the Language and Logic of Theology*. London: SCM Press, 1967.

Manson, T.W. *The Teaching of Jesus*. Cambridge: Cambridge University Press, 1955.

Marshall, I.H. *The Gospel of Luke*. NIGTC. Grand Rapids: Wm B. Eerdmans, 1978.

_______. *New Testament Theology: Many Witnesses, One Gospel*. Illinois: Intervarsity Press, 2004.

Martin, Francis. *The Feminist Question: Feminist Theology in the Light of Christian Tradition*. Grand Rapids: Wm B. Eerdmans, 1994.

Martin, R.P. *Mark: Evangelist and Theologian*. Exeter: The Paternoster Press, 1979.

Mason, R. *Old Testament Pictures of God*. Oxford: Regent's Park College, 1993.

Matera, Frank J. *Passion Narratives and Gospel Theologies: Interpreting the Synoptics Through Their Passion Stories*. New York: Paulist Press, 1986.

_______. *New Testament Theology: Exploring Diversity and Unity*. Louisville: Westminster John Knox Press, 2007.

Mcfague, S. *Metaphorical Theology: Models of God in Religious Language*. Philadelphia: Fortress Press, 1982.

McNamara, M. *Intertestamental Literature*. Delware: Michael Glazier, Inc., 1983.

Meier, J.P. *The Vision of Matthew: Christ, Church and Morality in the First Gospel*. New York: Paulist Press, 1979.

_______. *Law and History in Matthew's Gospel: A Redactional Study of Mt. 5:17-48*. Analecta Biblica 71. Rome: Biblical Institute, 1976.

_______. *A Marginal Jew II: Rethinking the Historical Jesus*. New York Doubleday, 1994.

Metzger, B.M. *A Textual Commentary on the New Testament: A Companion Volume to the United Bible Societies' Greek New Testament.* United Bible Societies, 1971.

_______. *The New Testament: Its Background and Content*. Nashville: Abingdon Press, 1983.

Meyers, C. "The Family in Early Israel." In *Families in Ancient Israel.* Edited by Leo G. Perdue, J. Blenkinsopp, J.J. Collins, C. Meyers. Louisville: Westminster John Knox Press, 1997, 1-47.

Michel, O. "The Conclusion of Matthew's Gospel: A Contribution to the History of the Easter Message." In *The Interpretation of Matthew*. Edited by G. Stanton. London: SPCK, 1983, 30-40.

Migliore, D.L. (ed.). *The Lord's Prayer: Perspectives for Reclaiming Christian Prayer.* Grand Rapids: Eerdmans, 1993.

Miller, Patrick D. *They Cried to the Lord: The Form and Theology of Biblical Prayer.* Minneapolis: Fortress Press, 1994.

Miller, J.W. *Biblical Faith and Fathering: Why We Call God "Father."* New York: Paulist Press, 1989.

Mills, J.P. *The Ao Nagas*. London: Macmillan, 1926; Second edition by Oxford University Press, 1973.

Minear, P.S. *Commands of Christ: Authority and Implications.* Nashville: Abingdon Press, 1972.

_______. *The God of the Gospels: A Theological Work Book*. Atlanta: John Knox Press, 1988.

Moffat, J. *The Theology of the Gospels*. London: Duckworth & Co, 1912.

_______. *Love in the New Testament*. London: Hodder and Stoughton, 1932.

Mollenkott, V.R. *The Divine Feminine: The Biblical Imagery of God as Female.* New York: Crossroad, 1984.

Moltmann, J. 'The Motherly Father. Is Trinitarian Patripassianism Replacing Theological Patriarchalism?' In *God as Father?* Edited by Johannes-Baptist Metz and Edward Schillebeecks. New York: T&T Clark, 1981, 51-56.

Moore, C.H. *The Religious Thought of the Greeks: From Homer to the Triumph of Christianity.* Cambridge: Harvard University Press, 1916.

Moore, G.F. *History of Religions* vol I. Edinburgh: T&T Clark, 1914.

_______. *Judaism in the First Centuries of the Christian Era The Age of the Tannaim.* 2 vols. Cambridge: Harvard University Press, 1932.

Morgan K.W. (ed.), *The Religion of the Hindus*. New York: The Ronald Press Company, 1953.

Murray, G. *Five Stages of Greek Religion*. Oxford: Clarendon Press, 1925.

Murthy, S.R.M. *Vedic View of the Earth*. New Delhi: D.K. Printworld, 1997.

Muthuraj, J.G. "New Testament and Methodology: An Overview." In *Interweaving Methodology and Praxis – Exploring Disciplinary Options in Today's World*. Edited by I. John Mohan Razu. Bangalore: BTESSC/SATHRI, 2007, 112-118.

_______. "Reading New Testament with a Pluralist Mindset." In *Light on Our Dusty Path*. Edited by Israel Selvanayagam. Bangalore: BTESSC / SATHRI, 2008, 30-57.

_______. *"...That They May Also be Sanctified In Truth:" A Response to the CSI Moderator's Paper "Wider Revitalization or Renewal of the Christ of South India."* Delhi: ISPCK, 2012.

_______. "The Bishops And Caste Reforms in The Nineteenth Century Indian Church." A Paper presented to the United Theological College Faculty Research Seminar dated July 26, 2013.

Myers, C. *Binding the Strong Man: A Political Reading of the Story of Jesus*. Maryknoll; New York: Orbis Books, 1988.

Neyrey, J.H. *Render to God: New Testament understanding of the Divine*. Minneapolis: Fortress Press, 2004.

Nickelsberg, G.W.E. *Jewish Literature between the Bible and the Mishnah*. Second Edition. Minneapolis: Fortress Press, 2005.

Nilsson, Martin P. *Greek Piety*. Translated by H. J. Rose. Oxford: Clarendon Press, 1948.

_______. *A History of Greek Religion*. Oxford: Clarendon Press, 1949.

Nolland, J. *Luke 9:21-18:34*. WBC vol 35b. Dallas: Word Books Publishers, 1993.

_______. *The Gospel of Matthew*. NIGTC. Grand Rapids, Michigan: Wm. B. Eerdmans, 2005.

Nygren, A. *Commentary on Romans*. Translated by Carl L. Rasmussen. Muhlenberg Press: Philadelphia, 1949.

_______. *Agape and Eros*. Translated by Philip M. S. Watson. New York: Harper & Row, 1969.

Ochs, Carol. *Behind The Sex of God: Toward a New Consciousness – Transcending Matriarchy and Patriarchy*. Boston: Beacon Press, 1977.

Olyan, S. M. *Asherah and the Cult of Yahweh in Israel*. SBL Series 34. Atlanta: Scholars Press, 1988.

Osborne, G.R. *Matthew: Zondervan Exegetical Commentary on the New Testament*. Grand Rapids: Zondervan, 2010.

Osthathios, Geevarghese Mar. *One Religion of Love: Globalization of Divine Love, Personalization of Conviction and Religious Faiths.* Thiruvalla: CSS, 2000.

Oswalt, John N. *The Book of Isaiah 1-39*. NICOT; Grand Rapids: Wm B. Eerdmans, 1986.

Otto, R. *Indian Religion of Grace and Christianity Compared and Contrasted.* New York: The Macmillan Company, 1930; Philadelphia: Fortress Press, 1976.

_______. "The Kingdom of God Expels the Kingdom of Satan." In *The Kingdom of God.* Edited by B. Chilton. London: SPCK, 1984, 27-35.

Overman, J.A. *Matthew's Gospel and Formative Judaism*. Minneapolis: Fortress Press, 1990.

Packer, J.I. *Knowing God.* London: Hodder and Stoughton, 1975.

Panikkar, R. *The Trinity And World Religions: Icon-Person-Mystery*. Madras: Christian Literature Society, 1970.

_______. *The Fullness of Man: A Christophany*. Translated by Alfred DiLascia. Delhi: ISPCK, 2006.

_______. *The Unknown Christ of Hinduism: Towards an Ecumenical Christophany.* Revised and Enlarged Edition; Bangalore: Asian Trading Corporation, 1982.

Patte, D. *The Gospel According to Matthew: A Structural Commentary on Matthew's Faith*. Philadelphia: Fortress Press, 1987.

Pennington, J. *Heaven and Earth in the Gospel of Matthew*. Grand Rapids: Baker Academic, 2007.

Perdue, Leo G. *Families in Ancient Israel.* Louisville: Westminster John Knox Press, 1997.

Perrin, N. "The Christology of Mark: A Study in Methodology." In W.R. Telford (ed.). *The Interpretation of Mark*. Edinburgh: T&T Clark, 1995, 125-140.

Plummer, A. *An Exegetical Commentary on the Gospel According to Saint Matthew.* Grand Rapids: Wm B. Eerdmans, 1953.

Pool, David De Sola (ed). *The Traditional Prayer Book for Sabbath and Festivals.* New York: Behrman House Publishers, 1960.

Powell, M.A. *God with Us: A Pastoral Theology of Matthew's Gospel.* Minneapolis: Fortress Press, 1995.

Prabhavananda, Swami. *The Sermon on the Mount according to Vedanta*. New York: Mentor Books, 1972.

Prabhu, G. M. Soares. *The Formula Quotations in the Infancy Narrative of Matthew.* Rome: Biblical Institute Press, 1976.

Ramshaw, Gail. *God beyond Gender: Feminist Christian God-Language.* Minneapolis: Fortress, 1995.

Rao, K.L. Seshagiri. *Mahatma Gandhi and Comparative Religion*. Delhi: Motial Banarsidass Publishers, 1978.

_______. and Henry O. Thompson *The Love of God in the World's Religions.* Delhi: ISPCK, 1984.

Radhakrishnan, S. *East and West in Religion.* London: George Allen & Unwin, 1933.

_______. *The Heart of Hindusthan.* Madras: G.A. Natesan & Co, 1936.

_______. *Recovery of Faith.* London: Allen & Unwin, 1956.

_______. *Eastern Religions and Western Thought.* London: Oxford University Press, 1939; Second Edition; 1940.

Radhakrishnan: Selected Writings on Philosophy, Religion, and Culture. Edited by Robert A. McDermott. New York: Dutton, 1970.

Raghavan, V. *Prayers, Praises, and Psalms.* Madras: G.A. Natesan and Co, 1938.

Rawson, B. "The Roman Family." In *The Family in Ancient Rome: New Perspectives.* Edited by B. Rawson. London: Routledge, 1992, 1-57.

Reinhartz, A. *God the Father in the Gospel of John. Semeia* 85. Atlanta: SBL, 1999.

Rendtorff, R. *The Canonical Hebrew Bible: A Theology of the Old Testament,* Tools for Biblical Study 7. Leiden: Deo Publishing, 2005.

_______. *Canon and Theology: Overtures to an Old Testament Theology.* Translated and edited by Margaret Kohl. Edinburgh: T&T Clark, 1994.

Richardson, A. *An Introduction to the Theology of the New Testament.* London: SCM Press, 1958.

Richardson, N. *Paul's Language about God.* JSNT Supplement Series 99; Sheffield: Sheffield Academic Press, 1994.

Riches, John. *Matthew.* Sheffield: Sheffield Academic Press, 1996.

Riches, John. and D.C. Sim. *The Gospel of Matthew In Its Roman Imperial Context.* London: T&T Clark, 2005.

Ricoeur, P. "Fatherhood: From Phantasm to Symbol." In *The Conflict of Interpretations: Essays in Hermeneutics.* Edited by Don Ihde. Evanston: Northwestern University Press, 1974, 468-497.

Robinson, J.A.T. *Honest to God.* 40th anniversary edition; Louisville: Westminster John Knox, 2002.

Rowley, H.H. *The Faith of Israel.* London: SCM Press, 1973.

Ruether, R.R. *Sexism and God-talk: Toward a Feminist Theology.* Boston: Beacon, 1983.

Saigal, K. *God and Goddesses in Hinduism.* Delhi: Kalpaz Publications, 2007.

Saldarini, A.J. "The Gospel of Matthew and the Jewish-Christian Conflict." In *Social History of the Matthean Community.* Edited by D. Balch. Minneapolis: Fortress Press, 1991, 38-61.

_______. "Matthew." In *The Eerdmans Commentary on the Bible.* Edited by J.D.G. Dunn. Grand Rapids, Michigan: William B. Eerdmans, 2003, 1000-1063.

Samartha, S.J. *One Christ – Many Religions: Toward a Revised Christology*. New York: Orbis Books, 1991.

_______. "Dialogue in a Religiously Plural Society." In *The Multi-Faith Context of India: Resources and Challenges for Christians*. Edited by I. Selvanayagam. Bangalore: BTTBPSA, 1994, 1-16.

Sandgren, Leo D. *Vines Intertwined: A History of Jews and Christians from the Babylonian Exile to the Advent of Israel*. Peabody: Hendrickson Publishers, 2010.

Schillebeeckx, E. *Jesus: An Experiment in Christology*. Translated by H. Hoskins. New York: Crossroads, 1981.

Schnackenburg, R. *The Gospel of Matthew*. Grand Rapids; Michigan: Wm B Eerdmans, 2002.

Schnelle, U. *Theology of the New Testament*. Translated by M.E. Boring. Grand Rapids: Baker Academic, 2009.

_______. *Apostle Paul: His Life and Theology*. Translated by M.E. Boring. Grand Rapids: Baker Academic, 2005.

Schreiner, Thomas R. *New Testament Theology: Magnifying God in Christ*. Grand Rapids; Michigan: Baker Academic, 2008.

_______. *New Testament Theology: Magnifying God in Christ*: A Summary of New Testament Theology. Grand Rapids; Michigan: Baker Academic, 2010.

Schottroff, Luise. *The Parables of Jesus*. Minneapolis: Fortress Press, 2006.

Scott, Basil. *God Has No Favourites: The New Testament on First Century Religions*. Bangalore: Primalogue Publishing, 2013.

Selbie, W.B. *The Fatherhood of God*. London: Duckworth, 1936.

Selvanayagam, Israel. "Non-Biblical Resources for Theological Writing in India." In *The Multi-Faith Context of India: Resources and Challenges for Christians*. Edited by I. Selvanayagam. Bangalore: BTTBPSA, 1994, 24-40.

_______. *Relating to People of Other Faiths: Insights from the Bible*. Tiruvalla: CSS – BTTBPSA, 2004.

Senior, D. *What Are They Saying About Matthew? Revised and Expanded Edition*. New York: Paulist Press, 1996.

_______. *The Gospel of Matthew*. Nashville: Abingdon Press, 1997.

Shaw, John Mackintosh. *The Christian Gospel of the Fatherhood of God*. London: Hodder and Stoughton, 1924.

Sheffield, Julian. "The Father in the Gospel of Matthew." In *A Feminist Companion to Matthew*. Edited by Amy-Jill Levine. Cleveland: The Pilgrims Press, 2001, 52-69.

Smart, N. *The Religious Experience of Mankind*. New York: Charles Scribner's Sons, 1984.

Smith, M.S. *The Early History of God: Yahweh and other deities in Ancient Israel.* New York: Harper & Row Publishers, 1990.

Stanton, G.N. "The Origin and Purpose of Matthew's Gospel: Matthean Scholarship from 1945-1980." In *ANRW* II. 25.3 (1985), 1889-1951.

_______. *A Gospel for a New People: Studies in Matthew*. Edinburgh: T&T Clark, 1992.

Stein, R.H. *An Introduction to the Parables of Jesus*. Philadelphia: Westminster Press, 1981.

Stevenson, T.R. "Divinity of Caesar and *Parens Patriae*." In *Ancient History in a Modern University* I. Edited by T.W. Hillard, R.A. Kearsley, C.E.V. Nixon, et al. Grand Rapids: Eerdmans, 1998, 257-268.

Strecker, G. "The Concept of History in Matthew." In *The Interpretation of Matthew*. Edited by G. Stanton. London: SPCK, 1983, 67-84.

_______. *Theology of the New Testament*. Translated by E. Boring and edited by F.W. Horn. Louisville: Westminster John Knox Press, 2000.

Suggs, M. J. *Wisdom, Christology, and Law in Matthew's Gospel.* Cambridge: Harvard University, 1970.

Takatemjen, *Studies on Theology and Naga Culture*. Mokokchung: Clark Theological College, 1997.

Talbert, C.H. *Reading the Sermon on the Mount: Character Formation and Decision Making in Matthew 5-7*. Grand Rapids; Michigan: Baker Academic, 2004.

Talitemjen, N. and A. Lanunungsang, *Naga Society and Culture: A Case Study of the Ao Naga Society and Culture*. Mokokchung: Nagaland University Tribal Research Centre Publications, 2005.

Telford, W.R. *Mark*. Sheffield: Sheffield Academic Press, 1995.

Tennis, D. *Is God the Only Reliable Father?* Philadelphia: Westminster Press, 1985.

Theissen, G. *The Sociology of Early Palestinian Christianity*. Philadelphia: Fortress Press, 1978.

_______. *The Miracle Stories of the Early Christian Tradition*. Edinburgh: T&T Clark, 1983.

_______. *Social Reality and the Early Christians: Theology, Ethics, and the World of the New Testament*. Trans. by M. Kohl; Minneapolis: Fortress Press, 1992.

_______. *The Gospels in Context: Social and Political History in the Synoptic Tradition*. Trans L.M. Maloney; T&T Clark: Edinburgh, 1992.

Tiede, David. *Luke*. Minneapolis: Augsburg, 1988.

Thielman, F. *Theology of the New Testament: A Canonical and Synthetic Approach*. Grand Rapids: Zondervan, 2005.

Thompson, M.M. *The Promise of the Father: Jesus and God in the New Testament.* Louisville: Westminster John Knox Press, 2000.

_______. *The God of the Gospel of John*. Grand Rapids: Wm B. Eerdmans, 2001.

Tolbert, M.A. *Sowing The Gospel: Mark's World in Literary-Historical Perspectives.* Philadelphia: Fortress Press, 1996.

Tuckett, C.M. *Q and the History of Early Christianity: Studies on Q.* Edinburgh: T&T Clark, 1996.

VanderKam, James C. *The Dead Sea Scrolls Today*. Grand Rapids: Eerdmans, 1994.

_______. *The Book of Jubilees*. Sheffield: Sheffield Academic Press, 2001.

Vermes, G. *Jesus and the World of Judaism*. London: SCM Press, 1984.

_______. *The Religion of Jesus the Jew.* London: SCM Press, 1993.

_______. *Jesus the Jew*. London: SCM Press, 1994.

Veyne, Paul (ed.). *A History of Private Life I: From Pagan Rome to Byzantium.* Cambridge: Harvard University Press, 1987.

Visser't Hooft, W.A. *The Fatherhood of God in an Age of Emancipation*. Philadelphia: The Westminster Press, 1982.

Volf, Miroslav and Michael Welker (ed). *God's Life in Trinity*. Minneapolis: Fortress Press, 2006.

Volf, Miroslav., Ghazi bin Muhammad, Melissa Yarrington (eds). *A Common Word: Muslims and Christians on Loving God and Neighbor*. Grand Rapids; Michigan: Wm B. Eerdmans, 2010.

Von Furer-Haimendorf, Christoph. *The Naked Nagas: Head-hunters of Assam in Peace and War.* London: Methuen and Co, 1939, Indian reprint, 2004.

Von Rad, G. *Old Testament Theology*. 2 vols. London: SCM Press,.1975.

Walton, John H. *Covenant, God's Purpose, God's Plan*. Grand Rapids: Zondervan, 1994.

Watson, F. *Text and Truth: Redefining Biblical Theology*. Grand Rapids; Michigan: Wm B. Eerdmans, 1997.

Weinstock, Stefan. "The Father." *Divus Iulius*. Oxford: Clarendon Press, 1971.

Wicks, Henry J. *The Doctrine of God in the Jewish Apocryphal and Apocalyptic Literature*. New York: Ktav Publishing House, 1971.

Witherington III, B. *Matthew*. Smyth & Helwys Bible Commentary. Macon; GA: Smyth & Helwys, 2006.

Witherington III and Laura M. Ice. *The Shadow of the Almighty: Father, Son, and Spirit in Biblical Perspective*. Grand Rapids; Michigan: Wm B Eerdmans, 2002.

Wooden, R. Glenn. "Guided By God: Divine Aid in Interpretation in the Dead Sea Scrolls and the New Testament." In *Christian Beginnings and the Dead Sea Scrolls*. Edited by J.J. Collins and C.A. Evans. Grand Rapids; Michigan: Baker Academic, 2006, 101-120

Wren, Brian. *What Language Shall I Borrow? God-Talk in Worship: A Male response to Feminist Theology*. New York: Crossroad, 1991.

Wright, C.J.H. *Knowing Jesus Through the Old Testament*. London: Marshall Pickering, 1992.

Wright, N.T. *The New Testament and the People of God*. Minneapolis: Fortress Press, 1992.

__________. *Jesus and the Victory of God: Christian Origins and the Question of God* 2. Minneapolis: Fortress, 1996.

Articles

Arokiasamy, S. "Your Father in heaven ... makes his sun rise on the evil and the good, and sends the rain on the righteous and the unrighteous' (Mt 5:48)." In *Vidyajyoti* 63 (1999): 381-384.

Barr, J. "Abba Isn't 'Daddy.'" In *JTS* 39 (1988): 28-47.

Bassler, J.M. "God in the New Testament." In *ABD* II. Edited by D.N. Freedman. New York: Doubleday, 1992, 1049-1055.

Batto, B. "The Sleeping God: An Ancient Near East Motif of Divine Sovereignty." *Bib* 68 (1987): 153-77.

Bertram, G. "νηπίοις," *TDNT IV*. Edited by G. Kittel and G. Friedrich. Grand Rapids; Michigan: Wm B. Eerdmans, 1968, 912-923.

Bietenhard, H. "Heaven." In *NIDNTT* II. Edited by Colin Brown. Exeter: The Paternoster Press, 1976, 188-196.

Borgen, Peder. "Philo of Alexandria." *ABD* V. Edited by D.N. Freedman. New York: Doubleday, 1992, 333-342.

Bowley, J.E. "Pax Romana." In *DNTB*. Edited by C.A. Evans & Stanley E. Porter. Illinois: InterVarsity Press, 2000, 771-775.

Brueggemann, W. "Israel's Social Criticism and Yahweh's Sexuality." In *JAAR* Supplement 45/3 (September 1977): 739-765.

Bultmann, R. "μεριμνάω." In *TDNT* IV, 592-593.

Burnett, F.W. "Wisdom." In *DJG*. Edited by J.B Green, S. McKnight, I. H. Marshal. Leicester: InterVarsity Press, 1992, 873-877.

__________. "Exposing the Anti-Jewish Ideology of Matthew's Implied Author: The Characterization of God as Father." *Semeia* 59 (1992): 611-630.

Conzelmann, H. "συνίημι." In *TDNT* VII. Grand Rapids: Wm B. Eerdmans, 1971, 888-896.

Cope, L. "Jesus' Radical Concept of God." In *The Christian Century* 90 (1973): 448-450.

D'Angelo, M. Rose. "Abba and 'Father:' Imperial Theology and the Jesus Traditions." In *JBL* 111/4 (1992): 611-630.

________________. "Theology in Mark and Q: Abba and 'Father' in Context." In *HTR* 85/2 (1992):149-174.

De Boer, Martinus C. "Ten Thousand Talents? Matthew's Interpretation and Redaction of the Parable of the Unforgiving Servant (Matt 18:23-35)." In *CBQ* 50 (1988): 214-232.

De Jonge, Henk J. "Sonship, Wisdom, Infancy; Luke 2:41-51a." In *NTS* 24/3 (April 1978): 317-354.

Delling, G. "teleios." In *TDNT* VIII. Edited by G. Friedrich. Grand Rapids; Michigan: Wm B Eerdmans, 1968, 49-87.

Deutsch, D. "Wisdom in Matthew: Transformation of a Symbol." In *NovT* 32 (1990): 13-47.

Dillon, R.J. "Ravens, Lilies, and the Kingdom of God (Matt 6:25-33/Luke 12:22-31)." In *CBQ* 53 (1991): 605-627.

Donahue, J.R. "A neglected factor in the Theology of Mark," in *JBL* 101 (1982): 563-94.

Duling, D.C. "Kingdom of God, Kingdom of Heaven." In *ABD* IV. Edited by D.N. Freedman. New York: Doubleday, 1992, 49-69.

Dunn, J.D.G. "Prayer." In *DJG*, 617-625.

Ellingworth, P. "'In Secret?' (Matthew 6.4, 6, 18)." In *BT* 40 (1989): 446-447.

Fiorenza, E.S. "Luke 2:41-52." In *Int* 36 (1982): 402-403.

Forster, R. "Why on Earth Use 'Kingdom of Heaven?': Matthew's Terminology Revisited." In *NTS* 48 (2002): 487-499.

Garlington, D. "The 'Better Righteousness:' Matthew 5:20." In *BR* 20/4 (2010): 479-502.

"God." In *DBI*. Edited by L. Ryken, J.C. Wilhoit, T. Longman III. Leicester: InterVarsity Press, 1998, 332-340.

Grant, R.M. "The Sermon on the Mount in Earliest Christianity." In *Semeia* 12 (1978): 215-231.

Grundmann, "δεῖ." In *TDNT* II. Edited by G. Friedrich. Grand Rapids; Michigan: Wm B. Eerdmans 1964, 21-25.

Guterbock, H. "The Composition of Hittite Prayers to the Sun." In *JAOS* 78 (1958):240-242.

Guttmacher, Adolf. "Family and Family Life." In *The Jewish Encyclopedia* V. New York: Funk & Wagnalls, 1925, 336-338.

Hagner, D.A. "hlios." In *The NIDNTT*, Vol. III. Edited by Colin Brown. Exeter: The Paternoster Press, 1978, 730-733.

Hemer, Colin. "ἐπιούσιος." In *JSNT* 22 (1984): 81-94.

Hill, D. "Son and Servant: An Essay on Matthean Christology." In *JSNT* 6 (1980): 2-16.

Hofius, O. "Father." In *NIDNTT* I. Edited by Colin Brown. Exeter: Paternoster Press, 1975, 614-621.

Hubner, H. "τέλειος." In *EDNT* III. Edited by H. Balz and G. Schneider. Grand Rapids; Michigan: Wm B. Eerdmans, 1994, 342-344.

Hurtado, L.W. "God." In *DJG*, 270-276.

Karris, Robert J. "Luke 23:47 and the Lucan View of Jesus' Death." In *JBL* 105/1 (March 1986): 65-74.

Kasemann, E. "The Problem of a New Testament Theology." In *NTS* 19/3 (1973): 235-245.

Keerankeri, G. "Fulfilling All Righteousness: The Baptism of Jesus." In *Vidyajyoti* 69/2 (2005): 144-151.

___________. "The Mighty Deeds of Jesus." In *Vidyajyoti* 69/4 (2005): 298-308.

Kingsbury, J.D. "The Title 'Son of God' in Matthew's Gospel." In *JBL* 95/2 (Dec 1976): 591-602.

Kittel, G. "αβ βα." *TDNT* I. Grand Rapids; Michigan: Wm B. Eerdmans, 1964, 5-6.

Kleinknecht, "Qeos." In *TDNT* III. Edited by G. Kittel. Grand Rapids; Michigan: Wm B. Eerdmans, 1965, 65-79.

Lassen, E.M. "The Use of the Father Image in Imperial Propaganda and I Corinthians 4:14-21." In *TynBul* 42/1 (1991): 127-136.

Levias, Caspar. "Father." In *The Jewish Encyclopaedia* V. New York: Funk & Wagnalls, 1925, 351-352.

Mark, Noll. "God at the Center: Jonathan Edwards on True Virtue." In *The Christian Century* September 8-15 (1993): 854-858.

Matera, F.J. "New Testament Theology: History, Method, and Identity." In *CBQ* 67 (2005): 1-21.

Meier, J.P. "Salvation History in Matthew; In Search of a Starting Point." In *CBQ* 37 (1975): 203-215.

Michel, O. "Πάτερ." In *EDNT* III, 53-57.

Montefiore, H.W. "God as Father in the Synoptic Gospels." In *NTS* 3.1 (Nov 1956): 31-46.

Mowery, R.L. "God, Lord and Father: The Theology of the Gospel of Matthew." In *BR* 33 (1988): 24-36.

__________. "From Lord to Father in Matthew 1-7." In *CBQ* 59 (1997): 642-656.

__________. "Son of God in Roman Imperial Titles and Matthew." In *Bib* 83 (2002): 100-110.

Muthuraj, J.G. "Economic Scenarios of the NT Christianity: A Socio-Economic Reading of Luke-Acts." In *IJT* 38.1 (1996): 49-59.

Myrick, Anthony A. "'Father' Imagery in 2 Corinthians 1-9 and Jewish Paternal Tradition." In *TynBul* 47.1 (1996): 163-171.

Nilsson, M.P. "Zeus." In *OCD*. Edited by M. Cary, A.D. Nock, W.D. Ross et al. Oxford: Clarendon Press, 1968, 966.

Osiek, Carolyn. "'When You Pray, God into Your ταμεῖόν' (Matthew 6:6): But Why?" In *CBQ* 71 No. 4 (2009): 723-740.

Owen, S.G. "Ovid (Publius Ovidius Naso)."In *OCD*, 630-632.

Pamment, M. "The Kingdom of Heaven According to the First Gospel." In *NTS* 27/2 (1981): 211-232.

Paradkar, Balwant A.M. "Hindu Interpretation of Christ from Vivekananda to Radhakrishnan." In *IJT* 18 (Jan-Mar 1969): 65-80.

Perkins, P. "God in the New Testament: Preliminary Soundings." In *T Today* 42 (1985): 332-341.

Popkes, W. "δεῖ." In *EDNT* I. Edited by H. Balz and G. Schneider. Grand Rapids; Michigan: Wm B. Eerdmans, 1990, 279-81.

Powell, M.A. "Toward a narrative-Critical Understanding of Matthew." In *Int* 46 (1992): 341-346.

Quell, "The Father Concept in the Old Testament." In *TDNT* V, 959-974.

Ringgren, בָּא (Father). In *TDOT* I. Edited by G.J. Botterweck and Helmer Ringgren. Grand Rapids; Michigan: Wm B Eerdmans, 1974, 1-19.

Rowe, C. Kavin. "New Testament Theology: The Revival of a Discipline." In *JBL* 125/2 (2006): 393-419.

Sabourin, L. "Why Is God Called "Perfect" in Mt 5:48?" In *BZ* 24 (1980): 266-268.

Schneemelcher. "υἱὸς." In *TDNT* VIII, 392-397.

Schrenk, G. "Πάτερ." In *TDNT* V. Edited by G. Friedrich. Grand Rapids; Michigan: Wm B. Eerdmans, 1967, 945-959, 974-1022.

Schuller, E. "4Q372 I; A Text about Joseph." In *Rev Q* 14/55 (1990): 343-370.

__________. "The Psalm of 4Q372 I Within the Context of Second Temple Prayer." In *CBQ* 54 (1992): 67-79.

Schweizer, E. "υἱὸς." In *TDNT* VIII, 363-392.

Temple, Patrick J. "'House' or 'Business' in Lk. 2:49?" In *CBQ* 1 (1939): 342-52.

Vernant, Jean-Pierre. "Greek Religion." In *The Encyclopedia of Religions.* Edited by M. Eliade. Vol 6. New York: Macmillan Publishing Company, 1987, 99-118.

Von Fritz, Kurt. "Cleanthes." In *OCD*, 199.

Widdicombe, P. "Fatherhood and the Conception of God in Early Greek Christian Literature." In *ATR* 82/3 (2000): 519-536.

White, E.O. "That 'Cry of dereliction' ...?" In *ExpT* 113 (2002): 188-189.

Williams, D.J. "Mercy." In *DJG*, 542-543.

Wilson, W. T. "Seen in Secret: Inconspicuous Piety and Alternative Subjectivity in Matthew 6:1-6, 16-18." In *CBQ* 4 (2009): 475-497.

Witherington III, B. "Birth of Jesus." In *DJG*, 60-74.

Wright, C.J.H. בָּא . In *NIDOTT* I. Edited by Willem A. VanGemeren. Carlisle: Paternoster Press, 1997, 219-223.

Yarnold, E. "*Teleios* in St. Matthew's Gospel." In *SE* 102 (1968): 269-273.

Newspaper

The Times of India, Bangalore, dated Tuesday, the 14th August, 2012

The Times of India (Sunday Times), May 12, 2013

The Times of India, Thursday, December 12, 2013

The Times of India / Bangalore Times, Wednesday, December 18, 2013

Webliography

Cesim: The Non-Proliferation Monthly 73 (Dec 2012), *http://www.cesim.fr/observatoire/eng/73/article/7*; accessed on 7 Jan, 2014.

Kaufman, Gordon D. "Re-conceiving God and Humanity in Light of Today's Ecological Consciousness: A Brief Statement," *www.crosscurrents.org/kaufman.htm*; accessed on Jan 12, 2014.

Naik, Zakir. "Concept of God in Hinduism," *http://www.irf.net/irf/comparativereligion/index.htm*; accessed on Dec 18, 2013.

Orphic Hymn 8 to Helios, trans Taylor (Greek hymns c. 3rd B.C.E. to 2nd C.E.), *http://www.theoi.com/Titan/HeliosGod.html*; accessed on 14 April, 2013.